Turtles, Wolves, and Bears

A
Mohawk
Family History

Barbara J. Sivertsen

HERITAGE BOOKS
2006

HERITAGE BOOKS

AN IMPRINT OF HERITAGE BOOKS, INC.

Books, CDs, and more—Worldwide

For our listing of thousands of titles see our website
at
www.HeritageBooks.com

Published 2006 by
HERITAGE BOOKS, INC.
Publishing Division
65 East Main Street
Westminster, Maryland 21157-5026

Other books by the author:

*The Legend of Cushetunk: The Nathan Skinner Manuscript
and the Early History of Cochecton*
Barbara J. Sivertsen and Barbara L. Covey

International Standard Book Number: 978-0-7884-0484-9

To Steven, for all his help and love

Contents

CONTENTS

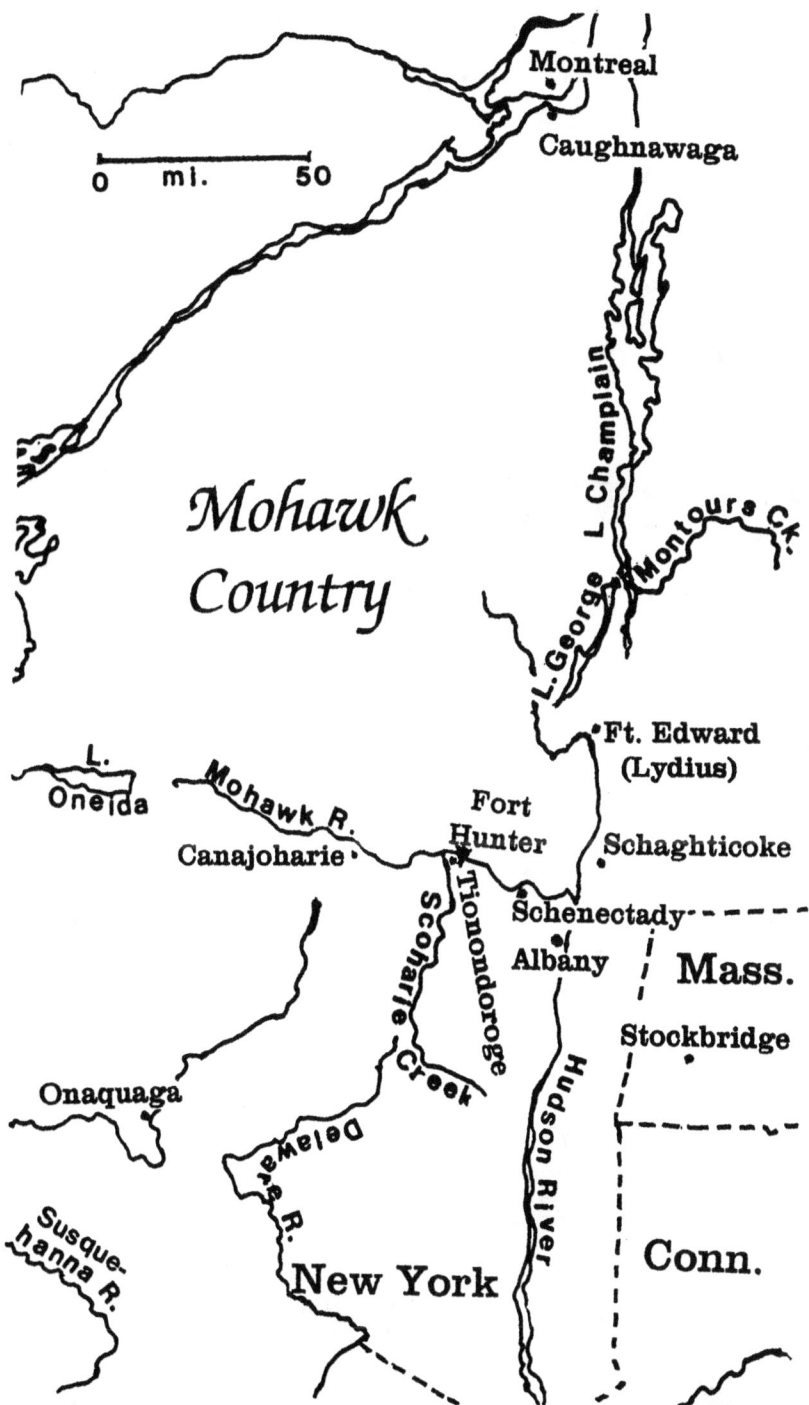

Montreal

Caughnawaga

0   mi.   50

*Mohawk
Country*

L. Champlain

L. George

Montours Ck.

Ft. Edward
(Lydius)

L.
Oneida

Mohawk R.

Fort
Hunter

Schaghticoke

Canajoharie

Tionondoroge

Schenectady

Schoharie Creek

Albany

Mass.

Stockbridge

Onaquaga

Delaware R.

Hudson River

Conn.

Susque-
hanna R.

New York

Acknowledgments

This work would have never been possible without the help of many people, either individual researchers or librarians and archivists at various institutions. First and foremost of these is Barbara L. Covey who since 1988 has been of invaluable assistance in ways too numerous to mention. She not only introduced me to many genealogical source records but sent me many of the fruits of her own decades of genealogical research. Most important has been her encouragement and support through years of correspondence.

A second major thank you goes to Dr. David Faux, who unselfishly sent me useful items and sources and shared with me insights from his extensive genealogical work into the eighteenth- and nineteenth-century Mohawks. His unfailing politeness throughout the lively discussions and disagreements in our correspondence is gratefully appreciated.

Other individuals who have kindly given me help include Mr. Robert S. Alexander, historian of the First Church in Albany, who examined the original church records and relayed his findings to me; Lois Feister of the New York State Office of Parks, who made available to me part of her own list of the Indian baptisms in the Albany church; Christine Beauregard of the New York State Library who advised me on various records and helped me secure some of them through interlibrary loan; Violet Fallone, Montgomery County Archivist who made a copy of the Barclay Register available to me. Others who either supplied material or answered questions include (in alphabetical order): Shirley Atterbery, James Corsaro (New York State Library), Ella Greene (Schenectady Historical Society), Dr. Barbara Graymont, Marjory Hinman (Broome County Historian), Donald Keefer, Arthur Kelly, Dr. Isabel Kelsay, Sarah Montgomery (National Archives Canada), Dr. Daniel Richter, Stephanie Shultes (New Iroquois Indian Museum), Susan Watkins, and Barbara Wright, U.E.

Introduction

For more than a century and a half, historians and ethnologists writing about the seventeenth and eighteenth century Iroquois have found themselves limited by the scarcity of reliable contemporary information. Virtually all of this information was from white sources, and nearly all of it was about a few male Indian leaders who appeared at councils or otherwise had contact with whites. Although in recent decades there have been a number of useful studies on the Iroquois, one vital collection of contemporary material on the easternmost tribe of the Iroquois League, the Mohawks, has been virtually ignored by scholars, possibly because it comes under the heading of "genealogy," a subject few historical and anthropological researchers take seriously. This collection consists of the baptismal, marriage, and sometimes even death records compiled by the contemporary Protestant ministers of Albany, Schenectady, Schoharie, and Fort Hunter.

The Mohawks (like the other Iroquois) were a matrilineal, kinship-based society whose principal women appointed many of the tribal leaders, the League chiefs. Many other Mohawk leaders, I have found, were also connected with the elite families. Kinship played a crucial role within Mohawk society and markedly affected their relationships with whites. Whites who were familiar with the tribe knew this and worked within the Mohawks' kinship system, but detailed knowledge of the various family relationships have not survived. Using the entries in the local church registers, however, a surprising amount of kinship information can be deduced.

In the course of my decade or so of research on the eighteenth-century Mohawks, I not only used church records from 1689 to 1777 (found in Appendices A–E) but also cross-indexed them on my computer. Family relationships, definite and probable, appeared in these indices which, when combined with other contemporary sources, can pin down specific key Mohawks and their families. From decade to decade certain families appear over and over in important roles in Mohawk society, and these connections can now be documented and related to historical events that affected the Mohawks in the late seventeenth and eighteenth centuries. I have not tried to present a broader ethnohistorical work—this is beyond my own expertise; instead I hope that my research and analysis will aid ethnohistorians and anthropologists in their own work.

A second major group who, I hope, will find this book useful consists of individuals who wish to trace their Mohawk ancestry. The records and narrative presented here, and the extensive references in the chapter notes, will be helpful to those who attempt this difficult project and, I hope, provide them with a sense of their ancestors and the rich family heritage they are heir to.

CHAPTER I

Hilletie

In 1679 two members of a small Protestant sect called the Labadists sailed from Holland to New York in search of a place for their co-religionists to settle. One of the men, a Hollander named Jasper Danckaerts, kept a journal of his travels which resurfaced in an Amsterdam book seller's in the mid-nineteenth century. It was purchased by a New Yorker and brought to America. In his journal Danckaerts records a particularly vivid encounter in Schenectady in April of 1680.

He was approached there by a woman with a little boy about four years old. The child's tongue had grown attached to the base of his mouth and the boy was mute. Could Danckaerts help him? Danckaerts could do nothing more than offer advice, but the woman herself intrigued him. He was told that her name was Hilletie and that she was of mixed Indian and European parentage. She had left the Indians, been taught by the Christians, and had been baptized in the Dutch church.

> Not contenting myself with this account, and observing something in her that pleased me, I asked her to relate to me herself how it had gone with her from the first of her coming to Christendom, both outwardly and inwardly.[1]

Hilletie, encouraged by the piety of the visiting Labadist, related her story. She had been born of a white father and a Mohawk mother and lived with her mother, brothers, and sisters in the Indian country. According to Hilletie, she soon attracted attention from the Christians who made offers to take and raise her. Her mother, angry and seemingly bitter against the Dutch, refused, but the little girl's curiosity was piqued. Life with her family became increasingly difficult as she continued to voice her

1

interest in her father's people. In 1663 she went to live with a Dutch woman, possibly as a servant. There Hilletie learned to speak the Dutch language, and later to read and write it. Catechized in the New Testament, she was baptized and became a devout Christian.

This process was not achieved without some difficulty, she confided to Danckaerts. She was abused by both Indians and whites. Her brothers and sisters despised and stoned her, her mother abused and maltreated her, and eventually the tribe compelled her to leave them. When she finally made her profession of faith and was baptized in the Dutch church, her life as an enthusiastic convert was not always easy. In attempting to rebuke the more drunken and disorderly of Schenectady's citizenry she was met with comments such as: "Well how is this, there is a sow converted. Run, boys, to the brewers's and bring some swill for a converted sow."

Evidently Danckaerts and his companion impressed Hilletie as much as she had impressed him. Danckaerts wrote:

> Looking at me she said, "How glad am I that I am so fortunate; that God should permit me to behold such Christians, whom I have so long desired to see, and to whom I may speak from the bottom of my heart without fear; and that there are such Christians in the world. How often have I asked myself, are there no other Christians than those amongst whom we live, who are so godless and lead worse lives than the Indians, and yet have such a pure and holy religion?"[2]

Hilletie had voiced a question that had puzzled the Mohawks for decades. In the 1640s a Dutch minister at Albany, Dominie Johannes Megapolensis, gained a certain knowledge of the neighboring Mohawks, but his efforts to convert them to Christianity were nullified by the behavior of the Christian Dutch, who set the worst of examples for the heathen observers. Megapolensis told the Indians that Christians ought not steal, nor commit lewdness, nor get drunk, nor commit murder. The Indians then asked him, "Why do so many Christians do these things?"[3]

Nine years after Danckaerts' visit, Hilletie would become the interpreter for the dominie of the Albany church and with him convert a great number of the nearby Mohawks to Christianity in the Dutch Reformed Church. The reasons for this singular success, after the Mohawks had successfully resisted Dutch efforts at conversion for over seventy years, are as complex as were Hilletie's own origins. Danckaerts describes her as a half-breed. Other sources confirm that she was the oldest daughter of Cornelius Antonisen (Theunise) van Slyck (or Schlick) and Otstock, a Mohawk. Cornelius Antonisen was from Breuckelen, near Utrecht, in the Netherlands. Born about 1604, he came to New Amsterdam in 1634, his passage paid for by the patroon, Kiliaen van Rensselaer, in return for three years of service carpentry, bricklaying, and farming. Van Slyck was appointed the patroon's *voorspraecke*, or representative, on May 12, 1639, along with Arent van Curler and Peter Cornelisz. His duties evidently brought him into contact with the Mohawks, for in 1640 his oldest son, Jacques (or Ackes) van Slyck was born at the Mohawk town then equivalent to the later-named Upper Mohawk Castle of Canajoharie. Although a man named van der Donck took over as *voorspraecke* in 1641, Cornelius Antonisen retained close ties with the Mohawks. While at Manhattan on August 22, 1646, he received a patent for land at Catskill in return for bringing about a general peace and securing the return of prisoners from the Indians. On September 23, 1650, Cornelius Theunise was appointed, along with Arent van Curler, Gerrit Wencom, Thomas Chamber, and Volckert Hansz, as a commissioner "to repair with a present to the Maquas [Mohawk] country, to renew the former alliance and bond of friendship." In his later years Cornelius van Slyck was a member of the court of the Dutch colony. He died in 1676.[4]

Hilletie's mother, Otstock, has usually been described as a full-blooded Mohawk, "a right Mohawks squaw." Tradition describes Otstock as the daughter of a chief. Another tradition, however, says that she was born about 1620, the daughter of a Frenchman named Hertell or Hartell and the Mohawk Queen of the (Van Slyck's) Island. Hertell and the Queen of the Island had two daughters: Otstock, "a large coarse-looking squaw like [her] mother" who married Cornelius Antonisen van Slyck; and Keuntze (or Kinetis) who may have had an Indian "marriage" to Arent Bradt.[5]

This tradition does not give a first name to the Frenchman Hertell, but an Hertel does appear in the early records of New France. He is named Jacques, the name given to Otstock's oldest son. Jacques is a French name, the Dutch equivalent being Jacob, and its appearance in a Mohawk village around 1640 is quite odd unless the Hertell tradition is accurate.

The Quebec Colony, called New France, had been founded by Samuel de Champlain in 1604. Champlain soon made friends with the local

Algonquian-speaking tribes and enemies of the more distant Iroquois, or Five Nations, leading hostile expeditions against the Iroquois in 1609, 1610, and 1615.[6]

Jacques Hertel was born at Fecamp, in Pays-de-Caux in Normandy, France, in 1603, the son of Nicholas Hertel and Jeanne Nirriot (or Miriot or Mirior). Jacques Hertel first appears on a list of those in Quebec in the winter of 1626-27. He may, however, have come to New France as early as 1615. His father, Nicholas Hertel, came to the New World at an unknown date but on December 20, 1637, sponsored (a position equivalent to today's godparent) an Indian child at Trois-Rivières. Nicholas was dead by August 23, 1641, when Jacques married Marguerite Marie Romain at Trois-Rivières.[7]

Jacques Hertel was the first settler at Trois-Rivières (between Quebec and Montreal) and was granted 200 *arpents* (roughly 170 acres) of land there on December 3, 1633. The Recollet priests had an Indian mission at Trois-Rivières as early as 1615, and it was they who initiated the policy of having certain Frenchmen learn the Indian languages. Jacques Hertel became an Indian interpreter, first for the Recollets and later for the Jesuit missionaries. He evidently spent a good deal of time with the Indians and sponsored several Indian children for baptism in the late 1630s.[8]

How, then, could he have been in contact with the Mohawks as early as 1620 or so, the reputed date of Otstock's birth? In 1621 the Iroquois, almost certainly the Mohawks, attacked a boat containing a Recollet priest, Father Poullain, and another Frenchman (his interpreter?) en route to the Nepissing Indians. The two Frenchmen were captured by the Mohawks at Sault St. Louis and later released. Later that year a Mohawk raiding party attacked the Recollet convent at Quebec and was driven off. It seems to me possible that the young Hertel could have been captured in this raid and brought to the Mohawk country, since accounts of both raids are rather sketchy.[9]

In 1622 the Mohawks sent two delegates to Quebec to sue for peace with the Montagnais, Indian allies of the French. The French commander, Samuel de Champlain, sent two of that tribe back with the Mohawks. As a second alternative, it is possible that Hertel accompanied this 1622 mission with the Montagnais. In any case, peace existed between the Mohawks and Montagnais—and the French—from 1624 until the winter of 1626-27. When war between the Algonquins and the Mohawks again commenced, Hertel would have made his way back to Quebec, to appear on the 1626-27 list previously mentioned.[10] Both Otstock and her sister could have been conceived during this four-year period.

Jacques Hertel died on August 10, 1651 at Trois-Rivières, leaving a son, François (born July 3, 1642), and two daughters. François was captured by the Iroquois in 1661 and given the preliminary torture generally dealt to prisoners: a finger of one hand was burnt and the thumb of the other hand was cut off. Rather than being executed, François seems to have been adopted. He returned to Trois-Rivières before 1664, when he married. On July 28, 1666, François wrote to the Fort Orange (Albany) magistrate Jacob de Hinsse thanking the magistrate for the good treatment given to the released prisoner. In the letter François asked to be remembered to many inhabitants of Albany, including the minister and his daughter. He also asked to be remembered to his "best friends Ganadtoc and his brother." In late 1689 "Ertel" was reported to have interceded for the Iroquois with the governor of Canada, Count Frontenac, and in 1695 the Iroquois sent a message to the French that Oraasa—François Hertel— could speak their language very well and asked that he be sent as a messenger to Onondaga. François was ennobled in 1716 and became the progenitor of a distinguished Quebec family.[11]

It would seem that after a traumatic capture, François Hertel's association with the Mohawks grew steadily more friendly. One wonders if he had been lucky enough to meet some of his Mohawk relatives at a critical point and they had intervened to adopt him.

Jacques Hertel's Mohawk daughters, Otstock and Kinetis, may have been adopted by their mother's parents, a practice not uncommon in the Iroquois; thus the tradition of their being daughters of a chief would coincide with their fathering by a Frenchman. This would probably account for their being thought of as full-blooded Mohawks. The fact that both Otstock and Kinetis married (at least in the Indian sense) whites suggests however that they were half-breeds.

Hilletie and her brothers Jacques and Martin Maurice and sister Leah would thus be only one-fourth Mohawk (Fig. 1-1). All but Martin eventually lived with the Dutch and married whites. They must have also had at least one half-sibling, a child of Otstock and an Indian father, because Jasper Danckaerts' account mentions Wouder (Walter), a full-blooded nephew of Jacques Cornelisen van Slyck's.[12] Possibly this half-sibling and other half-siblings were the source of Hilletie's trials with her Mohawk family.

Figure 1-1. *Hilletie's Family Tree*

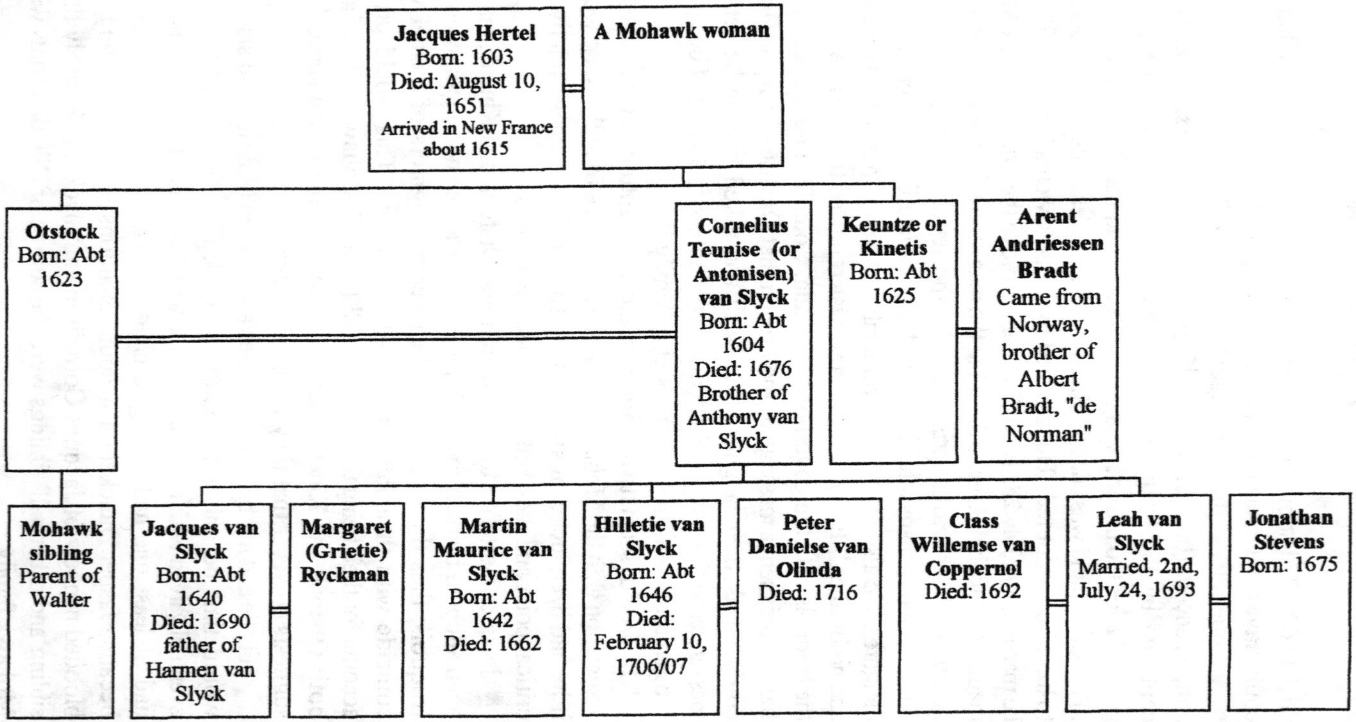

Jacques Hertel
Born: 1603
Died: August 10,
1651
Arrived in New France
about 1615

A Mohawk woman

Arent
Andriessen
Bradt
Came from
Norway, brother of
Albert Bradt, "de
Norman"

Keuntze or
Kinetis
Born: Abt
1625

Cornelius
Teunise (or
Antonisen)
van Slyck
Born: Abt
1604
Died: 1676
Brother of
Anthony van
Slyck

Otstock
Born: Abt
1623

Jonathan
Stevens
Born: 1675

Leah van
Slyck
Married, 2nd,
July 24, 1693

Class
Willemse van
Coppernol
Died: 1692

Peter
Danielse van
Olinda
Died: 1716

Hilletie van
Slyck
Born: Abt
1646
Died:
February 10,
1706/07

Martin
Maurice van
Slyck
Born: Abt
1642
Died: 1662

Margaret
(Grietie)
Ryckman

Jacques van
Slyck
Born: Abt
1640
Died: 1690
father of
Harmen van
Slyck

Mohawk
sibling
Parent of
Walter

Jacques Cornelisen van Slyck, Itsychoquachka (or Hisycho-saquachka), was evidently Hilletie's oldest brother. He was living at Schenectady as early as 1658 and was a licensed tapster there in 1671. Jacques was often employed by Albany authorities and the New York governor as an interpreter and messenger to the Iroquois. By 1687 he was acting as one of the two official colony interpreters at an Indian conference. Jacques and his younger brother Martin Maurice van Slyck farmed the Big Island (called Van Slyck's island) immediately west of Schenectady. Jacques married Margaret (Grietie) Ryckman and died sometime after May 18, 1690, when he wrote his will.[13]

Hilletie's youngest sister, eventually called Leah (or Lea), first married Class Willemse van Coppernol. Class died in 1692 and Leah was remarried, on July 24, 1693, to Jonathan Stevens. They had four children, Hendrick, Arent, Annatje, and Dina. Their second son, Arent, would become a Mohawk interpreter.[14]

Hilletie herself served as an interpreter to the Mohawks as early as 1666 at Schenectady, when she was called Hille *Cowenliche*. She married Peter Danielse van Olinda, a tailor who lived first at Beverwyck and later moved to Schenectady. The sachems of the Mohawks gave Hilletie the great island in the Mohawk River at Niskayuna (Canastagioene) on June 11, 1667. She and her husband sold it to Captain Johannes Clute, but the Mohawks later gave her other land. Hilletie had three sons, Daniel, Jacob, and Matthew. Matthew died unmarried, and he is likely the mute child brought by Hilletie to see Jasper Danckaerts.[15]

Schenectady had no resident minister until 1684, so it must have been the Albany dominie, the Reverend Gideon Schaets, who heard Hilletie's conversion and conducted her baptism. By 1681 Dominie Schaets was in considerable trouble with his congregation (or they with him, depending on how the situation was viewed) and was too old and feeble to carry out his duties. A request to Amsterdam for a new minister was answered in August, 1683, by the arrival of Dominie Godfridius (Godfrey) Dellius. In July, 1685, Dellius asked to be relieved of the Albany church, citing a call to a church in Holland. He agreed to stay on, however, since Dominie Schaets was too old to resume ministerial duties.[16]

There is no record of how this somewhat reluctant minister and the avid part-Mohawk Christian convert met or decided to join forces in an effort to convert the Mohawks. Dellius served as itinerant minister to

Schenectady before 1684 and may have become acquainted with Hilletie then. Perhaps she intrigued him as she had Danckaerts.

Part of the reason for the previous failures to convert the Mohawks was undoubtedly the problem of accurate interpretation. All the Iroquoian languages are "polysynthetic, fusional, and incorporating." Mohawk contains a number of inflections and strings a number of concepts together in one word. Its verbs, which are the most important part of the language, each have four parts: a prefix, a pronominal prefix, a base (which may contain a noun), and a suffix. Forms change as to whether the speaker is male or female and whether he or she is older or younger than the person spoken to. The language has no bilabial sounds (such as /b/, /p/ or /m/), quite different from Algonquian Indian languages. The sounds t/d and k/g are interchangeable in meaning in the Iroquois languages. This highly complex system defeated a number of Europeans attempting to master it. The Reverend Megapolensis wrote:

> This nation has a very difficult language, and it costs me great pains to learn it, so as to be able to speak and preach in it fluently. There is no Christian here who understands the language thoroughly; those who have lived here long can use a kind of jargon just sufficient to carry on trade with it, but they do not understand the fundamentals of the language. . . . One tells me the word in the infinitive mood, another in the indicative; one in the first, another in the second person; one in the present, another in the preterit. So I stand oftentimes and look, but do not know how to put it down. And as they have declensions and conjugations also, and have their augments like the Greeks, I am like one distracted, and frequently cannot tell what to do, and there is no one to set me right.[17]

What was needed "to set me right," was a comprehensive, adult-level understanding of both Mohawk and Dutch (or English, which like Dutch is a form of Low German). The Dutch who spoke the Mohawk language with any fluency were familiar principally with words and concepts relating to trade and war, not ethics or religion. Nuances of meaning, so important in explaining abstract ideas or spiritual matters, were not part of the repertoire of most of the white interpreters. Hilletie was a native Mohawk speaker into adulthood and raised in the spiritual traditions of her tribe. She then acquired years of exposure to the Dutch language and the Protestant Christian faith, including the ability to read the New Testament first-hand. Her dual knowledge of Mohawk and the Mohawk belief system on the one hand and Dutch and the Protestant Reformed Christian belief system on the other made her uniquely qualified as a religious interpreter. Hilletie would become, in the words of the Mohawks themselves, the "mouth and ears" of her mother's people.[18]

By the fall of 1689, Hilletie and Dellius had formed an alliance, with Hilletie interpreting between the dominie and certain Mohawks who were receptive to their message. He conducted public instructions in the faith, which were attended by a large number of Mohawks. She and Dellius would later translate large parts of the Christian liturgy and even parts of the Old and New Testaments into Mohawk. When the first converts were baptized into the Dutch church, Dellius recorded their Mohawk names and usually the translations of these names into Dutch. These are the first written records of a number of Mohawk names, including that of the first of the Mohawk chiefs, *Dekarihokenh* (Tekaniadaroge).[19]

A small start on this undertaking was made on December 26, 1689, when a blind forty-year-old Mohawk named Ock-kweese knelt and confessed his faith in the church at Albany and was baptized. Dominie Dellius recorded this momentous event in the Church's Registry Book:

DEN XXVI
Nae voorgaande openbaere belydenisse Is gedoopt, een seeker Heyðen, welke voor eenige jaren blint geworden was, & wiens naam onder syne natise OCK-KWEESE geweest is, van ouðerdom ontrent de 40 jaeren, & hem de naam was PAULUS, gegeven
de tolken der belydenisse waren
Aarnout Corneliis Viele
Hilletje Corneliis
[After a previous public confession was baptized a certain heathen who has become blind a number of years ago, and whose name in his nation had been Ock-kweese. He is about 40 years old, and the name Paulus was given to him.][20]

With Aarnout Viele, the province interpreter, Hilletie had translated Ock-kweese's confession of faith and acted as his sponsor. Ock-kweese's position in the tribe is unknown, but he is mentioned as one of the owners

of land behind Normanskill in a deed dated May 8, 1685 to Teunis
Slingerlant and Johannes Appel. He also appears in Evert Wendell's
accounts sometime between 1698 and 1704, with the notation that his new
name is Canaghquese or Canaghwase. He became a communicant of the
church in 1691 and died sometime before March, 1710.[21]

Paulus Ock-kweese was the first of hundreds of Mohawks who in the
ensuing years would publicly confess their faith and be baptized in the
Dutch church. Both Hilletie and the Mohawk converts would come to
trust the Albany minister, Godfridius Dellius, too much, for he would let
them down in the future. But even after he was gone, they would come to
the churches at Albany and Schenectady, and later to the Anglican chapel
at Fort Hunter, with their children and adult friends and relatives to be
baptized, a few to take communion and become actual church members,
and even a few to marry in a Christian ceremony. The records of these
baptisms, marriages, and church memberships survive to present a unique
history of these early Mohawks.

CHAPTER II

The People of the Longhouse

The League: Its Chiefs, Clans, and Lineages

The people of the extended longhouse, that is, the Five Nations of the Iroquois, had lived along the lakes and rivers south of Lake Ontario for many centuries before the Dutch sailed up the Hudson River or the French came exploring down Lake Champlain. Some time in the fifteenth or sixteenth centuries, perhaps as early as the year 1451, these five linguistically related tribes united to form a League or Confederacy.[1]

The traditional founder of the League, Deganawida, may have been a Huron—in some versions of the saga of the origin of the League he is called the man from the north. Other versions say that Deganawida was a spirit being, for through the centuries the origin of the League took on great spiritual significance for the people of the extended longhouse. Deganawida was greatly troubled with the incessant warfare amongst the tribes and, with the help of the Mohawk leader Ayonhwathah (Hiawatha), he spread his vision of a great tree of peace whose branches extended over many tribes and at whose roots the hatchet of war would lie forever buried, at least within the member tribes.[2]

To ensure this peace, and to settle matters that affected the various member tribes, a League council met in the main village of the central tribe, the Onondagas. Tradition says that this council was composed of fifty sachems, or League chiefs, from the five tribes. The Mohawks, *Kanyenkehaka* or "the people of the place of the crystals" as they called themselves, had nine seats in the League council. The Kanyenkehaka lived along the Mohawk River from just east of Schoharie Creek to just west of present-day Herkimer, New York, with an outlier at Onaquaga in present-day Broome County, New York. To the west of them were their "Younger Brothers," the Oneida, the "people of the standing stone" who also had nine sachemships. The Onondagas or "people on the mountain" were the keepers of the League council fire and had fourteen. The Cayugas, "the people at the landing" (or "of the great pipe") who lived west of the Onondagas, ten; and the westernmost tribe of the League, the Senecas, or "people of the great hill," eight sachemships.[3]

The offices of these League or federal sachems—the Mohawk name for them is *royaa'nehr* (or royaner in the Dutch church records)—belonged to individual lineages in the various clans of each tribe. There were three Mohawk clans: the Turtle (*anowara*), the Wolf (*okwaho*), and the Bear (*ohkwari*), and each had three separate lineages or *ohwachiras*. For example, the Bear clan had the Adult Bear, the Weanling Bear, and the Nursing Bear lineages. The Turtle and Wolf clan lineages were also composed of three different kinds of the clan animal. For the Mohawks, the Turtle was the senior clan. Their sachems acted as judges after issues had been discussed by sachems of the other two clans. The Turtle and Wolf clans shared one side of the council fire; the Bear clan, their "cousins," sat on the other side. The Turtle clan's senior League sachem was *Dekarihokenh* (or *Tekarihoke*), who was also the senior sachem of the tribe.[4]

Clan and *ohwachira* membership was determined by descent through the female line, and the clans were exogamous—individuals married outside of their own clan. Like the clans and *ohwachiras*, the League sachemships were inherited through the female line. As one twentieth-century author wrote:

> Strictly speaking these titles of chiefship belong to the mothers in the *ohwachira* over which the presiding matron held a trusteeship. ... The matron of an *ohwachira* is usually, not always, the oldest woman in it. But, by becoming incapacitated by age or other infirmity to manage the affairs of an *ohwachira* as its moderator, she may ask permission to resign so that a much younger woman of recognized ability and industry and integrity of character may be nominated and installed to preside over the *ohwachira* in her stead.[5]

It was the matron of each *ohwachira* who appointed the lineage's sachem, and it was she who could remove a sachem from office if he failed to conduct himself properly or attend to his duties. The senior women of the nine *ohwachiras* were called the clan mothers of the tribe. Their opinions carried a good deal of weight in the tribe, and they and other senior women of the lineages would hold councils and then let the male chiefs know what they had decided. The men would then hold their own council. The clan's women also owned the agricultural land, an important fact when it came to selling the land to whites.[6]

At the time of European contact, the Mohawk and other Iroquois clans were matrilocal: a husband lived with his wife, her sisters, her mother, her maternal aunts, their daughters, and the husbands and children of these women. These extended families resided in longhouses made from poles and covered with elm bark. The houses were gathered in towns or hamlets, usually surrounded by one or more palisaded walls. The fortifications were called castles by the Europeans. Each family of mother, father, and their children had a section along the length of the longhouse, partitioned off and sharing a fire with another nuclear family that lived directly across the central aisle where the fire was laid. For much of the year the men were away from the main towns or villages hunting, and the work of the villages was carried on by the women and their children. Thus the residence pattern, of related women living together, made a good deal of sense. The women planted and tended the crops (after the men had cleared the fields), skinned the animals and made clothing, and cooked the food. They also gathered wild plants and firewood, and made maple sugar in the spring.[7]

When Dominie Megapolensis first described the Mohawk settlements in 1644, he noted that each of the larger towns and its surrounding area belonged to a particular clan. The Turtle clan had the town farthest east, the Bear clan settlement in the center, and the Wolf clan the area farthest west. After 1693 the Turtle and Wolf clans switched territories, with the Wolf clan taking over the Lower (easternmost) Castle. Demographic and archeological evidence, however, indicates that men and women of all three clans lived in each of the villages. The tradition of a village being the domain of a particular clan was probably a holdover from previous centuries, when the Iroquois lived in small clusters of villages.[8]

Throughout the seventeenth and early eighteenth centuries, longhouses and the family groups they contained grew steadily smaller, as disease ravaged the Mohawk settlements. By the mid-1750s most of the dwellings in the Mohawk castles were probably single-family residences, built in the colonial fashion with boards or logs, shingle roofs, windows, and wooden doors. They were often better made than those of the surrounding white settlers, and glass windows and brick chimneys were not uncommon. This change in the physical house structure and the size of the families who lived together is not evident in the church records, because the ministers seldom made note of any extended family relationships in the first place. Only in a few instances can extended families be seen from the church records, when aunts or grandparents acted as sponsors at baptisms.[9]

None of the Mohawk clan relationships are mentioned in the church records. From the 1680s to the 1750s, however, individuals signing their marks to deeds would often draw a recognizable clan sign, or a least a sort of short-hand for their clan. In a few cases clan affiliations were preserved in council notes taken by colonial officials, the outstanding example being at the 1754 Albany Congress, where all the adult Mohawk males who attended were divided by clan affiliation. Another helpful list was compiled by Sir William Johnson's clerk (and eventual son-in-law) Daniel Claus in 1760, of Five Nations warriors who were given medals for accompanying Sir William to Montreal. For the Mohawks, the warriors were listed by clans. In a few, rare instances, individuals are described by their clan affiliation in the *Johnson Papers*.[10]

In addition to the "federal" or League sachems, there were "vice-chiefs" who seconded or spoke at council, other chiefs in the individual villages, and another class of leaders: "war chiefs" or "war captains." Governor Fletcher, in 1693, referred to "severall of the Chief Sachims and Captains of most note and bravery," and in the next century Cadwallader Colden and Conrad Weiser spoke of "sachems" and "captains." Colden wrote in the mid-1700s:

> Their great Men, both Sachems and Captains, are generally poorer than the common People; for they affect to give away and distribute all the Presents or Plunder they get in their Treaties or in War, so as to leave nothing to themselves. There is not a Man in the Ministry of the Five Nations, who has gain'd his Office otherwise than by Merit.[11]

David Zeisberger, who was intimately acquainted with both the Algonquian-speaking Indians of Pennsylvania and the Iroquois wrote this of the war captains:

The candidate must be resolute, brave, fearless, even in greatest danger. If a leader, who has not the rank of captain, has the good fortune not to lose a man of his troop in six or seven engagements and to bring scalps and prisoners to the camp, he is recognized and honored as a captain forthwith. If he loses a man he must secure a prisoner in his place. Should he lose more than one, responsibility weighs the more heavily upon him, and in default of showing an equal number of prisoners, his authority is at an end and he dare not think of continuing in the office.[12]

Despite nineteenth-century tradition, which held that the League sachems controlled the affairs of each tribe, the Iroquois leaders of the seventeenth and eighteenth centuries were most often the political and military leaders chosen by popular consent. Only in a few cases did known League sachems assume a principal leadership role with whites. Sir William Johnson, the Indian Superintendent, wrote in 1771:

The sachems of each tribe are usually chosen in a public assembly of the chiefs and warriors, whenever a vacancy happens by death or otherwise; they are generally chosen for their sense and bravery from among the oldest warriors, and approved of by all the tribe; on which they are saluted sachems. . . . The chief sachem, . . . is so, either by inheritance, or by a kind of tacit consent, the consequence of his superior abilities and influence. . . . Military services are the chief recommendations to this rank.

Only a few of the delegates mentioned in the records of Indian councils can be identified as *royaa'nehr* or League sachems. Most are referred to as sachems. In the case of the Mohawks, League sachems—and others—often used their informal names when dealing with whites, and thus League sachemship names seldom appear.[13]

The church records do give evidence of four or five *royaa'nehr*, but not *when* they were appointed to their office. Chiefs of various sorts, however, do make up a large proportion of the individuals who appear frequently in the church records. They probably saw the sponsoring of infants and baptism of their own children as part of their leadership role in their clan and tribe.[14]

It is not always possible to follow a distinction between "sachems" and "captains," for many if not most Mohawk leaders played both a political and a war role. I will use the term "sachem" if an individual was called one in a contemporary record or if he attended a political council. Mohawks who led war parties will be referred to as "war captains." The term "chief" will be used as eighteenth-century whites often used it, when it was unclear if a leader was a peace or war leader, or both.

Relatives, Marriages and Divorces, Adoptions
The Iroquois names for relatives differed between the mother's and father's sides of the family. Originally, an Iroquois would call his or her mother, "mother," and he would also call his mother's sister and his maternal grandmother's sister's daughter, "mother." However, more distant female relatives in the *ohwachiras* had a different name. He would likewise call his father's brother and his paternal grandfather's brother's sons, "father." Children of his mother's sisters *and* his father's brothers were called "brother" and "sister" just the same as his own siblings.[15]

One can imagine the confusion Europeans must have felt when they encountered this system, so radically different from their own. If the early Dutch and English ministers were like their later counterparts—the Moravians, for example—they would have attempted to ferret out the "real" relationship between individuals. Hilletie van Olinda, familiar with both types of terminology, could—and undoubtedly did—separate the two systems for the Dutch dominies. Individuals who appear in one church record as, for example, siblings, or parent and child, appear in other records in accordance with this relationship. The ministers were less successful in penetrating another ubiquitous Iroquois kinship custom, that of divorce.

Unlike their white contemporaries, the Iroquois would often divorce a spouse, usually in the first few years of marriage. Each spouse could—and usually did—remarry. The ministers, whatever their denomination, strongly disapproved of this practice. One supposes that some of the couples who appear in the church records had previously been recorded with another spouse, but there is no hint of this in the records themselves. If a couple had several children, they usually made an effort to stay together, and these couples formed the meaningful core of discernable Mohawk family groups.[16]

Adoption was a major aspect of Iroquois society in the seventeenth and early eighteenth centuries, when the tribes of the League sought to replace deceased family members with prisoners captured from enemy tribes. These captive adoptions sought to ritually replace specific individuals who had died. Other adoptions occurred when children whose parents had died were taken in by relatives. Adoptions were sometimes noted in the records, particularly if they were of the second type. Some adopted captive children undoubtedly were brought in to be baptized in the Dutch churches, but in most cases that type of adoption can only be inferred when a child was baptized with no parents listed. On other occasions, on which a group of children appear with parents who are unlikely to be their biological parents, adoption is also inferred. In a few cases children are described as being adopted by a male relative, after the European fashion. Most often, their wives were the true adopters and are sometimes listed as such.[17]

History of Iroquois Warfare

Although the central idea of the League was peace, or more accurately a consensus of ideas on important issues, in practice League members also banded together to carry out warfare against other non-League tribes. Since the early seventeenth century when the French and their Indian allies led by Champlain had defeated a large force of Mohawks, the tribes of the Five Nations had been in intermittent warfare with the French and most of the tribes to the north and west of Iroquois country. There were two principal reasons for this warfare: the insatiable need for beaver skins to exchange with the Dutch traders in Albany for guns and other white-produced goods, and the need to replenish their depleted populations, decimated by epidemic waves of European diseases.[18]

The Dutch had established a trading post at Fort Orange as early as the second decade of the seventeenth century. This land belonged to the Algonquian-speaking Mahican peoples, but immediately to the west of the Mahicans were the Mohawks. In 1634 Harmen Meyndertse van den Bogaert, surgeon at Fort Orange, and two companions went into the Mohawk Valley to try and establish trading relations with the Mohawks and their allied tribes.[19]

Soon the Mohawks had pushed the Mahicans from the vicinity of Fort Orange and had become the principal trading partners of the Dutch, trading beaver for guns, powder and shot, iron kettles, and other metal tools that soon became necessities for the Native Americans. By the 1640s the Iroquois had exhausted the beaver in their own country, and they began a series of attacks on the Huron confederacy in Canada, principal trading partners of the French at Montreal and Quebec. They soon wiped out the Huron villages and brought hundreds of Huron captives back to their own villages to replace through adoption the large numbers of Iroquois who had died from disease.[20]

European diseases, principally measles and smallpox but also influenza, typhoid, hepatitis, and other ailments, had unwittingly been spread to Indian populations that had absolutely no resistance to them. With cumulative mortality reaching as high as 90 percent (and initial mortality at 50 to 60 percent), the Iroquois sought, using their traditional practice of adopting war captives, to replace those who had died. By the mid-1660s, Jesuit missionaries estimated that as many as two-thirds of the Iroquois were adopted war captives.[21]

In the fall of 1666 a French expedition devastated the Mohawk country, destroying three villages south of the river and all of their crops. The Mohawks rebuilt their towns the next year: Caughnawaga, the Lower Castle of the Turtle clan just outside of present-day Fonda, New York; Gandagaron, the Middle Castle of the Bear clan three miles west of Fonda; and Tionnontoguen, the Upper Castle of the Wolf clan between Root and Canajoharie, New York. As part of their peace settlement with the French in that year, they also welcomed Jesuit missionaries into their villages, particularly Caughnawaga, for the first time.[22]

Many of the Mohawks' Huron captives and others were receptive to conversion by the Jesuits. By 1673 Catholic converts from the lower Mohawk village near Auriesville migrated to La Prairie just outside of Montreal. In 1676 the Mohawk settlement moved upriver to Sault St. Louis to form the core of what would become the Caughnawaga ("at the rapids") Mohawk settlement. Throughout the 1670s and early 1680s the tribe lost a great deal of its population to the new settlements set up in Canada by the priests. By 1677 one English observer estimated that the Mohawks had only about three hundred fighting men in their four castles: Cahaniaga, Canagora, Conajorha, and Tionondogue.[23]

Ties between the Mohawks and the Dutch—and English, after New Amsterdam had become New York in 1664—at Albany had been strengthening since the late 1670s, when the enforcement of new trading regulations eliminated the worst of the trading abuses practiced by the Dutch. One result of the improved trading practices was that Dutch traders were no longer such horrible examples of practicing Christians, at least to their Indian trading partners.[24]

By the mid-1680s French influence was on the wane. A new pro-English faction began to exert its political power among the Iroquois, particularly the Mohawks. The Jesuits were expelled from the Mohawk villages in 1684, and warfare over access to beaver hunting grounds recommenced between the western Iroquois and the French in the middle years of that decade. By 1689 France and England entered the struggle, now called King William's War.[25]

In June of that year an Iroquois raiding party attacked and destroyed the village of Lachine in French Canada, killing a number of the inhabitants and burning the houses. The possibility of retaliation by the French and their Indian allies, who now included a sizeable number of Catholic Mohawks, was very real with the arrival in New France later that year of the highly competent and agressive Count Frontenac as the new governor.[26]

By 1680 Mahicans and remnants of other New England tribes had been settled at Schaghticoke (North Albany) on the Hoosic River twenty miles northeast of Albany under the protection of the governor of New York and of the Mohawks. In reality, they served as a buffer between the French and both the white and Mohawk towns.[27]

Events in the New York colony also affected the relationship between the Mohawks and the English and Dutch at Albany. After the Glorious Revolution of 1688 in England had replaced the Catholic king James II with the Protestants William and Mary, a dissident group of New Yorkers had overthrown the royal governor and ruled the colony in his place. The rebel leader, Jacob Leisler, sent his cousin, Jacob Milborne, to Albany to try and secure that town for his government. Most of the citizens of Albany supported Leisler, but the mayor, Peter Schuyler, did not. Schuyler holed up in the fort just outside the town of Albany. Milborne marched out to the fort on November 15, 1689, with a company of armed men. Milborne thrust his foot inside the fort's gate; Schuyler and his men thrust him out. Milborne retreated to the city walls, where his followers loaded their guns and prepared to attack the fort.[28]

These antics were watched by a company of Mohawks standing upon a nearby hill. They had come to Albany for English assistance in their war with the French. Instead they found themselves the deciding voice in this internecine struggle. Hilletie was with them, and it was she who probably explained the significance of these actions to the Indians. The warriors wanted no part in a citizens' revolt. They needed military help from the English, and that help, they knew, was at the fort, not in the town. Hilletie relayed the Mohawks' message to the fort: the Mohawks were bound by a Covenant Chain to the mayor and the gentlemen at the fort, which was built for "our and there Defence, Desyred yt ye said Hille should tell them if any of those men came without ye gates to approach ye fort they [the Mohawks] would fyre upon them." To emphasize this point, while the message was being delivered, the warriors charged (loaded) their guns.[29]

One of those with the mayor in the fort was Dominie Dellius, a strong anti-Leislerite. Such was his influence with the Mohawks that Mayor Schuyler send Dellius and his interpretrer back to the warriors to quiet them. They did not succeed, for the Indians repeated their threat to fire upon any Leislerite approaching the fort. Dellius relayed this message to Milborne, with a certain degree of satisfaction no doubt, and the armed company threatening the fort disbanded.[30]

How much Hilletie and the dominie had done to persuade the Indians to take such a strong stance in this quarrel is not known. From this time forward, however, Dellius realized that his relationship with the Mohawks gave him both political influence and protection from the followers of Leisler. His baptism of Paulus on December 26 of that year was heralded by the Albany officials in a memorial to the government of Massachusetts.[31]

For their part, the Mohawks' need to strengthen their ties with the English in order to protect themselves from the French became even more evident when a party of French and their Indian allies, including Caughnawaga Mohawks, attacked the village of Schenectady in the early morning hours of February 8, 1690. Sixty persons were killed, the town was burned, and twenty-seven people were taken prisoner. A hastily gathered party of whites from Albany marched to overtake the raiders, reinforced by 140 Mohawks and River Indians (i.e., Mahicans). The leader of these Mohawks was a Christian war chief named Lawrence. This rescue party, while not recapturing the prisoners, killed about twenty-five Frenchmen and took an additional ten of them prisoner.[32]

While the relief party tried to catch up with the French and Canadian Indians, eight Mohawk sachems went to Albany to condole with the magistrates and mayor, Peter Schuyler, for the death of the people of Schenectady. Sinerongnirese (Sinnonquirese), a sachem of the Bear clan, was the speaker. The senior sachem (in age) was probably Rode of the

Turtle clan from the first or easternmost castle of Cangnewage (Cahaniaga. His age, from his later baptism, revealed that he had been born in 1615. Rode was followed by Saggoddiochquisax, another Turtle clan sachem, from the second castle or Canagere (Canagora). Oquedago or Aquedagoe was a sachem at an Albany council ten years later. Tosoquatho, another sachem of the Bear clan at this meeting, would appear at other conferences in the next twelve years. Odagerasse may have been Thodorasse, a sachem of the first castle who signed a deed on March 4, 1682 as a grandson of Caniachkoo. Of the other two, Aridarenda and Jagogthare, nothing more is known. The translator was Hilletie, who was obviously allied to the pro-English element of the tribe.[33]

Mayor Schuyler's response at the conference led the Mohawks to suppose that the English would offer real assistance against the French. The tribe's leaders decided to send another party of warriors, again under Lawrence, to accompany a force of New Yorker and New England men to French Canada that summer. With them went some of the principal women of the tribe, a few of their children, the dominie, and Hilletie. In a gesture both political and religious, three of these women, three men, and four children were baptized at North Albany—or Schaghticoke—while the Indians and New Yorkers were awaiting the arrival of the New England troops.[34]

CHAPTER III

The First Converts

While awaiting the arrival of additional troops from New England, the Reverend Dellius baptized the first group of Mohawks at the church at North Albany on July 11, 1690. Most of them were members of one extended family, probably from the same longhouse.

> Tekaniadaroge, that means *lack-scheydinge* (division of the wax?) about 22 years old, now called Isac.[1]

Tekaniadaroge is *Dekarihokenh*, the first of the Turtle clan League sachems. The title has been translated elsewhere as "It separates or divides the matter," "Of two opinions," "Between two statements," or "Double speech." Supposedly the original *Dekarihokenh* was of two opinions whether to join the League or not, and was appeased with the head chieftainship of the tribe. There is some question what *lack-scheydinge* means in English, but the idea of division (of *something*) in the name's meaning was clear 300 years ago.[2]

> A heathen woman, Karanondo, i.e., Lifter (*opligster*, which may also mean sharper), about 50 years old, now called Lidia.
> A ch. 12 years old, of whom this Karanondo, now Lydia, is the grandmother, and who, after the ch.'s mother (her daughter) died, adopted him as her own. The name of this ch. among its people was Kaadsjihandasa, i.e., Runner from the fire (*vier-upt loper*), now called Seth.

Karanondo, Dekarihokenh's mother, was the chief woman of the Mohawks, head of the Turtle clan. Her maternal grandson—and adopted son—Seth would become *Dekarihokenh* when Isaac died, sometime between March, 1704, and March, 1710.[3]

Tejonihokarawa, i.e., Open the door, about 30 years old, now called Henderick.

This baptism is listed following Isaac and just before Lydia Karanondo. *Tejonihokarawa* is also the name of the last of the Seneca League sachems, but Hendrick, as he became known, was a Mohawk of the Wolf clan. As the years passed, Hendrick would become a leader of the Christian Mohawks and a frequent voice at councils, and the "King Hendrick" who, with two other Mohawks and a River Indian, went to England in 1710. His wife's name was Catharine, baptized by the Jesuits, and probably the Catharine, aged thirty years, admitted into membership in the Albany church on June 26, 1696. Their only recorded child was Lysbet (Elizabeth), baptized in the North Albany church in December, 1690.[4]

In a deposition made nine years later, Hendrick mentions his mother-in-law, although not by name, as one of the Reverend Dellius' converts. Circumstantial evidence overwhelmingly suggests that his mother-in-law was Lydia Karanondo (see Fig. 3-1).[5]

A heathen called among his people Swongara, i.e., Little Board, aged about 40 years, now called David. A heathen woman, the wife of Swongara, now David, called among her people Kowajatense, about 30 years old, now called Rebecca.

David Swongara and Rebecca Kowajatense were the first Mohawk couple to be baptized. They brought no children with them and appeared to be childless. Both were admitted to communion on the 22nd of October, 1691. David last sponsored (with Gideon and Josine) Elias son of Joseph and Jacomine on April 13, 1696, and died in Albany that December (he was buried by the church). Rebecca was the adoptive mother of Elizabeth baptized on July 16, 1698. She was remarried, to Asa Onasiadikha (Pasture Burner), baptized on December 25, 1697, then aged thirty-five. They were the parents of Rebecca, baptized on October 6, 1700, at Albany. Because of a younger woman baptized with the same Christian name in 1692, Rebecca Kowajatense was also called Rebecca Senior by 1710. With Harmen van Slyck she sponsored Peter, son of

Figure 3-1. Matrilineal Descendants of Lydia Karanondo

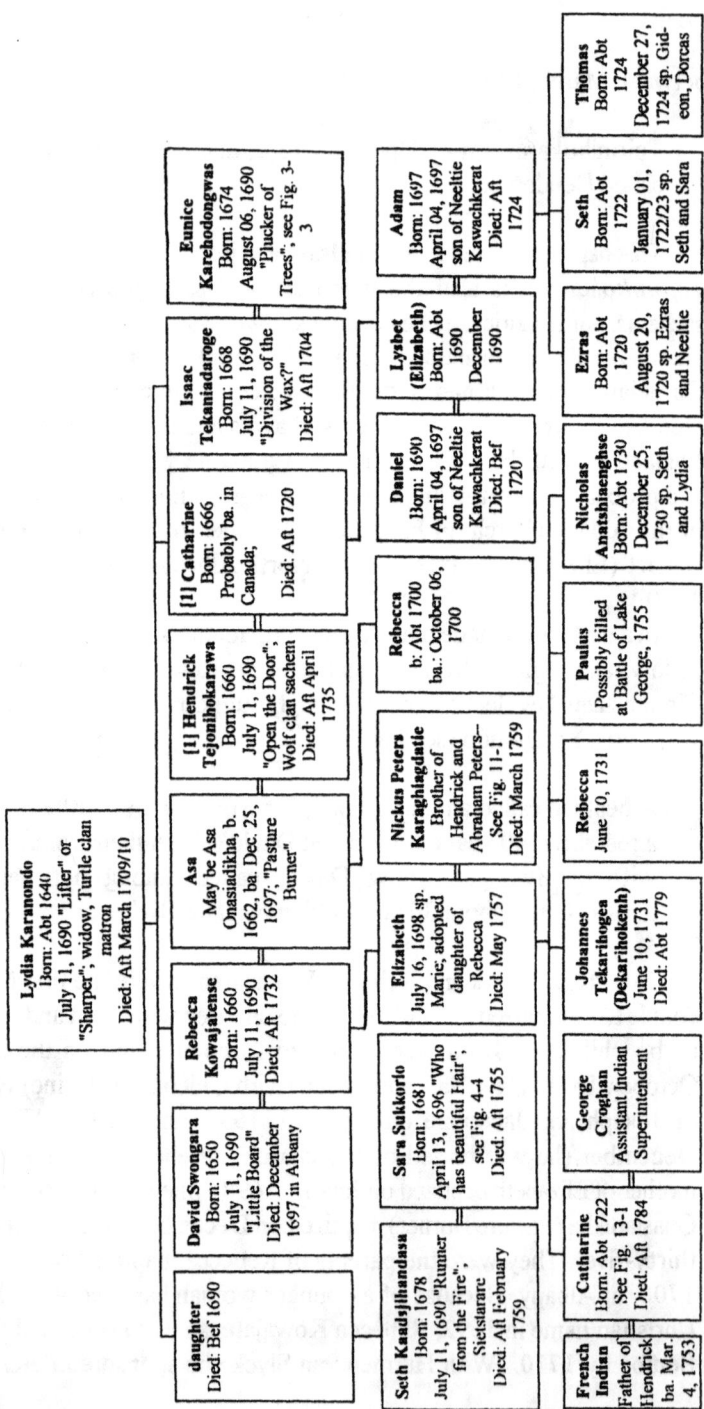

Lydia Karanondo
Born: Abt 1640
July 11, 1690 "Lifter" or "Sharper", widow, Turtle clan matron
Died: Aft March 1709/10

David Swongara
Born: 1650
July 11, 1690 "Little Board"
Died: December 1697 in Albany

Rebecca Kowajatense
Born: 1660
July 11, 1690
Died: Aft 1732

Asa
May be Asa Onasnaditha, b. 1662, ba. Dec. 25, 1697. "Pasture Burner"

[1] Hendrick Tejonihokarawa
Born: 1660
July 11, 1690 "Open the Door", Wolf clan sachem
Died: Aft April 1735

[1] Catharine
Born: 1666
Probably ba. in Canada;
Died: Aft 1720

Isaac Tekaniadaroge
Born: 1668
July 11, 1690 "Division of the Wax?"
Died: Aft 1704

Eunice Karebodongwas
Born: 1674
August 06, 1690 "Phucker of Trees", see Fig. 3-3

---

daughter
Died: Bef 1690

Sara Sukkorlo
Born: 1681
April 13, 1696 "Who has beautiful Hair", see Fig. 4-4
Died: Aft 1755

Elizabeth
July 16, 1698 sp. Marie, adopted daughter of Rebecca
Died: May 1757

Nickus Peters Karaghiagdatie
Brother of Hendrick and Abraham Peters—See Fig. 11-1
Died: March 1759

Rebecca
b: Abt 1700
ba.: October 06, 1700

Daniel
Born: 1690
April 04, 1697 son of Neeltie Kawachkerat
Died: Bef 1720

Lysbet (Elizabeth)
Born: Abt 1690 December

Adam
Born: 1697
April 04, 1697 son of Neeltie Kawachkerat
Died: Aft 1724

Seth Kaadsjlhandass
Born: 1678
July 11, 1690 "Runner from the Fire", Sietsiarare
Died: Aft February 1759

George Croghan
Assistant Indian Superintendent

Johannes Tekarihogea (Dekarihokenh)
June 10, 1731
Died: Abt 1779

Rebecca
June 10, 1731

Paulus
Possibly killed at Battle of Lake George, 1755

Nickolas Anatshiaenghse
Born: Abt 1730
December 25, 1730 sp. Seth and Lydia

Ezras
Born: Abt 1720
August 20, 1720 sp. Ezras and Neeltie

Seth
Born: Abt 1722
January 01, 1722/23 sp. Seth and Sara

Thomas
Born: Abt 1724
December 27, 1724 sp. Gideon, Dorcas

French Indian
Father of Hendrick
ba. Mar. 4, 1753

Catharine
Born: Abt 1722
See Fig. 13-1
Died: Aft 1784

Jacob and Jacomine on November 9, 1707. Harmen was a nephew of Hilletie's, Jacques van Slyck's oldest son. Kowajatense sponsored Seth's daughter Lydia on April 13, 1707, and was the Rebecca who signed the 1714 deed to Margaret and Edward Collins with a tortoise sign. After the death of Hendrick's wife Catharine in the mid-1720s Rebecca Kowajatense married Hendrick, which is in accordance with the Mohawk custom of a man marrying his dead wife's sister. These pieces of evidence indicate that Rebecca Kowajatense and Hendrick's wife Catherine were Lydia Karanondo's daughters.[6]

More than anything else, the baptisms of *Dekarihokenh*, his mother, sister, and nephew (adopted brother) underscore the great social and political importance of these conversions, over and above their genuine religious import. By the very nature of their position in the tribe, *Karanondo* and her sons represented a traditional position. It is known that earlier, traditionalists had resisted the French and Jesuit influences in the tribe. Now certain of the traditionalists had decided to ally themselves with the people of Albany and their church.[7]

After *Karanondo* and her family came another couple

A heathen woman, Sion heja, i.e., Lively, about 25 years old, now called Rachel. Her husband was ba. by the Jesuits and called Joseph, but was thereafter instructed by us in the faith of J.C. His name among his people was Skanjodowanne, i.e., Eagle's beak. Their ch. about 4 years old was also ba. and called Manasse.

Joseph and Rachel would bring their daughter Maria to be baptized on June 1, 1691, and their twins Helena and Hester to be baptized on April 11, 1694. Rachel was admitted to communion in Albany on March 24, 1692, and later was godmother to several children and an adult in the Schenectady church, but Joseph disappeared from the records. He probably was one of those killed in the bitter ten years of fighting with the French.[8]

Another warrior present at North Albany was the war captain Lawrence who led the relief party the previous winter. Lawrence and his wife Maria had been baptized in Canada by the Jesuits, but on this July 11 they brought their adopted twelve-year-old son to be baptized and were both admitted to communion. Governor Henry Sloughter himself would sponsor their son Henry on July 5, 1691, but this child probably died, since

Lawrence and Maria Iose had another son christened Hendrick on April 15, 1704, sponsored by Catharina. It's conceivable that Maria was another of Lydia's daughters, at least in the Mohawk sense (i.e., a sister's daughter).[9]

The final woman to bring her children for baptism to the North Albany church that day was Canastasi or Canastasie (spelled many ways), which was probably a rendition of the French name Anastasie. She was a widow who had been baptized in Canada. Her son, a boy of about eight, was baptized as Jacob and her daughter, aged three, was called Sara. She may have had another daughter, Cornelia, baptized on March 28, 1692. Canastasi Koaroni (or Neoni) would be married to Ezras Sonihoware (or Sogjowanne), a member of the Turtle clan, by 1701 and have daughters Mary or Maria and Margaret, and sons Ezras and Josua (see Fig. 3-2). She sponsored several Bear clan children and may have been herself a member of the Bear clan. Like Rebecca, this Canastasi would also be joined by at least one more woman of the same name, likewise baptized in Canada. Both Canastasis would become communicants of the Dutch Church. The second, Canastasi Kanawaakoha, was a slightly older woman (thirty-six years old in 1699), the wife of Amos Harogiechta (One who descended dead from Heaven). Together, she and Amos sponsored a number of children. Both were obviously prestigious women in the tribe.[10]

Hilletie interpreted these confessions and the baptism ceremonies on July 11, 1690, but it was probably a second group of converts baptized on August 6 which gave her an even deeper personal satisfaction.

The first of these was the oldest woman of the Mohawks to be baptized: Lea Kwaowarate (the name means passage or "overgang"). Kwaowarate was sixty years old, a widow and the mother of two more of the converts, Alida Karehojenda (Fallen Tree), aged thirty and married to a heathen, and Eunice Karehodongwas (Plucker of Trees), aged sixteen and the wife of Isaac Tekaniadaroge. Eunice also brought their son of nine months for baptism, christened Simon. With Lea was her sister, Wanika (Loaned), aged forty and christened Iosine (or Josine). Wanika's children, Josua (aged seven) and Jacomine (reportedly aged nine) were also baptized (see Figs. 3-3 and 3-4).[11]

The dominie did not record any special relationship between these women and the interpreter, but I do not think it coincidental that Karehojenda was given Hilletie's name (Hilletie is a diminutive of Alida) and that Kwaowarate was given the name of Hilletie's sister, Leah Stevens.

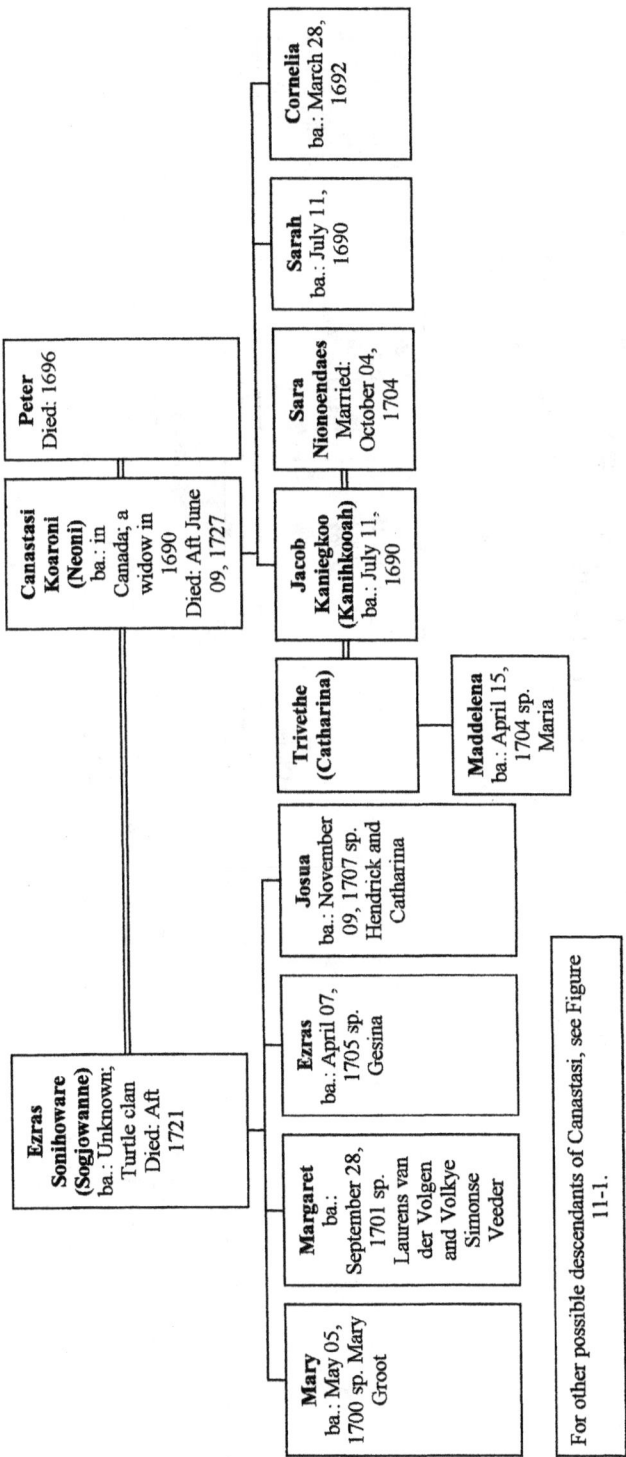

Figure 3-2. Some Descendants of Canastasi Koaroni

Ezras Sonihoware (Sogjowanne)
ba.: Unknown; Turtle clan
Died: Aft 1721

Canastasi Koaroni (Neoni)
ba.: in Canada; a widow in 1690
Died: Aft June 09, 1727

Peter
Died: 1696

Mary
ba.: May 05, 1700 sp. Mary Groot

Margaret
ba.: September 28, 1701 sp. Laurens van der Volgen and Volkye Simonse Veeder

Ezras
ba.: April 07, 1705 sp. Gesina

Josua
ba.: November 09, 1707 sp. Hendrick and Catharina

Trivethe (Catharina)

Maddelena
ba.: April 15, 1704 sp. Maria

Jacob Kaniegkoo (Kanihkooah)
ba.: July 11, 1690

Sara Nionoendaes
Married: October 04, 1704

Sarah
ba.: July 11, 1690

Cornelia
ba.: March 28, 1692

For other possible descendants of Canastasi, see Figure 11-1.

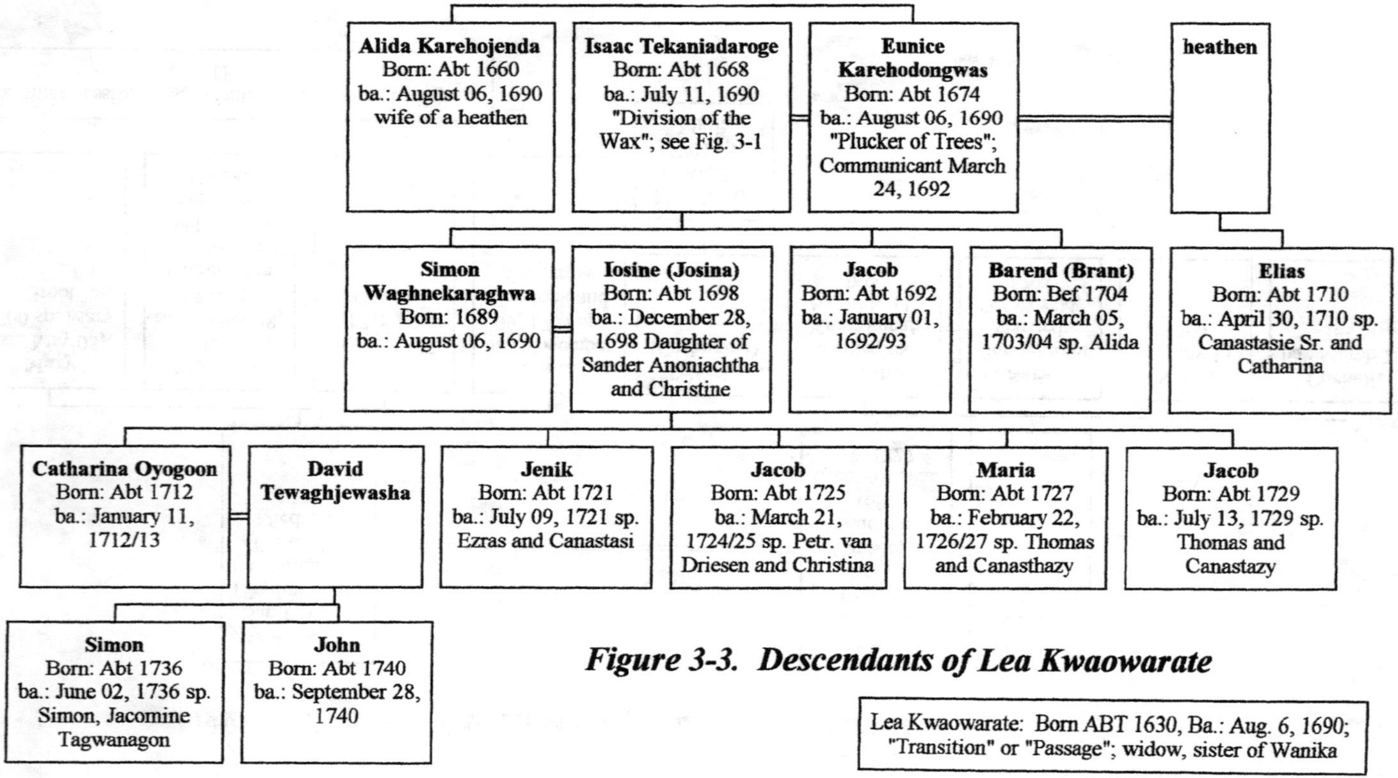

Figure 3-3. Descendants of Lea Kwaowarate

Lea Kwaowarate: Born ABT 1630, Ba.: Aug. 6, 1690; "Transition" or "Passage"; widow, sister of Wamka

Figure 3-4. Descendants of Josine Wanika

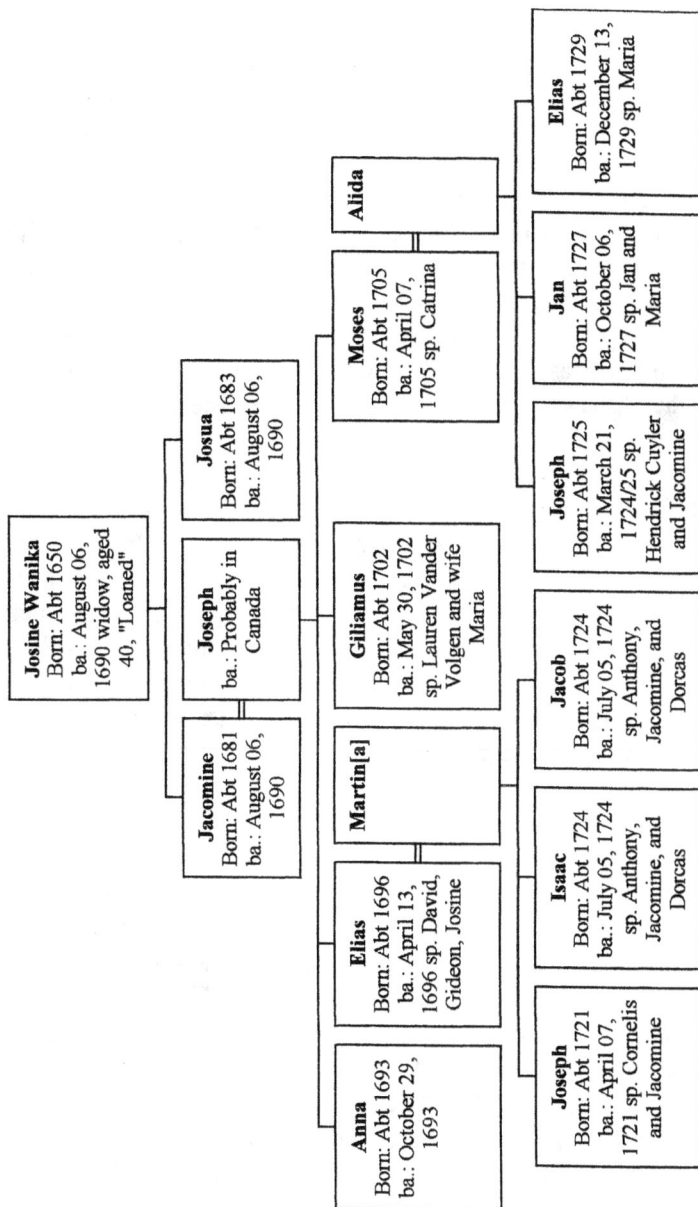

Josine Wanika
Born: Abt 1650
ba.: August 06, 1690 widow, aged 40, "Loaned"

Jacomine
Born: Abt 1681
ba.: August 06, 1690

Joseph
ba.: Probably in Canada

Josua
Born: Abt 1683
ba.: August 06, 1690

Anna
Born: Abt 1693
ba.: October 29, 1693

Elias
Born: Abt 1696
ba.: April 13, 1696 sp. David, Gideon, Josine

Martin[a]

Giliamus
Born: Abt 1702
ba.: May 30, 1702 sp. Lauren Vander Volgen and wife Maria

Moses
Born: Abt 1705
ba.: April 07, 1705 sp. Catrina

Alida

Joseph
Born: Abt 1721
ba.: April 07, 1721 sp. Cornelis and Jacomine

Isaac
Born: Abt 1724
ba.: July 05, 1724 sp. Anthony, Jacomine, and Dorcas

Jacob
Born: Abt 1724
ba.: July 05, 1724 sp. Anthony, Jacomine, and Dorcas

Joseph
Born: Abt 1725
ba.: March 21, 1724/25 sp. Hendrick Cuyler and Jacomine

Jan
Born: Abt 1727
ba.: October 06, 1727 sp. Jan and Maria

Elias
Born: Abt 1729
ba.: December 13, 1729 sp. Maria

They may have been in the same *ohwachira* or, at the very least, in the same clan.

Because Eunice Karehodongwas, age sixteen, was the wife of Isaac, and Isaac was *Dekarihokenh*, Eunice and all the other members of this group cannot have been Turtles. A clue to their clan is given in two deeds, one to Margaret and Edward Collins signed on July 10, 1714, and another, to the reverends Peter Van Driessen and John Jacob Ehle in 1732. In both these deeds a Simon appears, and on both he (or they) is(are) of the Wolf clan. Thus Lea, her daughters, her sister, and her sister's children were probably all members of the Wolf clan; and by inference, so was Hilletie. Hilletie's brother Jacques van Slyck was said to have been born at the Canajoharie castle, but in 1640 when Jacques was born, the Upper Castle of the Mohawks was held by the Wolf clan. The name Canajoharie itself was not used until the 1670s.[12]

The women of this group also reveal the temporal limits of fertility in Mohawk women at the time. Lea was forty-four when Eunice was born, and Eunice herself was fifteen when she had Simon. One mid-eighteenth-century missionary wrote: "marriages are contracted early in life, when men are from eighteen to twenty years of age and women fourteen or fifteen." This information is useful in attempting to assign a birth date to a woman, but it would seem from the women whose birth dates are known that a first child at about seventeen and a last at about thirty-seven or thirty-eight was more typical.[13]

****

The expedition against the French in the summer of 1690 foundered for want of more men from Massachusetts, but a small group of New Yorkers and Indians went up Lake Champlain and managed to kill about twenty-eight French and burn sixteen houses. Upon returning to Albany they found the rebel governor himself, Jacob Leisler, in the town and Dominie Dellius gone from it. Dellius had fled with his family to Long Island, fearing Leisler's persecution, probably with some justification. In late December Dellius and his family went by an overland route to Boston, the dominie intending to return to Holland and lay his troubles before the classis of Amsterdam. He stopped on the way at North Albany, where he encountered Hendrick and his wife Catharina and their daughter who was baptized. At Boston Dellius discovered that a new royal governor for

New York, Henry Sloughter, was about to land. Instead of returning to Holland, the dominie returned to Albany, where he arrived some time in April, 1691.[14]

Governor Sloughter hung both Leisler and his cousin Milborne for treason and in late May, 1691, held a conference with the Five Nations at Albany. Here for the first time the Christian Mohawks made a separate proposition to the governor, informing him that they were settling fifty-six miles above Albany at Tionondoroge on the Mohawk River. They also thanked the governor for the return of Dellius, and asked that ministers would be sent into the Mohawk country to instruct their people.[15]

The other sachems of the Mohawks told the governor that they had gone to Canada and tried to make peace with the French governor and the "praying Indians of Canada," their close kinsmen the Caughnawaga Mohawks. Needless to say, Governor Slaughter was not happy with this peace initiative, and it came to nothing.[16]

That summer another raiding party of 260 men, including ninety-two Mohawks and sixty-six River Indians, went up to Canada. They were led by Peter Schuyler, and the Mohawk leaders were Cristagie, Lawrence, Kanagaragayda, Adoeanoketta, Anoetsendie, and Kanayediero. The heads of the River Indians were Eetewapo, Eetowacamo, Wannesackes, and Magatawa. Of these last four men, Eetowacamo (Etowaucum) would join three Mohawks in being presented to Queen Anne in 1710. Schuyler claimed to have killed 200 French and Indians on the raid, but the real result was negative, since it made enemies of the Caughnawaga Mohawks.[17]

Another raid, in December of that same year, ended with the killing of fifteen Mohawks and Oneidas, including Caristase (Cristagie—one of the leaders of the summer raid), the Mohawk chief sachem of Trenondoge (Tionondoroge), his son Ianodathe and brother Kaakhare, Wannegreo a captain, and "several other the best Indians very well known amongst us." It was also reported that "most of our praying Indians are now killed, 15 we have lost this summer whom we could most confide in."[18]

This reference to the praying Indians being killed is interesting, because all of the adult male converts in the church records appear after this raid. Only Cristagie, who served (with a Mohawk warrior incongruously named Jannetie or Jeannetie) as a messenger from Schuyler and Dellius to Onondaga shortly after the Schenectady massacre, had known connections with Dellius. Since Tionondoroge was the Wolf clan's castle, the Upper Castle of the Mohawks at that time, members of the Wolf clan (such as those of Lea's lineage) were probably most receptive to the Protestant message and were either contemplating baptism or had been baptized in Canada. By June 15, 1693, Dellius wrote that he could count 200 converts, yet only fifty-three baptisms were recorded. The discrepancy between his totals and the actual number of baptisms was either because of sloppy record-keeping (the surviving record book is actually a copy made in 1699 of a former book, and Dellius notes that some names are omitted or not well registered) and/or made up by those baptized in Canada.[19]

Caristase, referred to as the chief sachem of Tionondoroge, fits Sir William Johnson's idea of a chief sachem picked for military prowess rather than as any sort of a peace chief. Later in the decade Hendrick, also then a sachem, refers to his having gone out on raids. That this pattern was typical of pre-seventeenth-century Mohawk society is unlikely, but one reason for the shift was probably the decimation of the Mohawk men by disease and war—there simply weren't enough leading men left to serve as separate war and peace leaders, and hence these leadership roles were in many cases combined. It was reported in December, 1691 that the Mohawks and Oneidas had lost ninety men in two years of warfare, and that the Mohawks had only 130 men left.[20]

There were only three baptisms in 1691, but twenty-six in 1692. Among the most important of these were on February 7, 1692: Rebecca Jokeÿha (She who shells), aged twenty, Jan Onodaka (Gamekeeper), aged sixteen, and Cornelis Aanasjadago (Plucker of feathers), twenty-two. Rebecca was also known by another Mohawk name, Dewaysidis or Deiudhodawae, and she appears in the next twenty years with at least ten and possibly as many as fourteen children (Fig. 3-5). Several of these were probably adopted children. Her husband was Johannes Owajadatferrio, who also had another Mohawk name, Tejejachso or Tejasse. The later was a formal name of the Turtle clan, for an Isaac Tayayake appears on the 1754 Albany list as a Canajoharie *anowara* (Turtle) and a Moses Teyeyagse appears on the 1760 list of Turtle clan Mohawks who accompanied Sir William Johnson to Montreal. On the other hand, the Thomas Thayonusyo who was the witness of Nicus Onweriyonghsere's baptism at Fort Hunter records in 1745 may have been Johannes Tejejachso's son Thomas, for by the mid-eighteenth century some Mohawks had taken their father's names (either Christian or Indian) as surnames, following the old Dutch custom.[21]

Given that Johannes Tejejachso was a Turtle, Rebecca was either a Bear or a Wolf. There is a Rebecca who appears on a 1730 deed to Peter Brown (or Brower) with the mark of a howling wolf. This is most likely Rebecca Jokeÿha.[22]

Cornelis Aanasjadago, also baptized on February 7, 1692, and made a church member on April 13, 1693, most likely was the sachem Cornelis Tirogaren who was present at an Albany conference on July 12, 1701, and signed several deeds from 1700 to 1717 with a tortoise or turtle sign. He and wife Maria had one daughter, Maria, baptized on October 19, 1711, at Schenectady, a son, Ezras, baptized on May 29, 1720, and a second daughter, Eva, baptized on October 13, 1723.[23]

Jan Onodaka (Onoda) was the first recorded Indian to have a child baptized at Schenectady; Christine, on October 19, 1698, sponsored by Gideon and Rebecca. He signed a deed to Abraham Cuyler dated July 19, 1711, for lands on Schoharie Creek, but the individual clan designations on this document are unlisted.[24]

Another important woman baptized in 1692 was Teianjeharre (Two Heights), about forty-eight years old and given the name Marta (Martha). Martha's ten-year-old daughter Quaktendiatha (One who is being driven) was also baptized, as Alette. In the next twenty years Marta would sponsor ten children, more than any other woman in the tribe. This degree of prominence suggests that she was a clan matron.[25]

One of the most inconspicuous baptisms of 1692 was that of a one-year-old child, called Wänis or Wäms (Long Bow) and christened Hendrick. There are no parents listed. This child is possibly an adoptee, and there is a tradition that a famous Mohawk, Hendrick Peters, Theyanoguin or Tiyanoga, was the son of an adopted Mahican father. Another version of this tradition has it that Hendrick himself was adopted into the Mohawks. Wänis may thus be Theyanoguin. Hendrick Peters was a speaker of the Six Nations, Chief Sachem of Canajoharie, and a member of the Bear clan. He was killed during the Bloody Morning Scout at Lake George on September 6, 1755. Because both he and Hendrick Tejonihokarawa went to England (Hendrick Tejonihokarawa in 1710, Hendrick Peters Theyanoguin in about 1740), historians have heretofore confused the two.[26]

Despite the ongoing war with the French, 1693 promised to be a good year for more Mohawk conversions. On January 1, Isaac Tekaniadoroge

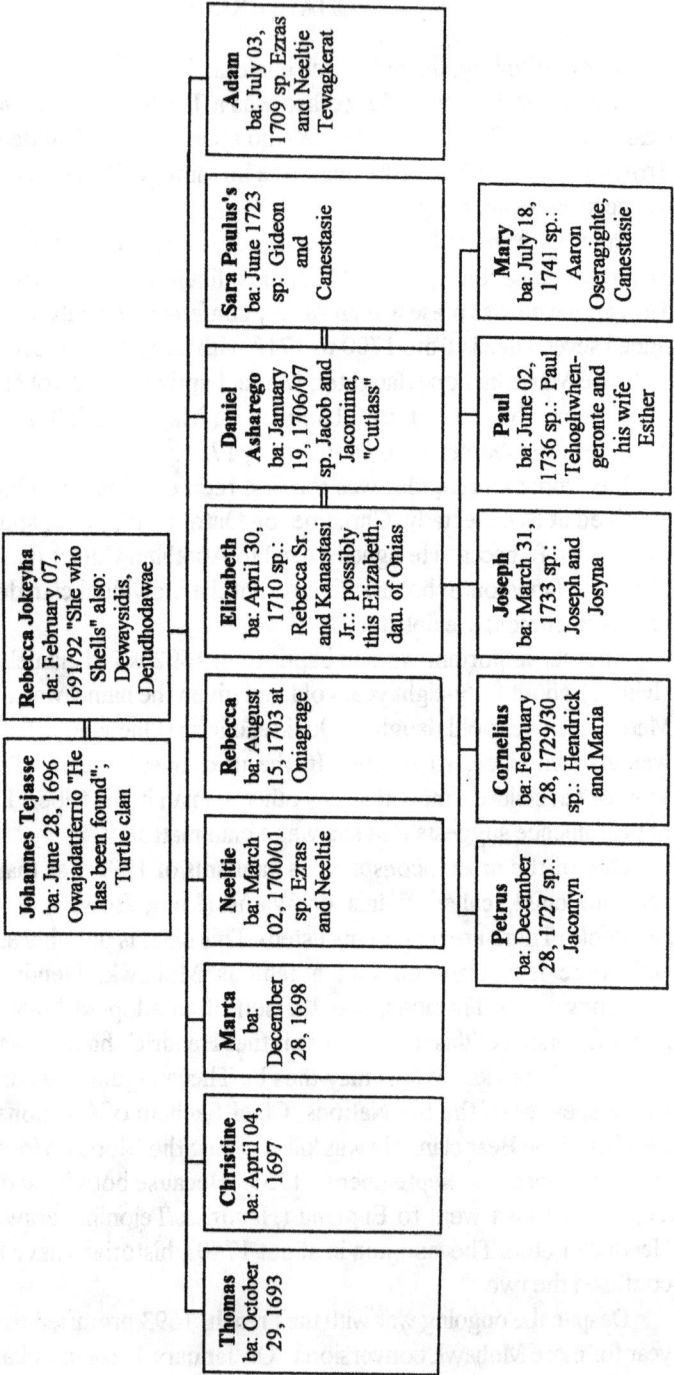

Figure 3-5A. Family of Johannes Tejasse and Rebecca Jokeyha

Figure 3-5B. Probable Adopted Children of Johannes Tejasse and Rebecca Jokeyha

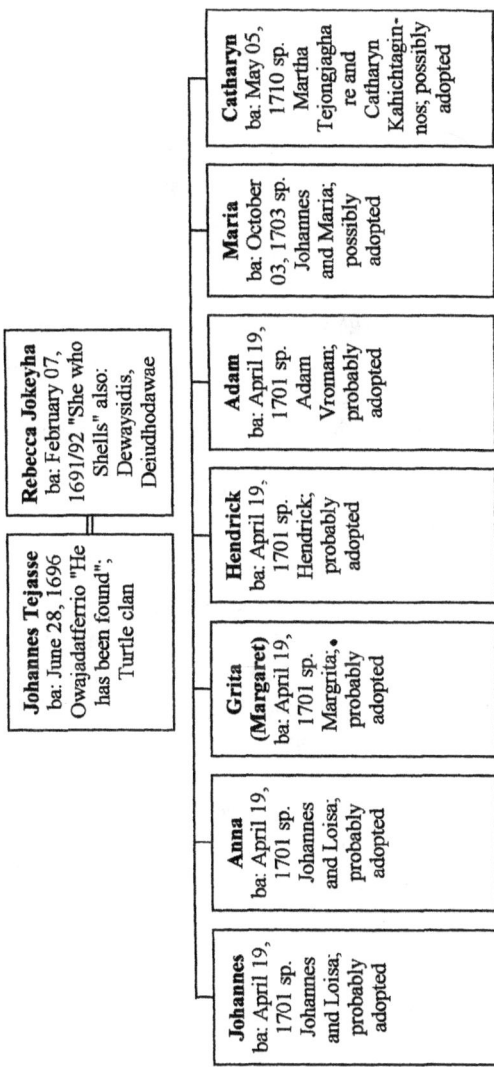

Johannes Tejasse
ba: June 28, 1696
Owajadatferrio "He
has been found";
Turtle clan

Rebecca Jokeyha
ba: February 07,
1691/92 "She who
Shells" also:
Dewaysidis,
Deiudhodawae

Johannes
ba: April 19,
1701 sp.
Johannes
and Loisa;
probably
adopted

Anna
ba: April 19,
1701 sp.
Johannes
and Loisa;
probably
adopted

**Grita
(Margaret)**
ba: April 19,
1701 sp.
Margrita;
probably
adopted

Hendrick
ba: April 19,
1701 sp.
Hendrick;
probably
adopted

Adam
ba: April 19,
1701 sp.
Adam
Vroman;
probably
adopted

Maria
ba: October
03, 1703 sp.
Johannes
and Maria;
possibly
adopted

Catharyn
ba: May 05,
1710 sp.
Martha
Tejongiagha
re and
Catharyn
Kahichtagin-
nos; possibly
adopted

and his young wife Eunice Karehodongwas brought their second son to Albany to be baptized. He was given the name Jacob.[27]

On February 13, almost exactly three years after the burning of Schenectady, a French army of nearly 600 regular soldiers, Canadian militia, and Indian allies attacked the Mohawks' three principal towns, taking 300 Mohawks prisoner and burning the towns to the ground. Only a pursuing party made up of whites and western Iroquois, led by Peter Schuyler, made the French give up most of their prisoners. The Mohawks returned to the ashes of their homes and their destroyed stores of food. The entire tribe spent the winter on Tribe's Hill overlooking the Mohawk River.[28]

Later that year the Turtle and Wolf clans switched locations and the Bear Castle merged with the Turtle. Tionondoroge was moved to a hill overlooking Schoharie Creek and became known as the Lower Castle of the Mohawks, and Canajoharie further up the river as the Upper Castle. The Protestant Mohawks were still located at Tionondoroge, with the Wolf clan still a substantial force among them: on October 23, 1693, a young man of twenty-three years, Tonidoge or Split Moon, was baptized by Dominie Dellius and given the name of Gideon. Gideon was or would later become *Sharenhowaneh*, the first League sachem of the Mohawk Wolf clan. Rebecca Jokeÿha brought her son (Thomas) to be baptized that same day, and Anna, a daughter of Joseph and Jacomine, was also baptized.[29]

The only Jacomine heretofore mentioned in the Albany records was Josine's daughter, reportedly about nine years old in 1690. Jacomine is not a name the Jesuits would have given a convert. Joseph and Jacomine's second son, Elias, was sponsored by David, Gideon, and Josine on April 13, 1696, which would suggest that this Jacomine was indeed Josine's daughter. Perhaps the Reverend Dellius made a mistake in copying Jacomine's baptism in 1699 when he transferred the information to the now-existing book and recorded her age inaccurately. Had she been but a few years older in 1690, she would have been old enough to have a child baptized in late 1693.[30]

The final member of this group baptized on October 23 was Anthony Akerrijehe (One who continuously turns something around), aged fifteen. Anthony, who may eventually have become Gideon's brother-in-law, was the first of the Bear clan Mohawks baptized in the next three years who would become influential members of the Christian Mohawk community.[31]

CHAPTER IV

Dominies and Deeds

On December 26, 1694, a group of six young men and women were baptized in Albany: Kanarongwe (Drawer-out of arrows—Peter), aged twenty, Anoniachtha (Dancer—Sander), also twenty, Thowariage (One whose fence has been broken—Brant), aged twenty-one, Sakkoherriho (One who re-enters the bushes—Dorcas), aged twenty-three, Tsike (Seer—Christine) aged eighteen, and Kanianaundon (Who lifts cones—Amirant), aged twenty. At the same time, seventeen-year-old Margaret Kviethentha (baptized on December 31, 1693) and forty-nine-year-old Eva Sowasthoa (Little one, baptized on April 11, 1694) were admitted to communion. A year later, on January 1, 1696, Eva's twenty-one-year-old son Sondagerakwe (Who digs up the soil—Lucas) would be baptized along with Brant Thowariage's and Margaret Kviethentha's small daughter Marie.[1]

Brant and Lucas were members of the Bear clan, as was Dorcas. It is quite possible that all of those baptized on December 26, 1694, belonged to the Bear clan, perhaps all "brothers" and "sisters" and Eva Sowasthoa their "mother"—in the Mohawk sense of these terms. Brant Thowariage would later appear in the Albany and Schenectady church records with the formal Bear clan name Saquainquaragton—Disappearing Smoke or Old Smoke. the first of three known Mohawk Bear clan leaders to bear this respected name (see Chapter 5). Brant would also be one of the four "kings" who went to England in 1710. Eva would be dead by March, 1710, but not forgotten—on October 13, 1723, Dorcas would sponsor a child baptized Eva in the Albany church.[2]

Dorcas appeared at church on September 20, 1696, as the wife of Gideon Tonidoge and the mother of a young son baptized Natan. A Jonatan Takaradi (aged twenty) was baptized on the same day as Natan, and Natan is undoubtedly short for Jonatan or Jonathan. Gideon had previously brought his son Moses (whose mother was then unbaptized) to be baptized on April 11, 1694. On June 28, 1696, two days after Dorcas was admitted to membership in the Dutch church, Thomas (aged five) and Antonette (aged two), children of Gideon and Catrina were baptized (Fig. 4-1). Catrina, Gideon's first wife, may have died, or the couple may have divorced. Many years later, Jonathan Cayenquerigo (or Cayenqueregoa), a sachem of the Bear clan, and Moses Contjochqua were mentioned as adopted Mohawk brothers of the Pennsylvania interpreter, Conrad Weiser. The church records make it probable that Weiser's adopted brothers were Moses and Natan (Jonathan), Gideon's sons (see Chapter 11). Dorcas and Gideon brought three other sons for baptism in the next decade, Laurens (baptized in Albany on September 1, 1700), David (baptized in Albany on May 30, 1703), and Dirk (Richard, baptized in Albany on April 4, 1708). Dirk would go on to be a Bear clan war captain ("Captain Dick" in the *Johnson Papers*). Gideon would also have a daughter, Mary (or Maria), mentioned in the Reverend Barclay's Fort Hunter records (see Fig. 4-2).[3]

On April 13, 1696, two sisters and another young woman were baptized in Albany. Moset, aged twenty, kept her original name—the only instance where such a thing happened. On December 27 of that year a Moset, probably this Moset, had an illegitimate son (the father was a white Christian) baptized with the name Johannes. Johannes' sponsor was Hilletie van Olinda. This young woman was quite likely the Moset Tassama (born in New England) who married the white John Harris (born in Old England) on May 3, 1701. She was probably an Algonquin-speaking Indian.[4]

The two sisters baptized on April 13, 1696 were undoubtedly part white. The older was named Kawachkerat, aged twenty-four (One who is whitish) and the younger Sukkorio (Who has beautiful hair), aged fifteen. Kawachkerat was given the name Neeltie and Sukkorio was baptized Sara. Neeltie Kawachkerat's two-year-old daughter was also baptized and given the name Catrina. A year later, on April 4, 1697, Neeltie's sons, seven-year-old Daniel and six-week-old Adam, were baptized. No father was listed, but Neeltie Kawachkerat appears in the Schenectady church records in 1701 as the wife of Ezras Kanneragh-tahare, a sachem of the Wolf clan. Unfortunately, there is no baptism recorded for Ezras. Ezras and Neeltie became two of the most constant members of the Dutch Protestant churches, and their dedication was

Figure 4-1. Descendants of Gideon Tonidoge and His First Wife Catrina

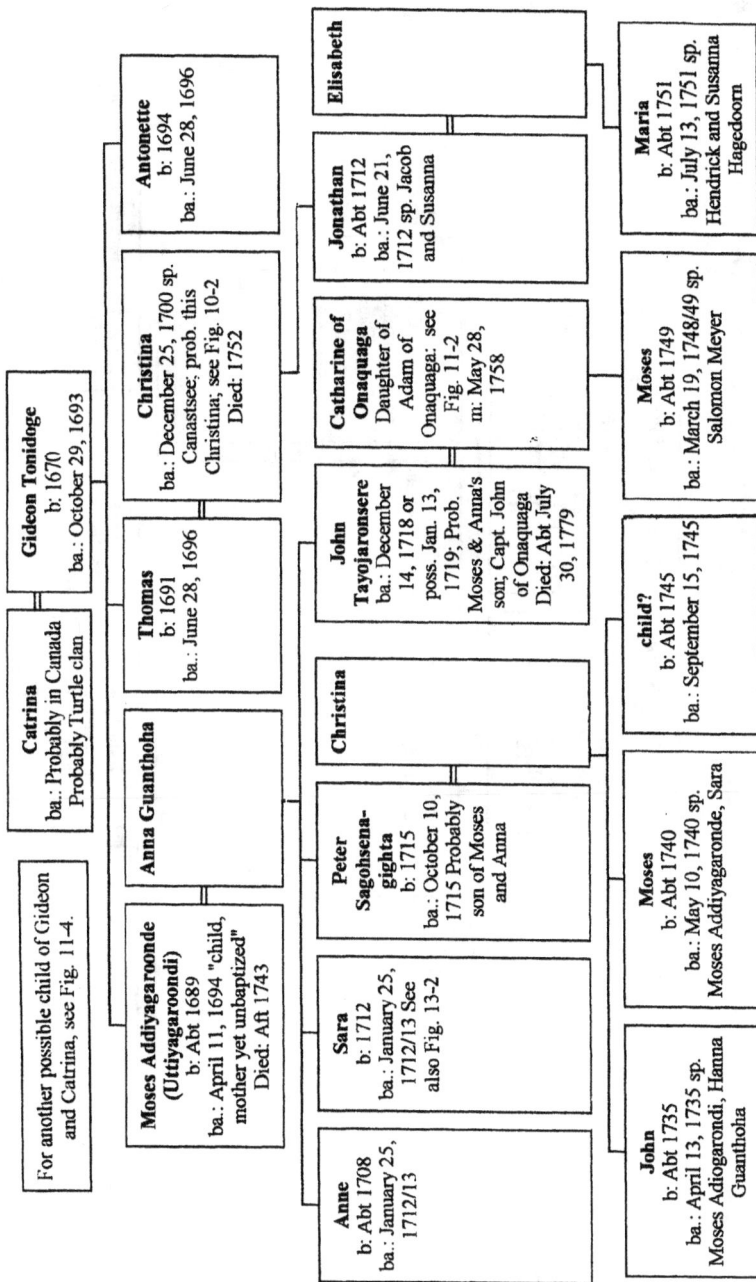

For another possible child of Gideon and Catrina, see Fig. 11-4.

Gideon Tonidoge
b: 1670
ba.: October 29, 1693

Catrina
ba.: Probably in Canada
Probably Turtle clan

Thomas
b: 1691
ba.: June 28, 1696

Christina
ba.: December 25, 1700 sp.
Canastsee; prob. this
Christina; see Fig. 10-2
Died: 1752

Antonette
b: 1694
ba.: June 28, 1696

Moses Addiyagaroonde (Uttiyagaroondi)
b: Abt 1689
ba.: April 11, 1694 "child, mother yet unbaptized"
Died: Aft 1743

Anna Guanthoha

Elisabeth

Jonathan
b: Abt 1712
ba.: June 21, 1712 sp. Jacob
and Susanna

Catharine of Onaquaga
Daughter of
Adam of
Onaquaga: see
Fig. 11-2
m: May 28,
1758

John Tayojaronsere
ba.: December
14, 1718 or
poss. Jan. 13,
1719; Prob.
Moses & Anna's
son; Capt. John
of Onaquaga
Died: Abt July
30, 1779

Christina

Peter Sagohsena-gightta
b: 1715
ba.: October 10,
1715 Probably
son of Moses
and Anna

Sara
b: 1712
ba.: January 25,
1712/13 See
also Fig. 13-2

Anne
b: Abt 1708
ba.: January 25,
1712/13

John
b: Abt 1735
ba.: April 13, 1735 sp.
Moses Adiogarondi, Hanna
Guanthoha

Moses
b: Abt 1740
ba.: May 10, 1740 sp.
Moses Addiyagaronde, Sara

child?
b: Abt 1745
ba.: September 15, 1745

Moses
b: Abt 1749
ba.: March 19, 1748/49 sp.
Salomon Meyer

Maria
b: Abt 1751
ba.: July 13, 1751 sp.
Hendrick and Susanna
Hagedoorn

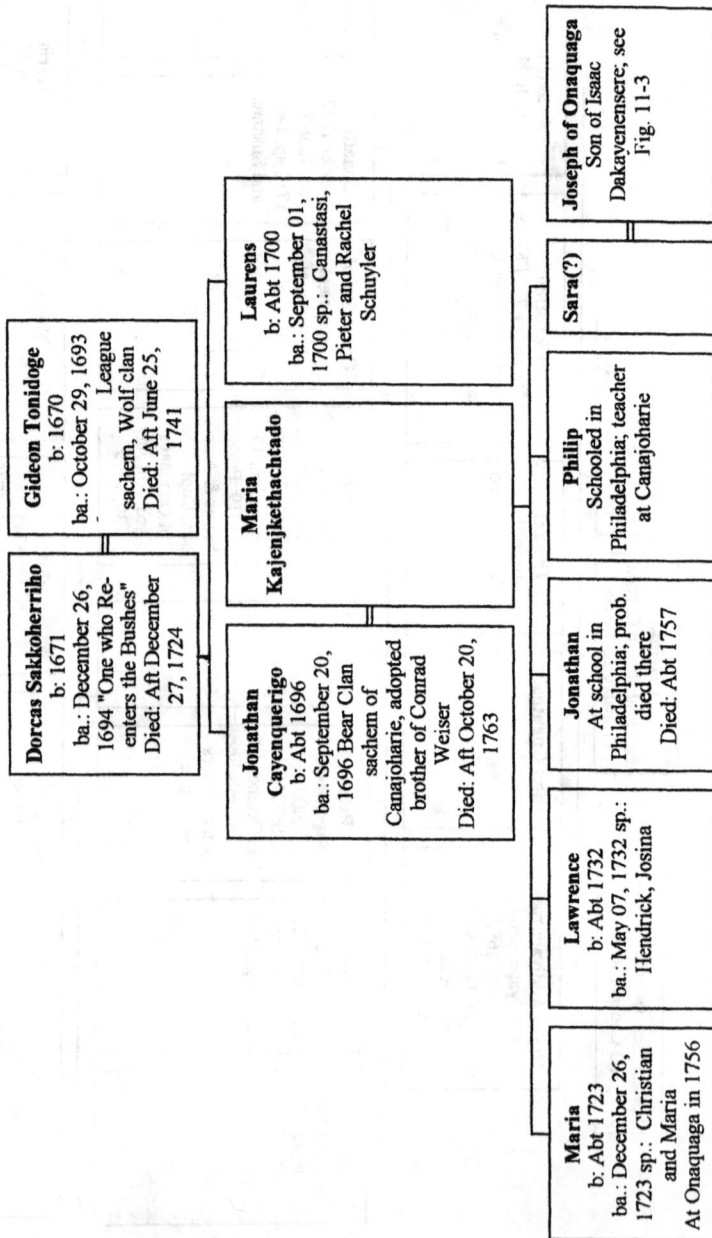

Figure 4-2. Descendants of Gideon Tonidoge and His Second Wife Dorcas Saktoherriho

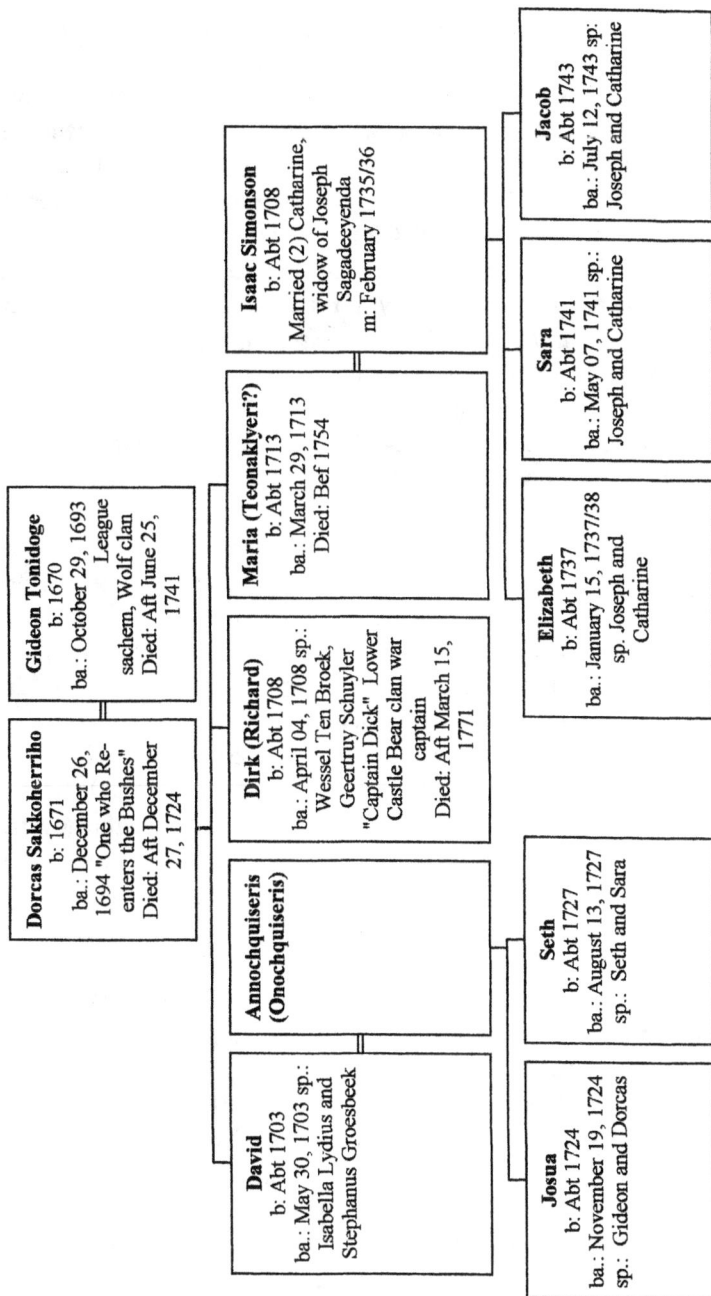

Figure 4-2. *Descendants of Gideon and Dorcas (Continued)*

Dorcas Sakkoherriho
b: 1671
ba.: December 26,
1694 "One who Re-
enters the Bushes"
Died: Aft December
27, 1724

Gideon Tonidoge
b: 1670
ba.: October 29, 1693
League
sachem, Wolf clan
Died: Aft June 25,
1741

Isaac Simonson
b: Abt 1708
Married (2) Catharine,
widow of Joseph
Sagadeeyenda
m: February 1735/36

Maria (Teonakiyeri?)
b: Abt 1713
ba.: March 29, 1713
Died: Bef 1754

Dirk (Richard)
b: Abt 1708
ba.: April 04, 1708 sp.:
Wessel Ten Broek,
Geertruy Schuyler
"Captain Dick" Lower
Castle Bear clan war
captain
Died: Aft March 15,
1771

Annochquiseris
(Onochquiseris)

David
b: Abt 1703
ba.: May 30, 1703 sp.:
Isabella Lydius and
Stephanus Groesbeck

Jacob
b: Abt 1743
ba.: July 12, 1743 sp.:
Joseph and Catharine

Sara
b: Abt 1741
ba.: May 07, 1741 sp.:
Joseph and Catharine

Elizabeth
b: Abt 1737
ba.: January 15, 1737/38
sp. Joseph and
Catharine

Seth
b: Abt 1727
ba.: August 13, 1727
sp.: Seth and Sara

Josua
b: Abt 1724
ba.: November 19, 1724
sp.: Gideon and Dorcas

reflected in their children, whose descendants can be traced through several generations (see Figs. 4-3 and 4-4).[5]

Dorcas, admitted to membership on June 26, 1696, became, with her husband Gideon, part of a small group of church members and communicants who were strongly influenced by Dominie Dellius and his interpreter, Hilletie van Olinda. The two most important men in this "inner group" of Protestant Christian Mohawks were Joseph Dehanochrakhas, Bear clan sachem probably baptized in Canada and admitted to membership in the Albany church on December 26, 1695; and Hendrick Tejonihokarawa, Wolf clan sachem baptized on July 11, 1690, and admitted to church membership on December 23, 1692. Joseph had served as Dellius' messenger between the officials at Albany, the French in Canada, and the Jesuit priest Father Millet at Oneida. Hendrick too served as the dominie's emissary to Canada with another Mohawk communicant named Tjerk.[6]

The success of baptizing the aged but important Turtle clan sachem Rode (whose name, paradoxically, meant Stupid) in June of 1695, and the possibility that Gideon may have been appointed a League sachem, *Sharenhowaneh* of the Wolf clan, during this period, may have suggested to the dominie that he secure for himself a considerable track of Mohawk land. On September 19, 1695, Dellius, along with Peter Schuyler, Dirk Wesselse Ten Broeck, and Evert Bancker petitioned New York Governor Fletcher for the right to purchase land of the Indians. Nine days later Nicholas Bayard of New York also petitioned the governor for the right to purchase Mohawk lands along Schoharie Creek. In giving their permission to Dellius, Schuyler, Ten Broeck, and Bancker, Fletcher and his council stipulated that William Pinhorne, a council member, be included in the transaction.[7]

On June 5, 1696, the Turtle clan sachem Rode, Tjerk, Joseph, and Gideon signed a deed giving Dellius title to an immense tract of land surrounding Schaghticoke east of the Hudson River. That summer Governor Fletcher appointed Dellius and his political allies Peter Schuyler, Evert Bancker, and Dirk Wesselse Ten Broeck commissioners to treat with the Five Nations. The four men went to individual Indians and, apparently in their capacities as commissioners, persuaded eight Mohawks to sign a bill of sale to most of the Mohawk country, including all the land of their towns. The signers of this deed were given to understand that these trusted whites (especially Dellius and Schuyler) would hold the land in trust for the Indians and not allow other whites to take it from the tribe.[8]

Word of these deeds caused uneasiness among the Mohawk leaders, particularly after Hendrick's and Joseph's complaints about a third deed, signed in 1695 and giving lands at Schoharie to Nicholas Bayard of New York, went unacted upon by the magistrates in Albany and later by Governor Fletcher. (The governor could hardly have cancelled the deed, since he had given Bayard permission to buy the land.) Dellius' religious efforts among the Mohawks slacked off during this period as well. Baptisms fell from thirty-seven in 1696 to ten in 1697. In the first months of 1698, only four children of proselytes—and no adults—were baptized.[9]

Britain had signed a peace treaty with France in 1697, but this did not end hostilities. In the spring of 1698, the New York colony got a new governor, the Earl of Bellomont, whose main mission was to repair the corruption of his predecessor, Governor Fletcher. Bellomont allied himself with the remnants of the pro-Leisler faction in the colony, which predisposed him against Dellius, Schuyler, and their political allies. Nonetheless, he sent Dominie Dellius and Peter Schuyler to Quebec to alert the French governor, Count Frontenac, of the peace and attempt to get him to stop French incursions into the Iroquois country. Their mission was unsuccessful, since Frontenac refused to admit that the Iroquois were covered under the peace treaty. The French governor demanded that the Iroquois negotiate a separate peace with him. He was surprised, however, to hear that at long last a Protestant minister had made inroads amongst the Iroquois.[10]

Dellius and Schuyler's absence prompted the pro-Leisler faction in Albany to approach the Mohawks with the idea of complaining directly to the new governor about the land deeds. On May 31, 1698, Hendrick and Joseph appeared in New York City before the governor, Bellomont, and the attorney general and related how they had been tricked into signing the 1697 deed. They also complained about the fraudulent 1695 Bayard deed to Schoharie lands. The Earl, looking perhaps for a scapegoat for the failure of English policy with the Indians for the last five to eight years, came to Albany in July to hold a council with the leaders of the Five Nations, right the wrong of the fraudulent land deals, and punish the perpetrators.[11]

Sinnonquirese, the Bear clan sachem, spoke for the Mohawk

Figure 4-3A. Descendants of Neeltie Kawachkerat and Ezras Kanneraghtahare

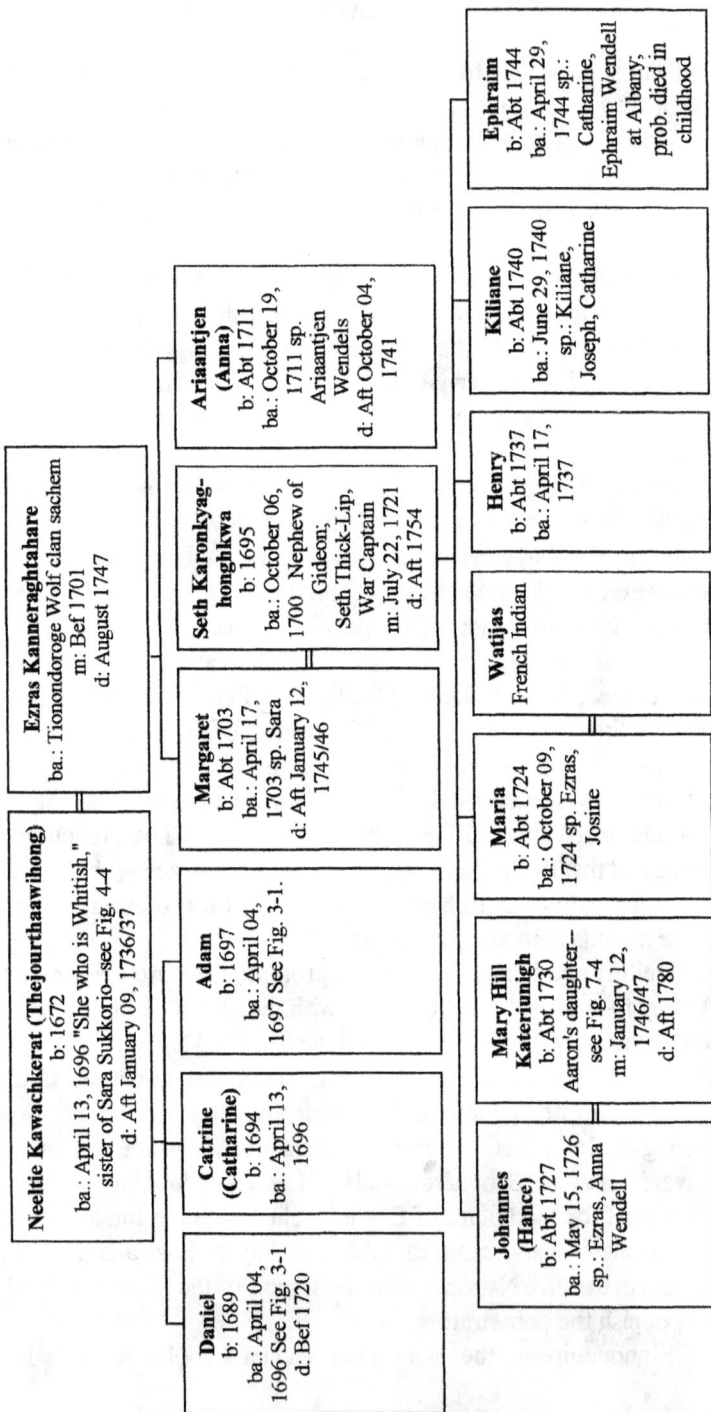

Neeltie Kawachkerat (Thejourthaawihong)
b: 1672
ba.: April 13, 1696 "She who is Whitish," sister of Sara Sukkorio—see Fig. 4-4
d: Aft January 09, 1736/37

Ezras Kanneraghtahare
ba.: Tionondoroge Wolf clan sachem
m: Bef 1701
d: August 1747

Daniel
b: 1689
ba.: April 04, 1696 See Fig. 3-1
d: Bef 1720

Catrine (Catharine)
b: 1694
ba.: April 13, 1696

Adam
b: 1697
ba.: April 04, 1697 See Fig. 3-1.

Margaret
b: Abt 1703
ba.: April 17, 1703 sp. Sara
d: Aft January 12, 1745/46

Seth Karonkyag-honghkwa
b: 1695
ba.: October 06, 1700 Nephew of Gideon; Seth Thick-Lip, War Captain
m: July 22, 1721
d: Aft 1754

Ariaantjen (Anna)
b: Abt 1711
ba.: October 19, 1711 sp. Ariaantjen Wendels
d: Aft October 04, 1741

Johannes (Hance)
b: Abt 1727
ba.: May 15, 1726
sp.: Ezras, Anna Wendell

Mary Hill Kateriunigh
b: Abt 1730
Aaron's daughter—see Fig. 7-4
m: January 12, 1746/47
d: Aft 1780

Maria
b: Abt 1724
ba.: October 09, 1724 sp. Ezras, Josine

Watijas
French Indian

Henry
b: Abt 1737
ba.: April 17, 1737

Kiliane
b: Abt 1740
ba.: June 29, 1740
sp.: Kiliane, Joseph, Catharine

Ephraim
b: Abt 1744
ba.: April 29, 1744 sp.: Catharine, Ephraim Wendell at Albany; prob. died in childhood

Figure 4-3B. Ezras Kanneraghtahare's Other Children and Grandchildren

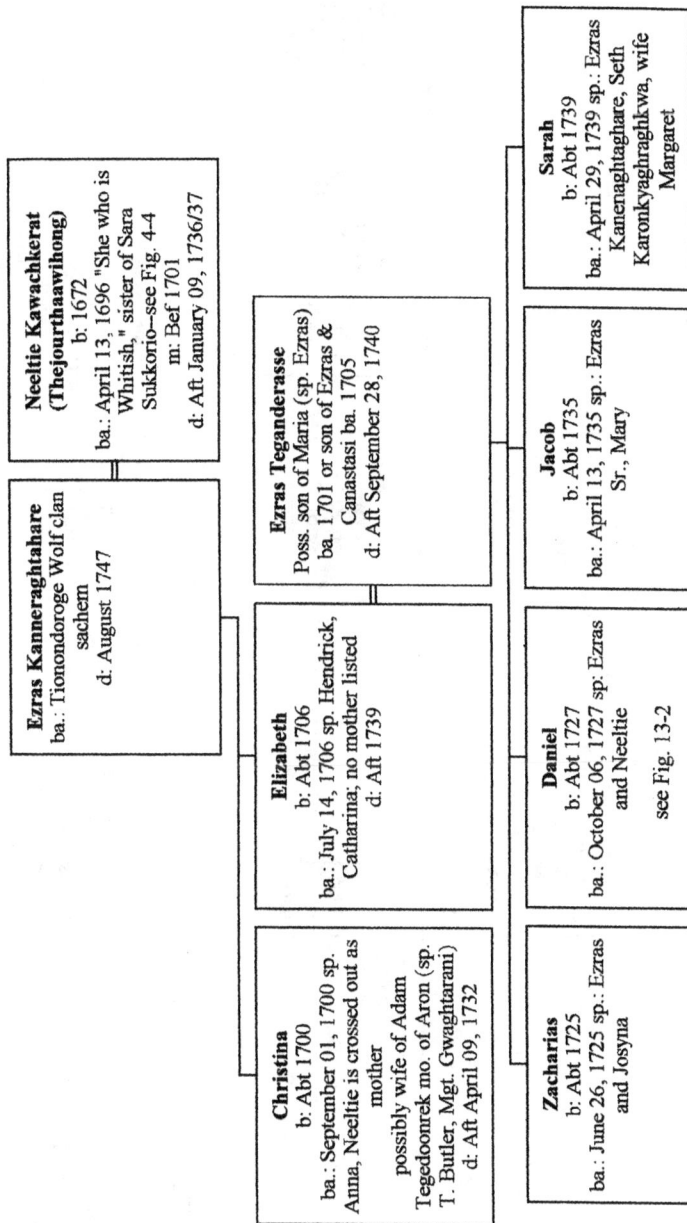

Neeltie Kawachkerat (Thejourthaaawihong)
b: 1672
ba.: April 13, 1696 "She who is Whitish," sister of Sara Sukkorio–see Fig. 4-4
m: Bef 1701
d: Aft January 09, 1736/37

Ezras Kanneraghtahare
ba.: Tionondoroge Wolf clan sachem
d: August 1747

Ezras Teganderasse
Poss. son of Maria (sp. Ezras) ba. 1701 or son of Ezras & Canastasi ba. 1705
d: Aft September 28, 1740

Elizabeth
b: Abt 1706
ba.: July 14, 1706 sp. Hendrick, Catharina; no mother listed
d: Aft 1739

Christina
b: Abt 1700
ba.: September 01, 1700 sp. Anna, Neeltie is crossed out as mother
possibly wife of Adam Tegedoonrek mo. of Aron (sp. T. Butler, Mgt. Gwaghtarani)
d: Aft April 09, 1732

Sarah
b: Abt 1739
ba.: April 29, 1739 sp.: Ezras Kanenaghtaghare, Seth Karonkyaghraghkwa, wife Margaret

Jacob
b: Abt 1735
ba.: April 13, 1735 sp.: Ezras Sr., Mary

Daniel
b: Abt 1727
ba.: October 06, 1727 sp: Ezras and Neeltie

see Fig. 13-2

Zacharias
b: Abt 1725
ba.: June 26, 1725 sp.: Ezras and Josyna

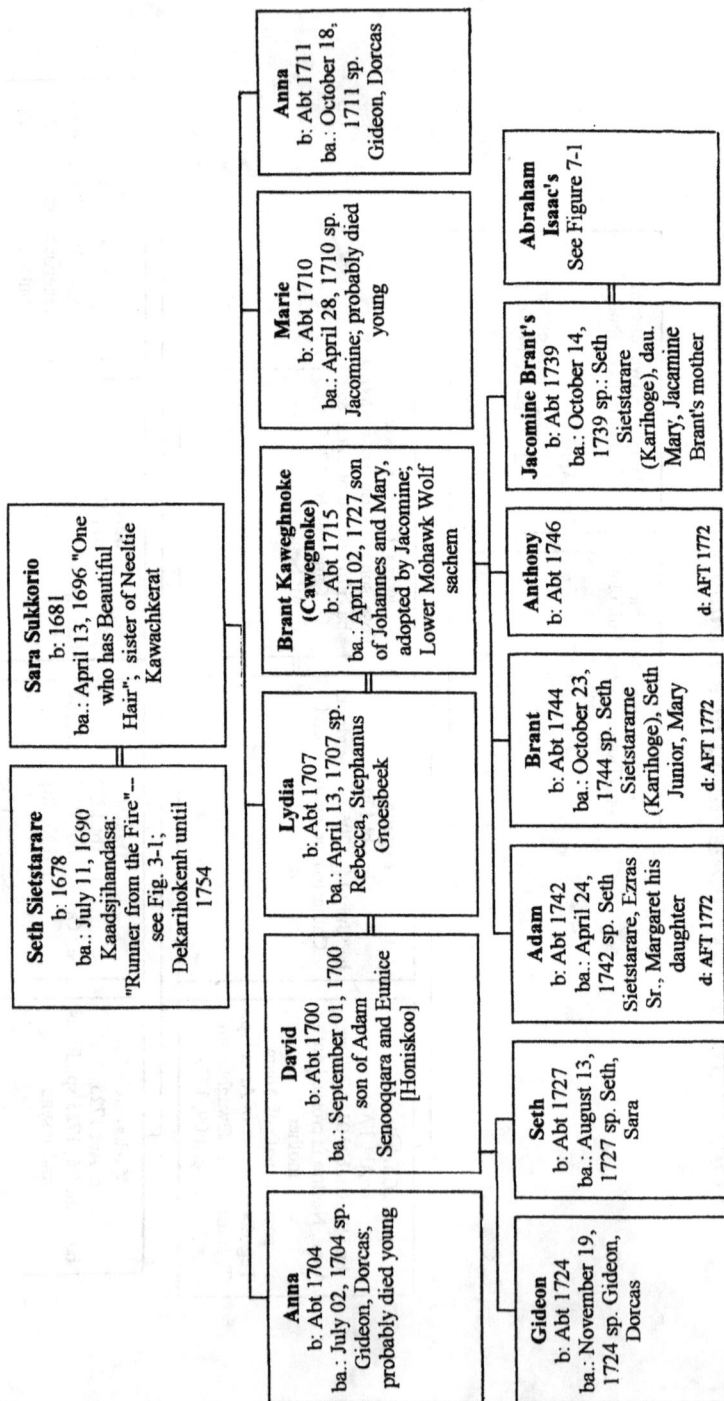

Figure 4-4. *Descendants of Seth Sietstarare and Sara Sukkorio*

Figure 4-4. Descendants of Seth and Sara (Continued)

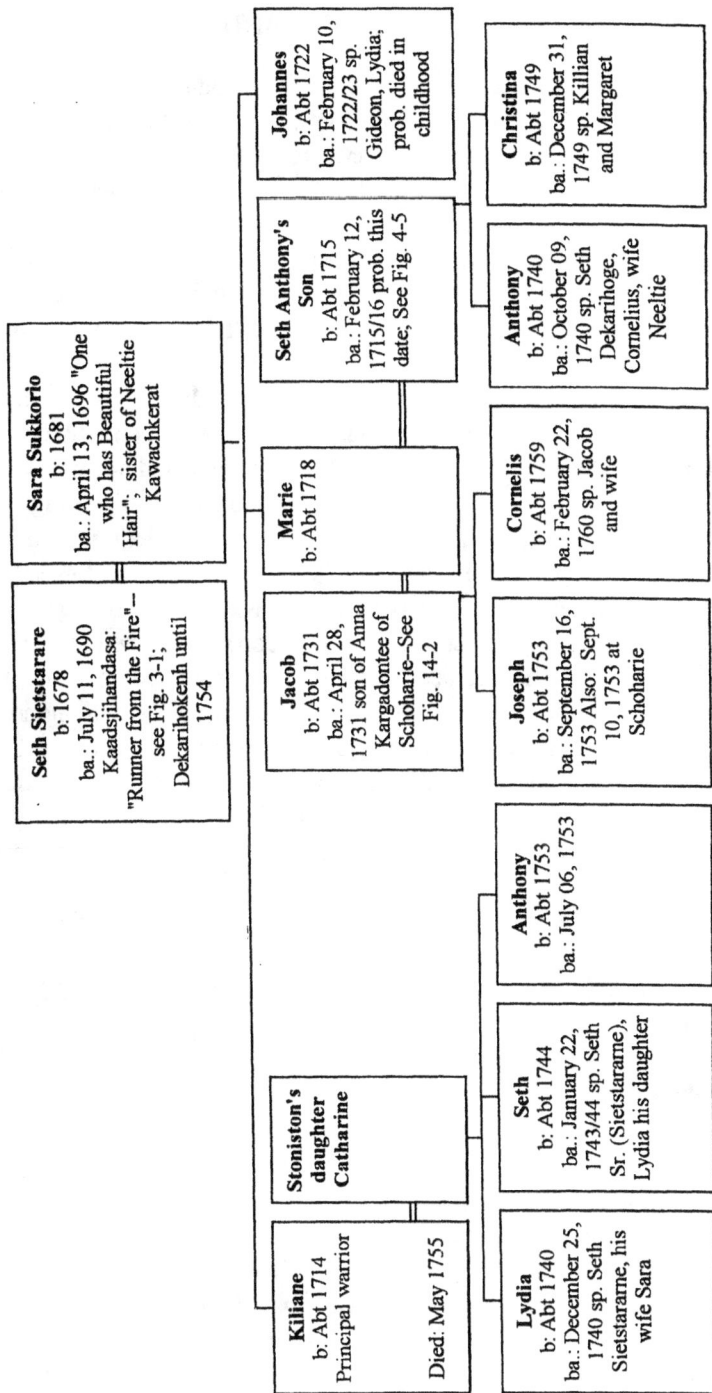

Seth Sietstarare
b: 1678
ba.: July 11, 1690
Kaadsjihandasa:
"Runner from the Fire"—
see Fig. 3-1;
Dekarihokenh until
1754

Sara Sukkorio
b: 1681
ba.: April 13, 1696 "One
who has Beautiful
Hair", sister of Neeltie
Kawachkerat

Johannes
b: Abt 1722
ba.: February 10,
1722/23 sp.
Gideon, Lydia;
prob. died in
childhood

Seth Anthony's Son
b: Abt 1715
ba.: February 12,
1715/16 prob. this
date; See Fig. 4-5

Marie
b: Abt 1718

Christina
b: Abt 1749
ba.: December 31,
1749 sp. Killian
and Margaret

Anthony
b: Abt 1740
ba.: October 09,
1740 sp. Seth
Dekarihoge,
Cornelius, wife
Neeltie

Cornelis
b: Abt 1759
ba.: February 22,
1760 sp. Jacob
and wife

Jacob
b: Abt 1731
ba.: April 28,
1731 son of Anna
Kargadontee of
Schoharie–See
Fig. 14-2

Joseph
b: Abt 1753
ba.: September 16,
1753 Also: Sept.
10, 1753 at
Schoharie

Killiane
b: Abt 1714
Principal warrior

Died: May 1755

Stoniston's daughter Catharine

Anthony
b: Abt 1753
ba.: July 06, 1753

Seth
b: Abt 1744
ba.: January 22,
1743/44 sp. Seth
Sr. (Sietstarame),
Lydia his daughter

Lydia
b: Abt 1740
ba.: December 25,
1740 sp. Seth
Sietstararne, his
wife Sara

leadership and denounced the 1697 deed, dramatically casting a copy of it into the fire. Schuyler and his political colleagues backed out of the grant, leaving Dellius and Hilletie to bear the brunt of the royal governor's denunciations. In 1699 Bellomont and the assembly formally revoked the three deeds, suspended the dominie from his pulpit, and removed Hilletie from her position as official interpreter to the province.[12]

Dellius, with thoughts of his political vindication in mind, made, through Hilletie, one last attempt to secure the support of his converts before he left for Europe, in June, 1699.

Hilletie encountered Gideon in Schenectady and urged her clan brother to go and bid Dellius goodbye, and more particularly to implore Dellius to return speedily. Gideon replied that he could not speak, for he had no present to lay down before the dominie, "according to our custom." The ever-resourceful Hilletie supplied Gideon with a beaver skin and sent him and his wife on their way to Albany. Several other Mohawk leaders and a number of Mohawk women also gathered at Albany. On the urging first of Dorcas (Gideon's wife), then of Hendrick's mother-in-law, then Rebecca and several other women, and finally Gideon, three Mohawk leaders: Hendrick, Joseph, and Sinnonquirese arrived at the dominie's kitchen. Hilletie, having come to Albany herself, and Dellius met with the Mohawks. The interpreter said to Hendrick and the others: "Speak now, Mr. Dellius is going over sea, speak hard, talk your best that he may return again to us in the spring for you are praying Indians."[13]

Before the Mohawks could reply on their own, Hilletie "took the word out of their mouth" and blamed the base people that "stir you up and draw you with a line." She then persuaded Hendrick and Joseph to sign what amounted to a recantation of their charges against the dominie concerning the deeds, asking forgiveness of Dellius and requesting his speedy return.[14]

When Dellius reached Europe he produced a sheath of memorials aimed at vindicating his conduct. Bellomont sent his own flow of papers to England against Dellius and was the more successful. The dominie never returned to America.[15]

The denunciation and revocation of the Dellius grant caused great disillusionment among the Mohawks toward the Protestants in Albany. With the Iroquois specifically left out of the treaty of peace between England and France, morale among the entire Five Nations was low, and more defected to the Mohawk settlements in Canada, following the urging of the French priests. Brant and Jacob were persuaded to stay in their homeland only by Hendrick. Tjerk, who with his wife Agnes Kajaidahje had brought their daughter Susanna and son Reineer to be baptized at Albany in 1693 and 1697, departed sometime in the ensuing years for Canada and "turned papist." Others did likewise. By 1700, two-thirds of the Mohawks had left.[16]

By the summer of 1701, delegates from all five Iroquois nations made peace with the French in Canada. At the same time they had also sent delegates to a conference with the lieutenant governor of New York, John Nanfan, at Albany. The Iroquois sachems at Albany realized the need for protection against the French, and thus they signed a deed turning over their western, "beaver" hunting grounds to the king of England, in return for his allowing them to hunt there unmolested. Hendrick, Joseph, and Cornelis Tirogaren signed this deed for the Mohawks, as did Tosoquathoa, Tsinago, Sinnonquirese, and the old sachem Onucheranorum. These last two were described as "the two principal sachems" of the Mohawks, neither baptized.[17]

This deed was drawn up to play the English off against the French rather than transfer land which the Iroquois had little claim to in the first place. These settlements with the French and English governors in the summer of 1701 inaugurated an Iroquois policy of neutrality which would last for over forty years.[18]

Meanwhile, the white Dutch church members in Albany and those in Schenectady sent petitions to the classis of Amsterdam requesting a new minister. Two officials of the classis met, and decided that the best solution was to send the minister of the church in Antwerp (in modern Belgium), Johannes Lydius, to Albany and have Dellius take over the Antwerp church. Lydius was given the appropriate letters of certification and sent to wait for the next appropriate ship.[19]

A third member of the committee, William Bancker, had been supposed to pick the new Albany minister. Instead he did something exceedingly odd. A native of New York, Bancker deliberately kept himself out of the meeting that chose Lydius and went instead to Westphalia (in what is now Germany) and picked an erstwhile tailor, Bernardus Freeman (or Freerman) to be hastily ordained there and sent to Albany on a ship leaving immediately. Freeman had previously failed the Amsterdam classis examination for minister, not even qualifying as a "comforter of the sick." But he ardently wanted to go to America.[20]

The two candidates arrived in New York within days of each other in July, 1700 and, with barely concealed hostility, sailed to Albany on the same schooner. They were met by the Albany church officials and Dominie Nucella of Esopus, who had been the interim pastor (when he could spare the time) to the Albany County Christians. Both candidates presented their credentials before the Albany church officials and preached a sermon.[21]

With the official backing of the Amsterdam classis, Lydius was installed as the minister of the Albany church. Not to be gainstayed in his search for a parish, Freeman went to Schenectady, by mid-August being accepted by this poor and isolated frontier church as its first minister since Dominie Tessenmacher had been killed by Indians in the 1690 raid.[22]

Lydius had been in the Albany pulpit for less than a month when Governor Bellomont held a council there with the Five Nations. Hendrick and others among the Protestant Mohawks thanked the governor for vacating the fraudulent land grants and then visited the new dominie. With Bellomont supplying an interpreter (probably Hilletie, who was reinstated as interpreter by 1701), Lydius conducted the "daily exercise of praying and singing" and expressed his wish to continue with Dellius' work. In a letter to the Amsterdam classis Lydius rather baldly expressed his resentment of Bernardus Freeman's installation at Schenectady: "How he could have done so [accepted the Schenectady post], on so insecure a foundation, I cannot comprehend. I . . . pointed out to him how such a way of doing things conflicted with all Ecclesiastical Regulations. But it seems that he [Freeman] cares for nothing, if he can only earn a stiver somewhere by preaching." Lydius lost no time in writing his fellow pastors of this highly irregular installation, perhaps in the hopes of having Freeman removed.[23]

In this he was disappointed, for Freeman had gained a powerful supporter, the Earl of Bellomont. Using his own judgement on the relative merits of the two ministers, Bellomont told the Iroquois sachems at the August, 1700, conference that he was appointing Freeman as their missionary. Whatever had so impressed William Bancker in Europe had also impressed the English Earl in Albany.

That fall Bellomont badly needed a source of masts and spars for the king's warships, and the Indians held claim to the forests which had trees large and straight enough for the ships' needs. The Earl, firmly distrusting "Schuyler or any of his party to make a bargain with the Mohacks for their woods—they would not [have] done it without finding their [own] account in it, to the King's cost," decided to circumvent the Albany anti-Leislerites. On November 15, 1700, Bellomont wrote Dominie Freeman at Schenectady, probably requesting his help in contacting the Mohawks. Freeman responded with a discrete letter promising his assistance.[24]

On December 26, 1700, eleven Mohawks ("sachems" in Bellomont's description—see Appendix F) who are described in the grant as "praying Mohawks and principal owners of the Mohawk country": Henry [Hendrick] Tejonihokarawa (Fig. 3-1), Joseph Dehanochrakhas, Amos Soocerhat, Hendrick Degandsiondagqua, Cornelis Tirogaren, Jacob Tohagigharigo, Brant Saquainquaragton (Fig. 5-1), Koor Sinhanawaght, Asa Onasiadikha, Ezras Kanneraghtahare (Fig. 4-3) and Sionhaytowane (or Soonagtowane, Ezras Sogjowanne) granted the king permanent right to cut down lumber in their country "in consideration that his excellency [Governor Bellomont] hath provided [the praying Mohawks] with a good Minister who teaches and instructs them." This contract did not, however, deed over the land itself, which remained in the "property and possession" of the Mohawks.[25]

In return the Earl of Bellomont attempted to get Freeman a salary from the Boston missionary society and a stipend for his interpreter. He also appointed Lydius as Freeman's assistant. When these funds were not forthcoming, the governor tried to get the New York assembly to supply the three men (the dominies and Freeman's interpreter), but as late as 1708 none had received anything like full compensation for their work.[26]

Despite the difficulty in securing a salary, for the next five years Dominie Freeman struggled among the poverty of the Schenectady living, lacking adequate funds for the gift-giving necessary for formal talks with the Indians. Without the backing of the Albany traders (who threw their support to Lydius, possibly because of Freeman's part in Bellomont's secret agreement with the Mohawks), but with the help of his own church member, the Mohawk-speaking Lawrence Claes, the Schenectady dominie proselytized the Mohawks, learned enough of the their language to give talks in Mohawk, and translated "a great part of our liturgy . . . into the Indian tongue; in particular morning and evening prayers, the litany, the creed of St. Athanasias, etc. besides several places of the old and new Testament." He even became the first minister to visit the Mohawk town of Ochniondage (or Ogniondage) where he baptized converts on May 23, 1701, and again on August 15, 1703.[27]

After his first year at Schenectady, Freeman's success was such that Hendrick reported to the acting governor (Bellomont had died) in July, 1701 that:

> we Maquase have now two Castles that are begun to pray or turn Christians; we desire that we may have a good large Church made in the first or nearest castle called Ochniondage which was promised us by the late Earl of Bellomont, and let it be so large as may contain us all. There is only a little Chapel made of bark now; a small number makes it full.[28]

During his five years at Schenectady Freeman baptized forty-two Mohawk adults and seventy-one children, admitted in the neighborhood of forty adults as communicants, and married at least six couples. Hendrick and Joseph, the two sachems who had protested Dellius' land grants, were frequent sponsors in Freeman's church, and Joseph and his wife Anna had the dominie baptize two of their children, Johannes on July 19, 1702, and Anna, on April 7, 1705. Ezras Kanneraghtahare and his wife Neeltie were communicants and prominent members, as were Rebecca Jokeÿha (Deiudhodawae) and her husband Johannes Tejejachso (Teiaiagse or Tejasse), and Canastasi Koaroni and her husband Ezras Sonihoware (Sogjowanne). On April 19, 1701, Lea Kwaowarate, her two daughters Alida and Eunice, and her sister Josine sponsored adults, who may have come from the upper (Canajoharie) castle of the Mohawks. Also there that day was Louisa, whose husband Onigoheriago would be baptized by Freeman in the "little chapel made of bark" at Ogniondage on May 23, 1701, and, as Johannes Onigoheriago the Wolf clan Mohawk from Canajoharie, be one of the four "kings" to visit England in 1710.[29]

A few Mohawks, however, continued to go to the church in Albany and to regard the Reverend Johannes Lydius as Dellius' legitimate successor. The leaders of this group were Gideon Tonidoge and his wife Dorcas Sakkoherriho and Asa and his wife Rebecca Kowajatense. Gideon and/or Dorcas were parents, adoptive parents, or sponsors of eight out of the sixteen individuals who were baptized by Lydius between

1700 and 1705. Despite the backing of Peter Schuyler, former Albany mayor, alderman Dirk Wesselse Ten Broeck, and the acting governor, Lydius could bring no more than a few Mohawks to his services. His rivalry with Freeman did, however, create a good deal of strife amongst the Protestant Mohawks. Awanay, a Mohawk sachem, spoke in a meeting with the acting governor in July, 1702, saying,

> There has been feuds and animosities among us Christian Indians, and last summer we were recommended to amity and Friendship, but it hath not had that good effect upon us as could have been wished for. We have been lately exhorted by your Lordship at Mr. Lydius's the minister's house to unite as Christians and not to live in envy and malice, which are the works of Satan, not becoming [to] Christians, but to live in Peace in concord, and then God would bless us, which last exhortation hath so wrought upon our spirits, that we are now all united and friends. . . .[30]

The fact that Gideon and Dorcas were Lydius' greatest supporters was to create long-term ties between the dominie's family and some of that couple's relations. On October 6, 1700, Dominie Lydius baptized three children adopted by Gideon and Dorcas, children of Gideon's brother (adopted in the sense that they would be raised by Gideon and Dorcas—they kept their original clan affiliations). Rotsiho, aged twelve, was given the name Johannes. The minister himself was probably the child's sponsor. His five-year-old brother Adanho was baptized as Seth and sponsored by Dirk Wesselse Ten Broeck, and their sister Kaken-harontje was baptized with Lydius's mother's name, Sara, and sponsored by the dominie's wife, Isabelle Lydius.[31]

Johannes would most likely become the head Turtle clan sachem of Tionondoroge, Johannes Segehowane, Seth Adanho the son-in-law of Ezras Kanneraghtahare, and Sara the wife of Anthony and mother of another Seth who would marry Seth Deharihokenh's daughter Mary (see Figs. 4-4 and 4-5). The dominie's grandchildren, Nicholas and (Isabella) Margaret Lydius (Fig. 8-5) would sponsor Seth Adanho's grandson Seth in the Albany church on July 10, 1748, and Johannes Segehowane's granddaughter Catharina on December 25 of that year.[32]

The dominie's only son, John Henry Lydius, would also make use of these ties, especially the relationship of his father with Johannes

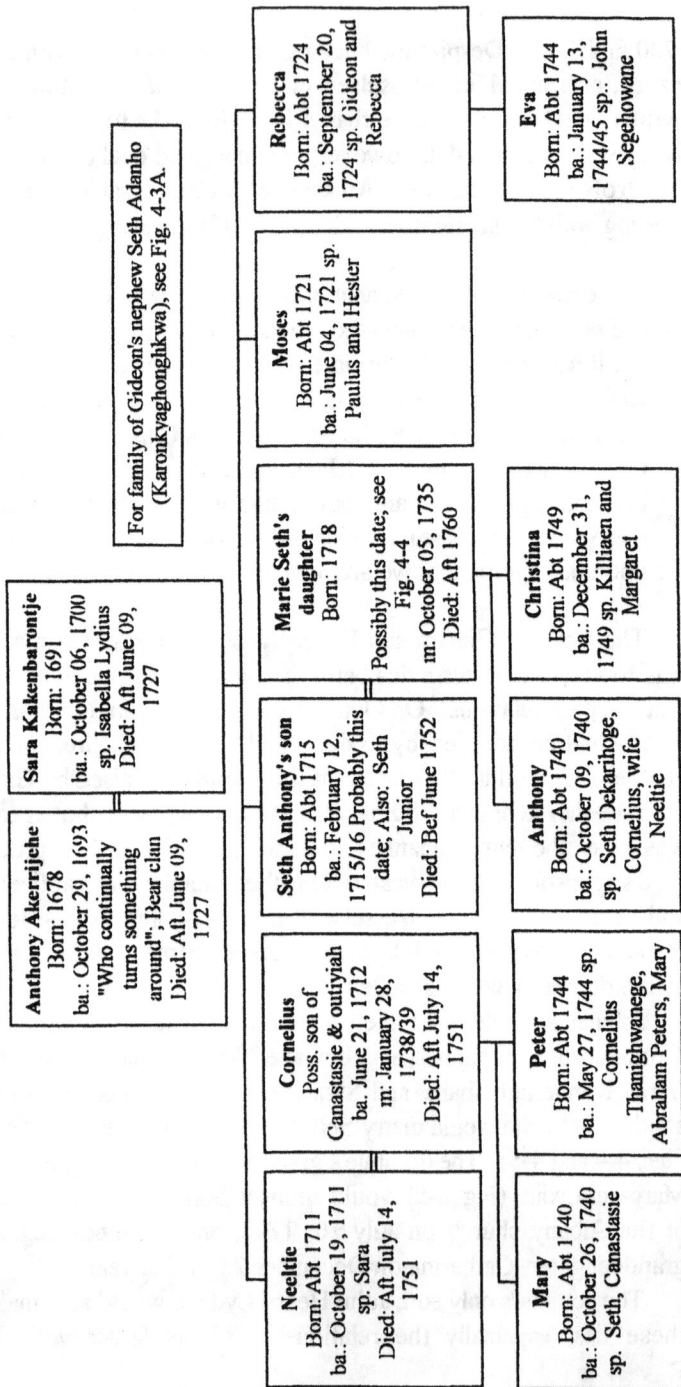

Figure 4-5A. *Descendants of Gideon's Niece Sara Kakenbarontje and Anthony Akerrijehe*

Anthony Akerrijehe
Born: 1678
ba.: October 29, 1693
"Who continually turns something around"; Bear clan
Died: Aft June 09, 1727

Sara Kakenbarontje
Born: 1691
ba.: October 06, 1700
sp. Isabella Lydius
Died: Aft June 09, 1727

For family of Gideon's nephew Seth Adanho (Karonkyaghonghkwa), see Fig. 4-3A.

Rebecca
Born: Abt 1724
ba.: September 20, 1724 sp. Gideon and Rebecca

Eva
Born: Abt 1744
ba.: January 13, 1744/45 sp.: John Segehowane

Moses
Born: Abt 1721
ba.: June 04, 1721 sp. Paulus and Hester

Marie Seth's daughter
Born: 1718
Possibly this date; see Fig. 4-4
m: October 05, 1735
Died: Aft 1760

Christina
Born: Abt 1749
ba.: December 31, 1749 sp. Killiaen and Margaret

Seth Anthony's son
Born: Abt 1715
ba.: February 12, 1715/16 Probably this date; Also: Seth Junior
Died: Bef June 1752

Anthony
Born: Abt 1740
ba.: October 09, 1740 sp. Seth Dekarihoge, Cornelius, wife Neeltie

Cornelius
Poss. son of Canastasie & outiyiah
ba.: June 21, 1712
m: January 28, 1738/39
Died: Aft July 14, 1751

Peter
Born: Abt 1744
ba.: May 27, 1744 sp. Cornelius Thanighwanege, Abraham Peters, Mary

Neeltie
Born: Abt 1711
ba.: October 19, 1711 sp. Sara
Died: Aft July 14, 1751

Mary
Born: Abt 1740
ba.: October 26, 1740 sp. Seth, Canastasie

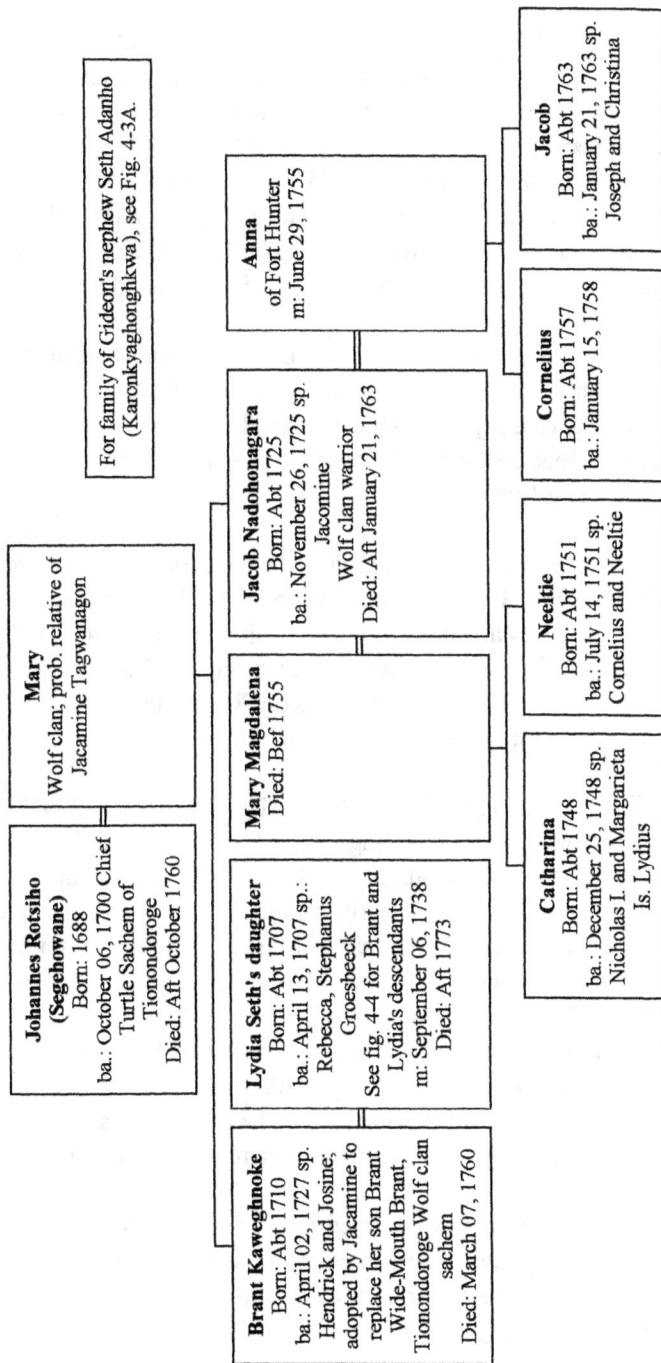

Figure 4-5B: Descendants of Gideon's Nephew Johannes Rotsiho (Segehowane)

Segehowane. John Henry Lydius became an adopted member of the Turtle clan and married a quarter-Indian Frenchwoman, Genevieve Massé, niece of the famous Madame Montour (see Chapter 8). He eventually became a fur trader, securing an extensive tract of land on Wood Creek north of Albany in 1732 with a deed which specifically mentions "John Lydius his ten years service among them [the Mohawks], instructing them in the Christian faith and performing all the offices of a minister of the Gospel among them." The deed goes on to state:

> As also in consideration of the great pains & diligence of the said John Henry Lydius in instructing several of them to read and translating & copying several of David's Psalms for them, his frequent visits, and many Christian and friendly offices performed and to be performed for them. . . .

The deed is signed by Caregohe, Tejonagarawe [Hendrick Tejonihokarawa, Fig. 3-1], Canneragtaherie [Ezras Kanneraghtahare, Fig. 4-3], Egnitee, Tewagnidoge [Gideon Tonidoge, Figs. 4-1 and 4-2], Testirrarie [Seth Sietstarare Dekarihokenh, Figs. 3-1 and 4-4], Tejasse [Johannes Tejasse, Fig. 3-5], Carogjarageon, Ragsotjata, and Canadagaye [probably Killian Canadagaye, baptized in the Albany church on April 9, 1732].[33]

Lydius became an Indian agent for Massachusetts, and in 1754 he would use his contacts among the Mohawks to orchestrate the Susquehannah Company purchase. In 1755 he would appeal to his "Turtle clan brothers," particularly Aaron, a Turtle clan war captain of Tionondoroge, to come to the aid of Massachusetts governor William Shirley, to the detriment of Indian Superintendent William Johnson (see Chapter 13).[34]

The poverty of the Schenectady church caused Freeman to accept a call to Flatbush, New York, in July, 1705. For the next five years the Mohawks kept asking for him back, "that he live [with us] in our Castle and not at Schenectady or Albany." Freeman's wife was opposed to this move, however.[35]

As early as 1703 a newly formed missionary society, the Society for the Propagation of the Gospel in Foreign Parts, had decided to appoint a Church of England missionary to minister to the Mohawks. They appointed Thoroughgood Moore to fulfill this duty. Moore arrived in

Albany in 1704 and sent a wampum belt with a message to the Mohawk country, requesting to live among them. The Mohawks eventually received him at their first castle, but refused the missionary's request to live with the Mohawks. Frustrated in his attempts to proselytize the Indians, Moore left the next year.[36]

After Freeman left, the Mohawks took their children to the Albany church to be baptized; twenty-two between Freeman's leaving and Lydius' death in early 1710. Lydius's demise left only one Protestant minister in Albany, the Reverend Thomas Barclay of the Church of England. The Reverend Barclay baptized children in the Dutch church, and in late April and May of 1710 he also baptized several Mohawk children who were brought to him for the sacrament.[37]

At the time of these baptisms, three Mohawks and one River Indian were making a sensational appearance at the English court.

CHAPTER V

The Four Kings

War between England and France had recommenced in May of 1702, but the Five Nations remained neutral. On July 23, 1702, the Mohawks asked the new New York governor, Lord Cornbury, for permission to send Awanay, one of their sachems, and Brant to Canada to exchange prisoners with the Canadian Indians. His lordship refused, but the Mohawks ignored him, sending four sachems to Canada in late summer/early fall of that year.[1]

Cornbury, a first cousin of Queen Anne, was singularly uncaring in his dealing with the Iroquois. He failed to send the 1701 deed of Iroquois beaver lands to London and moreover, he held no formal councils with them after July, 1702 and gave them no presents after the first council. He added insult to injury by failing to condole the death of the chief Mohawk sachem, Onucheranorum, in 1708 until the French had done so. He also failed for two years to confirm Robert Livingston's appointment to the office of Secretary of Indian Affairs when the latter returned from England in 1706.[2]

As the war dragged on in Europe one Boston merchant (and Robert Livingston's son-in-law), Samuel Vetch, formed a plan to rid the North American continent of the French. He sailed to England in 1708 with his scheme for a two-pronged attack against Montreal and Quebec. One arm of the attacking forces would sail down the St. Lawrence and the second would march north to Montreal from Albany. Queen Anne agreed that in the next year, 1709, a combined operation would be directed against the French in Canada. A fleet sailing from England would bring some regular British forces while two American forces would gather, one near Wood Creek and a second in Boston to await transportation to Quebec.[3]

In preparation for the attack, Killaen van Rennsselaer and Robert Livingston sent two Mohawks, "the most trust[ed] and most secret Indians you can get"—Ezras Kanneraghtahare and Cornelius Tha-

58

neghwanege (Tanechwanege)—to Montreal to spy out the fortifications, and three River Indians to Quebec with the same mission. With forces and supplies assembling at Boston for the expedition in August of 1709, five Iroquois sachems were invited to Boston to see the gathering of British might. One of them was Brant, almost certainly Brant Saquainquaragton (Fig. 5-1).[4]

The colonial army gathered in New England in the summer of 1709, eagerly awaiting the arrival of the English fleet. As they waited, sickness and desertions thinned their ranks. Word finally came that the fleet, essential to the invasion of Canada, was not coming—it had been diverted to Portugal! An Iroquois delegation, who were also at Wood Creak waiting with the colonial troops, went home in disgust.[5]

By that fall the New York commanders, Francis Nicholson, Peter Schuyler and others, knew they had to do something to repair the damage caused by the failure of the summer's expedition, for the Iroquois were more than ever opposed to intervening to aid the English. Thus in October the commanders wrote to a group of colonial governors meeting in Newport, Rhode Island, suggesting that representative sachems of the Iroquois should be sent to England to be impressed with British power and affluence, in an attempt to sway their adherence to neutrality. On October 14 the governors passed a resolution to this effect.[6]

These plans probably fitted in well with the wishes of the Iroquois leadership. Since 1701, when they had urged Robert Livingston, a commissioner for Indian affairs, to go to England and present their deed—and their troubles—before the queen, it was obvious to at least some of the Mohawks that they would greatly benefit by a direct approach to the Lords of Trade or even to the crown itself.[7]

Moreover, two other reasons had become important for the Mohawks themselves to approach authorities in England. The leaving of Dominie Freeman and the grave illness of Dominie Lydius (who by July, 1709 could not carry out many of his ministerial duties) demonstrated to the Protestant Mohawks the need for at least one permanent missionary in their territory. Having rejected the Reverend Moore in 1704-05, and probably not satisfied with the Reverend Thomas Barclay (whose duties in Albany left him little time for proselytizing the Indians), the Protestant Mohawks undoubtedly realized the usefulness of a direct appeal to religious authorities in England.[8]

A second issue was the great amount of rum which had made its way

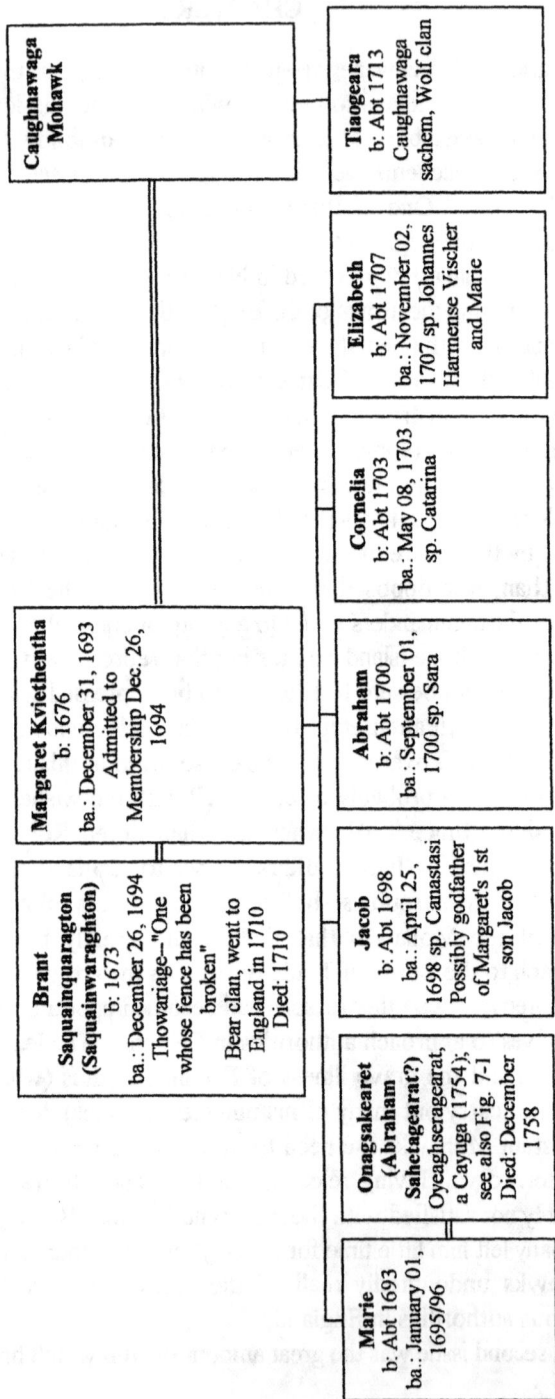

Figure 5-1. Possible Descendants of Margaret Kviethentha and Brant Saquainquaragton

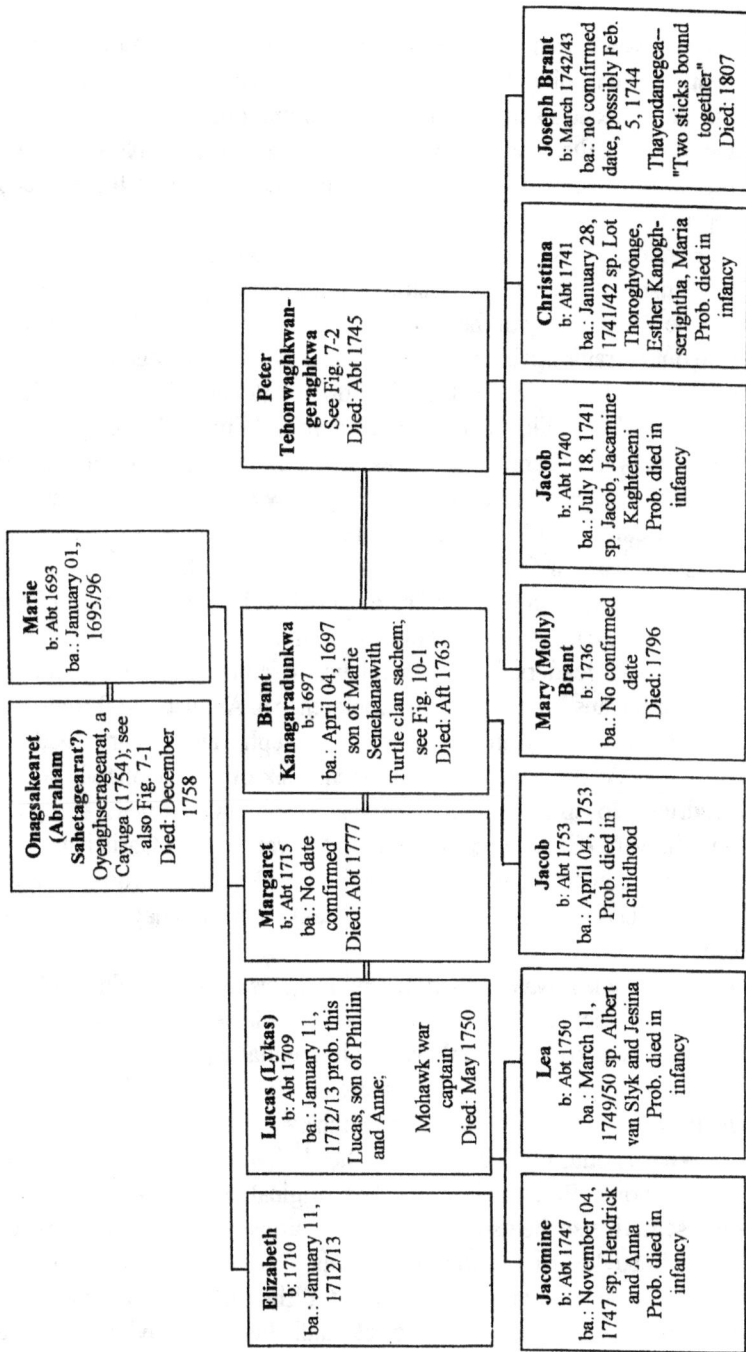

Figure 5-1. Possible Descendants of Margaret Kviethentha and Brant (Continued)

to the Mohawk castles. Under the maladministration of Lord Cornbury, questionable trading practices had again arisen in Albany in connection with an increase in the fur trade. Unscrupulous traders had used and abused rum in their dealings with the Indians. Responsible Iroquois and Algonquin (Mahican and River Indian) leaders wanted these excesses stopped.[9]

Hendrick Tejonihokarawa was probably one of these leaders. Since his baptism in 1690 and admission to communion in 1691, Hendrick had become a trusted ally of the important people in Albany. By 1695 he had gone out on raids against the French, and in 1697 he was one of Dellius' emissaries to Canada. In 1696 Hendrick had enough authority that his mark on the Dellius deeds gave them validity. By August, 1700, Hendrick was a sachem and speaker at a conference with the governor and later that year at another conference with the eastern Indians. He also appeared at the Albany conferences in July of 1701 and 1702. Hendrick was, in fact, the first Mohawk chief whose conversion and continued close links with the Protestant churches may have significantly furthered his career within Mohawk polity.[10]

Mohawk leadership in general was becoming more influenced by "praying Indians." At the Albany conference in August, 1700, only three sachems listed—Awanie (Awanay), Joseph, and Henry—had been baptized. At the next year's conference six of nine Mohawk sachems, Hendrick, Joseph, Gideon, Cornelis (probably Cornelis Tirogaren), Sidgsihowane (Ezras Sogjowanne), and Awanay were Christians. In the July, 1702 conference—headed as before by Onucheranorum—Hendrick, Tanograthask (Joseph Dehanochrakhas), and Awanay attended (see Table 5-1).[11]

By the time it was decided to send Iroquois leaders to England in late 1709, Hendrick was an obvious choice. Viewed, in part for religious reasons, as a "trusted" Mohawk by influential whites in New York, his value as an intermediary had also increased in the eyes of his own people (he may even have spoken some Dutch).[12]

What is odd, however, is the other Indians chosen by Indian affairs commissioner Peter Schuyler. The original resolution had called for representative sachems from all Five Nations. It is not known whether or not Schuyler tried to get any Oneida, Onondaga, Cayuga, or Seneca leaders to accompany the party. Of the other three Indians who eventually accompanied Hendrick and Peter Schuyler, his cousin

Table 5-1. Mohawk Sachems at Councils in Albany, 1690-1702

Feb. 25, 1690[a]	Aug. 27, 1700[b]	July 12-19, 1701[c]	July 18, 1702[d]
Sinerongnerese (speaker)	Sinonquirese	Sinnonquirese	Sinnonquirese
Rode			
	Onucheranorum	Onucheranorum (speaker)	Onucheranorum (speaker)
Saggoddiochquisax			
	Henry	Hendrick [Tejonihokarawa]	Hendrick
Oquedagoa	Aquedagoe		
	Joseph [Dehanochrakhas]	Joseph	Tanograthask [Joseph]
Tosoquatho	Tosoquathoa	Tolo Quatho	Toloquatho
Odagerasse			
Aridarenda			
Jagogthare			
		Gideon [Tonidoge]	
		Cornelis [Tirogaren]	
		Sidgsihowanne [Ezras Sogjowane]	
	Awanie	Awanay	Awanie
	Wadoene		
	Utsege		
	Dekanodasse		
	Aenruchtse		
			Orridigha

[a]*DHNY* 2:91.   [b]*DRCHNY* 4:728.   [c]*DRCHNY* 4:897.   [d]*DRCHNY* 4:985.

Abraham Schuyler, and Colonel Nicholson to England, two were Mohawks and one was a River Indian.

The second Mohawk was Brant Saquainquaragton. Called Thowariage in 1696, Brant had acquired the name Saquainquaragton (or Saquainwaraghton) by September, 1700. Brant was the first known holder of this important name, described 177 years later by its then holder as "the title of my chieftainship." Saquainwaraghton—Sayenquerachta—Soiengarahta—was the name given to a chieftain who carried a smoking brand from one village to kindle a council fire in another village. The "Disappearing Smoke" idea in this name perhaps relates to the brand disappearing into the forest. Although Brant was not a sachem, it is more than probable that he came from an influential family, and his near defection in 1700 was cause for alarm among the Mohawks at Tionondoroge. In 1703 Brant and another Christian Mohawk, the sachem Awanay, were named as emissaries to Canada in the redemption of prisoners. These two incidents make it likely that Brant had ties with the Canadian Mohawks. Perhaps this was the reason Brant had been one of the five Iroquois leaders to visit Boston in 1709 and chosen to go to England in 1710.[13]

Aged thirty-seven at the time of the voyage, Brant was, like Hendrick Tejonihokarawa, a church member and one who regularly appeared in the church records. He was married to another communicant, Margaret Kviethentha (or Kaietentha), and the father of five known children (see Fig. 5-1).[14]

The third Mohawk chosen for the trip to England was Johannes Onigoheriago, a member of the Wolf clan from the second castle of Canajoharie. Onigoheriago had been baptized on May 23, 1701, but his wife Louisa had previously brought in two of their children for baptism, Joseph on January 1, 1700, and Louisa on May 5, 1700. Given her name, she had probably been baptized in Canada. Four more children, Gideon, Rebecca, Jacob, and Martha, were baptized by 1712 (see Fig. 5-2).[15]

The fourth Indian chosen to go to England was a River Indian, possibly from Schaghticoke or from a Mahican settlement south of Albany on the Hudson. His name was Etowaucum. He was a war chief of the River Indians, having been one of the leaders of the expedition against the French in the summer of 1691. In August, 1695 Major John Abeel in Albany reported sending Etowaucum ("Itawacam") with one Gerrit Lucase to the sachems of the Five Nations with the request that

Figure 5-2. Descendants of Johannes Onigoheriago and Louisa

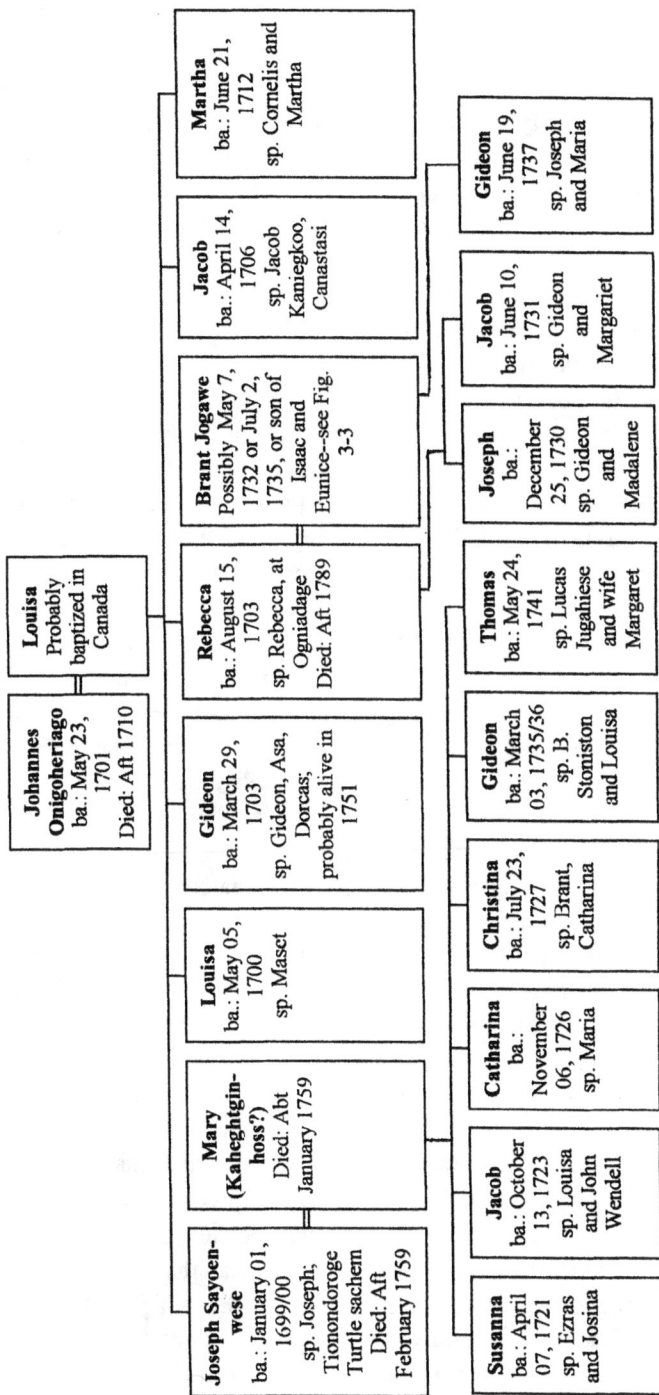

Johannes Onigoheriago
ba.: May 23, 1701
Died: Aft 1710

Louisa
Probably baptized in Canada

Joseph Sayoen-wese
ba.: January 01, 1699/00
sp. Joseph; Tionondoroge Turtle sachem
Died: Aft February 1759

Mary (Kaheghtgin-hoss?)
Died: Abt January 1759

Louisa
ba.: May 05, 1700
sp. Maset

Gideon
ba.: March 29, 1703
sp. Gideon, Asa, Dorcas; probably alive in 1751

Rebecca
ba.: August 15, 1703
sp. Rebecca, at Ogniadage
Died: Aft 1789

Brant Jogawe
Possibly May 7, 1732 or July 2, 1735, or son of Isaac and Eunice--see Fig. 3-3

Jacob
ba.: April 14, 1706
sp. Jacob Kaniegkoo, Canastasi

Martha
ba.: June 21, 1712
sp. Cornelis and Martha

Susanna
ba.: April 07, 1721
sp. Ezras and Josina

Jacob
ba.: October 13, 1723
sp. Louisa and John Wendell

Catharina
ba.: November 06, 1726
sp. Maria

Christina
ba.: July 23, 1727
sp. Brant, Catharina

Gideon
ba.: March 03, 1735/36
sp. B. Stoniston and Louisa

Thomas
ba.: May 24, 1741
sp. Lucas Jugahiese and wife Margaret

Joseph
ba.: December 25, 1730
sp. Gideon and Madalene

Jacob
ba.: June 10, 1731
sp. Gideon and Margariet

Gideon
ba.: June 19, 1737
sp. Joseph and Maria

they meet with Governor Fletcher (the Iroquois declined because of French activity at Cadarachqui). At an unknown time and place Etowaucum was baptized Nicholas (Nicus or Nickus). He was a member of his tribe's Turtle clan. His first wife was also a Mahican or Schaghticoke; his second wife was a Mohawk, Margaret or Griete, and their daughter, Catryn (Catherine), was baptized at Schenectady on June 21, 1712 (see Fig. 5-3 and Chapters 6 and 14).[16]

In discussing the choce of these four men as emissaries, previous writers have stressed the political necessity of impressing the Iroquois with the power of their erstwhile ally, England. Yet at least three of these men were already firmly in the English camp. What is evident, however, is the prominence of three out of the four in the Mohawk Protestant community. Hendrick as the natural spokesman was probably an obvious choice, politically and religiously. Brant, who seemed to have had ties with the Canadian (Caughnawaga) Mohawks, was nonetheless an active member of the Dutch church, as was Johannes Onigaroheriago. The latter was probably picked because he was from Canajoharie, the upper or second castle of the Mohawks. Only Nickus Etowaucum's political affinity to the English appears to have been greater than his religious observance, although his second wife may have been an active member of the praying Mohawks. The religious agenda of the Mohawks themselves must have been a considerable factor in who eventually accompanied Schuyler to England.

The four "kings" (as they were immediately called in England) sailed from Boston on February 28, 1710, and reached England at the beginning of April. On the 19th of that month, after being suitably applauded by wondering crowds, lodged in King Street, and clothed in European dress, they had an audience with Queen Anne. In their speech the sachems stressed their need of security and protection from the French, mentioned the nefarious influence of French priests, and requested that if the queen could send her own priests to instruct them, the Indians would give them "a most hearty Welcome." After their speech the Indians exchanged gifts with the queen, the sachems giving the queen necklaces, bracelets, and shells of wampum, Her Majesty reciprocating with 200 guineas.[17]

Of more importance to the Indians was that the queen turned over their requests to her secretary of state, the Earl of Sunderland, and to the Archbishop of Canterbury, who in turn sent a copy to the Society for the Propagation of the Gospel. The Society resolved to send two

Figure 5-3. Descendants of Nicholas Etowaucum

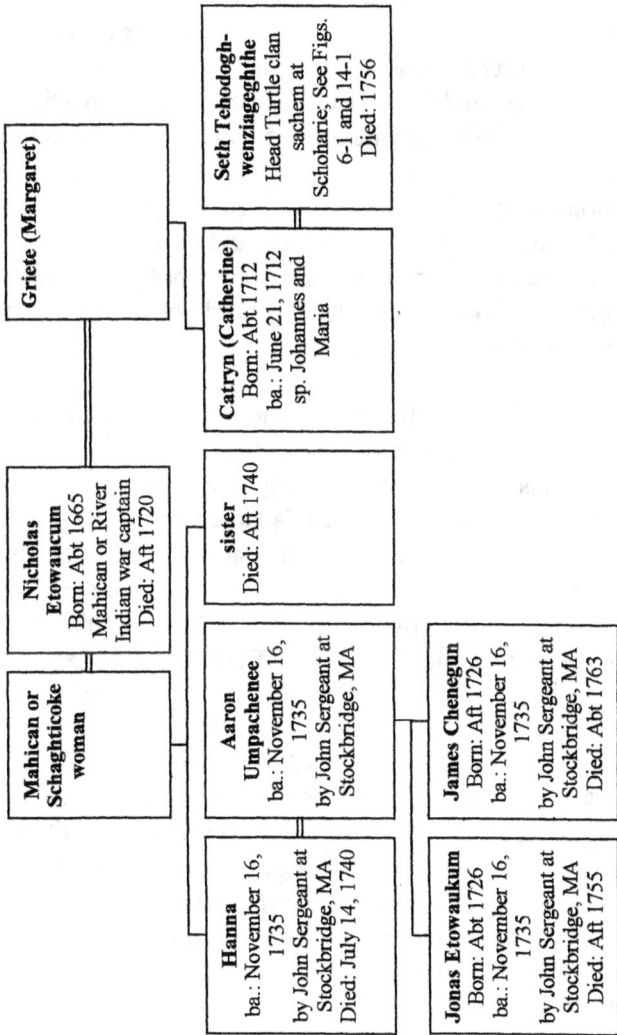

Griete (Margaret)

Nicholas Etowaucum
Born: Abt 1665
Mahican or River Indian war captain
Died: Aft 1720

Mahican or Schaghticoke woman

Seth Tehodogh-wenziageghthe
Head Turtle clan sachem at Schoharie; See Figs. 6-1 and 14-1
Died: 1756

Catryn (Catherine)
Born: Abt 1712
ba.: June 21, 1712
sp. Johannes and Maria

sister
Died: Aft 1740

Aaron Umpachenee
ba.: November 16, 1735
by John Sergeant at Stockbridge, MA

Hanna
ba.: November 16, 1735
by John Sergeant at Stockbridge, MA
Died: July 14, 1740

James Chenegun
Born: Aft 1726
ba.: November 16, 1735
by John Sergeant at Stockbridge, MA
Died: Abt 1763

Jonas Etowaukum
Born: Abt 1726
ba.: November 16, 1735
by John Sergeant at Stockbridge, MA
Died: Aft 1755

missionaries to the Iroquois and put a stop to the sale of intoxicating liquors to the Indians. The queen for her part agreed to erect a fort in the Mohawk country to house the chapel and protect the missionaries. She also sent two sets of Communion Plate to be used at the Mohawk chapel and at another proposed chapel in the Five Nations country. The Indian leaders were greatly pleased, since the fort would answer some of their military problems and the ministers and chapels their religious ones. No one explained how the missionaries would or could stop the sale of liquor.[18]

During their visit the four were feted, banqueted, and painted three times, they attended plays and concerts, and on a more serious note, they had conferences with representatives from the Society for the Propagation of the Gospel and the Lords of Trade. They departed England in May, arriving back at Boston on July 15 and Albany on August 7.[19]

On their return, the four men met varying fates. Johannes Onigoheriago seems to have "sunk into obscurity," but he left an active and vigorous family. His son Joseph became Joseph Sayoenwese, a Lower Castle sachem and father of a large family. The last reference to Joseph Sayoenwese is the sad note that he had "lost all his family" in 1759, undoubtedly to disease. Johannes and Louisa's daughter Louisa appears as a sponsor to two of her brother Joseph's children in 1723 and 1736, but nothing more is known of her. Johannes and Louisa's son Gideon signed the 1732 Ehle/Van Driessen deed to lands near Canajoharie and probably went with a group of Canajoharies to Stockbridge, Massachusetts, in 1751. Johannes and Louisa's daughter Rebecca had three sons, and her son Joseph had at least one child by 1751, when the family likewise visited Stockbridge. Rebecca lived to a great age, appearing as Rebecca Jayaweaye (her husband was Brant Jogawe) on the treaty of 1789 surrendering rights to lands on the Mohawk River. Her descendants are probably found among the descendants of the Mohawks who settled the Bay of Quinte after the American Revolution.[20]

Etowaucum was probably living at Schoharie after 1710, for his daughter Catharine, by local tradition, became the wife of the chief sachem of the Schoharie Mohawks (see Chapter 6). Another daughter by his first wife was the mother of a youth named Etowaucum who appeared at Yale in 1732 (see Chapter 11).[21]

Of the four "kings," Brant Saquainquaragton's children left the fewest traces, probably because of their father's untimely death, a few months after his return in 1710. This Brant has often been called the grandfather of the famous Mohawk war chief, Joseph Brant (1743–1807), but it would be a mistake to equate Joseph Brant with Brant Saquainquaragton because of the name, because the surname Brant was acquired from Joseph's stepfather. It is possible, nonetheless, that Joseph Brant was descended from Brant Saquainquaragton.[22]

When visiting England in 1776, Joseph Brant told James Boswell that he was the grandson of one of the four kings. Chronologically, he may have been the great-grandson of one, but the two kinship terms are identical in Mohawk. One late nineteenth-century tradition on the Six Nations Reserve in Canada said that Joseph Brant's mother was the granddaughter of Hendrick, but since Joseph and his mother were of the Wolf clan, and Elizabeth, Hendrick Tejonihokarawa's daughter, was a member of the *Dekarihokenh* Turtle *ohwachira*, this is impossible. It was Joseph Brant's *wife's* mother, not his own mother, who was Hendrick Tejonihokarawa's stepgranddaughter (Fig. 3-1). However, perhaps Katie Moses and Charlotte Smith, the Mohawk informants who spoke with Lyman Draper in 1879 and who remembered this tradition, were speaking of Hendrick Peters (whose ceremonial name was also Saquainquaragton); thus they confused the mid-eighteenth-century Saquainquaragton with the earlier holder of the name. If so, the two women meant that Joseph Brant's mother was a granddaughter of Brant Saquainquaragton.[23]

Joseph Brant reportedly came from Huron stock on both sides of his family. Although one story speaks of the capture of his grandmother in Canada, this tale probably relates to a more distant ancestress in the 1640s. By the 1660s Huron captives among the Mohawks made up much of the pro-Jesuit party in the tribe and formed the core of those who journeyed to Canada to start the Caughnawaga Mohawk settlements. Since Brant Saquainquaragton was intending to move to Canada in 1700 and was sent to redeem prisoners among the Canadian Mohawks a few years later, it is probable that he or his wife had relatives at Caughnawaga. Brant's wife Margaret Kviethentha was baptized on the same day as Tjerk's daughter Susanna. Since Tjerk did go to Canada and "turn papist," possibly it was Margaret who had the Caughnawaga relatives.[24]

On May 24, 1761, Daniel Claus reported that "Tiaogeara, the

Caghnawago Sachm., Brant's wife's uncle is coming a short time to see his relations." In this context, the Brant in question was Joseph Brant's stepfather Brant Kanagaradunkwa, and Kanagaradunkwa's wife was Joseph's mother. Tiaodaroo is later mentioned as a chief of the Wolf clan at Caughnawaga, and thus an uncle on Joseph's mother's mother's side. Given the generational difference, Joseph Brant's maternal grandmother would have been an older (or oldest) daughter and Tiaogeara a great deal younger (or youngest) son (see Fig. 5-1).[25]

Another genealogical relationship, noted by Claus, was that Joseph's sister Molly Brant and their mother Margaret had "relatives at Cayuga," implying a Cayuga in the maternal family tree. One Claus family tradition said that Molly Brant's father was a Cayuga, but circumstantial evidence points to her father being Peter Tehonwaghkwangeraghkwa, the father of Joseph Brant.[26]

There is no certain baptism for Margaret, the mother of Joseph and Molly Brant. Judging from the births of her children, she was born between 1713 and 1717. Margaret named her oldest child Molly or Mary, which may suggest that her own mother was named Mary or Maria. Molly Brant named her oldest daughter Elizabeth, which may harken back to an aunt or some other important woman in her family.

On January 11, 1713, Elizabeth, aged two, was baptized at Fort Hunter, the daughter of Maria and Onagsakearet. An Oyeaghseragearat attended the Albany conference in April, 1754. He was a Cayuga.[27]

All of this suggests that Margaret, Joseph and Molly Brant's mother, was a younger sister of the Elizabeth baptized in 1713, and that her parents were Onagsakearet (or Oyeaghseragearat), a Cayuga and Maria, the older (or oldest) sister of Tiaogeara, a Caughnawaga sachem or chief. Brant Saquainquaragton and Margaret's (note the name) oldest daughter Marie was baptized on January 1, 1696. She was a small child, probably two to four years old, just old enough to be the wife of Onagsakearet and mother of Elizabeth (named for Marie's sister Elizabeth, baptized on November 2, 1707), born in 1710 and baptized on January 13, 1713 (see Fig. 5-1). It's possible that, after Brant Saquainquaragton's death in 1710, Margaret Kviethentha moved to Caughnawaga to be near relatives. She could easily have had another son by a second husband between 1710 and 1715 or so, this son being Tiaogeara. This would explain Joseph Brant's telling James Boswell (the author of a sketch on Joseph that appeared in *The London Magazine*) that his "grandfather" (actually, great-grandfather) was one of the four kings.

Hendrick Tejonihokarawa, the principal "king," or "emperor" as he was sometimes termed in England, came back to yet another land controversy, this time over lands that bordered Schoharie Creek, which flowed into the Mohawk river from the south. At the heart of this particular dispute was the fate of a people from Germany who were being sent to North America. Because the majority were from the area of Germany known as the Palatinate, they became known as the Palatines.

CHAPTER VI

Schoharie and Its Mohawks

In Europe the wars between France and the Dutch and their German allies had, by 1708, produced great suffering amongst the peoples whose lands through which the armies marched. This was followed, in 1708-09, by one of the coldest winters in a century. Hardest hit were the people who lived along the Rhine River and its adjacent territories. Generally Protestant, the people of this area, the Palatinate, turned their attention to pamphlets which began to circulate in their country describing opportunities in the English colonies in America. The pamphlets led them to expect aid from Queen Anne in getting to America, once they had gotten themselves to England. Eager Palatine families packed their scanty goods and set off up the Rhine River toward the Netherlands, where ships took them across the channel.[1]

They came by the thousands. By July, 1709, over ten thousand German immigrants were camped outside London, fed at the public expense. Throughout the following fall and winter, the British government discussed what to do with them. The newly appointed governor of New York, Robert Hunter, sponsored a plan whereby the Palatines, to pay for their upkeep and passage to the New World, would be sent to live in pine forest regions in that colony and produce pitch for the Royal Navy. The government accepted this plan, and Hunter and the Palatines set sail for New York on April 10, 1710, just as Hendrick Tejonihokarawa and his companions arrived in England.[2]

Upon arriving in New York in early June, Governor Hunter decided that the Palatines could be settled on lands along Schoharie Creek, which he mistakenly believed had been purchased by the Nicholas Bayard grant in 1695. He directed the Commissioners of Indian Affairs to notify the Mohawk sachems of his plans, clear up any lingering claims the Mohawks might have on the land, and ask their assistance with surveying it.[3]

The Mohawk leadership received this unpleasant news on July 2, 1710. The next day they reminded the commissioners (who scarcely needed reminding) that the Earl of Bellomont and the New York assembly had revoked the Bayard deed to Schoharie and asked, "Do you think to deal with us like Children?"[4]

But the Mohawks were obviously thrown into disarray and uncertain about the request, supposedly from the queen herself, for their speaker also said, "We shall not be against her request to let her have ye land for poor people." Faced with such a momentous decision, the Mohawk leaders told the commissioners they would not allow the land to be surveyed before Hendrick and the others returned from England.[5]

On the 12th of July, however, two sachems arrived in Albany with the news that a general meeting of the Mohawks had been held, and it had been agreed that the land could be surveyed, these two messengers being sent to assist the surveyors. Secretary of Indian Affairs Robert Livingston informed the New York Council of this decision on July 20, as Governor Hunter prepared to go to Albany to have a meeting with the Five Nations.[6]

Faced with the impending purchase/grant of all the good flat land along Schoharie to the crown, on July 19 three Albany traders, Abraham Cuyler, Harmanus Wendell, and Evert Wendell, purchased about a mile of land along the west side of Schoharie Creek from Sogharowane, a member of the Wolf clan. The race for the Schoharie lands was on.[7]

The governor soon learned that the lands along Schoharie Creek had no trees appropriate for making pitch, for on July 24 he wrote the Lords of Trade that though the land along Schoharie had no pines, it was nonetheless being surveyed and other land would be found suitable for the Palatines to settle and make pitch. Hunter seemed not to realize that neither he, nor his government, nor Nicholas Bayard had any valid claim to the Schoharie lands.[8]

On August 22 Hendrick and the other Mohawk sachems met separately with Hunter. They were looking forward to the queen's making good her promises about the missionaries and the forts. Confidant of the queen's good faith, and perhaps reassured by her generous presents, Hendrick told the governor that the Mohawks would cede all the land along both sides of Schoharie Creek up to about five miles above the Falls to the queen, reserving only one planting plain and the adjacent woodland for themselves. However, Hendrick also prayed that no more land would be bought in a clandestine manner, and prayed that when land was sold it would be done so only with the approval of all three clans of the Mohawks: the Turtle, the Wolf, and the Bear. This was an attempt to regularize and partly control a practice that the Indians realized, even at this date, they could not halt. The Mohawk sachems left Albany without signing a formal deed for the Schoharie land; nor did they accept presents for it, an unheard of action and indicative of their deep dislike for the land concession.[9]

This dislike surfaced again, for the next year there was another conference with the governor about the Schoharie lands. Hunter claimed that the sachems had signed a deed for the land and reproached the Mohawks for "re-assuming the Gift." The Mohawks again consented to give it up, but again, despite the governor's claim, they signed no deed. By then, however, the Palatines were settled on 6,000 acres on the Hudson River, called Livingston's Bush, purchased from Robert Livingston. Governor Hunter was paying for their keep until they became self-supporting, and Secretary Livingston contracted to supply them with their wants until the venture had become profitable. Why Hunter had continued to press for the Mohawks' Schoharie lands in the face of the Palatines' settlement elsewhere is inexplicable, unless he hoped to use these lands to recoup the inroads into his personal fortune made by supporting the Palatines.[10]

On August 22, 1711, at Schenectady the Mohawks also deeded 260 acres of land near the hill called Onitstagrawa, on the west side of Schoharie Creek two or three miles above Middleburgh, N.Y., to Adam Vrooman, a wealthy Schenectady trader. The eighteen signers of this deed, apparently including six from each clan, included a number of familiar names: the sachem Sinnonquirese, Hendrick, Amos, Jacob, Cornelius, Johannes, and Ezras. By 1714, when the governor issued a patent on the basis of this deed and a second one signed that year, the 260 acres in the deed had expanded to over a thousand.[11]

Among the Palatines at Livingston's Bush the pitch pine project was progressing poorly. It was discovered first that trees had to be prepared for two years before they would produce pine tar, and later that the trees had been prepared incorrectly. Only the children, gathering pine knots, came up with a small but viable pine tar source. Their parents grew more and more hungry, restless, and angry, feeling they had been cheated of the farm land promised them. Somehow they had learned of the

Mohawks' cession of the lands along Schoharie Creek for their benefit. In the fall of 1712 Governor Hunter, having lost a fortune supporting the Palatines, told the immigrants they would now have to support themselves. A delegation of seven of the Palatine leaders made their way to the Schoharie Valley. They looked at the lush flatlands, met some of the Indians, and resolved to stay no longer at Livingston's Bush.[12]

One of these seven, John Conrad Weiser, soon brought his family to Schenectady, one of many Palatines intending to move to Schoharie in the spring. Weiser grasped the importance of friendly relations with the Mohawks and the need to communicate with them directly. When a delegation of Mohawk leaders passed through Schenectady from Albany after welcoming the new Church of England missionary, Weiser spoke with one of the sachems and requested that his oldest boy—also named John Conrad—go and live with the Mohawks to learn their language. The sachem agreed, and in late November, 1712, sixteen-year-old Conrad Weiser (as he became known) left with "a chief of the Maqua Nation named Qua y nant . . . to his country to learn the Maqua language."[13]

Quaynant, or Taquayanont as the name is often spelled, was originally from the Canadian Mohawk settlement of Caughnawaga, probably attracted back to the Mohawk homeland because of the trading opportunities which had opened up at Albany after the settlement of 1701. He signed the August 22, 1711, grant of land on Schoharie Creek to Adam Vrooman and the July 10, 1714, deed to Margaret Collins and her son. The mark he made on the latter deed was labeled a serpent, which might be a rearing wolf.[14]

In the Schoharie Valley in 1712 there were several Indian settlements. The main settlement, called Eskahare, was about twenty-four miles south of Tionondoroge and had about forty people in seven or eight houses. It was probably above Central Bridge on both sides of the creek and was later abandoned or moved several miles up the valley to the site of the old Schoharie railroad depot. The latter place was occupied by the Mohawks nearly to the time of the Revolution and contained a burying ground.[15]

Eight miles south of Eskahare was another Indian settlement called the Wilder Hook on about four hundred acres of land on the west bank of Schoharie Creek near Middleburgh. According to tradition, it was first settled by a Canadian Mohawk chief named Karighondontee who was captured by the Mohawks and married a chief's daughter. Karighondontee and his wife were placed so far from the other Mohawk settlements to protect them from the anger some Mohawks had against the Caughnawagas.[16]

Karighondontee (Tigreedontee) was one of the signers of a deed dated April 30, 1714, to Adam Vrooman for a parcel of land adjacent to the acreage purchased in 1711. He also signed (as DeGarydonde or Degarytunteey), for the Bear clan, a deed dated February 6, 1723, to three Palatine settlers. Karighondontee's wife Marie was a member of the Turtle clan, for their son, Seth, baptized in Albany on April 30, 1710, became chief sachem and chief of the Turtle clan at Schoharie from the 1730s until his death in late 1756 or early 1757.[17]

By 1712 there were also Mohegans living along Schoharie Creek in a small settlement on the east bank in present day Middleburgh. One tradition says that Etowaucum was the father of Karighondontee's wife, but church records make it evident that Etowaucum's daughter Catharine married Seth, Karighondontee's son. The Karighondontee tribe became quite numerous, for Karighondontee had at least three sons: Lawrence Nahohidaye (probably the oldest), Seth Tehodoghwenziageghthe, and Hans Ury Aghsunhaqacks, and four daughters: Anna, Catharine, Marie, and Margaret. Anna Kargadonte was born on the Mohawk river, according to the marriage record of 1745 when she married Pelles (or Bellis) Warreson. This husband, probably her second, was born on Long Island. His name might have been rendered as Paulus, Mary's son. Anna's first husband was Peter, by whom she had a son Jacob baptized in 1731. She probably also had an older son Seth, who signed a petition in 1754 (as Seth Karighondontee Jr.) with his Karighondontee aunts and uncles, indicating that his mother was dead by then. The second daughter, Catharine, married a Mahican ("Fichtahekan" in the Schoharie church records) and named her son Nicholas, either after Nikus Etowaucum or Nicholas Arighwanientha, probably head of the Wolf clan at Schoharie in the 1730s. Mary married Jan Ziniungino or Chawanguina, the head of the Bear clan at Schoharie by the 1730s, and Margaret (Margaret Gargadonde in the church records) married Jacob Quinebas (Fig. 6-1).[18]

Young Conrad Weiser spent the winter of 1712 and spring/early summer of 1713 with the Mohawks, becoming an adopted member of one of their families. His biographer, Paul A. W. Wallace, assumes that young Weiser stayed in the Schoharie Valley at Karighondontee's town, but later references to members of Weiser's adopted family are not to

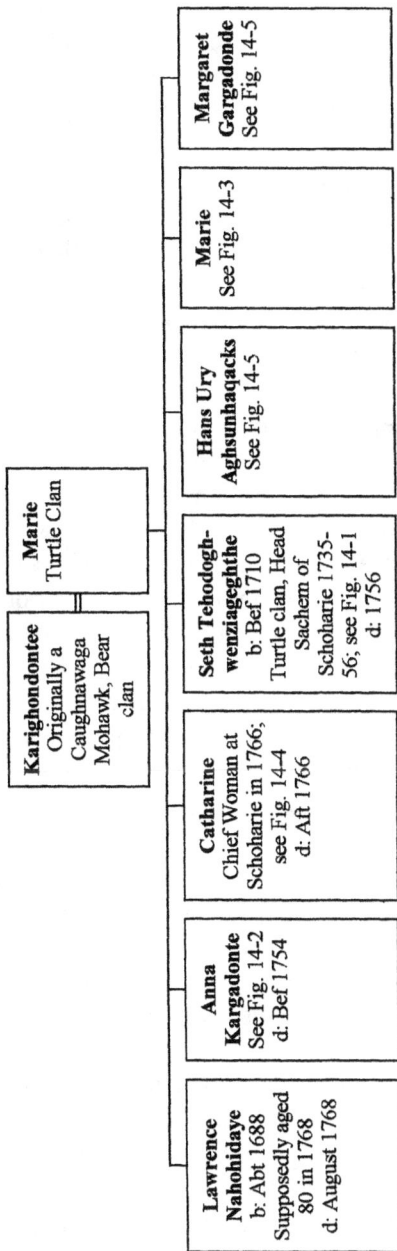

Figure 6-1. Children of Karighondontee and Marie

Karighondontee
Originally a
Caughnawaga
Mohawk, Bear
clan

Marie
Turtle Clan

Lawrence
Nahohidaye
b: Abt 1688
Supposedly aged
80 in 1768
d: August 1768

Anna
Kargadonte
See Fig. 14-2
d: Bef 1754

Catharine
Chief Woman at
Schoharie in 1766;
see Fig. 14-4
d: Aft 1766

Seth Tehodogh-
wenziageghthe
b: Bef 1710
Turtle clan, Head
Sachem of
Schoharie 1735-
56; see Fig. 14-1
d: 1756

Hans Ury
Aghsunhaqacks
See Fig. 14-5

Marie
See Fig. 14-3

Margaret
Gargadonde
See Fig. 14-5

Karighondontee and his family. Conrad's later familiarity with the Karighondontees stems from his father's settlement near the Wilder Hook, at Weisersdorp (Middleburgh), founded in the spring of 1713. One hundred and fifty Palatine families moved into Schoharie that spring.[19]

They broke ground for crops, but needed the Indians' assistance to find wild foods to subsist upon until their first harvest. In the meantime, they were not to be left in peace. To the Mohawks their presence was expected—hadn't their sachems, willingly or unwillingly, given the land to the queen for these poor families? To the whites in authority, especially Governor Hunter, the Palatines' presence was an affront and an illegality.[20]

Into the valley in the summer of 1714 came Samuel Bayard, son of the Nicholas Bayard who had secured a deed to Schoharie in 1695 from "idle drunk Indians." The son repeatedly petitioned the government to reinstate his father's voided deed. Now the younger Bayard declared to the Palatines that they must acknowledge him as their landlord. The outraged and angered Palatines chased him out of the valley. Bayard responded by selling his "interest" in the Schoharie lands to five wealthy Albany citizens, the "Five Partners": Myndert Schuyler, Peter Van Brugh, Robert Livingston Jr., John Schuyler, and Henry Wileman. They in turn petitioned Governor Hunter and the council for a patent on most of the Schoharie Valley in April of 1714, the same month that Adam Vrooman received a license on the basis of his 1711 and 1714 Indian deeds. Neither the governor nor the Five Partners had a deed from the Mohawks for this land, however, and the Indians had ceded the land to the queen, not to the governor for his personal disposal. Nonetheless, in November, 1714, the governor granted a patent to the Five Partners. Not until 1717 did these men secure a deed from the Mohawks for this land, which was described therein as "the lands at Schoharie." Lacking a precise description of the land in question, the Indian deed had no more legality than the governor's 1714 patent. Both the Mohawks and the Palatines had been, in effect, defrauded of the land.[21]

Some Palatine families stayed at Schoharie, often as tenants, others moved to the Mohawk River above the second Mohawk castle of Canajoharie, and another large group, including the Weisers, eventually moved south to Pennsylvania.[22]

The 1717 deed contains the marks of twenty-six individuals

(Appendix F): onowaroge, thanajons, orightaronim, Seth, Canagh-quasee, Sogohondightha, adjagoroende, Dehanadasse, Ahanignawege, Esseras, Esras thejoherede, Rowagjoidane, kaderade, adirwaghtha, Cagnawadigta (Cagnawedyggria), Targions, anongegtha (anonjightha), Canasquisacha, Gedion, Luycas, Canasquiackas, Totquaorese, Aria Canaghowende, Cornelius, Indian Witting[?], Wadonce, and Esseras. Turtles in various guises appear, often looking like many-rayed suns. Other turtles are drawn in profile, swimming. The elaborately drawn turtle with a cross on its back holding a tomahawk, shown in French documents in the late seventeenth century, does not appear. Odd-legged beasts and fat-bellied creatures seem to be bears. Lean and fat wolves appear, one resembling a deer or elk. Most puzzling are snakelike squiggles. Some resemble the line of the rearing head, arched back, and high tail of a wolf, as drawn by the Onondaga Achrireho on the 1701 deed to the king; others may be the line of a swimming turtle. Two Mohawks signed with crosses. The immeasurably helpful custom of signing deeds with clan totems gradually disappeared later in the century, to be replaced by cross marks, initials, and eventually, after the Revolution, by the written names of literate Mohawks.[23]

The lack of literacy of the Mohawk signers of these and later deeds makes it problematic how much they knew of the contents of the papers they signed. The Indians had to trust semi-literate interpreters, such as Leah Stevens, Hilletie's sister, who interpreted these early Schoharie deeds. It was not until the mid-century that a Mohawk, Paulus Peters Saghsanowano Anahario (or Oneahario), could read and write in English, although by that time many of the tribe could read and write in their own language.[24]

While all of this was going along the flatlands of Schoharie Creek, the Mohawks of Tionondoroge were getting used to their first continuous contact with whites, who had built and manned a fort where Schoharie Creek flowed into the Mohawk. Inside this fort was a chapel and parsonage, occupied by the first Church of England missionary to the Mohawks, the Reverend William Andrews.

CHAPTER VII

Fort Hunter

In October, 1711, Governor Robert Hunter signed a contract with five Schenectady men for the construction of a fort at the mouth of Schoharie Creek near the Mohawk castle of Tionondoroge. The plans called for a square fort with blockhouses at each of its corners. Each of the walls was to be 150 feet long and twelve feet high, built with logs a foot square piled "one upon another." The blockhouses were each to be seventeen feet high with two stories, built of smaller logs, nine inches in diameter, and shingled roofs. In the center of the fort would be the chapel, twenty-four feet on a side, ten feet high, with a cellar and garret, "the whole Chappel to be well floor'd." Also within the enclosure was the parsonage for the Anglican missionary. The Mohawk country fort was to be named after the governor.[1]

The fort and chapel were completed in the early fall of 1712, and the Reverend Thomas Barclay dedicated the chapel in the first week of October. The Reverend Barclay had baptized several Indian children in the Dutch church in April and May of 1710, but it is not known if he baptized any Mohawks in his own church during the next two years, for the early records of St. Peter's Church in Albany have not survived.[2]

On October 30, 1710, Jacob Depothonthode's and Jacomine Chagteljouny's daughter Christina was baptized in Schenectady by a visiting dominie, and in October of the following year nine Mohawk children and one adult were baptized there by Dominie Peter Vas. Vas was probably the dominie who baptized five more Mohawk children in Schenectady on February 13, 1712.[3]

Jacob Depothonthode (also called Tehotsogtade and Anonssontje) and Jacomine Chagteljouny (also known as Kowanoogwe and Kwanogweeoh) were one of two contemporary Mohawk couples named Jacob and Jacomine. Jacob Anonssontje had been baptized on July 13,

1701, and admitted to membership with his wife Jacomine in that year. One son, Isaac, was christened at Albany on April 14, 1706, and a second Isaac baptized on December 25, 1708, probably because the first child had died. Jacomine may have been baptized on December 21, 1700, at Schenectady, the mother of a child Christina (sponsored by Christina) who was also baptized on that date (see Fig. 7-1).[4]

The second Isaac became known as Isaac Anoghsookte, clearly his father's name, and was a member of the Bear clan. Isaac had two sons named Jacob (named for his father) and Abraham (named for his step-father), and a third son whose name was also Isaac Anoghsookte (or Aknosotah) or Captain Isaac Hill. A later source said that "Aknosotah" meant "to the end of the house." Isaac's mother, Jacomine (Kagh-tenoone, Kaghteneni, or Kaghteriooni), married as her second husband Abraham Sahetagearat on June 19, 1735. She sponsored Peter Tehon-waghkwangeraghkwa and Margaret's son Jacob on July 18, 1741. Since Peter Tehonwaghkwangeraghkwa and Margaret were the parents of Joseph Brant, Sahetagearat may have been Onagsakearet, Margaret's father (see Chapter 5) and Jacomine thus Margaret's stepmother. This would explain why Jacomine Kaghtenoone sponsored one of Margaret's children.[5]

The second Jacob in the early church records, Jacob Kajingwirage (Large Arrow), was baptized by Dominie Dellius on January 1, 1696, aged twenty-two. On December 27 of that year he brought his daughter Debora to be baptized at Albany. At that time the child's mother was receiving instruction, but there is no record of her baptism. This seems to have been one of the entries Dellius forgot to record. On January 5, 1700, Jacob and Jacomine brought their son Abraam (Abraham) to be baptized at Albany, and on July 4, 1703, a Jacob and Jacomine, probably this couple, had a son Brant baptized at Schenectady, probably an older child rather than an infant. On November 9, 1707, Jacob Kajingwirago's and Jacomine's son Peter was baptized, sponsored by Harman van Slyck (Jacques van Slyck's oldest son) and Rebecca Kowtayolduse (Rebecca Kowajatense) (see Fig. 7-2).[6]

The name Cayenquerago (Kajingwirago) or Swift Arrow was given to Governor Fletcher of New York in 1693, and in the eighteenth century is the name of at least one Bear clan sachem, Jonathan Cayenquerago; thus Jacob Kajingwirago was a member of the Bear clan. His wife Jacomine (probably Tagwanagon), was principal woman of the Wolf clan

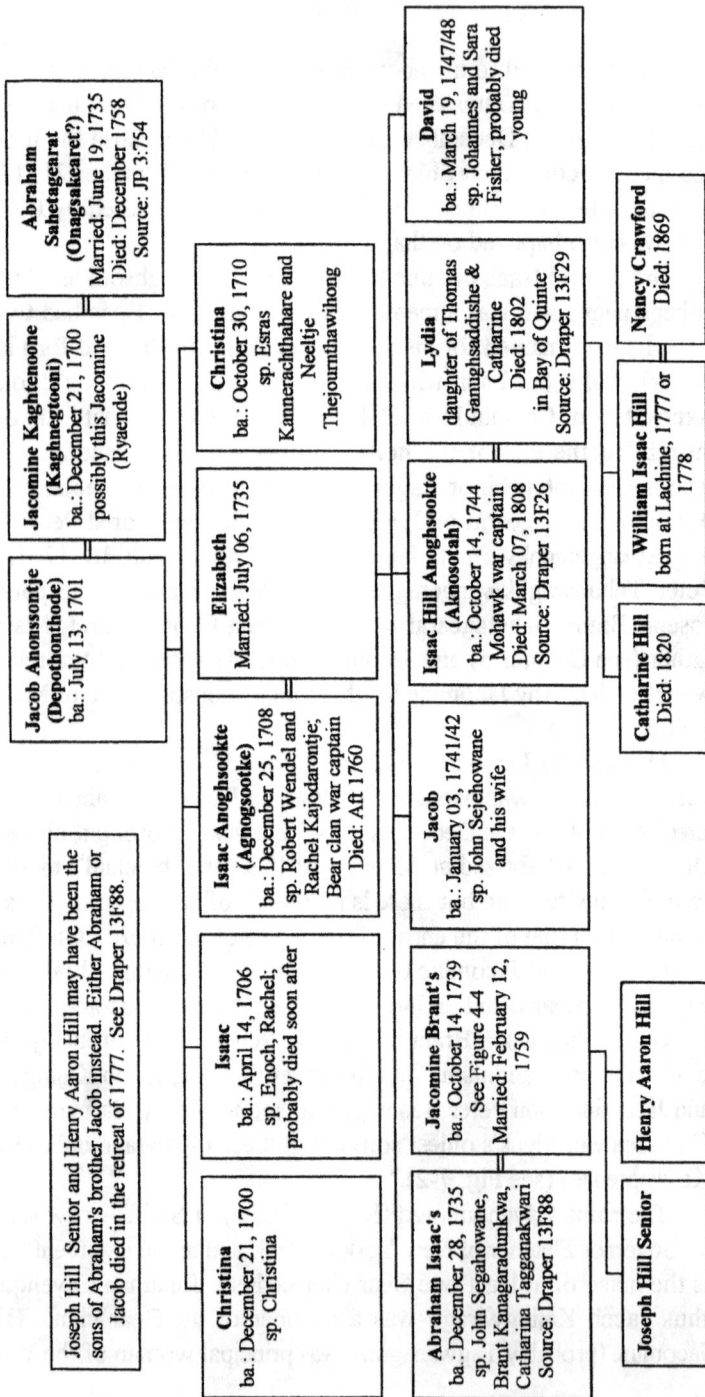

Figure 7-1. Descendants of Jacomine Kaghtenoone and Jacob Anonssontje

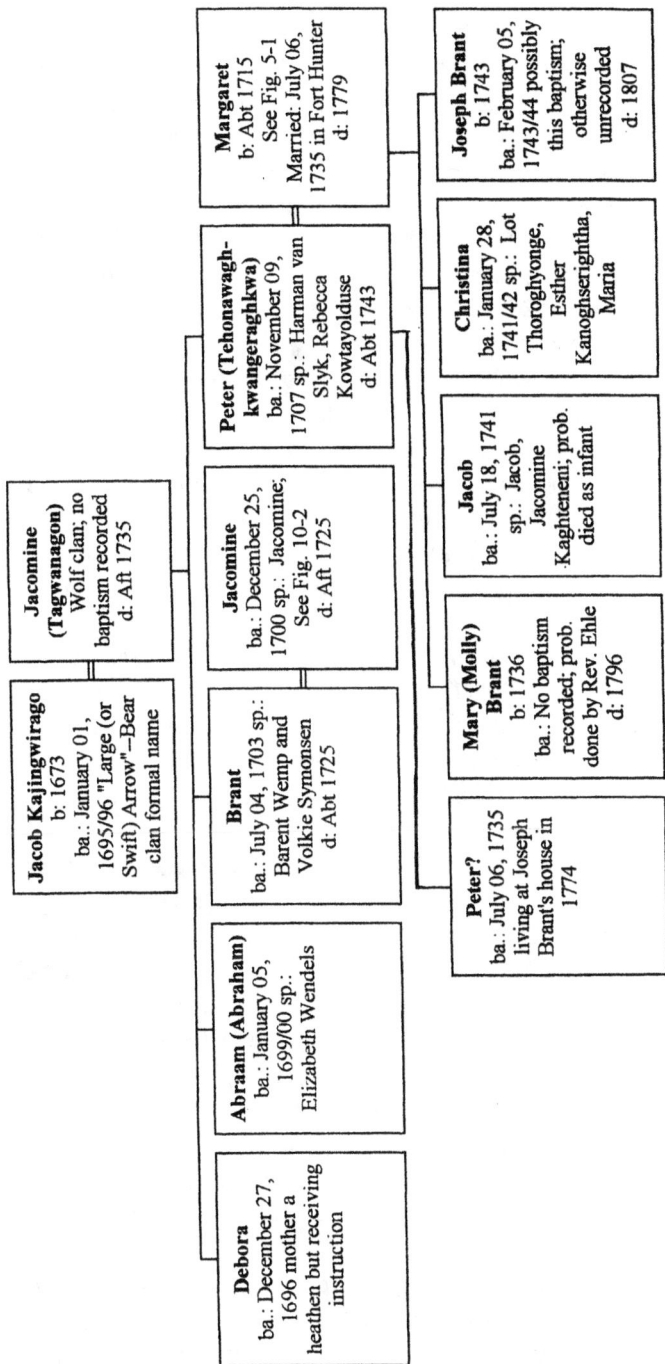

Figure 7-2. *Some Descendants of Jacob Kajingwirago and Jacomine*

at Tionondoroge in the 1720s and 1730s. This Jacomine was the adoptive mother of John (Segehowane) and Mary's son Brant who was baptized at Albany on April 2, 1727, probably adopted and called Brant to replace the son baptized in 1703. In 1727 the adopted Brant must have been a young man, for as Brant Kaweghnoke he married Seth Sietstarare's and Sara's daughter Lydia (see Figs. 4-4 and 4-5B). His adoptive mother Jacomine also sponsored Johannes and Mary's son Jacob on November 26, 1725. Possibly Mary was her daughter, at least in the Mohawk sense.[7]

While the Mohawks were waiting for the completion of the fort and the arrival of the Church of England missionary, a new dominie arrived at the Dutch church in Albany, Petrus (Peter) Van Driessen. Van Driessen baptized a number of Indian children in Schenectady on June 21, 1712, including four children of a Mohawk named Onihoenhoundi and his wife Anna: Alida, Margaret, Cornelius Kryn, and Catryna (Catharine). Kryn is Dutch for Quirine and was Onihoenhoundi's name. He signed, with the mark of a tortoise, the July 10, 1714, deed to Margaret Collins (wife of John Collins), and her son Edward. On January 28, 1722, Van Driessen would baptize Kryn and Anna's son Johannes, sponsored by John and Margaret Collins (this Margaret was Edward Collins' wife). This Johannes would grow up to become Johannes Aneqwendahonji (or Hance Kryn), the Mohawk Bear clan sachem also known as White Hans (see Fig. 7-3 and Chapter 13).[8]

There was an earlier Mohawk named Kryn, the war captain Togouiry, called the Great Mohawk by the French. The first Kryn became a Catholic convert, led two bands of Mohawks to Canada in the 1670s, and was one of the Caughnawaga leaders of the 1690 raid on Schenectady. He was killed on a raid on the Salmon River on June 4, 1690. There is no evidence that he was related to Kryn Onihoenhoundi.[9]

Calling Kryn Onihoenhoundi's son Cornelius Kryn follows the practice of the Dutch, who often used their father's name (with "se" or "sen" appended to it) as a surname. In contrast, Iroquois names, at least formal or "real" names, were handed down within clans. There were also informal or nicknames, many of which were the names Mohawks were known by to whites. This dual naming system is not dissimilar to the Delaware Indian practice, where a person had a deeply private name known only to close friends and family and one or more informal names by which he or she was known by to everyone else. In Iroquois tribes, however, when a person died the formal or real name was "requickened," by giving it to another member of the same clan. Thus a son would, amongst the Iroquois, never carry his father's formal name.[10]

Yet the Dutch practice, and the European practice generally of giving a child its father's name, began to affect the Mohawks. Kryn's son Johannes was often known as Johannes Kryn or Crine, and Aneqwendahonji, Johannes' Mohawk name, is actually Onihoenhondi, his father's Mohawk name. In the nineteenth century the Bear clan chief John Smoke Johnson (Sayenqueraghta) told informers that his father's name was Jacob Tekahionwake and that his grandfather's name was also Tekahionwake. Jacob Anonssontje's son Isaac used his father's Mohawk name, as did his own son Isaac. In 1760 Isaac Anoghsokte was listed as a Bear clan warrior, but by 1885 the name (Anonsokdah) was listed with the Wolf clan real names. It is probable that some formal Mohawk clan names migrated from one clan to the other in the late eighteenth and early nineteenth centuries because of white influence.[11]

By the mid-eighteenth century other Mohawks would use as surnames either their father's Mohawk name—the children of Karighondontee, for example—or his Christian name, such as Hendrick, Abraham, and Nickus Peters. The latter practice became a common method for the formation of permanent Mohawk surnames. Hendrick Peters' son Paulus, although he carried the Mohawk names of Sagsanowano and Onahario—presumably one a formal and the other an informal name—was most often known to whites as Paulus Peters.[12]

After the June 21, 1712, baptisms at Schenectady two more Indian baptisms appear in the Schenectady church records for 1712. These were the last Mohawk baptisms at the Schenectady church for thirty-five years.[13]

In November, 1712, the new missionary, the Reverend William Andrews, sailed up the Hudson River to Albany. As he came into sight of the town he saw his first Indians, Mohawks keeping watch on the riverbank awaiting his arrival. Five sachems, among them Hendrick, Terachjoris of Canajoharie, and Taquayanont, along with a number of other Mohawks, had come to welcome him.[14]

The next day, November 15, Andrews was introduced in a formal meeting. Terachjoris

stood up and Sayd that he was deputed by those of that Castle

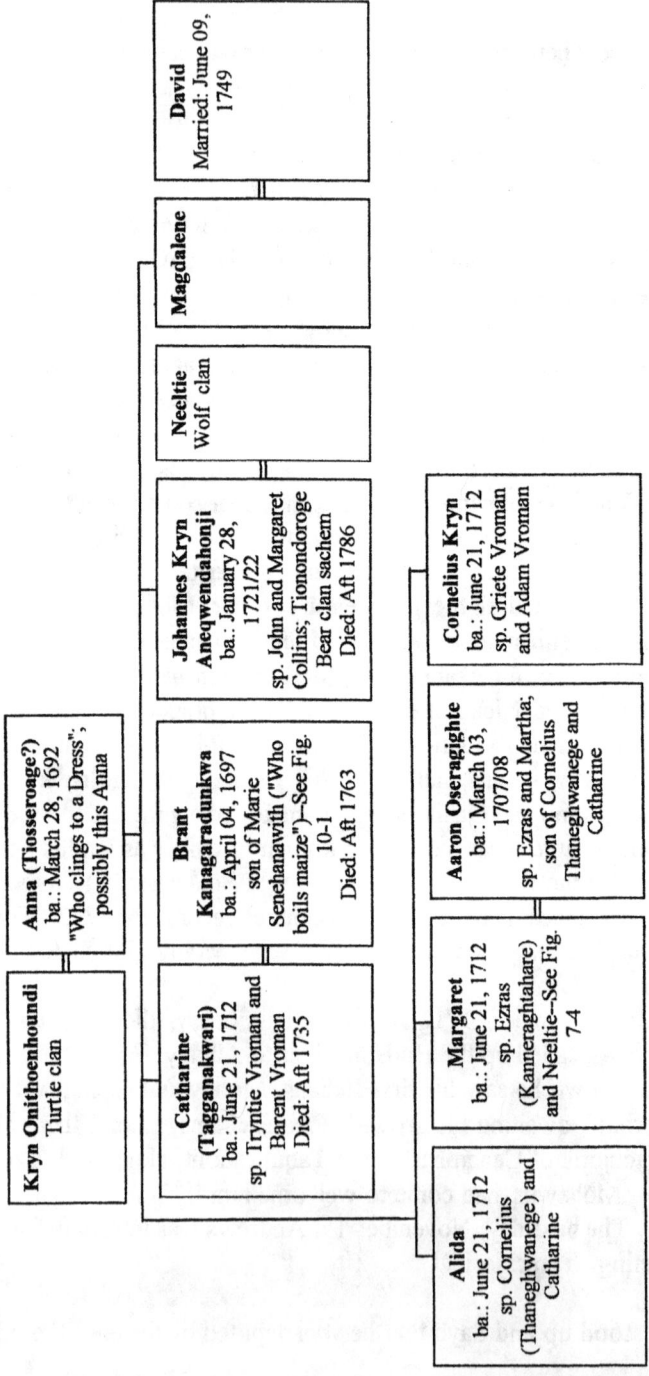

Figure 7-3A. Children and Spouses of Kryn Onithoenhoundi

Kryn Onithoenhoundi
Turtle clan

Anna (Tiosseroage?)
ba.: March 28, 1692
"Who clings to a Dress";
possibly this Anna

Catharine
(Tagganakwari)
ba.: June 21, 1712
sp. Tryntie Vroman and
Barent Vroman
Died: Aft 1735

Brant
Kanagaradunkwa
ba.: April 04, 1697
son of Marie
Senehanawith ("Who
boils maize")–See Fig.
10-1
Died: Aft 1763

Johannes Kryn
Aneqwendahonji
ba.: January 28,
1721/22
sp. John and Margaret
Collins; Tionondoroge
Bear clan sachem
Died: Aft 1786

Neeltie
Wolf clan

Magdalene

David
Married: June 09,
1749

Alida
ba.: June 21, 1712
sp. Cornelius
(Thaneghwanege) and
Catharine

Margaret
ba.: June 21, 1712
sp. Ezras
(Kanneraghtahare)
and Neeltie–See Fig.
7-4

Aaron Oseragighte
ba.: March 03,
1707/08
sp. Ezras and Martha;
son of Cornelius
Thaneghwanege and
Catharine

Cornelius Kryn
ba.: June 21, 1712
sp. Griete Vroman
and Adam Vroman

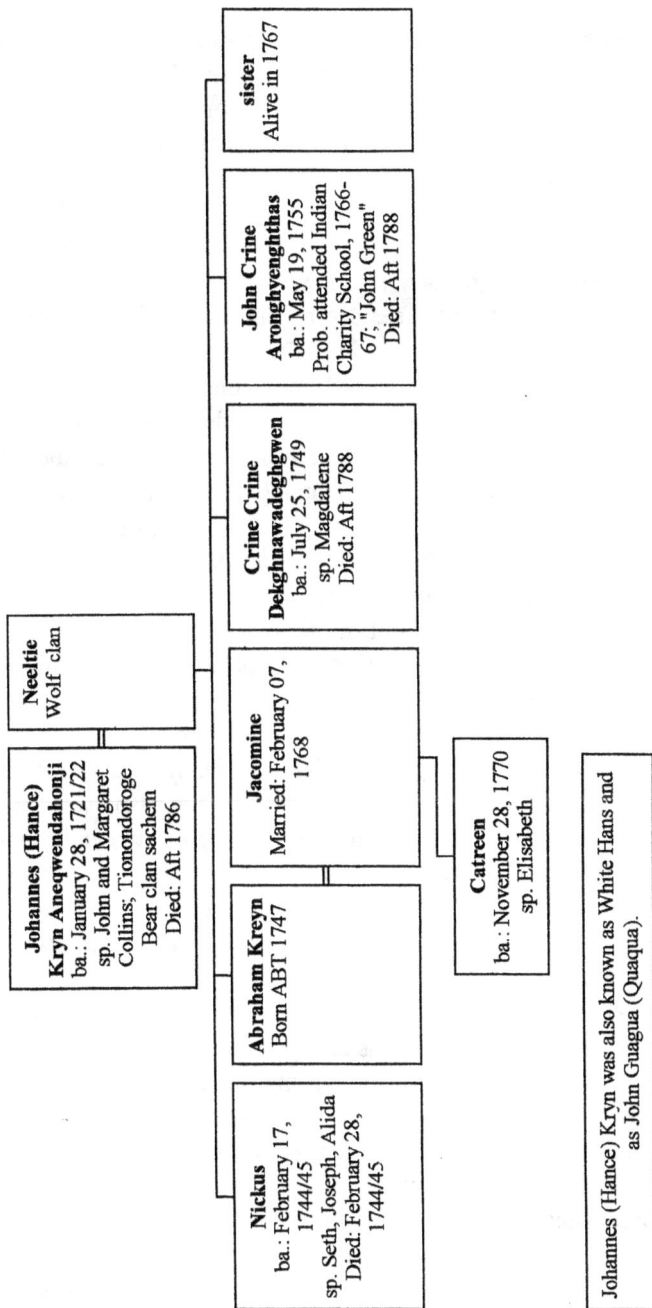

Figure 7-3B. Descendants of Johannes (Hance) Kryn

Johannes (Hance)
Kryn Aneqwendahonji
ba.: January 28, 1721/22
sp. John and Margaret
Collins; Tionondoroge
Bear clan sachem
Died: Aft 1786

Neeltie
Wolf clan

Nickus
ba.: February 17,
1744/45
sp. Seth, Joseph, Alida
Died: February 28,
1744/45

Abraham Kreyn
Born ABT 1747

Jacomine
Married: February 07,
1768

Crine Crine
Dekghnawadeghgwen
ba.: July 25, 1749
sp. Magdalene
Died: Aft 1788

John Crine
Aronghyenghthas
ba.: May 19, 1755
Prob. attended Indian
Charity School, 1766-
67; "John Green"
Died: Aft 1788

sister
Alive in 1767

Catreen
ba.: November 28, 1770
sp. Elisabeth

Johannes (Hance) Kryn was also known as White Hans and
as John Guagua (Quaqua).

[Canajoharie] to come to Albany to Receive in their name the
Reverend Mr. William Andrews for their Minister . . . and Gave
Mr. Andrews his hand and promised for those of that Castle to
give all the Protection and Incouragement unto him that shall lye
in their power.[15]

Terachjoris was "the chief war captain among the Mohawks" who
had distinguished himself in the wars against the French. In 1699
"Tarirjoris, a Maquase" attended a council at Albany and was given a
shirt as a gift. On March 1, 1711, Tarigjoris, Dotsigtade, and Anthony
were delegated to bring Hendrick Hansen, one of the Indian Commissioners, to a meeting in their country. As Turthyowriss, Terachjoris signed
the 1711 Schoharie deed to Adam Vrooman, and as Targiors the 1717
Five Partners deed with a swimming turtle sign. One of the two
settlements which became know as the Upper Castle of the Mohawks
(Canajoharie) was once known as Terrigories town, on the south side of
the river opposite a ford. It doesn't appear that Terachjoris was a
Christian, at least throughout this time period.[16]

After Terachjoris had made his formal greeting, Hendrick rose and
spoke for the Lower Mohawk Castle of Tionondoroge, welcoming
Andrews and thanking the queen, Governor Hunter, and Colonel
Nicholson for his coming. Hendrick then interjected a note of warning
into the formal greeting: he hoped that no more land would be bought
clandestinely of the Mohawks, for such purchases "would be an occasion
of leaving their Country and oblige them to go over to the Ottowawas or
far Indians where they would have no Christian Minister." Hendrick also
stated they they would not be like the Mohawks of Canada, obliged to
pay tenths (tithes) to the priests.[17]

The Reverend Andrews took pains to let the Mohawks know that he
demanded no tithe, getting his salary from the Society for the Propagation of the Gospel. Hendrick's warning must have been regarded by the
Mohawks as out of place in the greeting ceremony, for he was
temporarily relieved of his sachemship on that account, evidence of the
length the Mohawks would go to support their new missionary.[18]

Reverend Andrews' interpreter, Lawrence Claes, could speak no
English, and so he in turn needed an interpreter, John Oliver. On the
22nd of November they all departed to the fort for the winter. Andrews
sent the Society for the Propagation of the Gospel a long letter of his first

three-and-a-half months' sojourn in the Mohawk country on March 9, 1713, along with a detailed list of the children and one young man baptized. In his later baptismal lists, Andrews only included the baptismal names and the ages of the children, omitting the names of their parents or the Indian names of the adults. He also omitted the sponsors. His records, after his first list, are thus almost useless for genealogical purposes.[19]

In early September Andrews sent the Society more detailed information on the Mohawks: there were 360 men, women, and children at Teyawendarokough (Tionondoroge). Twenty miles up the river was the settlement of Canajoharie, and four miles farther on the village of Anadagie: "in both of these are about 180. In another [town] about 24 Miles from the fort called Eskahare about 40." He had also begun instructing the children (through his interpreter) to read and write in their own language.[20]

At that moment the Indian commissioners in Albany were more interested in whether the Five Nations would go to war with the whites of Carolina than in the state of the Mohawks' religious instruction. The central League council at Onondaga was about to meet to decide whether to help their kindred Iroquoian tribe, the Tuscaroras, attack European settlers in North Carolina. A group of 500 Tuscaroras had come north and settled near the Oneidas some years previously. A Tuscarora may have appeared in the Albany and Schenectady church records on May 26, 1708: Abraham Dsikeraha, wife of Catharine Dewadewanagkwa and father of Catharina. Between 1710 (when Hendrick referred to the Six Nations in his speech to Queen Anne) and 1714, the Tuscaroras were admitted into the League of the Iroquois under Oneida leadership. Henceforth the League was usually referred to as the Six Nations. In September, 1713, two commissioners, Hendrick Hansen and Johannes Bleeker, accompanied by the interpreters Lawrence Claes and Jan Patist (John Baptist) van Eps, and two young Cayugas were sent to attend the Onondaga council. Van Eps had received warnings about the danger of their mission, for many Iroquois felt they had no business interfering in League affairs.[21]

At Fort Hunter two Mohawks, Sander and Tanigwanega, were delegated to accompany the commissioners to Onondaga. One of them backed out, claiming sickness. Sander Anoniachta, baptized with Dorcas Sakkoherriho on December 26, 1694, was thirty-nine in 1713, married to

Christina and father of three daughters baptized at Schenectady: Iosene or Josine (December 28, 1698—see Fig. 3-3), Anna (November 25, 1701), and Martha (February 13, 1712). Sander's mark on the 1714 Collins Deed was described as a hedgehog; he was probably a Bear.[22]

The other Mohawk guide, Cornelius Tanigwanega (Thaneghwanege), had accompanied Ezras Kanneraghtahare on a secret mission to Montreal in 1709 and later became a Wolf clan sachem, but his origins are somewhat obscure. A Cornelius son of Arie and Catrina was baptized at Schenectady on October 5, 1700, age unknown, and a Cornelius son of Arie is mentioned in 1720. An Anna Thanigwanege (or Anna daughter of Thanigwanege) was baptized at Schenectady on April 19, 1701, but Anna seems to be the mother of Hindrik and Ephram, listed just below her.[23]

Cornelius or Kees Takonnigwannege married Magdalena Keragkwinon on October 4, 1704. Cornelius Thaneghwanege had two other wives, Catharine Karhages and Anna, and had children baptized as late as 1740. He was still vigorous in 1742, when he was schoolmaster and lesson-reader at Fort Hunter. If the Cornelius baptized on October 5, 1700 was about fourteen at that time, he might have been given the name Thaneghwanege sometime before 1704, upon the death of the earlier Thanigwanege. Then, as Cornelius Thaneghwanege, he first married in 1704. This idea is supported by the fact that the Cornelius baptized on October 5, 1700, was sponsored by Rachel and Martha, and two of Cornelius Thaneghwanege's daughters were sponsored by Rachel and Martha (see Fig. 7-4). Cornelius Thaneghwanege would then have been about sixty years old in 1744, the last time he is mentioned. In 1713, when he probably went with the commissioners to Onondaga, he would have been about twenty-seven. A young man, his prestige would not have been enough to guarantee the safety of the commissioners and their delegation.[24]

At Canajoharie the commissioners stopped again and requested other representatives to accompany them to Onondaga. Again one of the selected companions, Onogradicha, pleaded sick. Teadoius was appointed in his place, who with Taraghionis (Terachjoris, the Canajoharie sachem or war captain) accompanied the commissioners to Onondaga. Their mission was successful, since they succeeded in persuading the Five Nations not to join the Tuscaroras in their war.[25]

Probably because of his Caughnawaga origins, the sachem

Figure 7-4: Descendants of Arie and Catrina's son Cornelius Thaneghwanege

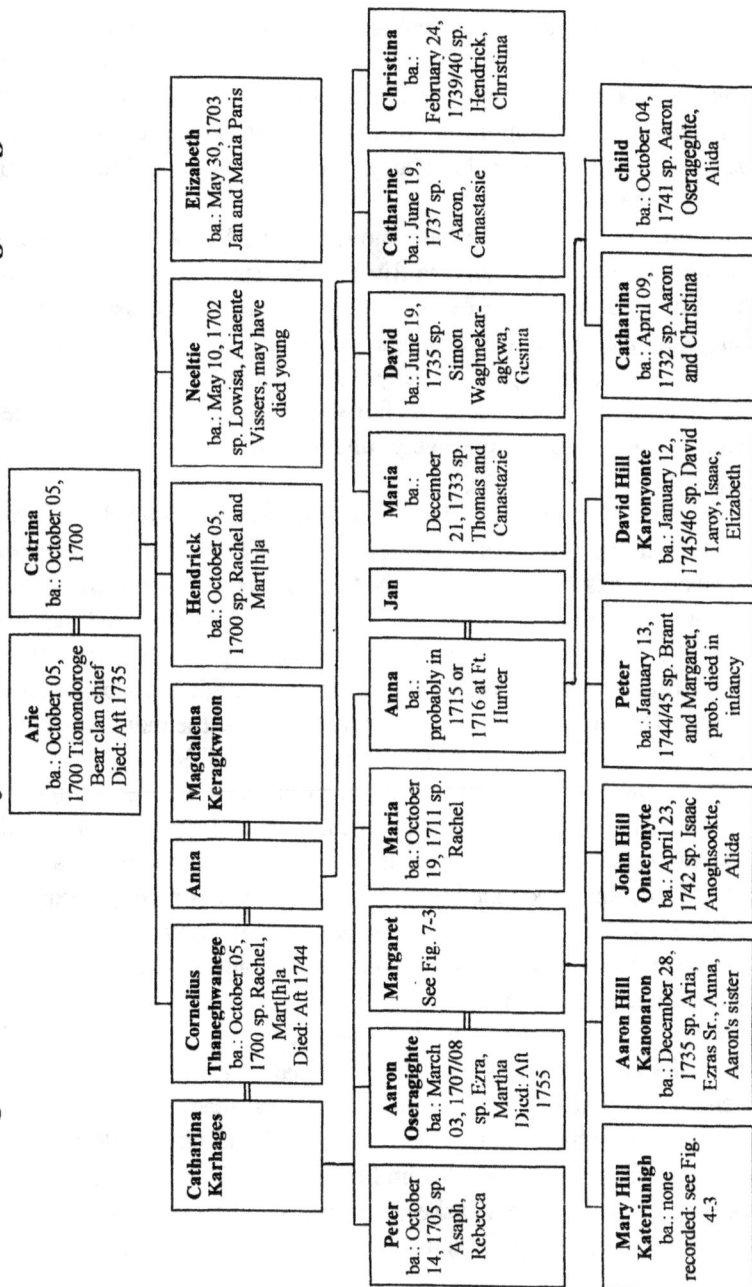

Catharina Karhages

Arie
ba.: October 05, 1700 Tionondoroge Bear clan chief
Died: Aft 1735

Catrina
ba.: October 05, 1700

Cornelius Thaneghwanege
ba.: October 05, 1700 sp. Rachel, Mart[h]a
Died: Aft 1744

Anna

Magdalena Keragkwinon

Hendrick
ba.: October 05, 1700 sp. Rachel and Mart[h]a

Neeltie
ba.: May 10, 1702 sp. Lowisa, Ariaente Vissers, may have died young

Elizabeth
ba.: May 30, 1703 Jan and Maria Paris

Peter
ba.: October 14, 1705 sp. Asaph, Rebecca

Aaron Oseragighte
ba.: March 03, 1707/08 sp. Ezra, Martha
Died: Aft 1755

Margaret
See Fig. 7-3

Maria
ba.: October 19, 1711 sp. Rachel

Anna
ba.: probably in 1715 or 1716 at Ft. Hunter

Jan

Maria
ba.: December 21, 1733 sp. Thomas and Canastazie

David
ba.: June 19, 1735 sp. Simon Waghnekaragkwa, Gesina

Catharine
ba.: June 19, 1737 sp. Aaron, Canastasie

Christina
ba.: February 24, 1739/40 sp. Hendrick, Christina

Mary Hill Kateriunigh
ba.: none recorded: see Fig. 4-3

Aaron Hill Kanonaron
ba.: December 28, 1735 sp. Aria, Ezras Sr., Anna, Aaron's sister

John Hill Onteromyte
ba.: April 23, 1742 sp. Isaac Anoghsookte, Alida

Peter
ba.: January 13, 1744/45 sp. Brant and Margaret, prob. died in infancy

David Hill Karonyonte
ba.: January 12, 1745/46 sp. David Laroy, Isaac, Elizabeth

Catharina
ba.: April 09, 1732 sp. Aaron and Christina

child
ba.: October 04, 1741 sp. Aaron Oserageghte, Alida

Taquayanont opposed the acceptance of the missionary sent over from England and eventually poisoned one of the Reverend Andrews' supporters, and according to Andrews was removed from office. This removal was only temporary, however, for by 1720 Taquayanont was again speaking as a sachem at a meeting with the Indian affairs commissioners at Albany.[26]

Taquayanont seems to have moved to the Mohawk settlement of Onaquaga on the Susquehanna River (in present-day Broome County, New York), for later in the century a David Taquayanont (aslo known as Utingwanlona) lived at Onaquaga and a sachem, Peter Taquayanont (French Peter), was also originally from Onaquaga. There was also a Jacob Taquayanont who was the father of Seth in 1746. These three—Peter, David, and Jacob—were undoubtedly sons of the original Taquayanont.[27]

At Fort Hunter, the Reverend Andrews maintained his work preaching to the Mohawks and teaching their children, but he was unable to extend his mission westward to the Oneidas. He had baptized eighteen Oneidas on May 19, 1714, but some of these children died, and that tribe grew suspicious of the English. More daunting was the influence of white traders, who continued to sell great quantities of alcohol to the Indians. The missionary railed against these abuses, the more so when an Indian, probably drunk, came into the chapel to kill Mr. Andrews while he was reading prayers. "When they are sober they are quiet enough, but when drunk [they are] like mad men." The traders, naturally, did everything they could to diminish the influence of the missionary. In addition, the Reverend found that his salary could not meet the expenses of feeding and gift-giving required of a person in his position.[28]

Reverend Andrews' influence continued strong among the Mohawks of Tionondoroge until the summer of 1716, when a smallpox epidemic produced a resurgence of pagan ceremonies. By late 1716-17 many Mohawks had ceased to heed the missionary and only twenty-four or twenty-five went to the chapel with any consistency. Only thirty-five individuals were baptized between April, 1716 and July, 1719, when the missionary filed his last report from Fort Hunter. Because of this hostile reaction, by 1718 Andrews asked to be transferred. He left Fort Hunter in 1719, although the garrison that had been at the fort since its inception remained.[29]

After his leaving, the more church-going Mohawks went to Albany, and the Reverend Van Driessen resumed his baptisms among them. The Albany church records once again record Indian baptisms and marriages through the mid-1730s, when the advent of another Church of England missionary, the Reverend Henry Barclay, (son of the Reverend Thomas Barclay of Albany), induced the Mohawks once again to worship at the little chapel at Fort Hunter.

CHAPTER VIII

Montours in Fact and Fiction

Notwithstanding his troubles with the Palatines, Robert Hunter remained governor of New York until the year 1720. His relations with the Iroquois during this period were immeasurably improved through the assistance and intervention of the wife of one of the Oneida war chiefs. This chief, Carundawana, changed his name to Robert Hunter out of respect for the governor. Carundawana's wife has come down in colonial history as Madame Montour.

Madame Montour first interpreted a conference between the governor and the Six Nations in 1711, and during the next decade Governor Hunter used her interpretative skills to check on the province's official interpreter and his allies, the Albany Dutch. Colden states that Hunter

> had so great a diffidence [i.e., distrust] of all the people at Albany that at the public meetings with the Indians he had allwise a French woman standing by him who had married one of our Indians to inform him whether the interpreters had done their part truly between him and the Indians, notwithstanding that Col. Schuyler was present at the same time. This woman commonly called Madame Montour had a good education in Canada before she went among the Indians and was very useful to Mr. Hunter on many occasions for which reason she had a pension and was sometimes admitted to his table in her Indian dress.[1]

In 1744 in Pennsylvania, Madame Montour told a young New Englander, Witham Marshe, that she was a Frenchwoman, the daughter of a French gentleman who had been governor. She said that she had been captured by the Five Nations when she was ten years old and raised by them, married to a war captain and had several children by him. It being nearly fifty years since she had been captured, she remembered neither her birthplace nor her parents.[2]

Very little of the information related by and about Madame Montour was true, for she took great pains to cover up her past. First, she was not wholly French, being half-Algonquin. Second, her father was neither a governor nor a gentleman but a commoner from the town of Cognac, France. Third, she was not ten but twenty-one years old when she was captured by a party of Iroquois (probably Mohawks) and Mahicans. She undoubtedly remembered both her birthplace and parents, for she maintained close ties with various members of her family through most of her life, notwithstanding the fact that most of them lived in Canada. Indeed, shortly before Hunter was to resign his post and leave for England, Madame Montour demanded the arrears of her pension from the governor. She told Hunter that the French governor of Canada considered her influence with the Six Nations so important that her sister had been sent from Quebec to persuade her to return to her native land and allegiance.[3]

One wonders which sister; she had five full sisters and two half-sisters, although one had been murdered in 1679 and one or both of her half-sisters may have actually been full sisters. She also had two brothers, one of whom was assassinated on the express orders of the Canadian governor, M. de Vaudreuil. Her last name was not Montour, and she seemed to have been reluctant to let her first name be known at all. It was actually Elizabeth, but she preferred its variant form, Isabelle.

The fictions about the Montours persisted down through the generations. Witham Marshe reported that Madame Montour had one son and two daughters. Other sources credit her with as many as twelve children. One "son" was probably a grandnephew or grandson. One woman commonly called her daughter, French Margaret, was actually her niece. Of the three daughters credited to French Margaret, one wasn't a "Montour" at all, except by marriage. In Canada, two of Madame Montour's children scarcely acknowledged her while various nephews and their families, for no particular reason that can now be ascertained, took the name Montour, though it was not the name of any of their fathers' relatives.

All in all, they were a remarkable family. Their descendants include a good many members of the Kanawake (Caughnawaga) Mohawks, a number of Delawares, and many families on the Six Nations Reserve, as well as a number of whites of French Canadian descent. Since their family history has been so closely connected with much of the history of the Six Nations, it would be well to separate, as much as possible, the facts from the fictions.

The investigator who uncovered the true antecedents of Madame Montour was the late Archivist of the Moravian Archives, William Hunter. He discovered Madame's true name and parentage, her connection to Louis Montour, and by inference, her reasons for leaving Canada. Other French records provide additional genealogical and historical detail.[4]

The family's story starts with Pierre Couc La Fleur, born in Cognac, France, in 1627, the son of Nicholas Couc and Elizabeth Templair. The earliest record of Pierre Couc in the New World is in 1651, when at Trois-Rivières on August 27 he sponsors the daughter (called Pierrine after her godfather) of Marie Kitarangoukoe, an Indian. Trois-Rivières was a settlement on the St. Lawrence River about midway between Montreal and Quebec. The child's father is listed as an Amerindian, but since the name of the mother is quite similar to the woman Pierre married six years later, one wonders if the child was actually his. That Pierre Couc was a soldier is noted the next year, when on May 21, 1652, he was wounded by Iroquois on the south side of the St. Lawrence opposite Trois-Rivières. That same year, on November 1, Marie Mite-ouamegoukoue, an Algonquin Indian at Trois-Rivières, had her daughter Catharine baptized. Catharine's father is listed as an Amerindian named Assababich.[5]

On April 16, 1657, Pierre Couc La Fleur and Marie Miteouame-goukou married at Trois Rivières. She was twenty-six (born in 1631) and two of the witnesses were Algonquins: Charles Pachirini and Barthelemy Anaraoui.

> Pachirini was the Algonquin chief who had given (1634) a piece of land for the erection of the first Christian (Jesuit) chapel at Three Rivers. This lot . . . is still the same under the name of Pachirini. In the tongue of the Algonquin Pachirini means a little man whose body keeps straight up—like a military man if you like. The family of Pachirini lived in Three Rivers during the whole of the XVIIth century.[6]

Pierre Couc and his wife Marie had eight children, the first (Jeanne) baptized on July 14, 1657, and the second (Louis) baptized November 27, 1659. These were followed by five daughters: Marie Angelique, born about 1661; Marie Anne, born about 1663; Marguerite, baptized June 1, 1664; Elizabeth, born in 1667; and Madeleine, born about 1669. A second son, Jean Baptiste, was born in 1673 (see Fig. 8-1).[7]

Pierre Couc was an Indian interpreter at Trois Rivières by 1659, when he came to blows with the drunk son of the merchant Loyseau. Another time he complained to authorities of being set upon by three other men. He was also in debt for 450 livres for European goods, possibly trading stock.[8]

In 1660 Couc arranged to buy some land at Cap de la Madeleine close to Trois-Rivières and by 1664 was living there with his family. About the year 1674 he was one of the settlers recruited by Jean Crevier, the seigneur or landowner, to develop Saint Francis du Lac near Sorel, having been granted a land concession there on October 3, 1673. St. Francis is approximately midway between Trois-Rivières and Montreal, on the south side of the St. Lawrence. Pierre Couc's lands were on Fort Island. On April 22, 1676, Louis Couc obtained a piece of land next to his father's.[9]

Pierre and Marie's eldest child, Jeanne, was confirmed on May 22, 1664 and sponsored a child on December 31, 1677. Two years later, on October 23, 1679, Jeanne was mortally wounded and her father grievously injured in a scuffle or brawl at St. Francis. She was buried two days later, with her mother and her sister Angelique looking on.[10]

A man named Jean Rattier was convicted of the murder on the 31st of October, but he appealed and was sent to the prison in Quebec. The seigneur of St. Francis, Jean Crevier, was accused of complicity in the attack, along with Crevier's servant Pierre Gilbert and two others. Judgement was rendered on December 31, 1680 against Rattier, who was sentenced to hang and pay a large fine. He was pardoned however and stayed in Quebec, as did another accused man, Jacques Dupuis.[11]

During the inquiry Gilbert, Jean Crevier's servant, said that his master had been the cause of all that had occurred. The authorities ordered Crevier to pay 486 livres to Pierre Couc. Couc blamed Jean Crevier for instigating the affair, and one French Canadian historian went so far as to call Jeanne's death an assassination. The reason for such agressive action is unknown, but one must remember that Pierre Couc had a record of

Figure 8-1. *Children of Marie Miteouamegoukoue and Pierre Couc (La Fleur)*

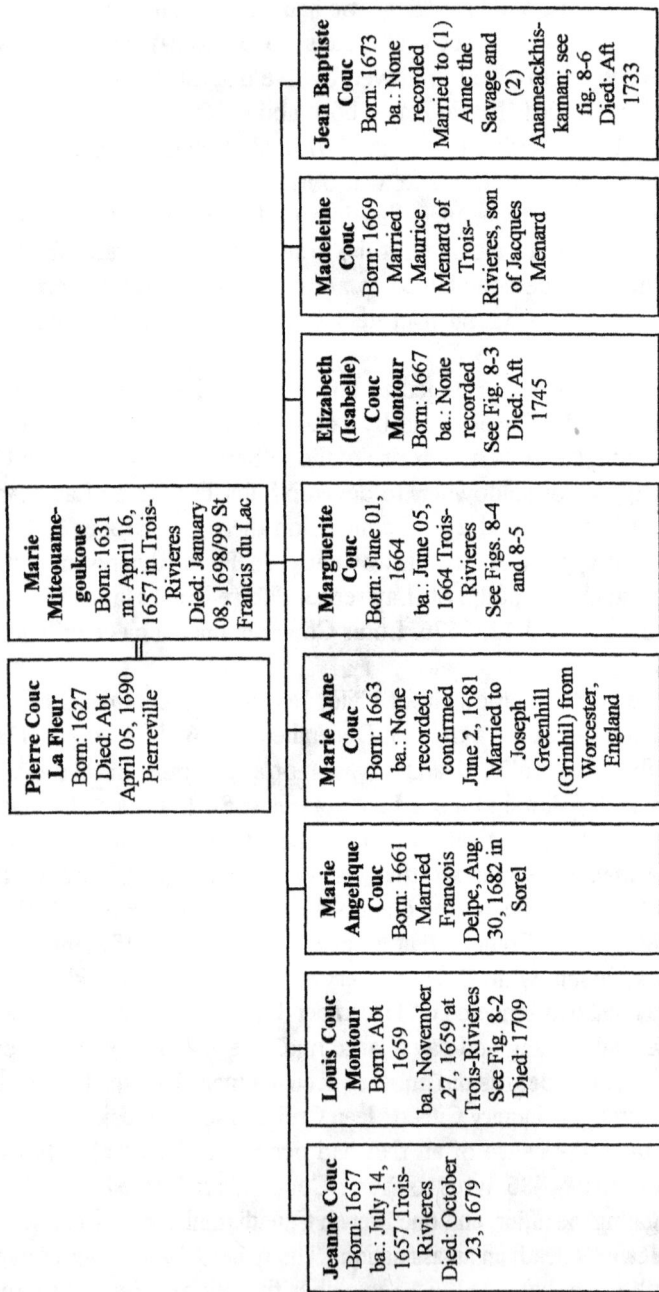

Pierre Couc La Fleur Born: 1627 Died: Abt April 05, 1690 Pierreville		**Marie Miteouame-goukoue** Born: 1631 m: April 16, 1657 in Trois-Rivieres Died: January 08, 1698/99 St Francis du Lac

Jeanne Couc Born: 1657 ba.: July 14, 1657 Trois-Rivieres Died: October 23, 1679

Louis Couc Montour Born: Abt 1659 ba.: November 27, 1659 at Trois-Rivieres See Fig. 8-2 Died: 1709

Marie Angelique Couc Born: 1661 Married Francois Delpe, Aug. 30, 1682 in Sorel

Marie Anne Couc Born: 1663 ba.: None recorded; confirmed June 2, 1681 Married to Joseph Greenhill (Grinhil) from Worcester, England

Marguerite Couc Born: June 01, 1664 ba.: June 05, 1664 Trois-Rivieres See Figs. 8-4 and 8-5

Elizabeth (Isabelle) Couc Montour Born: 1667 ba.: None recorded See Fig. 8-3 Died: Aft 1745

Madeleine Couc Born: 1669 Married Maurice Menard of Trois-Rivieres, son of Jacques Menard

Jean Baptiste Couc Born: 1673 ba.: None recorded Married to (1) Anne the Savage and (2) Anameackhis-kaman; see fig. 8-6 Died: Aft 1733

violent altercations.[12]

Jeanne's death must have been a severe blow to the family, not helped by the fact that the murderer was left unpunished. It may have been the first wedge that was eventually to separate some of Pierre's family from their French allegiance.

Another wedge may have been in the person of an English son-in-law, Joseph Greenhill (born in Worcester, England), who married Marie Anne Couc. Virtually nothing is known of this couple except that they had a son, also named Joseph (Grinhill), born about 1683 in British America. Joseph Jr. was a shoemaker who married twenty-one-year-old Marie-Louise Paille in Montreal in 1711. He was granted French citizenship in 1713 and by 1716 had two sons, Joseph and Jean Baptiste. By 1727 Joseph Jr. had deserted his wife and sons to live in New England.[13]

Like his father, Louis Couc occasionally used the surname La Fleur. In 1679 a La Fleur, probably Louis, is described as an inhabitant of St. Louis—Sault St. Louis, the Caughnawaga Mohawk settlement of Kanawake. While hunting near Lake Champlain that year he heard the rumor that "the French have no longer freedom to trade at Orange [Albany]," news which he confirmed himself and reported to French authorities in Canada. There is an implication that La Fleur himself was one of the Frenchmen trading at Albany.[14]

On August 30, 1682, the Coucs were in Sorel where a son of Louis Couc's was baptized and given the name François. The mother was an Amerindian (see Fig. 8-2). On that same day Marie Angelique Couc married François Delpe Saint-Cerny of St. Francis, aged thirty-four. In Canada, as in the rest of colonial North America, there was a surfeit of single white men looking for wives. Pierre Couc's half-Indian daughters all married Frenchmen, at one time or another. His sons found partners only with the Indians. Marie Angelique and her husband François would have seven children. Their son Maurice would take the surname Montour, the name of Marie Angelique's brother Louis.[15]

Louis Couc adopted the surname of Montour in the early 1680s, for when another of his natural children, Jacques, was baptized at Trois-Rivières on May 1, 1684, Louis is recorded as Montour rather than Couc. The mother of this child was a Sakokie Indian by the name of Madeleine. The Sakokies were a branch of the Abenaki Indians who had migrated to the St. Francis area after 1669 from what is now Vermont. One of the creeks or small rivers that flows into Wood Creek on the west side of

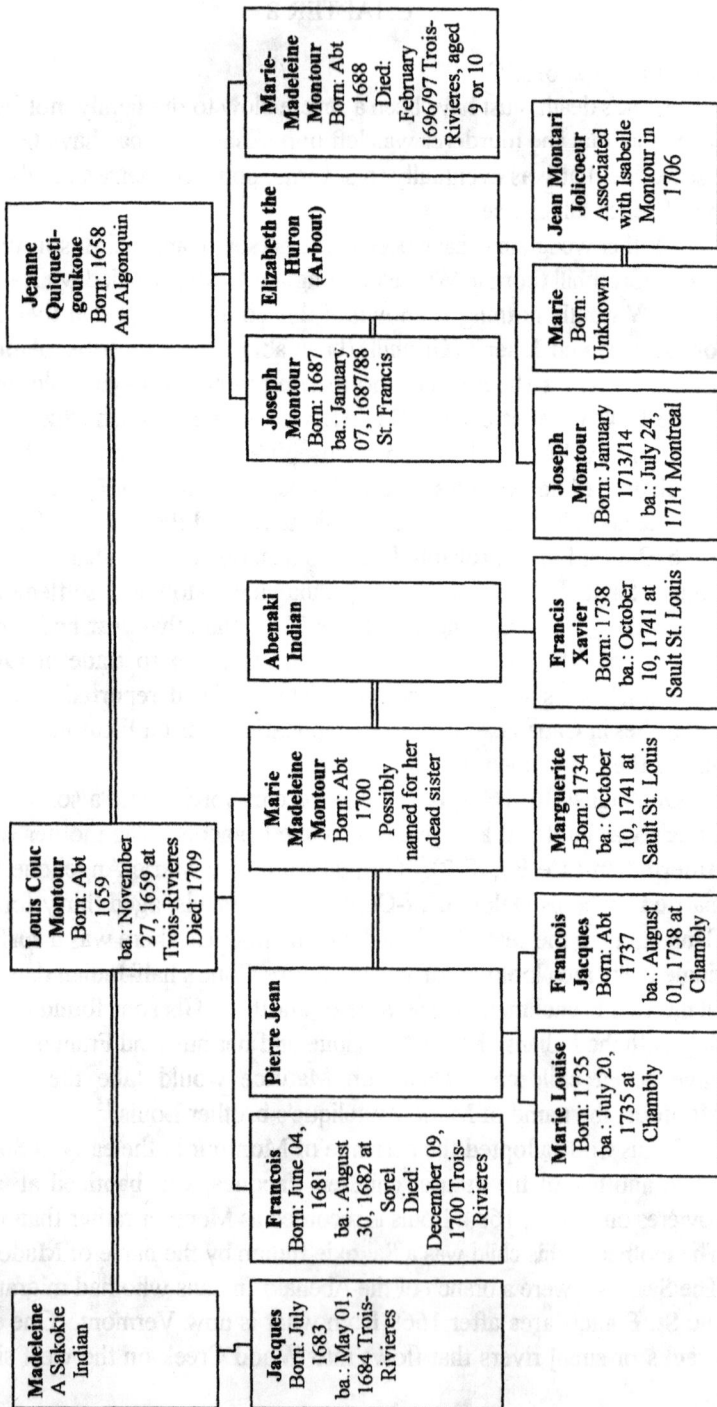

Figure 8-2. Descendants of Louis (Couc) Montour

Louis Couc Montour
Born: Abt 1659
ba.: November 27, 1659 at Trois-Rivieres
Died: 1709

Jeanne Quiqueti-goukoue
Born: 1658
An Algonquin

Madeleine
A Sakokie Indian

Jacques
Born: July 1683
ba.: May 01, 1684 Trois-Rivieres

Francois
Born: June 04, 1681
ba.: August 30, 1682 at Sorel
Died: December 09, 1700 Trois-Rivieres

Pierre Jean

Marie Madeleine Montour
Born: Abt 1700
Possibly named for her dead sister

Abenaki Indian

Joseph Montour
Born: 1687
ba.: January 07, 1687/88 St. Francis

Elizabeth the Huron (Arbout)

Marie-Madeleine Montour
Born: Abt 1688
Died: February 1696/97 Trois-Rivieres, aged 9 or 10

Marie Louise
Born: 1735
ba.: July 20, 1735 at Chambly

Francois Jacques
Born: Abt 1737
ba.: August 01, 1738 at Chambly

Marguerite
Born: 1734
ba.: October 10, 1741 at Sault St. Louis

Francis Xavier
Born: 1738
ba.: October 10, 1741 at Sault St. Louis

Joseph Montour
Born: January 1713/14
ba.: July 24, 1714 Montreal

Marie
Born: Unknown

Jean Montari Jolicoeur
Associated with Isabelle Montour in 1706

Lake Champlain—probably Metawee Creek (former Sakokie territory)—was once named Montour's Creek. His union with Madeleine did not last, for on January 7, 1688 Louis married the thirty-two-year-old Jeanne Quiquetigoukoué, an Algonquin; their son Joseph having been born at St. Francis the previous November (Fig. 8-2). In August, 1698 Louis enlisted for a western trading expedition (*voyage*).[16]

In April, 1684 Elizabeth or Isabelle Couc, daughter of Pierre Couc and Marie Miteouamegoukou, was married to Joachim Germaneau of Rivière de Loup, a settlement near St. Francis. A native of the Perigord region of France, Germaneau had arrived in New France on June 18, 1666, a soldier in the Carignan regiment. For a few years prior to 1684 he had been farming a small piece of land at Rivière de Loup (Louiseville). He must have been at least twenty years older than Isabelle.[17]

According to a deposition written twenty years later by Antoine Laumet (de Lamothe Cadillac), former commandant of Fort Michilimacknac and founder of Detroit, Isabelle was married once in the rites of the church but at the end of a year she left her husband and betook herself to the English and married a savage of the Loup (Mahican) tribe, with whom she remained twelve years and had several children.[18]

However, Cadillac's writing is untrustworthy. In this instance he was attempting to make Isabelle as disreputable as he could to defend himself against official charges of irregularities in fur-trading. Instead of running off to the English as he states, it is more than likely that she was captured by Mohawks and Mahicans raiding Rivière de Loup (Louiseville) in July, 1688, when she had been married four years. Although most of the inhabitants had left to convey food to Fort Frontenac, some prisoners were taken on the raid and not returned to Canada. English sources identify the raiders as Mohawks and Schaghticoke Indians. That Isabelle Germaneau lived with the Mahicans and had a son by one is true, for in 1747 a Mahican named Germaneau left the French raiding party that was attacking Saratoga, New York, and defected to the English in Albany.[19]

Cadillac also wrote that,

during the last war this woman was captured among the English by our Iroquois from the Waterfall. She was ransomed by one of her brothers-in-law, a Frenchman named Maurice Menard, who took her to the Utavois [Ottawa Indians] where her first husband was, to whom she would not go back.[20]

There is no reason to doubt that Isabelle was recaptured by Caughnawaga Mohawks and ransomed by her brother-in-law, Maurice Menard. Menard had married Isabelle's sister Madeleine sometime before 1692 and was the official interpreter at the fort of Michilimackinac. Their son Antoine was baptized there on April 28, 1695. It was here that Laumet must have first met Isabelle; he was commandant at Michilimackinac between 1694 and 1697. During that time he sold unlimited quantities of brandy to the Indians, trading it for furs. He also fleeced the *coureurs de bois* (white hunters and fur traders), "few of whom dared to complain."[21]

Two *coureurs de bois* were Isabelle's brother and her husband, who were together on a western trading expedition (*voyage*) in 1692. In 1694 Germaneau was on another such *voyage*. This would explain Cadillac's statement that her husband was among the Ottawa Indians, who frequented the area of Michilimackinac. That Isabelle went willingly with her brother-in-law to her husband at Michilimackinac and briefly reconciled with Germaneau is suggested by the existence of Michael Germaneau, certainly Isabelle's child and possibly Joachim's, who later gave his birthdate as 1695. Another child of Isabelle's, a daughter Marie Anne born about 1697, occasionally used the name Germaneau, but it is unlikely that Joachim was her father. There was also a Marguerite Germaneau, but her parents are unknown (see Fig. 8-3).[22]

According to Cadillac, at Michilimackinac Isabelle led a licentious life and accused her brother-in-law Menard of trying to seduce her. She brought her complaint against Menard to Cadillac, the commandant there, who says he recognized "the imposture of that wicked woman." The theme of Isabelle's dissoluteness is a major part of his defense against charges that he used her as an interpreter in one of his shady deals— surely no one could believe that he used as wanton a woman as this! If she was as dissolute as he claimed, why would she bother to go to the fort's commandant with a charge against her brother-in-law? Menard is spoken well of in regard to his relations with the Indians by Father Marest, the Jesuit priest at Sault St. Marie.[23]

Cadillac continues with his commentary on Isabelle:

> She afterwards enticed away two Canadians to take them to the English, and when she set out with them I had her pursued. She was caught with these two young men, who confessed the fact,

Figure 8-3. Descendants of Elizabeth (Isabelle) Couc Montour

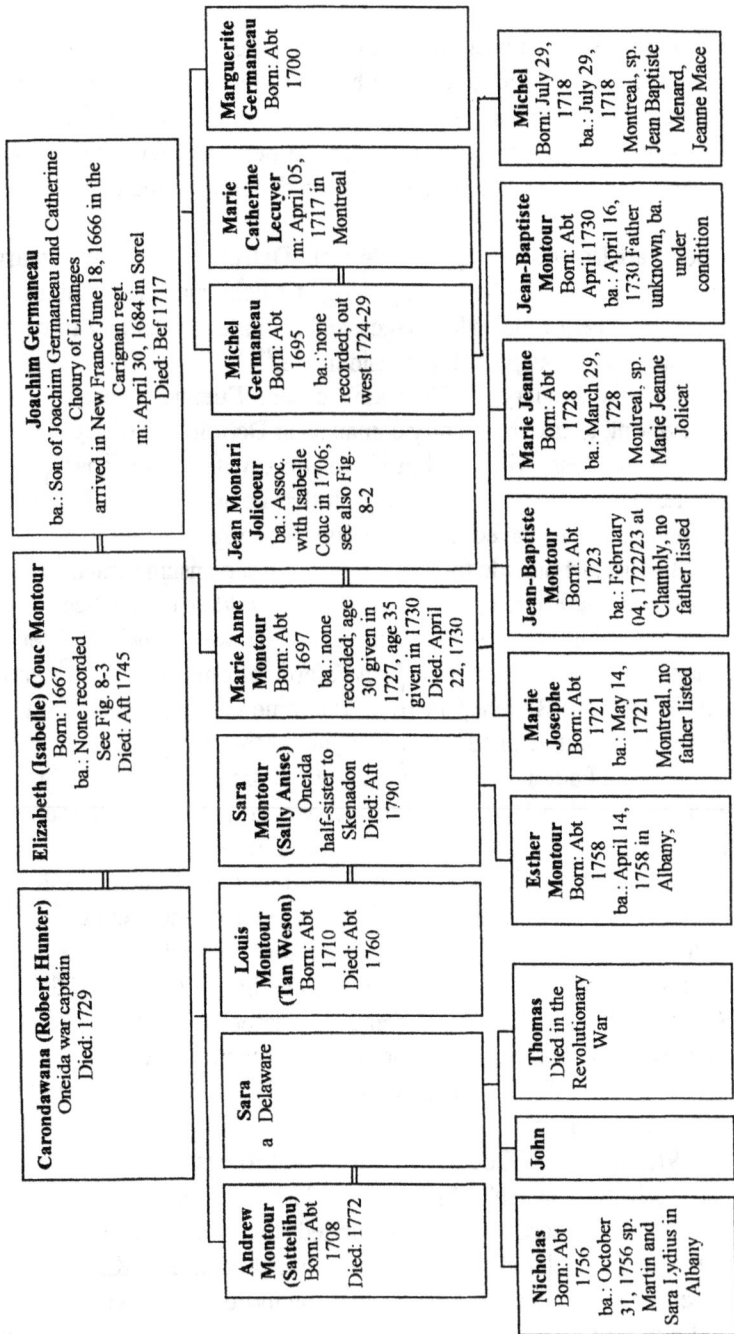

Figure 8-3. Descendants of Elizabeth (Isabelle) Couc Montour

Carondawana (Robert Hunter) — Oneida war captain. Died: 1729

Elizabeth (Isabelle) Couc Montour — Born: 1667. ba.: None recorded. See Fig. 8-3. Died: Aft 1745

Joachim Germaneau — ba.: Son of Joachim Germaneau and Catherine Choury of Limanges arrived in New France June 18, 1666 in the Carignan regt. m: April 30, 1684 in Sorel. Died: Bef 1717

Marguerite Germaneau — Born: Abt 1700

Andrew Montour (Sattelihu) — Born: Abt 1708. Died: 1772

Sara — a Delaware

Louis Montour (Tan Weson) — Born: Abt 1710. Died: Abt 1760

Sara Montour (Sally Anise) — Oneida half-sister to Skenadon. Died: Aft 1790

Marie Anne Montour — Born: Abt 1697. ba.: none recorded; age 30 given in 1727, age 35 given in 1730. Died: April 22, 1730

Jean Montari Jolicoeur — ba.: Assoc. with Isabelle Couc in 1706, see also Fig. 8-2

Michel Germaneau — Born: Abt 1695. ba.:none recorded; out west 1724-29

Marie Catherine Lecuyer — m: April 05, 1717 in Montreal

Michel — Born: July 29, 1718. ba.: July 29, 1718 Montreal, sp. Jean Baptiste Menard, Jeanne Mace

Nicholas — Born: Abt 1756. ba.: October 31, 1756 sp. Martin and Sara Lydius in Albany

John

Thomas — Died in the Revolutionary War

Esther Montour — Born: Abt 1758. ba.: April 14, 1758 in Albany,

Marie Josephe — Born: Abt 1721. ba.: May 14, 1721 Montreal, no father listed

Jean-Baptiste Montour — Born: Abt 1723. ba.: February 04, 1722/23 at Chambly, no father listed

Marie Jeanne — Born: Abt 1728. ba.: March 29, 1728 Montreal, sp. Marie Jeanne Jolicat

Jean-Baptiste Montour — Born: Abt 1730. ba.: April 16, 1730 Father unknown, ba. under condition

[and] I sent her under guard to the Chevalier de Calliere who sent her down to Quebec to send her to France. As no precautions were taken, the man Jean le Blanc, . . . took her off, brought her back to Missilimakinak and married her. She left him to take another, and has been kept by more than a hundred men.

When Cadillac was writing, in 1704 from Detroit, Isabelle was "married" to a man named Techenet and living at Michilimackinac. By now she knew a number of Indian languages, and her influence among some of the western tribes was probably considerable.[24]

In early January, 1706, Cadillac sent Etienne Venary, Sieur de Bourgmont, to take temporary command at Detroit. He brought Isabelle, now his mistress, with him but his relations with the Indians there were hostile. The Ottawas in particular felt that he and Isabelle, known as La Techenet, had betrayed them and consequently attacked their enemies, the Miamis, just outside the French fort. In the ensuing fracas a number of Indians, the French priest, and a French soldier were killed.[25]

Also living at Detroit by the year 1702 was Isabelle's older sister Marguerite, who had married Jean Fafard "of one of the oldest and best families of Trois-Rivières" in 1690, the same year that Pierre Couc died. Marguerite and Jean had one daughter, Marguerite, born in the early 1690s. Jean Fafard died at some unknown date, but in 1702 Marguerite was remarried in Detroit to Michael Massé and had another daughter, Genevieve Massé, born about 1705 (see Fig. 8-4).[26]

In August, 1706, the Sieur de Bourgmont, with Isabelle and several soldiers of the Detroit garrison, deserted the fort and went to live in the wilderness. Isabelle's brother, Louis Montour, joined her, for he had been trading furs with the Mississagua Indians in the vicinity of the Grand River, north of Lake Erie. Over a year later one of the deserters was interrogated at Detroit and reported that Techenet and Bourgmont were going to the English to live there forever, and that Montour would follow the next summer.[27]

Why did Louis Couc Montour decide to cast his lot with his sister and with the English? As late as 1695 he was in the vicinity of Lake Champlain, where he was wounded by two Mohawks when he patriotically declared himself to be a Frenchman. But King Louis XIV issued a royal edict in 1696 forbidding any more trading with the Indians, and much of Montour's source of livelihood was consequently cut off.

Figure 8-4. Family of Marguerite Fafard Turpin (French Margaret)

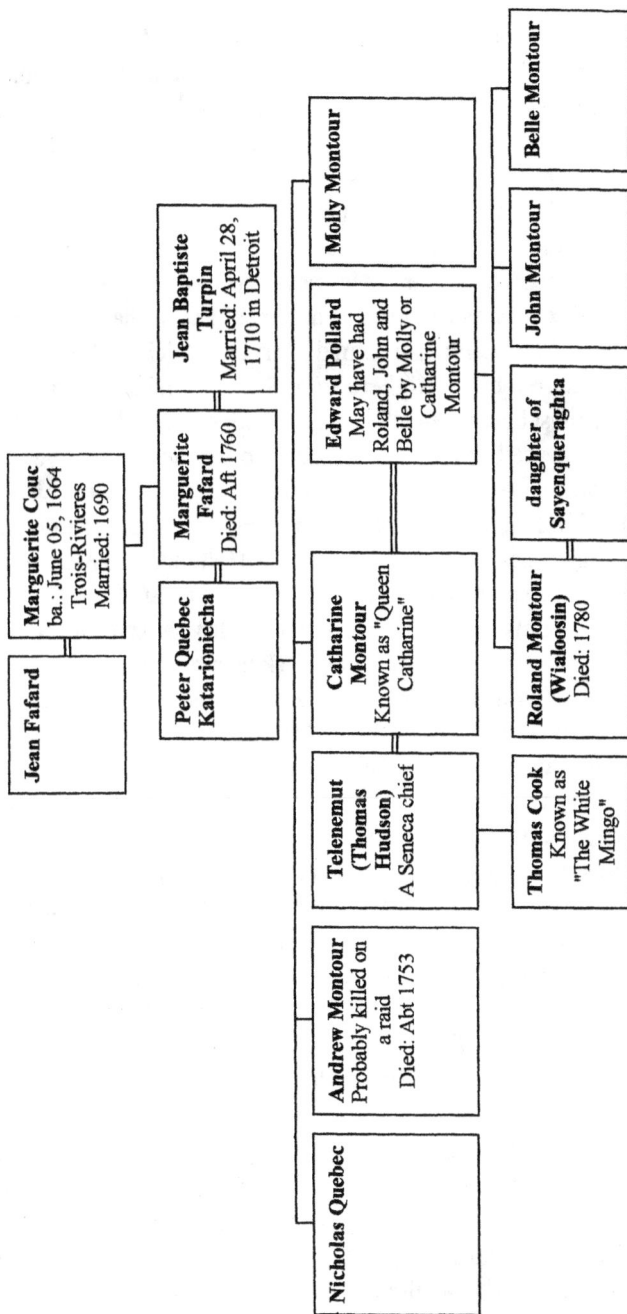

Jean Fafard

Marguerite Couc
ba.: June 05, 1664
Trois-Rivieres
Married: 1690

Jean Baptiste
Turpin
Married: April 28,
1710 in Detroit

Peter Quebec
Katarioniecha

Marguerite
Fafard
Died: Aft 1760

Molly Montour

Nicholas Quebec

Andrew Montour
Probably killed on
a raid
Died: Abt 1753

Telenemut
(Thomas
Hudson)
A Seneca chief

Catharine
Montour
Known as "Queen
Catharine"

Edward Pollard
May have had
Roland, John and
Belle by Molly or
Catharine
Montour

Thomas Cook
Known as
"The White
Mingo"

Roland Montour
(Wialoosin)
Died: 1780

daughter of
Sayenqueraghta

John Montour

Belle Montour

Moreover, he may actually have owned land in Albany County, possibly north along the Hudson, for a La Fleur is listed as a freeholder there in 1701 and a fort where La Fleur once lived is described in that general area in 1709. Evidently Louis used this fort as a base for trading furs with Albany.[28]

In the late 1690s Louis's family was probably at Trois-Rivières, for his daughter Marie Madeleine was buried there in 1697 and his son Francis three years later. He may also have had a family at Sault St. Louis, since he was reported as an inhabitant of that settlement in 1679, and in the 1730s an Indian named Marie Madeleine Montour had several of her children baptized there (Fig. 8-2). Cadillac's founding of Detroit in 1701 must have seemed like a good opportunity to start trading again, with the peace between France and the Iroquois in that year.[29]

It soon proved to be something other than what was promised. Cadillac's tyrannical rule made him even more hated than he had been at Michilimackinac. His extortionate ways extended to Montour's brother-in-law, Michael Massé, and to other tradesmen in the fort, who had to pay large sums just to carry on their trades. Massé had to pay Cadillac 150 livres just to do occasional work as a blacksmith.[30]

The fur trade at Detroit, unlike that at Michilimackinac, soon found its way to Albany rather than Montreal. Anglo-Dutch merchants paid more for furs than did French merchants, and furs coming into Detroit went on to the Iroquois country. Louis had already appeared at Albany in June, 1707 with a party of "far Indians" who came to trade their furs. He was paid five pounds for his services and promised to return to the "far nations" again and bring down more Indians with their furs.[31]

An inquiry into Cadillac's governorship and the situation at Detroit was instituted in 1708 by the Sieur d'Aigremont, acting for the king's minister in France. His report "was a crushing indictment of Cadillac as a profiteer and of his policy as a menace to French control of the interior." D'Aigremont wrote that

M. de La Mothe [Cadillac] told me that he had been accused of trading with the English, and of employing the Sr. Bourgmont for that purpose; but there is no ground for believing that that is so. He is too clever to put his interests in the hands of a man so dissolute as the Sr. Bourgmont, who deserted from Detroit to go after a woman called La Chenette, . . . with whom he is living in the woods like a savage.[32]

Here again is Cadillac's theme of dissoluteness as a defense, along with a second idea—that Bourgmont went after Isabelle into the wilderness. Could he have persuaded her not to go immediately to the English? Did she go with her brother Louis to Albany in 1707 only to find that her Mahican husband had remarried or died, her Mahican children dead, grown, or dispersed? Or was this another of Cadillac's blinds? Had he indeed been using Bourgmont to trade with the English? Cadillac did not send a force after Bourgmont and the other deserters for nearly a year and a half after they deserted, and the deserter who showed up at Detroit in November, 1707, apparently of his own volition, was queried closely about Louis Montour's cache of furs at Long Point. If the deserter could tell, he did not—he was executed.[33]

Contrary to what the deserter had said, Le Bourgmont did not go to Albany. He went west to the Missouri River, where he resurfaced fifteen years later. In 1728 a French trader, Jean or James Latort, reported that Madame Montour had lived for a time among the Miami Indians and that she had a sister who was married to a Miami. After leaving Detroit had Isabelle gone to a Miami settlement before she joined her brother headed for Albany, or is this another piece of fiction about the Montours?[34]

On August 20, 1708 New York Governor Cornbury reported that:

> there is come to Albany one Montour, who is the son of a French Gentleman, who came above forty Years ago to settle in Canada; he had to do with an Indian woman by whom he had a son and two Daughters: The man I mention is the son, who had lived all along like an Indian, some time ago he left the French, and had lived among the far Indians, and it is chiefly by his means, that I have prevailed with those far nations to come to Albany.[35]

The next year M. de Vaudreuil, the governor of Canada took swift and ruthless steps to stop the fur trade with Albany—and even more important, to scotch a peace agreement between France's western Indian allies and the Five Nations. In the spring of 1709 Vaudreuil ordered his agent in the Seneca country, Joncaire, to assassinate Louis Montour.[36]

Near Cayuga Castle, Joncaire and his men met Louis and his sister and brother-in-law who were heading to Albany with ten sachems from two of the western tribes to engage in trade. After failing to persuade Louis to turn back, Joncaire offered to smoke a peace pipe with him. When Montour was off his guard one of Joncaire's men killed him with a hatchet.[37]

Montour's brother-in-law prevented the sachems from killing Joncaire and his men, and his sister led the group to Albany anyway. Whether this brother-in-law was a brother of Montour's wife (who also appeared at Albany) or the husband of his sister is not known. The sister who had the fortitude to continue on the mission to Albany was undoubtedly Isabelle. The brother-in-law may have been her new husband, Carondawana, the Oneida war chief. Despite Cadillac's constant references to her as dissolute, she would live comfortably with her Oneida husband for the next twenty years and mourn his death.[38]

From the time of her brother's death, Isabelle was known as Madame Montour. She used her translating skills at a conference between the Five Nations and the lieutenant governor of New York in August, 1711. She and her husband would go among the Five Nations the next year to allay distrust against the new fort being built at Tionondoroge. She also later claimed a role in Hunter's efforts at getting the Six Nations to fight the Cawtabas, a southern tribe who were traditional enemies of the Iroquois. This last effort would have tragic repercussions in 1729 when her husband was killed on an expedition in which at least fifty-five Oneida raiders were assassinated by the Cawtabas after they pretended to negotiate peace.[39]

Although more than forty years of age at the time of her marriage, at least two sons have been attributed to Isabelle's union with Carondawana—Andrew (the oldest) and Louis Montour. The Moravian archivist Reichel said that she had two more: Henry and Robert. This is probably an error. Robert was the name taken by Madame Montour's husband. The editors of the *Johnson Papers* held that Andrew and Henry were one and the same person because Henry Montour's receipts appeared in Andrew Montour's account and both were referred to as Captain Montour. However, Andrew held a formal commission from Pennsylvania and Virginia, while Henry was appointed an Indian war captain by Sir William Johnson. Since Henry appeared as an adult only in the 1760s, he must have belonged to the generation after Andrew.[40]

Isabelle was forty in 1707 when she may first have gone through the Oneida country and met Carondawana. Her mother bore her last child at age forty-two, and thus Isabelle could have had two sons by Carondawana between 1708 and 1711. A possibility, since Andrew Montour's countenance was described as "decidedly European," is that Andrew, at least, was the son of Isabelle's Michilimackinac or Detroit years and that his father was white; however, Conrad Weiser (aged fifty-eight at the time) described Andrew as a "young man" in "the best of his time" in 1754, so Andrew could have been no older than his mid-forties then.[41]

By 1727 Madame Montour and Carondawana had settled in the area of Chenasky on the Susquehanna River, probably at Ostonwaken (present-day Montoursville, Pennsylvania). Madame interpreted a conference at Philadelphia the next year between the Pennsylvania governor and the Five Nations. In 1733 the Pennsylvania governor personally condoled her for the death of her husband, but in 1734 she was accused of duplicity by the Penns at the treaty meeting in Philadelphia. In 1736 at Ostonwaken she gave food and succor to Conrad Weiser and in 1744 she presented some of her fever medicine to him. Weiser later wrote that Madame "spoke french with her children . . . and was a very intelligent person, as were her children too."[42]

In 1742 Moravian missionaries Count Zinzendorf and his party passed through Madame's settlement, then known as Frenchtown. There they found Andrew and his mother and several grandchildren among a group of promiscuous French Indians. Madam told one of the Moravian women that she was tiring of Indian life.[43]

Madame Montour was present at the treaty at Lancaster in 1744 and by 1745 had moved to Shamokin (Sunbury, Pennsylvania) where Andrew lived. Andrew brought her to the Ohio River country in 1746, when she was blind, but she was living near Harris's Ferry in October, 1748. She probably died not long after.[44]

Isabelle's son Andrew would serve various colonial governments faithfully as an interpreter and later as a captain. He appears frequently in official Pennsylvania and New York records and in the *Johnson Papers*. His wife's name was Sara, and she was a Delaware. Their son Nicholas was baptized in the Albany church on October 31, 1756. Nicholas's sponsor was his second cousin, Martin Lydius. Andrew had two other sons, John and Thomas. The latter was killed in the Revolution and was the father of Montgomery Montour, who lived with the Moravians early in the next century.[45]

Andrew's brother Louis Montour (Tan Weson) had stayed in Canada during the 1744-48 war, but he returned to Pennsylvania by 1752. Louis's wife was also named Sara, and their daughter Esther was baptized by the Reverend Ogilvie in 1758. Louis probably died not long after, but Sara, a half-sister of the Oneida war chief Skenadon, retained the surname Montour for a considerable period until she took the name Sally Anise in Detroit after the Revolution. Even before Louis's death she became known as a liquor dealer and was often vilified for selling alcohol to the Indians. Her son Christian, by John Chamble, the commander of Fort Stanwix, was baptized at the Fort Herkimer church in 1762.[46]

In 1710 Marguerite Couc Massé's daughter Marguerite Fafard married Jean Baptiste Turpin in Detroit, witnessed by François Fafard, Marguerite's uncle (brother of the late Jean Fafard) and Michael Massé. Shortly after this marriage Massé sold two houses he owned in Detroit (one of them to Turpin) and headed out on a western *voyage* to Fort St. Louis in the Illinois country (now in Starved Rock State Park, Ottawa, Illinois). He later went back to Montreal, his home before Detroit, for in 1727 his daughter Genevieve was married to John Henry Lydius there (see Fig. 8-5).[47]

At Detroit Marguerite Fafard Turpin must have been unhappy in her marriage, for before seven years had passed she had, like her aunt, also run away to the English. This second Marguerite would become known as French Margaret, sometimes called a daughter but by the more meticulous Moravian missionaries the "sister's daughter" of Madame Montour. She would marry a Caughnawaga Mohawk named Katarioniecha or Peter Quebec. In 1733 they were living near Shamokin but moved, prior to 1745, to the Alleghany River. In 1745 the Moravian missionary Martin Mack met her in at Andrew Montour's lodge on a island in the Susquehanna near Shamokin. By 1753 Margaret had moved to a settlement adjacent to her aunt's at the mouth of Lycoming Creek, which became known as French Margaret's Town, where she prohibited liquor. Later Margaret moved to the Chemung River, about a half-day's journey from Assinisink (near Painted Post), Eghohowin's Munsee town (see below). She died sometime after 1760.[48]

French Margaret and her husband had two daughters, Catherine and Mary (or Molly) Montour, and two sons, Nicholas Quebec and Andrew Montour (see Fig. 8-4). Margaret's son Andrew and a son-in-law (Molly's husband?) were killed in a raid against the southern Indians in

Figure 8-5. Descendants of Michel Masse and Marguerite Couc

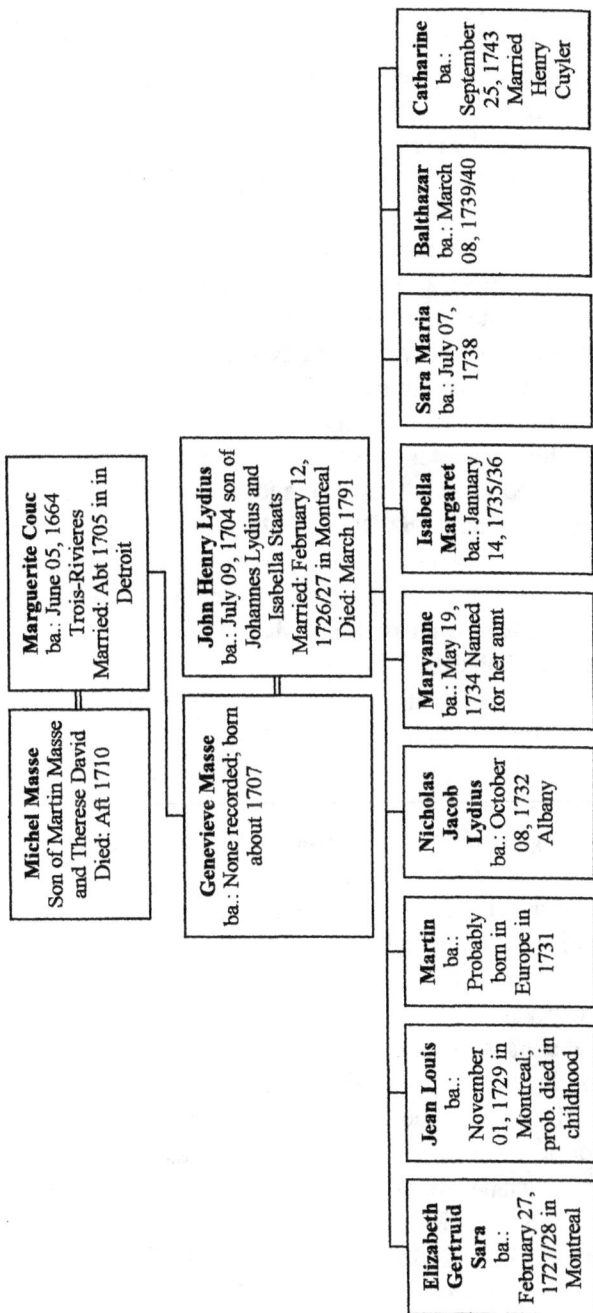

Michel Masse
Son of Martin Masse and Therese David
Died: Aft 1710

Marguerite Couc
ba.: June 05, 1664 Trois-Rivieres
Married: Abt 1705 in in Detroit

Genevieve Masse
ba.: None recorded; born about 1707

John Henry Lydius
ba.: July 09, 1704 son of Johannes Lydius and Isabella Staats
Married: February 12, 1726/27 in Montreal
Died: March 1791

Elizabeth Gertruid Sara
ba.: February 27, 1727/28 in Montreal

Jean Louis
ba.: November 01, 1729 in Montreal; prob. died in childhood

Martin
ba.: Probably born in Europe in 1731

Nicholas Jacob Lydius
ba.: October 08, 1732 Albany

Maryanne
ba.: May 19, 1734 Named for her aunt

Isabella Margaret
ba.: January 14, 1735/36

Sara Maria
ba.: July 07, 1738

Balthazar
ba.: March 08, 1739/40

Catharine
ba.: September 25, 1743 Married Henry Cuyler

the winter of 1752-53. Catharine Montour married Telenemut or Thomas Hudson, a noted chief among the Senecas. Thomas Hudson and and his father-in-law Peter Quebec were described at the conference at Easton, Pennsylvania in 1758 as "noted men, and their advice is often required by the Indian, they have distinguished themselves for the English always."[49]

Catharine and her husband moved to a Seneca town known as Sheoquaga (Havana, New York), which became known as Catharine's Town. It was destroyed by the Sullivan Expedition in 1779. Afterward she moved into the vicinity of Niagara, as did most of the Senecas. Catharine had a son known as Thomas Cook, the White Mingo, who by 1791 was living near Detroit.[50]

At the Lancaster Treaty in 1744 Witham Marshe met Madame Montour and French Margaret, and saw Margaret's two daughters and some of their children. Both of Margaret's daughters are described as being married to war captains of the Five Nations, but one of the children, a boy of about five years, is described as being not so tawney as the other Indians, with a delicate white skin, ruddy cheeks, and hazel hair. This was probably the "half-breed" Iroquois war captain Roland Montour (Wialoosin) or his brother Stuttering John, both children of Edward Pollard, a white Indian trader. A third child of Pollard's was Belle Montour, who married a white man. Stuttering John was wounded in the back during the Sullivan Campaign in 1779 and Roland, who was married to the daughter of the Seneca war chief Seyenqueraghta, was killed in the fall of 1780 on an expedition to the Catawisse Valley. These three children have usually been ascribed to Catharine Montour, but they may equally have been the offspring of her sister Molly. Molly Montour was also living near Detroit in 1791, when she wished to join the Moravian community there.[51]

Isabelle's remaining brother Jean Baptiste also went over to the English by the 1720s and also adopted the surname Montour. He led a party of Albany traders to Fort Oswego on the south shore of Lake Ontario in 1725. His son Jean Baptiste was baptized on November 27, 1706, at Lachine, near Montreal, the mother an Amerindian named Anne. Jean Sr., or John Montour as he was usually known, was probably the father of "Michael Montour, son of Montour the Indian," cared for by Mrs. Thomas Barclay in Albany in 1726 (see Fig. 8-6).[52]

By 1729 John Montour was in Pennsylvania, and in 1733 his wife

Figure 8-6. Descendants of Jean Baptiste (Couc) Montour

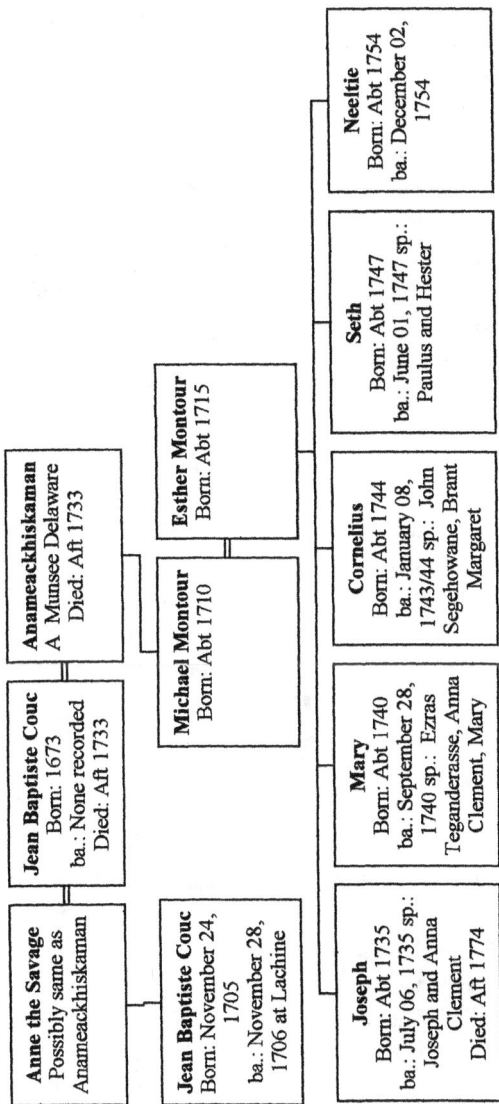

Anne the Savage
Possibly same as
Anameackhiskaman

Jean Baptiste Couc
Born: 1673
ba.: None recorded
Died: Aft 1733

Anameackhiskaman
A Munsee Delaware
Died: Aft 1733

Jean Baptiste Couc
Born: November 24,
1705

ba.: November 28,
1706 at Lachine

Michael Montour
Born: Abt 1710

Esther Montour
Born: Abt 1715

Joseph
Born: Abt 1735
ba.: July 06, 1735 sp.:
Joseph and Anna
Clement
Died: Aft 1774

Mary
Born: Abt 1740
ba.: September 28,
1740 sp.: Ezras
Teganderasse, Anna
Clement, Mary

Cornelius
Born: Abt 1744
ba.: January 08,
1743/44 sp.: John
Segehowane, Brant
Margaret

Seth
Born: Abt 1747
ba.: June 01, 1747 sp.:
Paulus and Hester

Neeltie
Born: Abt 1754
ba.: December 02,
1754

Anameackhiskaman, a Munsee Delaware, with her son claimed land on the Forks of the Delaware River. James Logan, the Penn family's agent, described John Montour as "being very noisy & troublesome, for he is a senseless fellow, and is like his sister as an oyster is to an apple." Madame Montour was "of another make, but ancient, & should be well treated."[53]

Michael Montour appears in the Fort Hunter records in the 1730s and 1740s, the father of Joseph, baptized on July 6, 1735; Mary, baptized on September 28, 1740; Cornelius, baptized on January 8, 1744; and Neeltie, baptized on December 2, 1754. Another son, Seth, was baptized at Schenectady on June 1, 1747. His wife's name is not mentioned in the Reverend Barclay's Register, but the Schenectady church records her as Esther. Because they evidently lived at Fort Hunter at that time, she may have been a Mohawk.[54]

Sponsors for Michael and Esther Montour's children during the Reverend Barclay's tenure included the Clement family (see Chapter 10), Ezras Teganderasse, John Segehowane, Mary, and several members of the family of Lawrence Delagger and Elizabeth (Fig. 10-2). Michael and Esther's last child was sponsored by Paulus and Hester; Paulus was a Mohegan or Mahican.[55]

Michael's wife has come down in history as the infamous Queen Esther Montour, who supposedly executed captured prisoners-of-war after the battle of Wyoming in 1778 by splitting their heads open with a stone maul in grief over the death of one of her sons in the battle. As Queen Esther, she first appeared shortly after the French and Indian war, the wife of Eghohowin, a Munsee Delaware chief. At that time she and her family moved from the West Branch to Assinisink on the North Branch of the Susquehanna River. After Eghohowin's death in 1772 she "took charge of his refugee Munsees at what became known as Queen Esther's Town." This was located opposite Tioga Point, present West Athens, Pennsylvania. The town was destroyed in the fall of 1778 on a raid led by American Colonel Hartley. She may have later married a Tuscarora chief named Steel Trap.[56]

Assuming that Michael Montour's mother was Anameackhiskaman, the Munsee Delaware, he would also be considered a Munsee, the Eghohowin who died in 1772. His wife Esther was thus a Montour only by marriage and not related, as has commonly been stated, to Catherine and Molly Montour. That she had a sister named Molly is reasonably certain, but this is a common Indian name.[57]

Michael Montour Eghohowin may have had a sister Cornelia, for he sponsored Cornelia's and Asaph's son Henry (with Renier and his sister Margaret, Sander Kensiago's wife, see Fig. 10-2) at Fort Hunter on January 15, 1744. Michael's son Joseph Montour sponsored a child of William and Anna's at Schenectady in 1774.[58]

Two of Isabelle's sister's sons also called themselves Montour. Her sister Marie Angelique's son Maurice Delpe St. Cerny was usually called Maurice Montour. His children by his wife Thérèse Petit—Charles, Pierre, Jerôme, Maurice, Veronique and Thérèse—were called Montour. Maurice even named a son who died for Andrew Montour, showing that the family still had ties with their turncoat relatives. Madeliene and Maurice Menard's son Jean Baptiste (born July 11, 1703, at Boucherville) was also called Montour.[59]

CHAPTER IX

An Interlude of Uneasy Peace

A minor ripple on the calm waters of Six Nations neutrality came in the early 1720s, when Massachusetts entered into a struggle with the Abenaki tribes of Maine known as Father Rasle's (or Rale's) War. The boundaries of Acadia, ceded to Great Britain under the Treaty of Utrecht in 1713, had been left undefined and were claimed both by New England and New France. Massachusetts' settlement in what is now Maine was resisted overtly by the local Abenaki Indians and surreptitiously by the French in Canada. By early 1722 the Abenakis had "captured a number of English at Different places, burned Brunswick, and continued their depredations under the direction of Father Rasle [a French Jesuit priest]. He as their religious leader had acquired almost unbounded influence over them, and his political and religious zeal combined to inflame the Abenakis against English and Protestant aggression."[1]

By September of 1722 both the Abenakis and Massachusetts tried to draw the Iroquois into the war. During a conference between the Iroquois and the governors of Virginia and New York, Governor Burnet of New York told ten Iroquois sachems (two from each of the Five Nations), that the Abenakis had broken the peace with the English. He gave them the present sent by the governor of Massachusetts, who wanted the Iroquois to go to war against the Eastern Indians. Hendrick Tejonihokarawa replied for the other sachems that the Abenakis had sent them a black wampum belt a year and a half earlier to try and get their help but that the Mohawks had stifled it. Governor Burnet, seeing the Iroquois' reluctance to get involved in the fight, suggested instead that they try and stop the war. An Iroquois delegation that included Hendrick and Taquayanont did go to Boston in October to try and mediate between the English and the Abenakis, but the Bostonians did not encourage their efforts. The sachems were feasted and then presented with guns in the Council Chamber at Boston, hardly an appropriate gesture to a peace delegation. The Iroquois delegates were kept at Boston while only one, Taquayanont, and a Massachusetts officer were sent (on October 3) to the Abenakis at Norridgewock. They returned without finding any Abenakis, and the delegates went home. While he was in Boston, Hendrick met botanist Thomas More, whom he had seen in London in 1710. Hendrick invited More to the Mohawk country to collect plant specimens.[2]

During two more conferences, in Albany in June, 1723, and at Boston in August, Massachusetts representatives sought to get the Six Nations to declare war against the Eastern Indians. The sum result was two Iroquois volunteers.[3]

In early 1724 Massachusetts established a fort near present-day Battleboro, Vermont, named Fort Dummer. On April 3 Hendrick and Ezeare (probably Ezras Kanneraghtahare) signed up to help garrison the fort. Despite the generous rations alotted to the Indians, only a few Schaghticokes under their sachem Apaumeet and six other Mohawks under Hendrick (and three Oneidas) joined them. The Mohawks were listed as Ezerus, Kewakcum, Cosannip, Christian, his son Christian, and Isaac. Among Apaumeet's men was Taukaquint. Possibly there was a mixup in the lists, for Kewakcum may have been Etowaucum and Taukaquint actually Taquayanont the Mohawk sachem. Hendrick and Taquayanont (and Ezras) seem to have been the only Mohawk leaders who favored involvement in the struggle, which ended with the Abenakis' defeat in 1725.[4]

The fort's commander was Captain Joseph Kellogg, a Mohawk-speaking resident of Deerfield who had been captured by the Caughnawaga Mohawks in the raid on that town in 1704. In 1710 he became a French citizen and went on a French trading expedition to the Mississippi River, and on the way became the first English-speaking American to pass the Chicago portage, which linked Lake Michigan to the Mississippi via the Des Plaines and Illinois Rivers. In 1714 Joseph and his brother Martin returned to Massachusetts, leaving two sisters, Joanna and Rebecca, behind with the Caughnawaga Mohawks. Joseph became employed by his home state both as a soldier and an interpreter to the Six Nations.[5]

One expedition was sent up the Connecticut River Valley in July 1724 with thirty whites and twenty Mohegan and Niantic Indians to help defend the colony. Its leader was Captain Walter Butler. A more agressive approach was taken in August, 1724, when 280 New Englanders and three Mohawks—Christian, his son Christian Jr., and Isaac, Christian Sr.'s brother—attacked Father Rasle and the Abenakis at Norridgewock. One of Father Rasle's Indian companions killed Isaac, only to be killed in turn by Christian Sr., who also burned the town after the New England officers had left. The senior Christian was married to Marie, possibly later known as Moye Mishe. Christian Jr. had a son, Isaac, baptized by the Reverend Ehle on April 17, 1737, and, with his wife Margaret, presented their daughter Margaret for baptism at Fort Hunter on September 30, 1739 (see Fig. 11-4).[6]

****

Beginning in April, 1720, Mohawks had returned to the Dutch church in Albany to have their children baptized by Dominie Petrus Van Driessen. The dominie recorded only the Christian names of the Mohawks (with one exception), and thus it is often difficult to determine who was who. Black slaves had also begun to appear in the church records, as they had in the Schenectady church records beginning in the second decade of the eighteenth century. Caution, and a careful examination of patterns of parents and sponsors from the cross-index of the Albany and Fort Hunter entries, can usually allow one to separate the Natives from the African Americans.

Ezras Kanneraghtahare and Neeltie Kawachkerat sponsored Cornelis Tirogaren and Marie's son Ezras on May 29, 1720 and Ezras, son of Adam and Elizabeth, on August 20. It seems likely that this Adam was Neeltie's son, baptized on April 4, 1697, at the age of six weeks. Elizabeth may have been married first to Adam's older brother Daniel, for a Daniel and Elizabeth were married at Schenectady on June 20, 1712, too early for the later couple of Daniel Asharego and his wife Elizabeth. Adam and Elizabeth also had a second son Seth, sponsored by Seth and Sara on January 1, 1723, and a third son Thomas, probably named for Gideon Tonidoge's son by his first wife, since Gideon and his second wife Dorcas sponsored the child on December 27, 1724 (see Fig. 3-1). The names and sponsors suggest that Elizabeth was a Turtle, and, if one accepts that she were first married to Daniel in 1712, she was most likely born between 1690 and 1695.[7]

Hendrick Tejonihokarawa's daughter Elizabeth was baptized in December, 1690. While at Fort Dummer in the spring of 1724 a message was passed to Hendrick that his daughter was well, a possible reference to Elizabeth's pregnancy, childbearing, or postpartum. This would fit with Adam and Elizabeth's third son, Thomas, christened later in the year. Thus Hendrick's and Ezras's joint stay at Fort Dummer may have been prompted in part by their familial ties.[8]

Ezras Kanneraghtahare and Neeltie Kawachkerat's daughter Margaret was one of the first Mohawks to have been married at the Albany church, on July 21, 1722. Margaret married Seth Karonkyaghonghkwa, also known as Seth Caronkycent or Seth Thick Lip, a Mohawk war captain. They had a numerous family, and through the 1720s Margaret sponsored many children with her father. Ezras also sponsored many children of Ezras Teganderasse and his wife Elizabeth, and it is likely that she was his daughter, baptized on July 14, 1706 (see Fig. 4-3B).[9]

Gideon Tonidoge sponsored a child of David and Onochquiseris on December 26, 1723, and (with Dorcas) a son of David and Lydia on November 19, 1724. Lydia was the daughter of Seth Sietstarare and Sara (Fig. 4-4), and thus a member of the Bear clan. Since Gideon and Dorcas' son David (baptized in Albany on May 30, 1703, see Fig. 4-2) was also a Bear, he was not likely to have been Lydia's husband. David, son of Adam and Unisse (Eunice) baptized at Schenectady on September 1, 1700, is a likely candidate for Lydia's husband and David the husband of Onochquiseris (or Annochquiseris) probably Gideon and Dorcas' son (see Figs. 4-2 and 4-4).[10]

The sachem Hendrick Tejonihokarawa and his wife Catharine were also present on August 20, 1720, to sponsor Cornelia daughter of Anna. This is the last mention of Catharine, and she may have died not long after. Hendrick then married Rebecca Kowajatense sometime before April, 1726, when they sponsored Daniel and Susanna's daughter Maria— it was a Mohawk custom for a widower to marry his dead wife's sister. On June 10, 1731, at Albany Hendrick and Rebecca sponsored Jan and Rebecca, children of Elizabeth. These were probably Rebecca's grandchildren, and not infants at the time of baptism. Elizabeth was married to a Canajoharie Wolf clan sachem Nickus Karaghiagdatie, and on December 25, 1730, their son Nickus was baptized at Albany, sponsored by Seth Sietstarare and his daughter Lydia (see Fig. 3-1). Nickus Karaghiagdatie and Elizabeth do not otherwise appear in the

Albany or Fort Hunter records.[11]

In contrast to Nickus and Elizabeth, another Canajoharie leader and his wife who did appear regularly at the Albany church were Daniel Asharego ("Cutlass") and his wife Elizabeth, who brought their three sons and a daughter to be baptized at Albany before 1735. In the early 1740s Daniel Asharego served as a schoolmaster to the children of Canajoharie. Daniel and Elizabeth's son Paul and daughter Mary were baptized at Fort Hunter (see Fig. 3-5A).[12]

The Canajoharie Mohawks, however, did not have to go to Albany or even to Fort Hunter for a minister shortly after 1723. In 1722 another minister came to the Mohawk Valley, the Reverend John Jacob Ehle. The Reverend Ehle was originally from Hachenburg (in Westphalia) in Germany, baptized there on May 15, 1689. The son of Hachenburg's schoolmaster, Ehle went to the nearby Reformed University (later theological seminary) of Herborn in 1706. Dominie Ehle, a Reformed minister, arrived in England in 1722 to go to America. Reverend Ehle must have been of an ecumenical mind, for while waiting in England for a ship to New York he took orders in the Church of England on August 10, 1722, and agreed to serve the Society for the Propagation of the Gospel as a missionary in New York.[13]

Reverend Ehle resided briefly at Kingsburgh, New York, then went on to Albany, where he met Petrus Van Driessen and also his future wife, Johanna Van Slyck. Ehle soon married Johanna, and the dominie and his wife went on to Schoharie, where he preached to both Reformed and Lutheran congregations. He also ministered to the Palatines now settled at Stone Arabia. In 1723 Reverend Van Driessen was authorized to establish a small mission in the Mohawk country, and probably not long afterward a log mission house was erected on the site of the future Ehle homestead. This was on the north side of the Mohawk, beside the ford that crossed the river and just below the present Prospect Hill, Nelliston, New York. This hill, on the south side of the river and called Taraghjorees or Hill of Health by J. R. Simms, was the spot of a village headed by the Mohawk sachem Tarraghioris and called variously the Middle Castle or the Lower Canajoharie castle. Here the Reverend Ehle made periodic visits to the Upper Mohawks.[14]

In 1727 the log mission was replaced by a one-room stone structure with a huge fireplace at one end, a partial loft, and an earthen floor. The services held here were apparently appreciated by hitherto unbaptized

Indians, for starting in 1729 there were a number of adult baptisms listed in the Albany church records; five on December 13, 1729 (including Nickus Canaquase, a prominent member of the Canajoharie Turtle clan and his wife Sara), four on December 25 the next year, and four more April 18, 1731. It was in 1732, however, that the most impressive numbers of adult baptisms were recorded: nineteen on May 7 and thirteen more on July 23. These were evidently performed at the Canajoharie mission by Ehle and Van Driessen.[15]

On May 9, 1732, two days after the first group of adult converts were baptized, the Canajoharie Mohawks signed a deed to the Reverends Ehle and Van Driessen granting about 2,000 acres, including the mouth and lower part of East Canada Creek and East Creek, "in consideration of the love, good will, and affection which we have and bear for the Revd's. Petrus Van Driessen and Johannes Ehle." Also that year, Ehle purchased 100 acres adjacent to the mission, and this became the Ehle homestead. He and his wife and their four children lived in the mission until their son Peter built a larger stone house (connected to the first) in 1752. The house was in the path of many Indian raiders during the Revolution but, probably because it was known as a Mohawk mission/church, was not harmed. Reverend Ehle died in 1782, at ninety-three years of age. Unfortunately his records, containing over fifty years of christenings, marriages, and possibly burials, have not survived. With this loss goes a great deal of information on the Canajoharie Mohawks and many Palatine families as well.[16]

The May 9, 1732, Van Driessen-Ehle deed lists eighteen Canajoharie Mohawks under their proper clan figures: a fat wolf, a tortoise with its tongue darting out, and a furry bear. The Wolf list is headed by Sourence (Lawrence?) and followed by Symon (Fig. 3-3), Moses (Fig. 3-4), Anthony, Eliza (Elias, Fig. 3-4), and Jan. The Turtles are headed by Gideon (undoubtedly the son of Johannes Onigariago and Louisa—see Fig. 5-2), then Johannes, Adam, Willem, Nicolaes (Nickus Canaquase), and Argiadihha (or Aegiadihha). The Bear column starts with Abraham, then Onichanorum, Targioris, Annanias, Seth, and finally Hendrick. The Bear column is the most important, for Abraham is Abraham Canostens or Abraham Peters, and Hendrick (at the list's end) his younger brother Theyanoguin. These two men would become the political leaders of the tribe in the 1740s and early 1750s (see Chapters 10–13).[17]

Also in the Bear column was Targioris, and in the Turtle column

Willem. Later sources indicate that both of these men had the Christian name William. William Targioris was a Bear whose wife Eusenia (Gesina) was dead by 1758. Their son, Paulus Anotaragte (or Paulus Targioris) would sign a deed in 1753 with a Turtle sign. William Towaraghions (sometimes also referred to as Tarraghioris) was not the earlier sachem Terachjoris but his nephew, namesake, and successor. He was the chief of the Turtle clan at Canajoharie, killed at the Battle of Lake George in 1755 (see Appendix F).[18]

In a somewhat similar confusion, Canajoharie has been called the Middle (i.e., Bear) or Upper (i.e., Turtle) castle of the Mohawks. In fact, the Middle and Upper Castles had been combined by the first decade of the eighteenth century, but there remained two distinct settlements which together made up eighteenth-century "Canajoharie;" both were on the south side of the river. In addition some Mohawks continued to live on the north side of the river where the old Bear clan Canajoharie Castle had once stood. In his 1774 map of the Six Nations country, Indian Superintendent Guy Johnson labeled the north side of the river opposite Palatine Bridge "Canajoharie."[19]

Two other deeds obstensibly signed by the leaders of the clans at Canajoharie during this period were later contested by the Mohawks. The signs of Karaghkondie, Orighjadickha, Hanaharisso, and Kanaquatho, sachems for the *three* clans at Canajoharie, appear on a February 16, 1730, deed to Philip Livingston and others for a large tract of land south and west of Canajoharie. A later Karaghkondie (David Karaghkundy of the Canajoharie Wolf clan) went with Sir William Johnson to Montreal in 1760. Orighjadickha was Brant Aroghyiadecka, the head of the Canajoharie Bear clan, and Hanaharisso the Turtle clan sachem who signed the 1723 deed for lands near Schoharie Creek. Kanaquatho had signed the 1711 Adam Vrooman deed to lands at Schoharie. The 1730 deed would become the basis for the much-disputed Livingston Patent (see Chapter 15). A deed to Jacob Glen dated June 9, 1735 is in Dutch, contains none of the legal forms required for the time, has no interpreter listed and no confirming signatures. It is little more than a note scratched on a stray piece of paper and signed by Willem Tangyon (Towarghions) for the Turtle (William had evidently replaced Hanaharisso), Kangade (Karaghkondie?) for the Wolf, and Hanneyard(?) for the Bear.[20]

The most important Mohawk deed controversy of this period,

however, had to do with the lands of the Lower Mohawk Castle of Tionondoroge. In the 1686 charter to the City of Albany, New York Governor Thomas Dungan had granted the city the right to purchase 1,000 acres of the flats near and including Tionondoroge. The Mohawks, however, had other ideas. In 1721 Cornelius Thaneghwanege sold Abraham Cuyler part of the designated tract. On July 7, 1730, Peter Brown secured another parcel of this land on a ninety-nine-year lease. The body of the lease named David, Gideon, Jacob, Canestagie, Jacomyn, and Gesina as "sachems of the Moaks castle," yet the document was signed by Neeltie (with a bear's head), Canastasie (a slug-like sign), Mary (a circle or oval), Sara (a cross), and Rebecca (a rearing wolf) for the women and Johannes (with a turtle), Gideon (wolf), David (with a bear?), Aaron, Loures, and Hendrick. Presumably those listed in the body of the lease were owners of the land, but the signers represented leaders of the three clans. Because this was at least in part cleared agricultural land, the owners and signers of the deed included women.[21]

Word of these and other proposed purchases (the lease was functionally a purchase) of this prime land, termed the Mohawk Flats, brought the mayor of Albany and several of the city officials to Tionondoroge, possibly at the behest of three of the Lower Castle sachems. Later Albany officials claimed that the mayor and his minions had been asked by the Mohawk sachems to execute a deed of trust made out to the city for those lands and that the chiefs had done so. On September 12, 1733, however, the Mohawk owners of these lands—listed as Arie, Gideon, Hendrick, Ezras, Seth, Ezras, and Lawrence—requested that the current New York governor William Crosby read the actual text of this Albany deed and translate it to them. According to the governor's report to the Board of Trade, when they heard the actual text of the deed (granting the land to the city of Albany), the sachems were outraged and claimed that the deed had been obtained by trickery. They demanded the offending document and Arie, the Bear clan sachem, then threw it into the fire.[22]

The governor thus voided the deed, but to protect the lands, he had the principal Lower Castle Mohawks sign a deed granting the land to the king in trust for them. The first name on this 1733 grant to the king was that of Jacomine, obviously the chief woman at Tionondoroge. She was the adopted mother of Brant Kaweghnoke (or Cawegnoke) or Wide-Mouthed Brant (see Fig. 4-5) who married Lydia (Seth and Sara's daughter) and had a numerous family (see Fig. 4-4). Brant Kaweghnoke died in 1760, but Lydia is mentioned as late as the early 1770s.[23]

Other names on the 1733 deed include three Ezrases, probably Ezras Kanneraghtahare, Ezras Teganderasse, and Ezras Tekjerere (the head Bear clan sachem of the castle in 1740), Gideon (Tonidoge), and Cornelius (probably Cornelius Thaneghwanege, Fig. 7-4) and Seth (Seth Sietstarare Dekarihokenh, Fig. 3-1). There are also Sander (Sander Kinsiago, Fig. 10-2), Whisaw, Petrus, Aria, and two Johannes, one of whom had to have been Johannes Segehowane, head Turtle clan sachem at Tionondoroge (Appendix F).[24]

That Johannes Segehowane held the rank of "head of the Turtle clan" at Tionondoroge, yet Seth Sietstarare was *Dekarihokenh*, the first-ranking Turtle clan League sachem, illustrates the division between political leadership—the elected clan or town chief described by Sir William Johnson—and ceremonial leadership, which was hereditary. At this time there was also a designated chief sachem at Tionondoroge, Hendrick Tejonihokawara.[25]

The city fathers of Albany did not take the voiding of their deed without protest, and on December 12, 1734, the Tionondoroge Mohawks petitioned the king about their deed of trust made out to him. This petition was signed by thirty-nine of the leading adults at Tionondoroge, including eleven sachems. Hendrick as sachem in chief signed first, and Rebecca as wife of "ye chief sachem" signed last. Several names that appear on the 1733 deed to the king do not appear on this petition: Cornelius, Whisaw, and Petrus. Other sachems appear on the petition but not on the deed: Carigory, Sodionquase, Honuchtenorum (the Bear clan signer of the Ehle-Van Driessen deed), and Brant (with a turtle mark). The last, Brant, became one of the leaders of Tionondoroge in the 1740s.[26]

In 1735 six Mohawks (Johannes Segehowane, Gideon Tonidoge, Asarus [Ezras Tekjerere], Seth, Joseph, and Thomas) signed another deed ceding the woodland around Fort Hunter along Arie's Creek to Walter Butler, the fort's commandant. Originally from Connecticut, Butler had crossed over to New York and by 1730 held the rank of lieutenant at Fort Hunter. He had obviously acquired the Mohawks' trust, for Mohawk leaders expressed their pleasure when he was reinstated as the fort's commander in 1733 after a brief interlude. Because of Butler's deed, 86,000 acres on the south bank of the Mohawk

River were ceded to various white speculators, one of whom was Governor William Crosby who acquired 14,000 acres nearest to where Schoharie Creek meets the river itself.[27] In the first part of 1733 another missionary was in the Mohawk country learning their language. He was Henry Barclay, son of the Reverend Thomas Barclay of Albany and his Dutch wife. Proficient in Dutch and English, the young Barclay would become passibly fluent in Mohawk, as his fellow missionary, New Jerseyan John Sergeant, wrote of him on November 25, 1734:

> Mr. Barclay, an ingenious and religious young gentleman, has been about a year and a half among the Mohawks, and is learning their language and designs to get Episcopal ordination to be a Missionary among them, if the Society for Propagating the Gospel in Foreign Parts will support him. Mr. Barclay . . . now reads to them every Lord's Day the prayers in the Liturgy which are translated into their language, with some lessons out of the New Testament, besides some Manuscript Discourses made by a former Missionary, which he has got.[28]

During this period, in fact, the Society for the Propagation of the Gospel was employing the Reverend Miln, pastor of St. Peter's in Albany, as its missionary to Fort Hunter. Mr. Miln reported that he visited the Mohawks four times a year until forced to return to England in 1734 for health reasons. In April of 1735 the Society officially appointed Henry Barclay as Catechist to Fort Hunter and began to pay him for services he had previously done at his own expense.[29]

With this appointment Barclay began his "Register of Baptisms, Marriages, etc." at Fort Hunter, which contains the most complete information on both the Mohawks and the early white settlers in the Mohawk Valley.[30]

In the fall of 1737 Barclay went to England to be ordained, returning to Albany in April of 1738 to take up his post as minister of St. Peter's and Mohawk missionary. During his absence the Reverend Ehle performed several baptisms and marriage rites for the Mohawks, which Barclay recorded in his Register Book. Later in that year he informed the Society that his congregation had been increased by the settlement of some Protestant Irish in the area, "very honest, sober, industrious, and religious."[31]

Twelve Protestant Irish families had indeed settled on the Mohawk River that year, led by the nephew of British admiral Sir Peter Warren. Sir Peter Warren, an Anglo-Irishman, had married Susannah, daughter of James De Lancey, Governor William Crosby's chief justice. After Crosby's death Sir Peter acquired the governor's acres on the Mohawk River near Tionondoroge. In the spring of 1738 the admiral sent his maternal nephew and the Irish to settle his tract. Sir Peter's twenty-three-year-old nephew was William Johnson.[32]

CHAPTER X

An Irishman among the Mohawks

William Johnson spent his first years in the Mohawk Valley surveying, subdividing, and selling his uncle's land or setting up tenant farmers on it. He also opened a trading post and began to engage in the fur trade with the passing Indians. John Henry Lydius was his Albany agent. Johnson's activities so impressed the Mohawks that they named him *Warraghiyagey*, he who undertakes big (or great) things.[1]

In the spring of 1739 Johnson formed a liaison with a seventeen-year-old runaway German indentured servant, Catharine Weisenberg. They had a daughter, Ann, baptized by the Reverend Henry Barclay on June 8, 1740, and sponsored by Anna Clement and two others. The Clements were a Dutch family who had settled on the north side of the Mohawk not far from where Johnson built his new house in the early 1740s. In November, 1741, Johnson had a son by Catharine Weisenberg, baptized by Reverend Barclay on February 7, 1742, and named John. Isaac Wemp, Elizabeth Clement Powell (Anna Clement's daughter), and her husband William Powell (an Irishman and Indian trader) sponsored the boy. William Johnson and Catharine Weisenberg had a third and last child in 1744, named Mary.[2]

In the fall of the same year that William Johnson arrived in the Mohawk Valley, the Reverend Henry Barclay married two high-ranking Mohawks at Fort Hunter. The couple was Brant Kanagaradunkwa, a sachem of the Turtle clan who had signed the 1734 petition to the King, and Christina, a principal woman of the Bear clan. Brant was probably the son of Marie Senehanawith (She who boils maize) who was baptized at two months in Albany on April 4, 1697.[3]

Brant Kanagaradunkwa became William Johnson's closest friend among the Tionondoroge Mohawks, the two probably beginning their relationship as trading partners. Certainly Brant was open and eager to contacts with whites, for he learned to read and write in Mohawk and later signed his own name to treaties. By the early 1750s Brant owned a wagon and horses, and his house was of the smaller style favored by white settlers who by then lived nearby. In 1745 Conrad Weiser, the official interpreter for the commonwealth of Pennsylvania, learned that Brant was one of the leading chiefs of Tionondoroge.[4]

Brant Kanagaradunkwa's first wife had been named Catharine (or Catharina), the daughter of Kryn Onihoenhoundi and Anna baptized at Schenectady on June 21, 1712. Their son Thomas Ganughsiddishe was baptized at Albany on February 12, 1721. This Thomas and his wife, another Catharine, were also married by Mr. Barclay in the fall of 1738. Through the 1720s no other children of Brant and Catharine were brought to Albany for baptism, but later baptismal and marriage records suggest that they had two daughters after Thomas, Mary (born about 1723), and Magdalene (born about 1725). About 1727 they had another son, Nickus Canadiorha, who became a Bear clan sachem and was known as Nickus Brant. On September 25, 1730, Brant and Catharine's daughter Esther was baptized at Albany, sponsored by Jacomine and Simon. On July 23, 1732 another daughter, Rachel, was baptized (probably at Canajoharie) by Reverend Van Driessen, and sponsored by Abraham Peters and his wife Gesina (see Fig. 10-1).[5]

The last time Brant Kanagaradunkwa's first wife Catharine appears in the church records is as Catharina Tagganakwari who sponsored Abraham son of Isaac and Elizabeth (Fig. 7-1) with Brant Kana-garadunkwa and John Segehowane on December 28, 1735. Catharine does not seem to have been related to Brant's second wife Christina.[6]

Christina, Brant's second wife, was of the family that Conrad Weiser was adopted into in 1713. Because of the families where she sponsored children, Christina was probably the daughter of Elizabeth and Laurence (Delagger) baptized at Schenectady on December 25, 1700, with her sisters Jacomine and Margaret (see Fig. 10-2). Perhaps Elizabeth was a sister of Dorcas, or perhaps Weiser only meant she was of the same Bear clan *ohwachira*. The likeliest possibility is that Christina's first husband was Thomas, Moses Uttiyagaroondi's brother, and the mother of the Jonathan baptized at Schenectady on June 21, 1712 (Figs. 4-1 and 10-3; Moses Uttiyagaroondi sponsored the children of Renier with Brant and Christina on January 14, 1740). There is evidence that Moses Uttiyagaroondi (and thus also his brother Thomas) was a Turtle. Since

Figure 10-1. Family of Brant Kanagaradunkwa and Catharina Tagganakwari

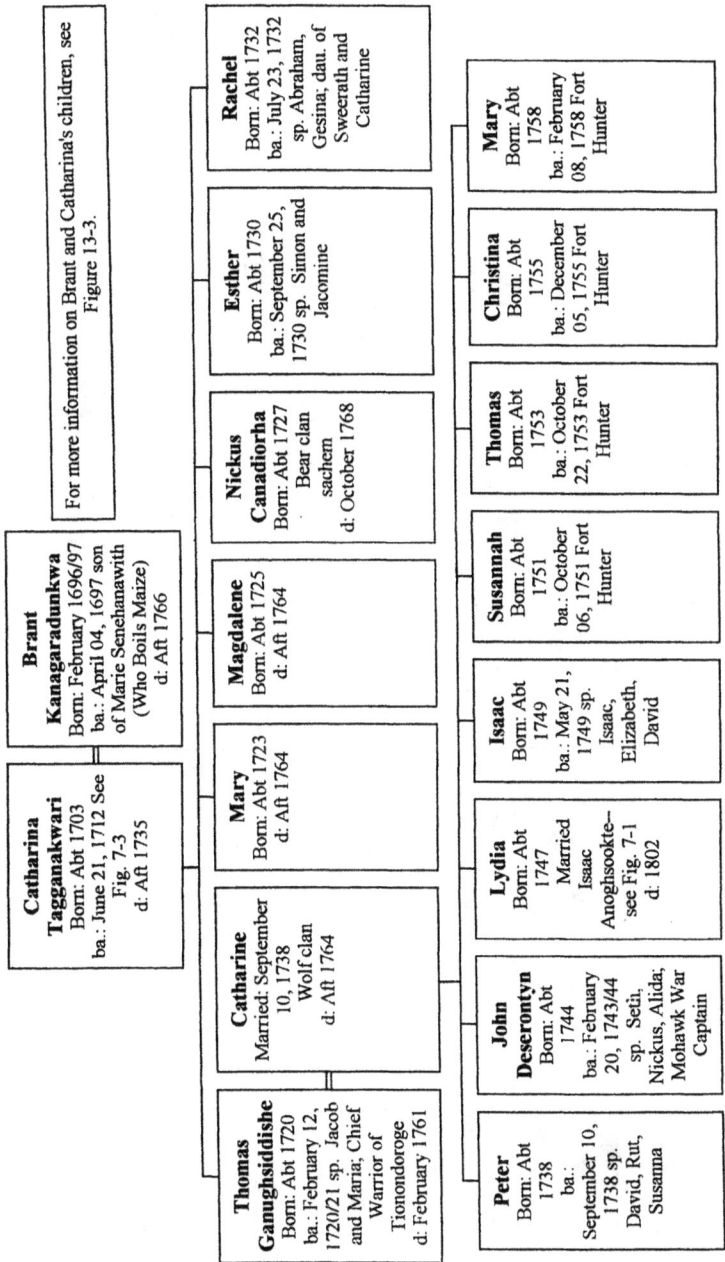

Catharina Tagganakwari
Born: Abt 1703
ba.: June 21, 1712 See Fig. 7-3
d: Aft 1735

Brant Kanagaradunkwa
Born: February 1696/97
ba.: April 04, 1697 son of Marie Senehanawith (Who Boils Maize)
d: Aft 1766

For more information on Brant and Catharina's children, see Figure 13-3.

Thomas Ganughsiddiishe
Born: Abt 1720
ba.: February 12, 1720/21 sp. Jacob and Maria; Chief Warrior of Tionondoroge
d: February 1761

Peter
Born: Abt 1738
ba.: September 10, 1738 sp. David, Rut, Susanna

John Deserontyn
Born: Abt 1744
ba.: February 20, 1743/44 sp. Setii, Nickus, Aliida; Mohawk War Captain

Lydia
Born: Abt 1747
Married Isaac Anoghsookte—see Fig. 7-1
d: 1802

Isaac
Born: Abt 1749
ba.: May 21, 1749 sp. Isaac, Elizabeth, David

Susannah
Born: Abt 1751
ba.: October 06, 1751 Fort Hunter

Thomas
Born: Abt 1753
ba.: October 22, 1753 Fort Hunter

Christina
Born: Abt 1755
ba.: December 05, 1755 Fort Hunter

Mary
Born: Abt 1758
ba.: February 08, 1758 Fort Hunter

Catharine
Married: September 10, 1738 Wolf clan
d: Aft 1764

Mary
Born: Abt 1723
d: Aft 1764

Magdalene
Born: Abt 1725
d: Aft 1764

Nickus Canadiorha
Born: Abt 1727 Bear clan sachem
d: October 1768

Esther
Born: Abt 1730
ba.: September 25, 1730 sp. Simon and Jacomine

Rachel
Born: Abt 1732
ba.: July 23, 1732 sp. Abraham, Gesina; dau. of Sweerath and Catharine

Figure 10-2. Family of Laurence Delagger and Elizabeth

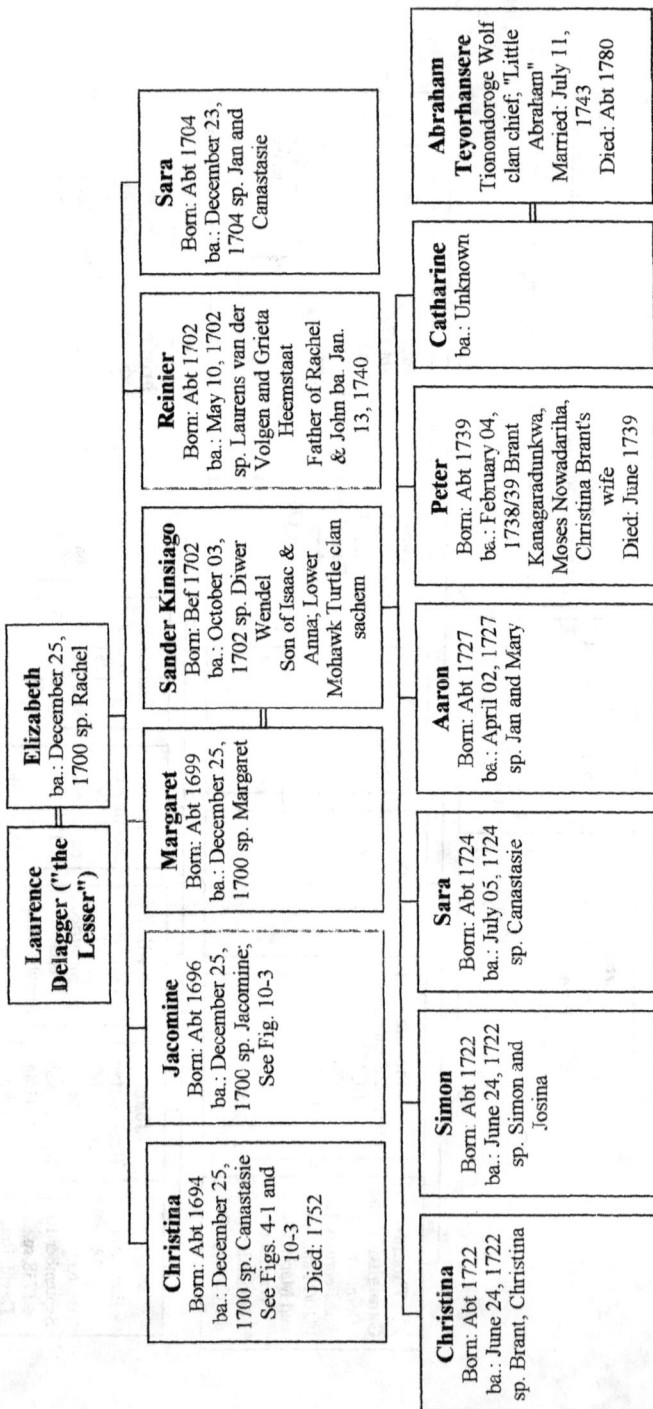

Laurence Delagger ("the Lesser")

Elizabeth
ba.: December 25, 1700 sp. Rachel

Christina
Born: Abt 1694
ba.: December 25, 1700 sp. Canastasie
See Figs. 4-1 and 10-3
Died: 1752

Jacomine
Born: Abt 1696
ba.: December 25, 1700 sp. Jacomine;
See Fig. 10-3

Margaret
Born: Abt 1699
ba.: December 25, 1700 sp. Margaret

Sander Kinsiago
Born: Bef 1702
ba.: October 03, 1702 sp. Diwer Wendel
Son of Isaac & Anna; Lower Mohawk Turtle clan sachem

Reinier
Born: Abt 1702
ba.: May 10, 1702 sp. Laurens van der Volgen and Grieta Heemstaat
Father of Rachel & John ba. Jan. 13, 1740

Sara
Born: Abt 1704
ba.: December 23, 1704 sp. Jan and Canastasie

Christina
Born: Abt 1722
ba.: June 24, 1722 sp. Brant, Christina

Simon
Born: Abt 1722
ba.: June 24, 1722 sp. Simon and Josina

Sara
Born: Abt 1724
ba.: July 05, 1724 sp. Canastasie

Aaron
Born: Abt 1727
ba.: April 02, 1727 sp. Jan and Mary

Peter
Born: Abt 1739
ba.: February 04, 1738/39 Brant Kanagaradunkwa, Moses Nowadariha, Christina Brant's wife
Died: June 1739

Catharine
ba.: Unknown

Abraham Teyorhansere
Tionondoroge Wolf clan chief; "Little Abraham"
Married: July 11, 1743
Died: Abt 1780

he was the son of Gideon Tonidoge's first wife, this is quite possible.[7]
Christina appears also to have been the wife of Aquirith and mother
of Peter christened on June 26, 1725. Aquirith, probably Amirant
Kanianaundon (Who Lifts Cones), was born in 1674 and baptized with
Dorcas, Gideon Tonidoge's second wife, on December 26, 1694. Peter's
sponsors were Brant and Jacomine—Christina's sister Jacomine and her
husband, another Brant. This second Brant and his wife Jacomine were
the parents of a daughter Margaret in 1722 and probably also parents of
Elizabeth, daughter of Jacomine, baptized on April 18, 1720. They may
also have had another daughter, Sarah, baptized about 1718 (Fig. 10-3).[8]
    This Brant and his wife Jacomine do not appear after 1725, and two
years later Jacomine Tagwanagon adopted Brant Kaweghnoke. Thus this
second Brant was probably Jacomine Tagwanagon's son Brant baptized
in 1703, a Wolf clan sachem who died between 1725 and 1727 and was
replaced by Brant Kaweghnoke.[9]
    On February 4, 1739, Christina and her husband Brant Kana-
garadunkwa and Moses Nowadarika sponsor Peter, son of Sander
Kinsiago and his wife Margaret. Margaret was also one of Christina's
sisters (Fig. 10-2). Moses Nowadarika appears to have been their
nephew, Jacomine and her husband Brant's son, born about 1714—Moses
is later called a sachem's son. On September 2, 1740 Christina, Gideon
Sr. (Gideon Tonidoge), and Jacomine Sr. (Jacomine Tagwanagon)
sponsored Moses Nowadarika's daughter Jacamine; Jacomine
Tagwanagon was thus the child's paternal grandmother (see Fig. 10-4).[10]
    It is worth remembering that the Mohawks had an exceedingly close
relationship with their mother's sister. Jacomine's children would thus
have had close ties to Christina, especially if their mother had died
sometime after 1725 (when Jacomine last appears in the church records).
Although both Moses and Sarah married on October 5, 1735, Elizabeth
and Margaret may have lived with her "mother" Christina, and after 1738,
also with Christina's new husband, Brant Kanagaradunkwa—soon to
become William Johnson's close friend.[11]
    On June 13, 1742 at Fort Hunter the Reverend Barclay baptized a
child whom he recorded as the son of Brant Kanagaradunkwa and his
wife Christina, who was almost certainly past the age of childbearing by
then. The boy was christened Brant and sponsored by Seth Karonkyaghonghkwa—Seth Thick Lip of the Turtle clan—and Seth's wife
Margaret (the daughter of Ezras Kanneraghtahare and his wife Neeltie,

Figure 10-3. Families of Christina and her sister Jacomine

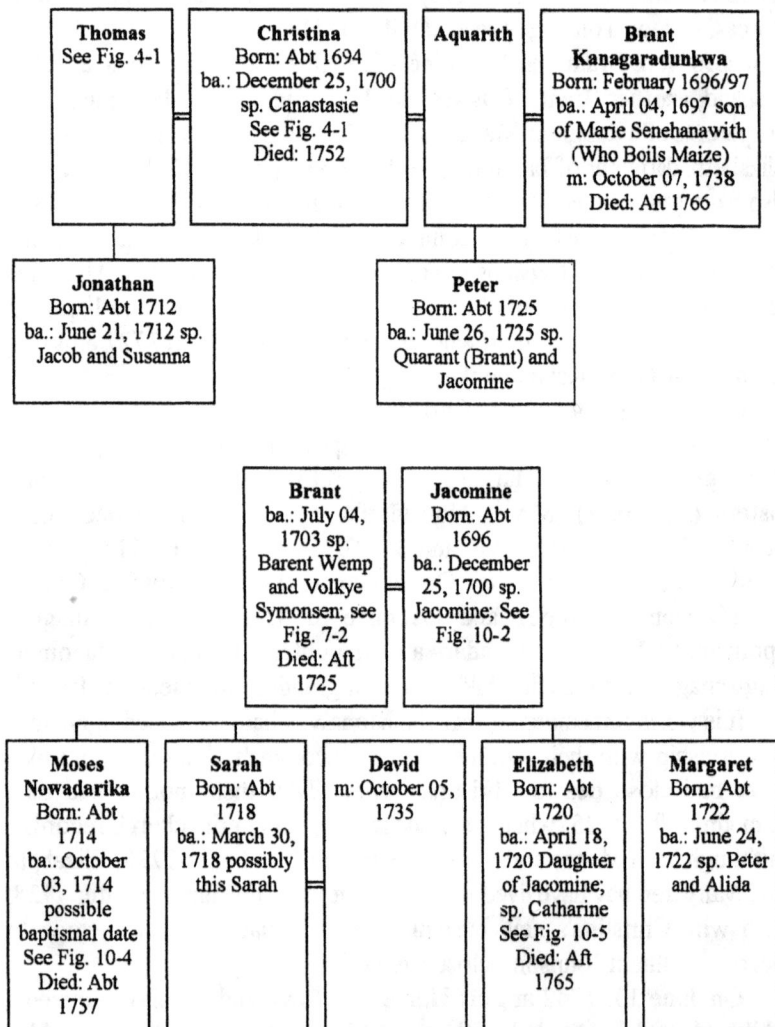

Thomas See Fig. 4-1	Christina Born: Abt 1694 ba.: December 25, 1700 sp. Canastasie See Fig. 4-1 Died: 1752	Aquarith	Brant Kanagaradunkwa Born: February 1696/97 ba.: April 04, 1697 son of Marie Senehanawith (Who Boils Maize) m: October 07, 1738 Died: Aft 1766

Jonathan Born: Abt 1712 ba.: June 21, 1712 sp. Jacob and Susanna	Peter Born: Abt 1725 ba.: June 26, 1725 sp. Quarant (Brant) and Jacomine

Brant ba.: July 04, 1703 sp. Barent Wemp and Volkye Symonsen; see Fig. 7-2 Died: Aft 1725	Jacomine Born: Abt 1696 ba.: December 25, 1700 sp. Jacomine; See Fig. 10-2

Moses Nowadarika Born: Abt 1714 ba.: October 03, 1714 possible baptismal date See Fig. 10-4 Died: Abt 1757	Sarah Born: Abt 1718 ba.: March 30, 1718 possibly this Sarah	David m: October 05, 1735	Elizabeth Born: Abt 1720 ba.: April 18, 1720 Daughter of Jacomine; sp. Catharine See Fig. 10-5 Died: Aft 1765	Margaret Born: Abt 1722 ba.: June 24, 1722 sp. Peter and Alida

a member of the Bear clan). This baby Brant had been born that spring and was in fact William Johnson's first Mohawk son. His Mohawk name was Keghneghtaga or Quahayack, which means either "on the bed" or "in the gun." He would grow up to marry a white woman named Margaret Campbell who had been captured by "Canadian Indians" during the French and Indian War and redeemed by William Johnson in the fall of 1764 (Fig. 10-5). Brant Keghneghtaga and Margaret Campbell Johnson would have four daughters: Jemima (an English form of the Dutch Jacamine), Elizabeth, Sarah, and Mary, a pattern nearly identical to Moses Nowadarika's four oldest daughters: Elizabeth, Jacamine, Mary, and Sarah. Assuming that Brant Johnson named one of his daughters after his mother, and because of the similarity of their names to Moses' daughters, it is more than probable that Brant Keghneghtaga Johnson's mother was Elizabeth, Christina's "daughter" (in our usage, her maternal niece). Indeed, Brant seems to have followed Moses Nowadariha's pattern of naming his first daughter for his maternal grandmother and his second for his mother. Margaret Campbell's parents are not known, but she may have been a cousin of Arthur Campbell, with him the two "Cantual children" taken by Indians on September 18, 1757, in Augusta County, Virginia. Arthur's father was one of seven sons, and the family records on the Virginia frontier are incomplete.[12]

Another likely Mohawk son of William Johnson and Elizabeth was christened on May 27, 1744: Thomas, son of Christina and sponsored by William, Gesina, and Christian. On June 23, 1745, the Reverend Barclay christened another boy, named Christian, the "adopted son of Brant," also sponsored by Christian. By now, one surmises, the reverend had seen through the fiction of Brant Kanagaradunkwa and Christina's parenthood, although they were the adoptive parents of these boys.[13]

Thomas may have died shortly after being baptized because Christian was baptized the next year (Mohawks spaced their births every three years or so unless the infant died). Young Christian died in late February or early March, 1747, when William Johnson, then Colonel of the Six Nations, made an unusually long and detailed entry in his accounts on March 7: "1 black stroud 30s[hillings], stockings, and shirt to clean Brant's house after the decease of his son before he could keep council in his house two pounds ten shillings." A year later (March, 1748), William Johnson met with leaders of the two Mohawk castles at Moses' house in Tionondoroge.[14]

Figure 10-4. Children of Moses Nowadarika and Margaret

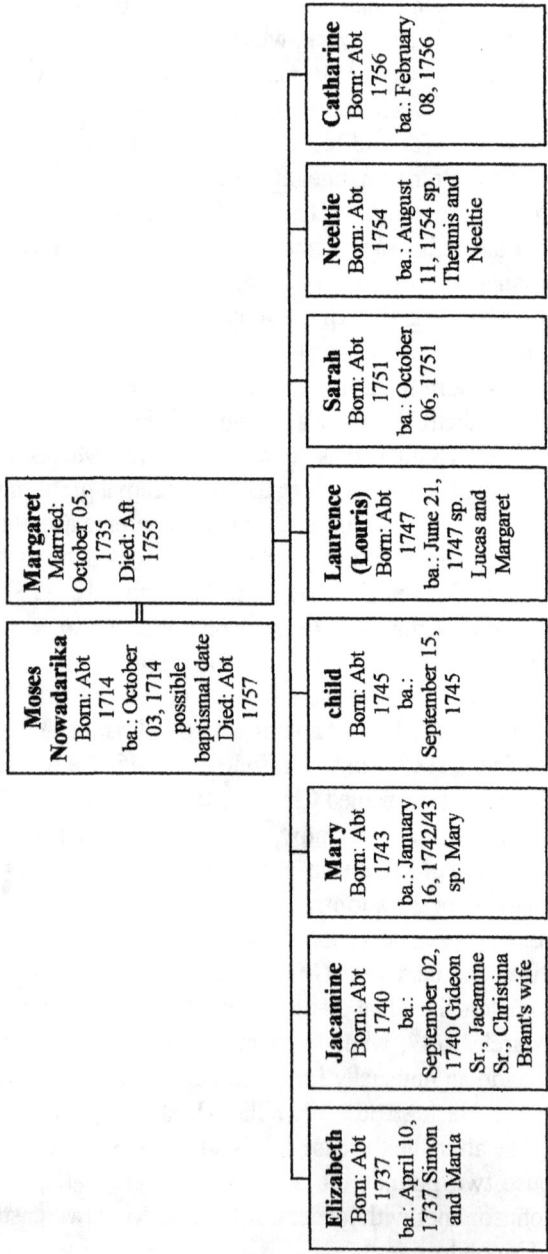

Moses Nowadarika
Born: Abt 1714
ba.: October 03, 1714 possible baptismal date
Died: Abt 1757

Margaret
Married: October 05, 1735
Died: Aft 1755

Elizabeth
Born: Abt 1737
ba.: April 10, 1737 Simon and Maria

Jacamine
Born: Abt 1740
ba.: September 02, 1740 Gideon Sr., Jacamine Sr., Christina Brant's wife

Mary
Born: Abt 1743
ba.: January 16, 1742/43 sp. Mary

child
Born: Abt 1745
ba.: September 15, 1745

Laurence (Louris)
Born: Abt 1747
ba.: June 21, 1747 sp. Lucas and Margaret

Sarah
Born: Abt 1751
ba.: October 06, 1751

Neeltie
Born: Abt 1754
ba.: August 11, 1754 sp. Theunis and Neeltie

Catharine
Born: Abt 1756
ba.: February 08, 1756

Figure 10-5. Descendants of William Johnson and Elizabeth

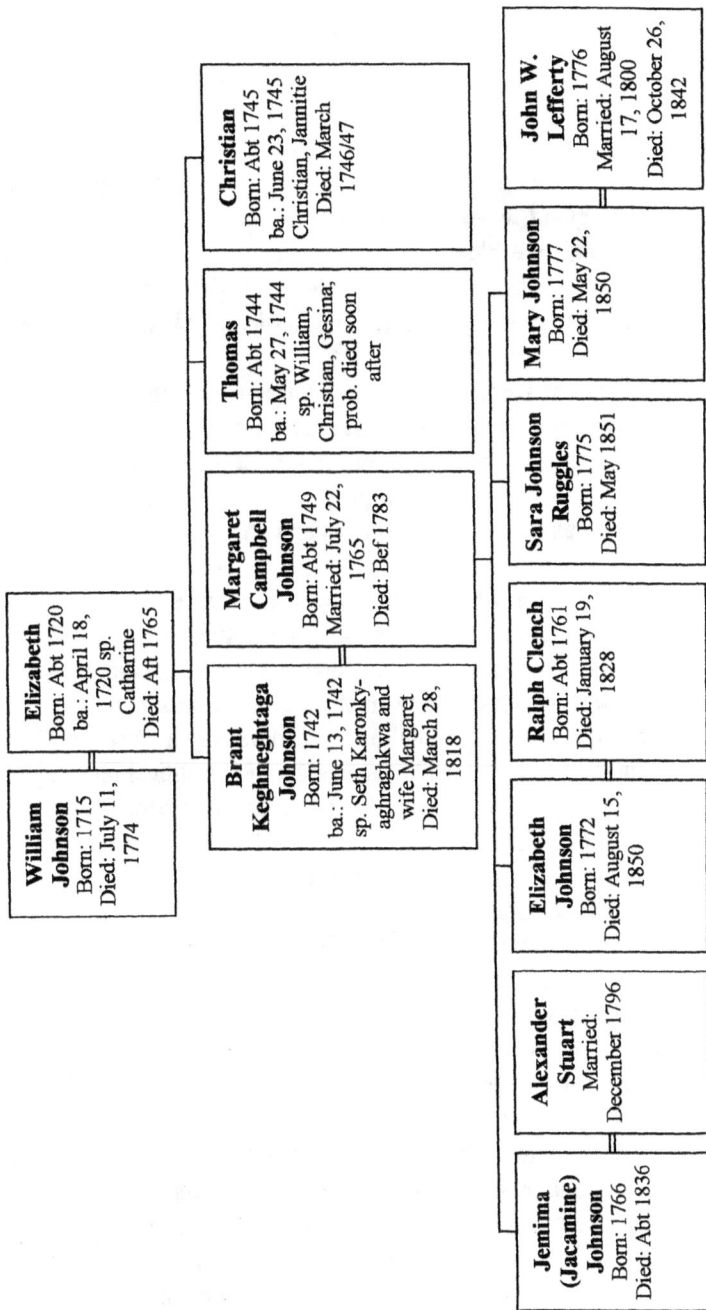

****

After the demise of Hendrick Tejonihokarawa, who last appeared in the records in April, 1735, a new leader and orator rose among the Mohawks. In about 1740 this Canajoharie Mohawk of the Bear Clan went to England, where he met with King George II and was given a laced hat and fine blue coat by the king. This new leader was also coincidentally named Hendrick, and thus historians have merged the two Mohawk leaders into one impossibly long-lived "Hendrick." They were, however, two very different men.[15]

The earlier Hendrick, Tejonihokarawa or Open the Door, was frequently concerned with religious matters, having ascended to leadership as part of the inner group of followers of Dellius and subsequent Dutch dominies, a group of followers commonly found in religious revitalization movements under a charismatic leader, in this case Dellius.   Such movements often occur when societies are under considerable stress, as were the Mohawks at the end of the seventeenth century.   Hendrick Tejonihokarawa's constantly-voiced concern for spiritual well-being (and his condemnation of alcohol among the Indians must be seen at least partly in this context) was part of the desired revitalization of his people by incorporating a foreign—Protestant Christian—belief system while maintaining their political integrity, as seen by his protests of unauthorized land sales.   Hendrick's own divergent behavior, bewailing land sales to whites but signing a number of often questionable deeds himself, reflects the conflict between these two often divergent goals. Hendrick Tejonihokarawa's face, as seen in his portrait by John Faber, shows rather sensitive yet melancholy features, as if he was deeply affected by the problems of his people and knew that his efforts were preordained to fail.[16]

The second Hendrick was of a different sort. His portrait, painted in England wearing the hat and coat the King had given him, shows a narrower face, with sharper features and a short lower jaw. There are tattoos on the sides of the cheeks near the ears. This Hendrick, Hendrick Peters Tiyanoga or Theyanoguin's formal clan name was Sayenquerachta or Soiengarahta, the chieftainship name—Saquainquaragton—that had once belonged to Brant Thowariage who visited England in 1710. Theyanoguin was a more aggressive personality entirely, known for his sharp and fiery oratory. Religious matters he left to his older brother Abraham Peters Canostens. He had no intense devotion to a particular white minister, or to Colonel of the Six Nations and later Indian Superintendent William Johnson, whom he saw as an ally rather than a superior.[17]

Hendrick Theyanoguin's wife was named Mary, a member of the Turtle clan. They had at least one son, Paulus Peters Sagsanowano Oneahario, a sachem at Canajoharie. Another son may have been the Hendrick Jr. of Canajoharie killed before the spring of 1747. There was also one daughter Mary or Maria, baptized on August 30, 1730, and probably another, Margaret, who married a Mahican in Stockbridge in December, 1750 (see Fig. 11-1).[18]

Hendrick Theyanoguin is first noticed in the colonial records at a conference in Boston in the late summer of 1744, where he made a speech demonstrating his formidable oratorical powers and was called a bold and intrepid fellow (another observer called him "very ready, pleasant, and intelligent"). On this occasion he was probably wearing the gold laced coat and hat given to him by the king. Hendrick was accompanied to this conference by Jonathan Cayenquerigo, Conrad Weiser's adopted brother.[19]

War between England and France had begun in the spring of that year, but the Six Nations wished to remain neutral. For the Mohawks, usually the most pro-English of the League, this decision in part reflected their fears that the Albany city fathers continued to have designs upon their land. One rumor had it that the city of Albany had obtained another deed to replace the one destroyed by Arie in 1733. A worse rumor began in the fall of 1744, when the Mohawks heard that the people of Albany were conspiring to kill them or drive them away from their lands. According to the rumor, ammunition and guns would be delivered to Fort Hunter when the Mohawks had gathered at Tionondoroge for winter, and then the Albany people and their allies from Schenectady would come and kill the Lower Mohawks or drive them all away.[20]

Sure enough, powder and musket balls were sent to the fort for the winter. In the middle of one cold January night in 1745 the Tionondoroge Mohawks were roused with the death call, and a warning that they should flee for their lives. Hearing the ruckus from the parsonage at Fort Hunter, Mr. Barclay went to the village to try and calm the Indians. Instead, "the authors of this sedition" turned on him, calling

Barclay "the chief contriver of the destruction intended against them" and accusing the minister of being in league with the devil, who authored the books the minister had given to the Mohawks. Barclay and others reported this disturbance to the Commissioners for Indian Affairs who then came to Fort Hunter to get to the bottom of the matter. The commissioners succeeded in getting some of the Indians to return to their homes, but not in easing the Mohawks' fears.[21]

As leader of the Canajoharie Castle, Hendrick Peters met with the commissioners on the 1st of March, along with Aaron Oseragighte, a Turtle clan sachem of the Lower Castle of Tionondoroge. During another meeting on April 17 between the commissioners and Aaron Oseragighte, John Segehowane, and two other Mohawk leaders, Aaron told the commissioners that he and the other three refused to act any longer as sachems, and all four Mohawks told of their peoples' uneasiness.[22]

The role of Aaron Oseragighte in all of this is significant. According to Aaron and Johannes Canadagaye's later account and a report Andrew Montour received from Brant's son Thomas Ganughsiddishe, Johannes Canadagaye (who could understand Dutch) overheard Arent Van Patten of Schenectady telling his Negro maid about the proposed death threat from the citizens of Albany. Johannes was also told by Van Patten to stay away from the Mohawk Castle. Instead he brought Aaron, who also understood Dutch, back to Van Patten's house where the warning was repeated. If this is accurate, Aaron and Johannes probably brought the alarm to Tionondoroge in January. Aaron was without a doubt deeply angered and alarmed by the threat, later telling Conrad Weiser that a reconciliation had been made in name only ("with our tongues, not our hearts").[23]

Aaron's role in regard to the denunciation of Reverend Barclay is less clear, for the Anglican missionary baptized most of this sachem's children. On December 28, 1735, Mr. Barclay had baptized Aaron, son of Aaron Oseragighte and his wife Margaret, and Abraham son of Isaac Anoghsookte and his wife Elizabeth (Figs. 7-4 and 7-1). These two couples lived on a hill overlooking the Mohawk River, and in time their families became known as "of the hill" (van den burgh in German or van den barrack in Dutch) and eventually by the surname Hill. Their children would become some of the most prominent Mohawks of the next generation.[24]

Aaron Oseragighte was probably the Aaron, son of Cornelius Thaneghwanege and his second wife Catharina Karhages, baptized in the Albany church on March 3, 1708. Aaron's wife Margaret was the daughter of Kryn Onihoenhoundi and Anna baptized in Schenectady on June 21, 1712; thus Aaron was a brother-in-law of Brant Kanagaradunkwa's. Margaret was a member of the Bear clan, as was one of Aaron Jr.'s sponsors—Arie, the Bear clan sachem who had thrown the City of Albany's deed claiming the Mohawk Flats into the fire in 1733. It seems likely that Arie was also Aaron Oseragighte's grandfather (see Fig. 7-4).[25]

The other couple, Isaac Anoghsootke ("to the end of the House") and Elizabeth, had been married by Mr. Barclay in July of 1735, and their son Abraham, baptized on December 28, 1735, appears to have been their first child. Isaac and Elizabeth would go on to have two other sons, Jacob and Isaac. This younger Isaac would also be known as Isaac Anoghsootke and as Captain Isaac Hill, but either Abraham or Jacob would be killed in the Revolution.[26]

Isaac Anoghsootke the elder, baptized in 1708 (the son of Jacob Anonssontje and Jacomine), was a Bear. His son Abraham was sponsored by John Segehowane, Brant Kanagaradunkwa, and Catharina Tagganakwari. Because John Segehowane was the chief of the Turtle clan at Tionondoroge and Brant Kanagaradunkwa another Turtle clan sachem, one suspects that Elizabeth, Isaac Anoghsootke's wife, was a Turtle, named for the Elizabeths in the *Dekarihokenh* Turtle *ohwachira*. She may have been baptized by the Reverend Andrews in 1717 or 1718, and her parents are unknown.[27]

The threat of Aaron Oseragighte and the other Lower Mohawk leaders to resign in April, 1745 was not carried out, but it reflected the serious nature of the disturbance in the minds of the Mohawks. The uneasiness continued, and the Six Nations were determined to send a belt to their relatives at Caughnawaga, informing them of the rumor. Pennsylvania's interpreter Conrad Weiser, coming to the Mohawk country in June, found the Mohawks still bitter and hostile against the Albany people. Of the Mohawk leaders only Abraham Canostens and Brant Kanagaradunkwa, Weiser was told, really believed the assurances that the rumor was groundless. It was probably not an accident that these two chiefs were closely linked to William Johnson.[28]

The Commissioners of Indian Affairs made a vigorous attempt to discover the source of the rumors which had caused the disturbance. Among their informants was John Henry Lydius, who had settled north of Albany near present-day Fort Edward, New York. Lydius reported that he had offered his son as hostage for the safety of the white informant, but the Mohawks would name no one. A Lydius neighbor, probably at his instigation, named William Johnson as the source of the rumor, but the Indian Affairs Commissioners seemed to have ignored this allegation, knowing that by now Lydius and Johnson were rivals in the fur trade. The Commissioners eventually hit upon Arent Van Patten as the supposed informant, but he vigorously denied the charge.[29]

At a conference in October, 1745 between the Six Nations and the commissioners of several colonies, the Mohawks again expressed their hostility through Weiser, using him as a neutral means to convey their message. Hendrick Peters Theyanoguin was not so subtle, ranting on for an hour against the governor until Weiser had to take the governor's belt of wampum into his own hand and told Hendrick to "forbear and hold his tongue." Hendrick's behavior was so rude that Weiser even began to suspect that the Mohawk speaker had been the source of the January rumors, although Hendrick blamed first the French spy Joncaire and then Van Patten, who had already denied the charge.[30]

The major effect of all this was to make the Mohawk leadership distrustful of the Indian Commissioners and the Albany Dutch. Hendrick told the October conference that five or six individuals had illegal deeds in their pockets and that the land had been secretly surveyed by night. Aaron Oseragighte or Brant Kanagaradunkwa told Weiser's fellow interpreter, Andrew Montour, that the Albany people had secured a deed to replace the one destroyed by Arie in 1733. The next year, in the spring of 1746, Aaron led a Mohawk delegation to Canada to treat with the French and confer with the Caughnawaga Mohawks. At a conference with Governor Clinton the following October, Aaron left without notifying the governor and was accused by Clinton of deceiving him and of spreading rumors "that a French army of great force was coming against us and them."[31]

The connections between the fatal Albany deed of 1733 and Arie, and between Aaron and the rumors of a replacement deed twelve years later, strengthen the possibility that Arie was Aaron Oseragighte's grandfather. Aaron's distrust of the Albany people and of the New York governor, and his being accepted as a friend of the French Mohawks, placed him in a rather ambiguous role in regard to the ensuing Mohawk war effort and in the departure of the Reverend Mr. Barclay. Aaron's peace efforts may have backfired, however, for he may have ended up as one of the Mohawk prisoners in Canada at the war's end (see Chapter 11).[32]

Probably because some Indians still harbored suspicions that the Reverend Barclay had been behind the supposed threats in January, 1745, his influence among the Mohawks, particularly those of Canajoharie, decreased greatly in 1745 and 1746. In 1744 he baptized twenty-four Indians, in the first half of 1745 ten, but in the second half of that year only five. The last Indian baptism in his Register was recorded on February 2, 1746. Barclay's own discouragement is evidenced by the increasing incompleteness of his entries in those two years. In October 1746 he accepted a call from Trinity Church, New York City, and left the Mohawk Valley.[33]

Because of their distrust of the Commissioners of Indian Affairs, the Mohawks turned instead to William Johnson. Johnson had volunteered to supply the British post of Oswego on Lake Ontario, and because of his influence with the Mohawks at the 1746 Albany conference he was made Colonel of the Six Nations. By the spring of 1747 he had begun to supply raiding parties of Mohawks going out to fight against the French.[34]

Hendrick Peters supported Johnson's efforts to arm his tribe but went on a supposed peace mission to the French governor in the fall of 1746. On the way home Hendrick raided a group of French in present-day Vermont. The next May he led a raiding party of Mohawks, Senecas, Oneidas and whites up to Montreal, but it was ambushed by a French force on June 15 and only he and a few others arrived home safely. The Wolf clan Canajoharie sachem Nickus Karaghiagdatie and fourteen other Mohawks were captured by the French.[35]

Throughout 1747 and early 1748 Johnson armed numerous bands of raiders headed for Canada. Among the war captains were Joseph Senior (probably Joseph Sayoenwese, see Fig. 5-2), Seth Cahungewana (probably Seth Karonkyaghonghkwa—see Fig. 4-3), and Isaac. Gideon's son David may also have been among the raiders, as was the famous war captain Gingego who was killed by French Indians in March, 1748.[36]

Not coincidentally, many of the Mohawk war captains were the sons of sachems. John Lydius stated in 1745 that "Moses and Killiaen, sachems' sons and Lucas all three sachem's sons who are those principal

warriors among ye young men . . .." The Moravian missionary David
Zeisberger wrote that the first intimation of the position of war captain
usually came in a dream, and that "occasionally, boys are prepared and
instructed for such a dream by fasting until they have a dream which
satisfies their elders that they are destined for this office." Successful
leadership on raids was needed to confirm this destiny, but it seems
obvious that those boys "prepared and instructed" were sons of chiefs or
sachems. Moses was the son of the Wolf clan sachem Brant and Killiaen
the son of Seth Dekarihokenh. Brant Kanagaradunkwa's son, Thomas
Ganughsiddishe, became the head warrior of Tionondoroge.[37]

A change relevant to the traditional Iroquois leadership structure
became apparent when William Johnson was made sole Indian
Commissioner by Governor Clinton in 1748: he was able to appoint
sachems.

> I shall send Arent Stephens up among the Indians immediately to
> give the Five Nations an account of the Peace, which requires a
> good deal of ceremony in their way; then he is to condole (in
> Your Excellency's name) the death of two old Sachems, one an
> Onondaga and the other an Oneida, and appoint two others of the
> best, in their room. This ceremony is also attended with a great
> deal of form; it was always neglected in the late Commissioners'
> time, which gave the french an opportunity of doing it, and
> appointing such in their room as would do everything for their
> interest. Wherefore I shall put a stop to that now.[38]

Undoubtedly the candidates for these appointments were already
approved by the Iroquois, but in the years to come Johnson was as good
as his word, routinely appointing numbers of sachems of the Six Nations.
When this prerequisite came to be granted to either English or French
authority was not mentioned, but the exercise of this duty would have
profound implications on Mohawk and Iroquois politics and result in a
Mohawk leadership closely allied to William Johnson for the next twenty-
five years.

Sometime during the war (called King George's War or the Old
French War) William Johnson seems to have sent Catherine Weisenberg
and their three children to a safer residence than the threatened Mohawk
Valley. Free of his domestic partner, he formed new liaisons with a white

woman and another Mohawk. Mary Connor McGrah, widow of the late Sergeant Owen Connor of Fort Hunter and wife of Christopher McGrah, produced a child named Mary McGrah, later mentioned in Johnson's will. This child, undoubtedly Johnson's, was probably conceived in the four years, 1746-50, when Christopher McGrah was a prisoner in Canada.[39]

Around 1748 Johnson had a son by a Mohawk woman other than Brant Keghneghtaga's mother. This boy is first mentioned in April 1750 as "little Will" and, with Brant Keghneghtaga, accompanied William Johnson to Montreal in 1760. Named William after his father, his Mohawk name was Tagawirunte, which means "Two Infants Stand Out." This probably corresponds to Tekarohhonte, a Mohawk Bear clan name. William Tagawirunte was almost certainly baptized by the Reverend John Jacob Ehle, the only "Anglican" cleric in the valley at that time. Clues to William Tagawirunte's mother are thus scarce, but the boy's clan and his close associations to Brant Keghneghtaga (they appear together with Bear clan Lower Mohawks in 1760) and later to Mohawk chief Joseph Brant make it likely that William's mother was connected in some way to one of Brant Kanagaradunkwa's first two wives, both members of the Bear clan. Possibilities include Brant Kanagaradunkwa's daughter Esther, baptized in 1730, and Elizabeth's younger sister Margaret, baptized in 1722.[40]

When the war ended in the summer of 1748 William Johnson was appointed to arrange for the exchange of prisoners. There was little problem repatriating the white prisoners, but the French would not release the Mohawks until 1750. The French governor requested that the Indians themselves arrange for the release of these men, kept in chains under conditions so severe that three of them died. The English authorities demanded that the Iroquois, as subject of England's king, be exchanged through them. Faced with this impasse, the French governor released the prisoners of his own accord in the summer of 1750 after encouraging them to believe that the English were responsible for the delay and were once again were conspiring to destroy the Mohawks.[41]

CHAPTER XI

From Stockbridge to Onaquaga

At the meeting in Albany in October, 1745, at which he scolded Governor Clinton, Hendrick Peters Theyanoguin stated that his father had once or formerly resided at Westfield, Massachusetts. We know that "some of the tribes on the Westfield River had relocated among the Hudson River Mahicans a year before the outbreak of the war [King Philip's War, in 1675-76] . . . and were probably early occupants of Schaghticoke." Schaghticoke, located where the Hoosic River joins the Hudson twenty miles northeast of Albany, was the starting point of various raids and expeditions by the Mohawks and their allies the "River Indians" (the collective term for the Mahicans and Schaghticoke remnants from the Westfield River area) against the French as early as 1688. It was also the site of the first group baptism of Mohawks by the Reverend Dellius in 1690.[1]

Among those July, 1690, Mohawk converts at North Albany or Schaghticoke were the widow Canastasi and her children Jacob and Sara (born in 1682 and 1687, respectively—see Chapter 3). On March 28, 1692, a Canastasi, probably this woman, brought her six-week-old daughter Cornelia to the Reverend Dellius for baptism. Just before the entry for Cornelia is that of Hendrick Wänis, aged one. No parent is listed, but the proximity of the two entries (following a trio of adolescents) makes it likely that Canastasi was Hendrick's mother, in the real or adoptive sense.[2]

Since Hendrick Theyanoguin and his brother Abraham Canostens or Kaneghstase used the surname Peters, their father probably had the Christian name Peter (a Mahican tradition said that his Mahican name meant "wolf"). Canastasie's son Peter was baptized on January 3, 1697, and the Reverend Dellius noted that the infant's father, also named Peter, had been killed a few months before. Thus Canastasi's husband Peter, killed in 1696, could easily have been Hendrick's and Abraham's father, one of the Westfield River tribesmen who settled with the Mahicans at Schaghticoke, joined the Mohawk raiders in King William's War, and was killed in the fighting. Abraham was most likely baptized in Canada with his mother, who may not have been formally married to Peter at the time; however, the early records of the Mohawk mission at Sault St. Louis have been lost or destroyed and this cannot be confirmed.[3]

Daniel Claus, who knew this family extremely well, stated that the Wolf clan Canajoharie sachem Nickus Karaghiagdatie, who was also known as Nickus Peters, was Hendrick and Abraham's brother. If so, Nickus must have also been a son of Peter the Schaghticoke Indian, but with a different mother, a Mohawk of the Wolf clan (see Fig. 11-1). Peter may even have been adopted into the Mohawk's Turtle clan, since Rebecca sponsored the infant Peter baptized on January 3, 1697. Circumstantial evidence indicates that Hendrick, Abraham, and Nickus Peters were indeed brothers, since the three men and their families all went to the mission at Stockbridge, Massachusetts, starting in 1750.[4]

The mission at Stockbridge had begun in 1734, when a Yale graduate named John Sergeant arrived on the Hoosic River to preach to the two Mahican settlements that were under the leadership of Kuncapot and Umpachenee. Sergeant baptized Kuncapot and Umpachenee and their families, including Umpachenee's wife (who was Etowaucum's daughter), her sister, and young Etowaucum, who was Umpachenee's son and the earlier Etowaucum's grandson (see Fig. 5-3). Not long after Sergeant's coming another young man, Timothy Woodbridge, joined the community as the Mahicans' schoolmaster.[5]

During the next several years the government of Massachusetts set aside for the Indians a township that encompassed Kuncapot's town and some choice meadowland, and both Mahican leaders settled their people there. By the end of the 1740s over 200 Indians, some from Schaghticoke, and some whites lived in Stockbridge township. There was a meeting house and school, and a boarding school had begun to be built when John Sergeant wrote William Johnson on July 1, 1749: "I have all along proposed in my own mind, if possible, to have some Mohawk Children in this School, to be educated in the manner proposed, and perhaps to bestow on some of them a liberal Education."[6]

Sergeant died less than a month later, on July 27, 1749, and plans for

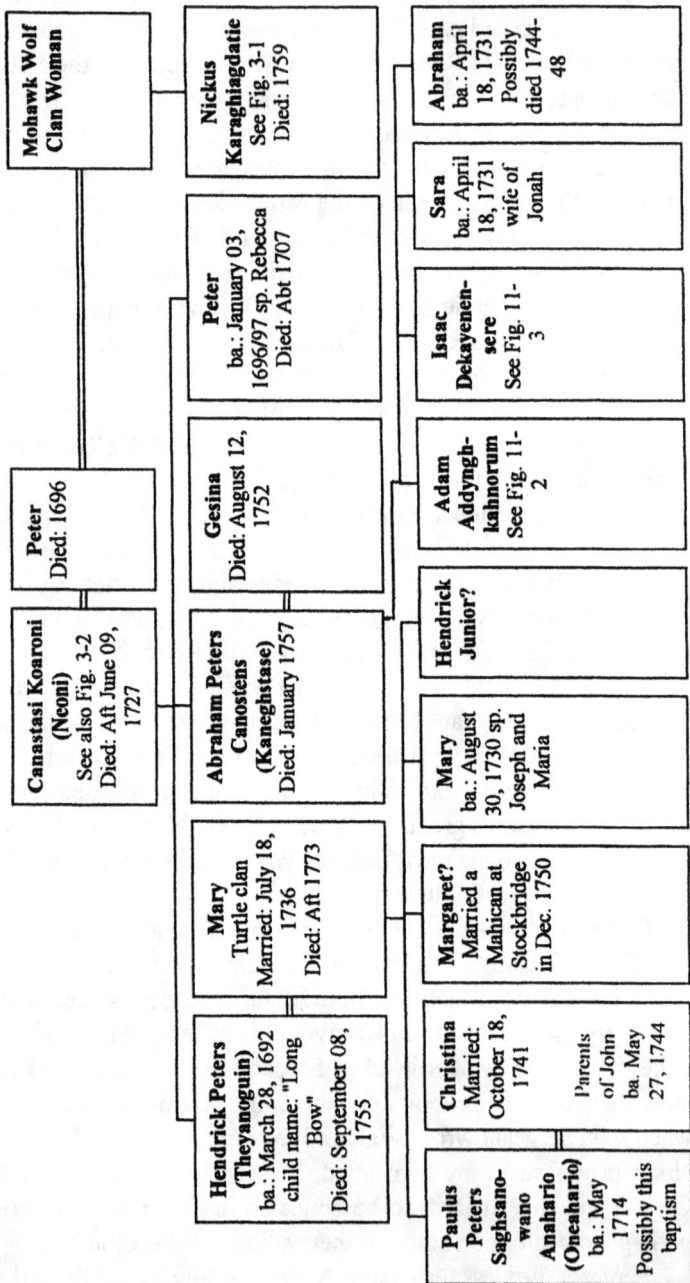

Figure 11-1. Suggested Lineage of the Peters Family

the Mohawks to come with their children to Stockbridge were put on hold. In the summer of the next year, however, the Mohawk prisoners headed by Nickus Karaghiagdatie returned from Canada. The French governor had told Nickus and his fellow prisoners that the English had wanted the French to join in a plot to kill all the Mohawks (the governor naturally refused, he said). Nickus, incensed, stormed into William Johnson's house with Hendrick and Abraham. Only three days of persuasion by Johnson could convince them that the French governor had lied. Dispirited, nonetheless, by their long imprisonment, Nickus and two others who had been prisoners went with Hendrick, his sister Mary, and their families, to Stockbridge in late August. Rebecca, Brant Jogawe's wife, and her son Joseph, and her son or brother Gideon (see Fig. 5-2) had been at Stockbridge since early August. The identities of the other two former prisoners are not given, but two Mohawk men who do not appear to be related to Nickus, Hendrick, or Rebecca appear in the Stockbridge accounts that fall and winter: Aaron and Christian. At Albany the Stockbridge-bound Mohawks met Conrad Weiser, who commiserated with the two Peters brothers and treated them to several bottles of wine at a local tavern. Nickus' family stayed until January of 1751. At some point, probably during the Stockbridge years, Nickus' sister's daughter married the Mahican war captain Jacob.[7]

The Mohawks were, apparently, under the care of Martin Kellogg, another of the Deerfield captives of 1704 and older half-brother of the Joseph Kellogg mentioned in Chapter 9. His sister, Rebecca Kellogg Ashley, was their interpreter. During this period there was no permanent minister at Stockbridge, though the settlement was visited by Moravian missionaries, and Massachusetts ministers rotated their services. In February, 1751, a new missionary to Stockbridge was elected, Jonathan Edwards.[8]

That summer commissioners from Massachusetts along with Edwards met Hendrick and Nickus at Albany and persuaded them to bring the chiefs of the Mohawks to Stockbridge in August to hear the proposal for the education of Mohawk children at the boarding school. On August 13, seven chiefs from Canajoharie and six from Tionondoroge arrived at the town with seventy-nine other Mohawks. After listening to the proposal the chiefs left on the twenty-second, leaving fifty Mohawks and the promise that others would send their children there in the fall.[9]

At this meeting the learned Puritan divine, Jonathan Edwards, met a

Mohawk leader he called "a remarkable man . . . Abraham Caunauh-
stansey, Hendrick's elder brother." Edwards went on to describe
Abraham as

> A man of great solidity, prudence, devotion, and strict conversa-
> tion; and acts very much as a person endowed with the simplicity,
> humanity, self-denial and zeal of a true Christian.[10]

This, coming from the notoriously rigorous Edwards, was praise indeed.
Nor was he alone in this character estimation. Conrad Weiser said that
Abraham "is looked to be the most sincere Indian of that Nation." Others
suggested that he was a better Christian than most whites.[11]

Abraham was a lay preacher among the upper Mohawks, and in
September, 1749, William Johnson suggested to New York governor
Clinton that he be paid a small salary for this service, "which may support
him and his old wife in their old age, as he is past hunting." In this letter
Johnson goes on to make a curious mistake: he identifies Paulus Peters,
Hendrick's son, as Abraham's son. Paulus was acting as schoolmaster at
Canajoharie, and Johnson must have gotten mixed up with the Mohawk
kinship terminology, since both older men would have been called
"father" by Paulus Peters. This error was compounded by the Reverend
Ogilvie, the newly-appointed missionary at Fort Hunter, who correctly
identifies Paulus as Hendrick's son but goes on to say that the only son
of Abraham he'd heard of had been killed in the war. Abraham had two
other sons still living, but they resided at Onaquaga, which explains why
the new Anglican missionary had not heard of them.[12]

By the summer of 1751 Abraham had been duly appointed a Reader
in the Church of England "to carry on divine service in the absence of the
minister," and given a salary of five pounds per year. He was firmly allied
to the English interest, and twice during conferences that year, first in
Albany and later at Stockbridge, he expressed fears of French influence
among his people. To offset this influence Abraham exhorted his fellow
Mohawks to bring their children to Stockbridge.[13]

By November of 1751 both Abraham and Nickus had brought their
families to Stockbridge and by December, 1751, Abraham's son Isaac
Dekayenensere and his wife Sophia (called Nugea in Martin Kellogg's
accounts) arrived. In the next few months Abraham's other son, Adam
Addynghkahnorum, also came to Stockbridge. By the end of 1751

ninety-five boys were enrolled in the boarding school.[14]

Dominie Van Driessen of Albany had baptized Adam, Sara, Isaac, and Abraham, adult proselytites, on April 18, 1731, the same day Abraham Peters and his wife Gesina sponsored a child. I think it likely that these adults were Adam Addynghkahnorum, Isaac Dekayenensere, their sister Sara and younger brother Abraham (Fig. 11-1). This younger Abraham may have died in the 1744-48 war. Adam and Isaac have been called Tuscaroras, and Isaac was involved in a major Tuscarora migration to Onaquaga in 1767. It is quite possible that Abraham's first wife (a predecessor to Gesina) was a Tuscarora whose children, following the Iroquois practice of matrilineality, would be Tuscaroras.[15]

Among those at Stockbridge in 1751-52 was Jonah T'han-hanagwanageas, a half-French Indian who lived at Schoharie, his wife Sara, and their children Adam and Bitsy (another child, Sara, baptized July 13, 1751, was probably also there). Sara was a Tuscarora, and I think it likely that she was the Sara baptized on April 18, 1731, Adam and Isaac's sister. She must have died not long after (she is last mentioned in May, 1753), for in 1755 Jonah and another wife, Elizabeth, had a son William baptized at Schoharie.[16]

The Mohawks and Onaquagans left Stockbridge in April of 1752 for their spring planting, but Abraham and his son Adam had returned by late July. On August 12 Martin Kellogg's accounts record the death of Abraham Peters Canostens's wife Gesina. A Rachel died the next day, which may indicate some kind of infectious cause in both deaths. Kellogg's accounts with the Mohawks end in that month.[17]

On February 5, 1752, a Yale, graduate named Gideon Hawley had been appointed teacher of the Mohawks, Oneidas, and Tuscaroras at Stockbridge to replace the semi-literate and aging Martin Kellogg. Kellogg, however, had refused to give up his post, enlisting the aid of an influential local family, the Williamses, to whom he was related by marriage. The feud between Martin Kellogg and the Williams family— Ephraim Williams Sr., his daughter Abigail (John Sergeant's widow) and her new husband Joseph Dwight, and Ephraim Jr.—on the one hand and Timothy Woodbridge, Jonathan Edwards, and now Gideon Hawley on the other seriously compromised efforts to keep the Mohawk students and their families at Stockbridge. The boarding school, where Hawley lived and taught his Indian students, burned down the following February, possibly under the instigation of the Williams family. Many of the

Mohawks left in 1753, and Hendrick directed that the rest leave by the spring of 1754.[18]

With an eye on becoming a missionary, young Hawley journeyed to the Mohawk country for a brief stay in September, 1752. He met Jonah and his family at Schoharie and preached to some of the Indians who were in the area gathering ginseng for sale to whites. Among these were Sherrick or Shadduck, husband of Isaac's daughter Eve, and the Oneida chief Peter Agwrondougwas, whose mother had been educated by Catholics and baptized at Caughnawaga. Hawley used these connections in good stead when he set out on May 22, 1753, to establish a mission at Onaquaga. With him as interpreter was Rebecca Kellogg Ashley (her Mohawk name was Wausaunia), sister of Joseph and Martin Kellogg, and her husband Benjamin Ashley.[19]

Onaquaga was a Six Nations settlement on the Susquehanna River in present-day Broome County, New York. It may have originally been a Mohawk settlement, but by 1753 the population was mostly Oneida in the central village. Two smaller villages to the north (Cautourot) and south (Caunoiaugaurotreh) held Tuscaroras. There were also Delawares settled nearby. Adam Addynghkahnorum was the chief sachem of Onaquaga, and his brother Isaac Dekayenensere the religious leader. In later decades Isaac was known as Isaac the Priest. While the main settlement at Onaquaga was on the east side of the Susquehanna, Adam lived on the west side and farmed on an island in the river. This probably reflects the fact that most of the Onaquagans were Oneidas and Adam was originally from Canajoharie. His wife, Eva, may have been an Oneida. Their son Jacob Canadiorha became a war captain. Canadiorha is a Bear clan name among the Mohawks; possibly it was likewise among the Oneida (if Eva was an Oneida their children would be regarded as Oneida).[20]

Jacob Canadiorha was married to Margaret, Isaac's daughter, on August 21, 1760, although their daughter Josina (Gesina) was baptized on March 18, 1759. (Josina was named for her [step?] great-grandmother, on both maternal and paternal sides.) Adam, the husband of Lea, was also probably one of Adam and Eva's children (see Fig. 11-2).[21]

Adam's daughter Elizabeth married another Onaquagan, Hendrick son of Jannetie, on July 20, 1751. Elizabeth may have later married Seth, a Tuscarora sachem of Onaquaga who returned there after the Revolution. Another daughter, Catharine, was probably married to Captain John

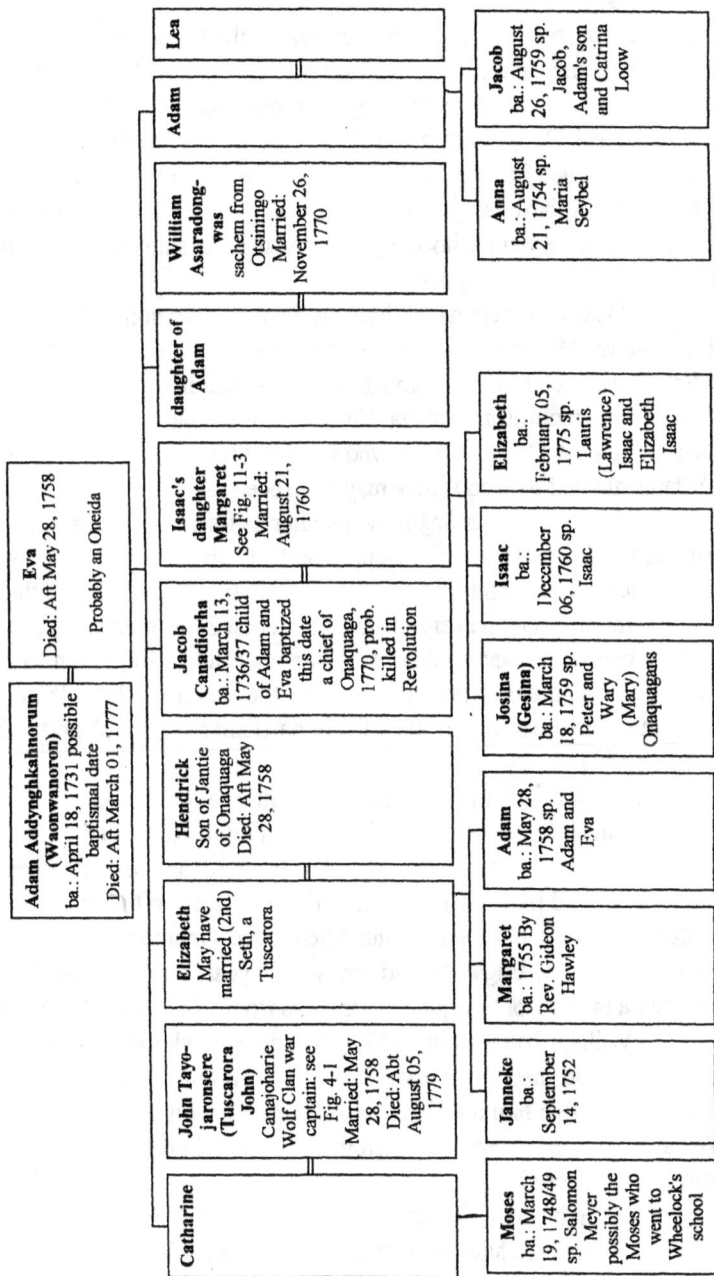

Figure 11-2. Descendants of Adam Addynghkahnorum (Waonwanoron)

Tayojaronsere. Captain John is usually termed a Tuscarora or Tuscarora John but is also listed as a Canajoharie Mohawk of the Wolf clan by Daniel Claus and called "John the Mohawk" by Joseph Brant. On several occasions he served Gideon Hawley as interpreter to the Tuscaroras and later, in the 1770s, became one of the political leaders of Onaquaga. Captain John died in August, 1779, from a wound received at the battle of Minisink. A third daughter of Adam's married William Asaradongwas, an Onondaga sachem who originally lived at Otsiningo (Binghamton, NY) but moved to Onaquaga.[22]

Isaac Dekayenensere had at least two wives, two sons, and a number of daughters. His sons were Joseph and Lawrence, husband of Elizabeth of Schoharie (see Figs 11-3 and 14-4). His daughters were: Margaret, who married Jacob Canadiorha; Elizabeth, who married Thomas son of Alida on August 11, 1754; Eva, who married Sherrick (or Shadduck) and was later married to Jacob (they may have been the same person) on May 5, 1759; Neggan Aoghyatonghsera, and her half-sister Susanna, who both married the Mohawk chief, Joseph Brant. Neggan died of tuberculosis in 1771, leaving two children, Isaac and Christina Brant. When the Fort Hunter missionary, Reverend Stuart, refused to marry Joseph and Susanna because it was against Anglican church law for a man to marry his wife's sister, the enterprising Brant had the Reverend John Jacob Ehle (who may have been ignorant of this particular stricture) perform the ceremony.[23]

By 1748 Christian rites were important enough to the Onaquagans that early in the year they appointed the Dutch Reformed minister of Schoharie, Dominie Johannes Schuyler, to come and visit three or four times a year and perform baptisms and marriages. In the same year the Boston Mission Board sent Elihu Spencer to Onaquaga to establish a mission. The New Englander did not last the year, but Dominie Schuyler recorded a number of Onaquagan baptisms from 1747 to 1755. As Adam noted to William Johnson in 1757: "Parson Schuyler at Schoharie used to Christen and marry our people and we paid him for it, but he told us if we would give him a little piece of Land he would do it for nothing. We gave him a piece but since then we have heard nothing from him and don't know where he is."[24]

Dominie Schuyler objected to Gideon Hawley's mission at Onaquaga in 1753 but seems to have been ineffective at ousting him. More effective were hunger and disease, which drove Hawley from his mission twice

Figure 11-3. Descendants of Isaac Dekayenensere

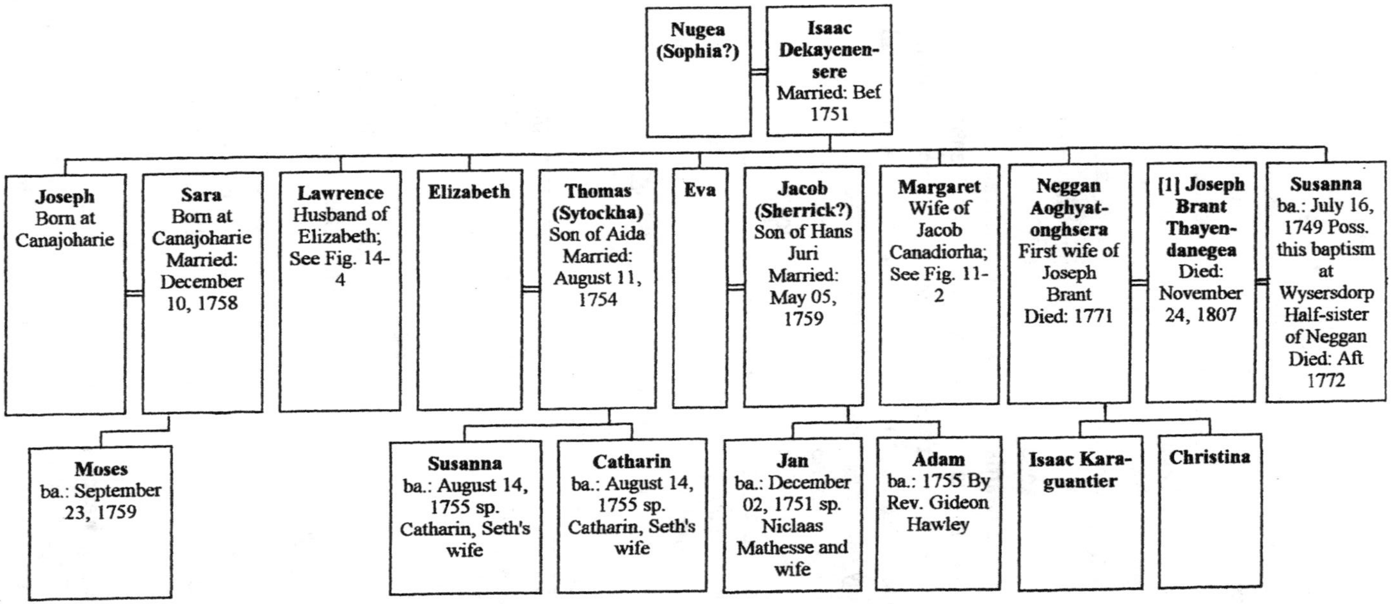

Nugea (Sophia?)

Isaac Dekayenen-sere
Married: Bef 1751

Joseph Born at Canajoharie

Sara Born at Canajoharie
Married: December 10, 1758

Lawrence Husband of Elizabeth; See Fig. 14-4

Elizabeth

Thomas (Sytockha) Son of Aida
Married: August 11, 1754

Eva

Jacob (Sherrick?) Son of Hans Juri
Married: May 05, 1759

Margaret Wife of Jacob Canadiorha; See Fig. 11-2

Neggan Aoghyat-onoghsera First wife of Joseph Brant
Died: 1771

[1] Joseph Brant Thayen-danegea
Died: November 24, 1807

Susanna ba.: July 16, 1749 Poss. this baptism at Wysersdorp Half-sister of Neggan Died: Aft 1772

Moses ba.: September 23, 1759

Susanna ba.: August 14, 1755 sp. Catharin, Seth's wife

Catharin ba.: August 14, 1755 sp. Catharin, Seth's wife

Jan ba.: December 02, 1751 sp. Niclaas Mathesse and wife

Adam ba.: 1755 By Rev. Gideon Hawley

Isaac Kara-guantier

Christina

during the year. By November, 1753, Hawley was back at Onaquaga, however, preaching to the Oneidas and Tuscaroras and settling a dispute between Adam and his wife. He was accused of influencing the Indians in the Susquehannah Company's purchase the next year (see Chapter 12) but seems to have been more concerned with rum brought into the community, with the physical hardships of his mission, and in the next year, with the worsening war.[25]

By the end of 1755 it had become very dangerous for Hawley to remain at Onaquaga, and on the 6th of January, 1756, he left with Jonathan Edwards' son and Thomas Spencer. He returned briefly in April, but it was still too dangerous, there being hostile Indians within raiding distance of the settlement. Adam and his fellow Onaquagans requested that he return in 1757, but conditions were still unsettled and Hawley had settled into a parish elsewhere.[26]

Hawley kept no register of his baptisms and recorded christening only two Onaquagans in his diary—Hendrick's (and Elizabeth's?) daughter Margaret and Shadduck and Eve's son Adam, both in 1755. After he left, the Onaquagans resumed their custom of going to the Schoharie churches for marriages and baptisms up to the time of the Revolution.[27]

Other part-Mohawk families at Onaquaga in the mid-1750s included the three daughters of Jonathan Cayenquerigo, Conrad Weiser's adopted brother. Born in 1696 (the same year as Weiser), Jonathan had learned to read and write in Mohawk, probably from the efforts of Reverend Andrews, the first Anglican missionary. His wife's name was Maria Kajenjkethachtado. Their daughter Mary was baptized at Albany on December 26, 1723, and their son Lawrence on May 7, 1732. At this time Jonathan and Maria were probably living at Canajoharie. The Sara (born at Canajoharie) who married Joseph (also born at Canajoharie) on December 10, 1758, at the Lutheran church in Schoharie was another likely daughter of Jonathan's, married to Joseph, Isaac Dekayenensere's son. Two other sons, Phillip and Jonathan, were educated in Philadelphia in the mid-1750s and one, probably Jonathan, died there in 1757.[28]

Although Jonathan accompanied Hendrick Peters to the conference in Boston in 1744, he seems to have moved to the Ohio country in the ensuing years; he appeared at Logstown in 1751. In 1753 Jonathan was at the conference at Carlisle, Pennsylvania and later obviously assumed a pro-English stance, for he had to flee the Ohio (where the French were building a fort) and in 1754 was living on Big Island on the West Branch of the Susquehanna. He became a loyal ally in Weiser's efforts to hold Indian allegiances for the English, which put him in some danger from pro-French Indians, particularly Delawares. In November, 1755, he and his wife were believed to have been killed by enemy Indians, but they turned up hunting near Shamokin and accompanied the Oneida half-king Scaroyady and Andrew Montour to Onondaga and thence to the Mohawk castles, to Albany, and on to Philadelphia.[29]

With Jonathan, Scaroyady, and the others when they reached Philadelphia was Moses Moye Mishe's son who died there on the 29th of March, 1756, of food poisoning. Richard Peters, the Pennsylvania Indian commissioner, called this Moses Conrad Weiser's adopted brother, but he confused the issue. Jonathan's family, after the first Moses—Moses Uttiyagaroondi born about 1689—had several other members named Moses. Moye Mishe's Moses who died in Philadelphia was Moses Contochqua, Moses the Song, a Mohawk who lived at Logstown in the early 1750s. He was the Oneida half-king's Scaroyady's brother-in-law. Scaroyady's wife in the 1750s was named Eve, and their two children Aaron and Neeltie were baptized by the Reverend Ogilvie at Fort Hunter on February 15, 1756. Eve was a Mohawk of the Turtle clan, for two of the half-king's younger sons (Tsiuaye and Sose) are listed with the Turtle Mohawks in 1760.[30]

The Fonda accounts in the 1760s and 1770s refer to "Moye Mishe's Christian," "Moye Mishe's Daniel," "Moye Mishe's Eva," "Moye Mishe's Sara," and "Moye Mishe's Hess" (see Fig. 11-4), as well as to Moye Mishe herself, who died between 1762 and 1768. Moye Mishe's son Moses who died in Philadelphia in 1756 would thus be of the generation following Jonathan Cayenquerigo's, but probably within his family.[31]

The sponsors of Jonathan Cayenquerigo and Maria's daughter Maria on December 26, 1723 were Christian and Maria. Christian and Maria had a son Joseph baptized on May 11 that year sponsored by Jan (Jonathan) and Maria. Gideon Dewighnidoge (Tonidoge), Jonathan's father, sponsored Christian Jr.'s daughter Margaret in 1739. Maria, wife of Christian Sr. and mother of Christian Jr. was probably Moye Mishe, evidently a daughter of Gideon Tonidoge and his first Turtle clan wife Catrina. Thus she was a sister to Moses Uttiyargaroondi and half-sister to Jonathan Cayenquerigo.[32]

In later years Jonathan returned to live at Canajoharie where his son Phillip Jonathan was schoolmaster. He was the speaker at a meeting with

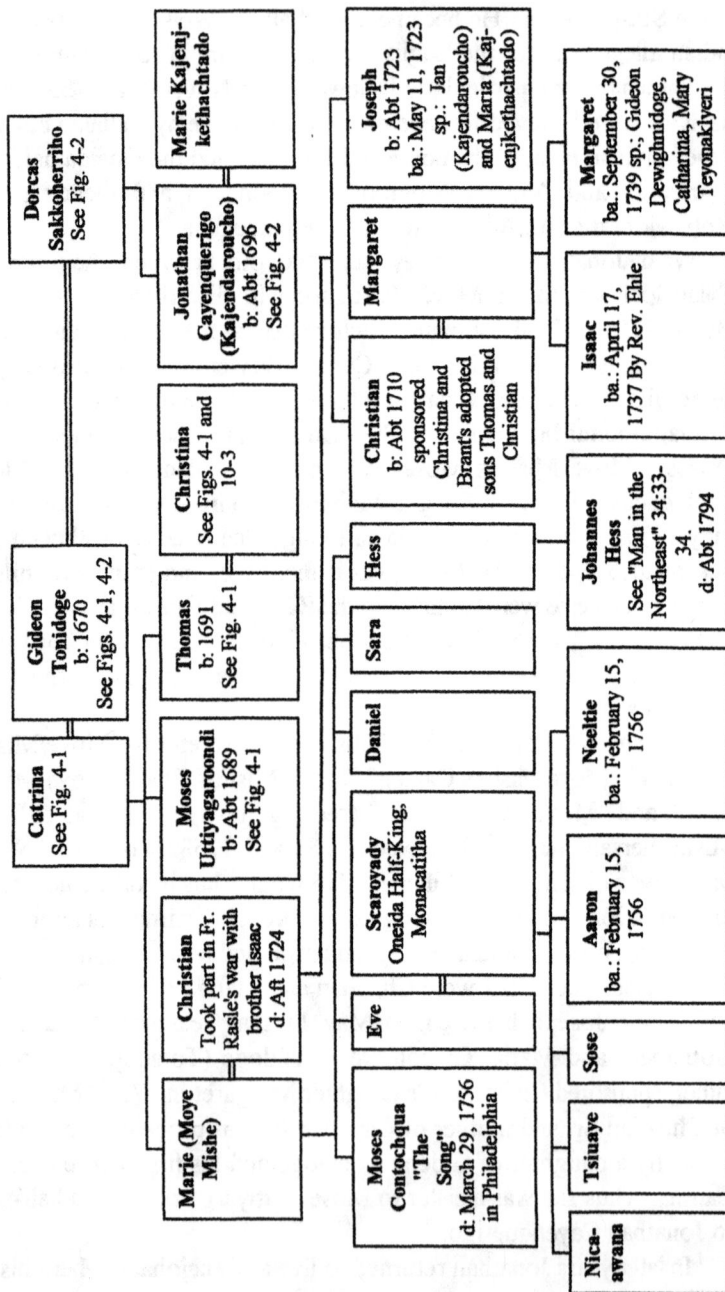

Figure 11-4. Moye Mishe and her Family Relationships

Sir William Johnson in which the perils of alcohol were graphically illustrated by Jonathan's throwing bottles on the ground instead of presenting belts or strings of wampum at important points of the speech.[33]

While the missionary efforts at Stockbridge and Onaquaga were taking place, larger events elsewhere were affecting the lives of the Mohawks, the other Indians, and the colonists as well. Problems with the Six Nations over land in the face of a renewed French threat in the Ohio Valley led the Lords of Trade and Plantation in Whitehall to instruct the colonial governors to convene an Indian conference in Albany in the summer of 1754.

CHAPTER XII

A Quest for Land

William Johnson's management of Indian affairs during and after King George's War had proved effective, but expensive. From his appointment as Indian Commissioner in 1748 to 1750-51 he spent nearly six hundred pounds, and there was no provision for its payment by the governor or assembly of New York, or by the Crown. Moreover, Johnson's accounts for the supply of Fort Oswego during the 1744-48 war had only been partly paid, leaving a balance of over seventeen hundred pounds. Frustrated by his unsuccessful efforts to get his expenses paid, Johnson resigned his position as Commissioner in May of 1751.[1]

Both Governor Clinton and the Mohawks reacted with alarm at this announcement. At a meeting in Albany with the governor, Hendrick Peters Theyanoguin told Clinton that Johnson

> was Like a Tree, that grew for our use, which now seems to be falling down, tho it has many roots; his knowledge of our affairs made us think him one of us and we are greatly afraid, as he has declined, your Excellency will appoint some person, a stranger both to us and our Affairs.

Hendrick's prediction proved to be true, for Clinton was forced to appoint new Commissioners from the Albany Dutch whom the Mohawks so distrusted.[2]

With the coming of peace the scramble for Mohawk land recommenced. Since nearly all of the good land near Tionondoroge had been sold, the Canajoharie Mohawks now bore the brunt of land purchasers and speculators.

On May 23, 1750, the Reverend John Christopher Hartwick received a deed for land between Schoharie Creek and Cherry Valley. It was signed by Hendrick and Abraham Peters (for the Bear), Nickus Peters (for the Wolf) and Nickus' oldest son Johannes (for the Turtle clan). Johannes, often called Big Hance, had been appointed to the office of *Dekarihokenh*, the first League sachem of the tribe, around this time. This office, which required extensive ceremonial duties, had probably become too rigorous for the aged Seth Sietstarare (born in 1678, see Chapter 3 and Fig. 3-1), although he still retained a place of leadership within the tribe. Seth's cousin Elizabeth, now the matriarch of the *Dekarihokenh* Turtle *ohwachira*, appointed her oldest son to the post.[3]

In the following year a number of other parcels were sold by the Canajoharie Mohawks, including a large grant of land along the Susquehanna River to William Johnson. Valid deeds and indentures carried the marks (or signatures) of the leading Mohawks at Canajoharie: Hendrick Peters Theyanoguin, Abraham Peters Canostens, and Brant Aroghyiadecka for the Bear Clan; William Tarraghioris, Joseph, Paulus Peters Sagsanowano Anahario (or Onahario) (Hendrick's son), Paulus Anotaragte (Paulus Tergiorus), Johannes Dekarihokenh, and David Aghnerageghta for the Turtle Clan; and Nickus Karaghiagdatie and Rut (probably Rutgert Kenderago) for the Wolf clan.[4]

False or misleading deeds were a problem, with unscrupulous whites getting Indians drunk and then having them make their marks on papers. An even bigger problem was that often, once the deed had been signed, the land actually included in the survey or the patent—or both—would be expanded beyond the scope of the purchase, at least as the Mohawks understood it. The old Indian Commissioners, ineffective and avaricious as they were, had been reinstated after Johnson's resignation, and so the Mohawks' complaints were ignored.[5]

One proposed land transfer, based on a license Governor Clinton issued on May 8, 1752, to Teady Magin, provoked an impassioned petition written in English by Hendrick's son Paulus Peters on February 8, 1753. It was signed by Hendrick, Abraham, and Nickus Peters, and Nickus' son Johannes Dekarihokenh. The petition asked the governor to "let our High Germans have part of the land Teady McGinnes intends to have. Our Christian brethren have had the promise of it these many years and at all time[s] supply us in our want." The land included one of the Palatines' churches, where evidently both Indians and whites worshiped, and Paulus wrote, "we will not have our church pulled down for we [the

Mohawks and the Palatines] are on[e] church and we will not part.
We are grown up together and we intend to live our lifetime together as
Brothers." Such noble sentiments came to naught twenty-four years later
when Mohawks and Palatines fought each other in the Revolution.[6]

By 1753 these deed problems were so disrupting that Hendrick led
a group of seventeen Mohawks to New York to see Governor Clinton on
June 12-13, 1753, shortly before the governor's departure for England.
Hendrick asked the governor:

> We desire our brother to let us see the Patents that we may shew our
> brother what Lands we have sold & what we have not, for sure
> brother there is no grant given out but that the names of the Persons
> who bought the Lands & of the Surveyor and interpreter are
> mentioned & by this we shall know who have cheated us.[7]

Hendrick went on to name a long list of complaints about land
purchasers. Among those listed were Arent Stevens, the provincial
interpreter, and Alexander Colden, son of Cadwallader Colden, the
provincial secretary. These, Hendrick added, "were the cases in which
they [the Mohawks] have been considerably cheated which were of too
great importance to be neglected, and that there are other instances
but being of little consequence they took no notice of them."[8]

Faced with the irate sachem and these blunt charges, Clinton
equivocated. First, he declared that it would be impossible to determine
whether the Mohawks had been cheated by looking at the grants
themselves. Second, he referred their complaints to the Commissioners
of Indian Affairs and forbade the Mohawks from turning anyone off the
disputed land.

Hendrick's reply was blunt, and of far-reaching proportions:

> When we came here to relate our Greivances about our Lands,
> we expected to have something done for us, and we have told
> you that the Covenant Chain of our Forefathers was like to be
> broken, and brother you tell us that we shall be redeemed at
> Albany [by the Commissioners], but we know them so well, we
> will not trust to them, for they are no people but Devils, so we
> rather desire that you'l say, Nothing shall be done for us.
> Brother, by and by you'l expect to see the Nations [come] down

which you shall not see, for as soon as we come home we will
send up a Belt of Wampum to our Brothers the Five Nations to
acquaint them that the Covenant Chain is broken between you
and us. So, brother, you are not to expect to hear of me any
more, and, Brother, we desire to hear no more of you.

With that Hendrick stalked out, followed by the other Mohawks.[9]

This ostensible severing of ties between the Iroquois and the English
drew a quick reaction in London, where government officials were keenly
aware of the importance of the Iroquois League in holding the western
frontier of North America. The British ministers knew that another war
with France was in the offing and that it was the worst time to lose Indian
allegiances. Because of Hendrick's action they directed seven of the
colonial governors to appoint delegates to a conference between the
colonies and the Iroquois in the early summer of 1754.[10]

****

The Albany conference was the first of its kind in British North
America. All of the colonies north of Virginia sent delegates. One of the
delegates from Pennsylvania, Benjamin Franklin, prepared "Short Hints
toward a Scheme for Uniting the Northern Colonies." Thomas
Hutchinson of Massachusetts brought a proposed plan of union. While
waiting for the Indian delegates to arrive, a committee was formed to
consider formation of a union, and a plan was devised and approved by
the colonial commissioners on July 10, who directed it be sent to the
various colonial assemblies. This was the first plan of colonial union ever
officially considered.[11]

The main object of the congress, however, was meeting with the Six
Nations. The Indians were slow in arriving, 200 appearing on June 22,
and Hendrick and the Canajoharies not until the twenty-eighth. Hendrick
was the Indians' principal speaker. He complained that

The Govr of Virginia, and the Govr of Canada are both
quarrelling about land which belongs to us, and such a quarrel as
this may end in our destruction; they fight who shall have the
land. The Govrs of Virginia and Pennsylvania have made paths
thro' our Country to trade and built houses without acquainting

us with it.

Hendrick went on to excoriate the English commissioners for their lack of preparedness against the French, saying "look at the French, they are Men, they are fortifying everywhere—but, we are ashamed to say it, you are all like women bare and open without any fortifications."[12]

While these general meetings were going on, the Pennsylvania commissioners were making overtures to the sachems about a purchase of lands below the forty-second parallel, from the Susquehanna River westward to that colony's western bounds, adjacent to Lake Erie. Hendrick told them that

> We will never part with the Land at Shamokin and Wyomink. . .
> Brother: We have heard since We came here, that our brother Onas [Penn] and our Brother of New England have some Disputes about the Lands of Sasquehannah, . . . but We desire You would not differ with one another about it, for neither of you shall have it.

Hendrick and the Six Nations sachems did agree, however, to sell the Pennsylvania agents the rest of the land that the Penns desired.[13]

On July 6, 1754, the Six Nations leaders signed a deed to the proprietors of Pennsylvania. The Mohawk signers of this deed were Hendrick, Abraham, and Nickus Peters, Hendrick's son Paulus, Brant Kanagaradunkwa, Johannes Segehowanne (Satsyhowano), Johannes Canadagaye (Kanadakoyon), Abraham Sastreghredchy, Lawrence Sonagaris, Moses Tegenondake, Cornelius Terakaru, William Tarraghioris, and Zacharias Tanaghsagoughita.[14]

On July 9, the Six Nations were shown a deed signed in 1736 in which the Iroquois promised not to sell any land within the boundaries of Pennsylvania to anyone but the Penns. A chief who had signed this deed was present at the Albany meeting and confirmed it to the rest of the assembled Indians. Paulus Peters Anonhario signed the written confirmation of this event.[15] Satisfied, the Pennsylvania commissioners departed for home.

Ironically, two days later, July 11, is the date affixed to the Susquehannah Company's deed to purchase the Wyoming Valley from the Six Nations.[16]

****

In 1753 a number of citizens of Connecticut had formed an organization, the Susquehannah Company, to purchase the Wyoming Valley in the watershed of the Susquehanna under the supposed aegis of their colony's charter. Shares in the company were sold in the various Connecticut counties, but word of these plans leaked to the other colonies. Faced with opposition from Pennsylvania lieutenant-governor Hamilton, New York acting-governor James De Lancy, and William Johnson, the Susquehanna Company directors granted a full share in the company to Timothy Woodbridge of Stockbridge to purchase the lands directly from the Six Nations.[17]

Woodbridge was present at the Albany congress as the interpreter for the Stockbridge Indians, and he was privy to the negotiations between the Pennsylvania commissioners and the Six Nations. Both he and Connecticut commissioner Elisha Williams were shown the 1736 deed in which the Six Nations promised to sell land within the Penn grant only to Pennsylvania. However, Woodbridge had enlisted an agent of his own, none other than John Henry Lydius, to purchase the Wyoming Valley from the Iroquois using $1500 in gold.[18]

Both sides agreed to that much. However, the manner in which the land was purchased from the Iroquois has been the subject of some debate between the advocates of Pennsylvania and those of Connecticut. Modern historians, and the evidence of the Iroquois themselves in their subsequent dealings with Lydius, tend to favor the account given by Pennsylvania agent Daniel Claus.[19]

Claus was a young man from a town in Wurtenburg in Germany who came over to Pennsylvania to make his fortune. Failing in this, he accompanied Conrad Weiser to the Mohawk country in 1751 when Weiser came to put his son Sammy in the home of a Mohawk sachem to have him learn the language, much as the elder Weiser had done in 1713. Claus, ostensibly Sammy's tutor, was also to learn the Mohawk language and use his ability to serve as an agent to Pennsylvania, much as the aging Conrad Weiser did.[20]

The Mohawk sachem who gave room and board to both Sammy Weiser and Daniel Claus was Brant Kanagaradunkwa, William Johnson's closest friend among the Mohawks and the adoptive father of William

Johnson's Mohawk son Brant Keghneghtaga. Brant Kanagaradunkwa's wife Christina was a member of the family into which Weiser was adopted in 1713. Claus roomed with Brant's son Thomas Ganughsiddishe in 1752, but by 1753 he was living with and working for William Johnson. His service for Pennsylvania in 1754 did not conflict, however, since Johnson wholeheartedly supported the Penns on this issue.[21] As Claus wrote:

> John Lydius of Albany engaged in to serve the Connecticut People in buying the Lands at Sasquehannah the said Province was contriving to buy of the Six Nations this year past, and that after the Sum of Fifteen Hundred Dollars being put in his Hands, . . . he went in the following clandestine manner to work, and with tempting the Indians he could prevail upon with Plenty of Dollars, got the following Subscriptions to his Deed. Vizt. Gahikdote alias Grote Younge the Head of the Senecas; Atsinoughiata alias the Bunt, and Canatisiagaye Two Onondagos; Those he got after the Treaty was over and the Commissioners gone, suppose when they were drunk.

> Afterwards he under a vain Pretence took a Ride to Canajochery as he told me himself . . . that he had been there to buy a Span of Horses, and by laying down the Bag of Dollars had Abraham, [and] Nickas, Hendrick's Brothers and Tarraghioris to sign.[22]

Lydius didn't dare to ask Hendrick himself, although Hendrick's name is listed in the body of the deed as a "granter" of the land. Claus continues:

> Then he [Lydius] passed in his way home the lower Mohock Castle and invited Four of the Sachems to his House about some Business he had to propose to them, and when they came there, he called one after another in a Room by himself and laid the Deed before them and shewed the Subscriptions of the other Nations, and by many false Persuasions, with the offer of Twenty Dollars each, brought them to sign their Names, which are Tsistarare [Seth Sietstarare], [Johannes] Canadagaye, Sotsihowano [Johannes Segehowane] and Gawegnoge [Brant Kaweghnoke].

According to Johannes Canadagaye, the Tionondoroge Bear clan sachem, Lydius told him that the lands were in Ohio. Lydius later brought a group of thirty Oneidas to Albany, got them drunk, and had their chiefs sign the deed.[23]

In an effort to get the Six Nations to renounce the deed, officials in Pennsylvania invited a delegation of Mohawk leaders to Philadelphia early in the new year. This expedition, headed by Hendrick Theyanoguin and guided by Daniel Claus, headed down Schoharie Creek to bypass Albany, reaching Philadelphia on Wednesday, January 8, 1755. Besides Hendrick there were Seth Sietstarare, Joseph Otchenuchyata, Johannes Dekarihokenh, his brother Nicholas Anatshiaenghse (see Fig. 3-1), and Jacob Sagotenjuchta (a Turtle clan Mohawk from Canajoharie). Also in the delegation were Brant Kanagaradunkwa, his son Nicholas Canadiorha, his adopted son Brant Keghneghtaga, and his new wife Margaret and her two children, known to history as Joseph and Molly Brant.[24]

As Joseph Brant's biographer Isabel Kelsay discovered, Joseph Brant's parents were Peter Tehonwaghkwangeraghkwa and Margaret, whose children Jacob and Christina were baptized at Fort Hunter in the early 1740s. Molly had been born in 1736, and Joseph was born in the Ohio country in March, 1743. Peter and Margaret may have been the Peter and ___ married by the Reverend Barclay on July 6, 1735, the same day Jacomine Kaghtenoone's son Isaac Anoghsookte married—Jacomine was probably Margaret's stepmother since June 19 that year (see Figs. 5-1 and 7-1).[25]

Peter Tehonwaghkwangeraghkwa and Margaret would need the blessing of the church, for they would not receive the blessings of the Mohawks. (In the next century an aged Oneida went so far as to call Joseph Brant a bastard.) Peter and Margaret's marriage violated the rule of clan exogamy—they were both members of the Wolf clan. This fact probably explains why the sponsors of their children were so obscure. It may also explain why the couple went west to the Ohio country, where Margaret may have had relatives among the Caughnawaga Mohawks who frequented that area (see Chapter 5).[26]

Peter died in the Ohio country, possibly of an epidemic. After his death Margaret came back to Canajoharie and married a war chief named Lucas (Lykas), giving him two children, Jacomine and Lea who must have died in infancy. Lucas was killed in May, 1750, on a raid to the

Catawba country.[27]

Margaret probably met Brant Kanagaradunkwa in 1752 while gathering ginseng, then a speculative cash crop for the Mohawks. Their son Jacob was baptized by the Reverend Ogilvie at Fort Hunter on March 4, 1753. Brant's wife Christina was probably dead by then, killed by a drunken Indian, but the child had been conceived adulterously, and the Reverend made Margaret do penance. A devout Mohawk Christian, she did so. Brant and Margaret were married by the Reverend on September 9, 1753. All of Margaret's children appear to have died in infancy or early childhood except for Molly and Joseph, who soon took their stepfather's name as their surname.[28]

In Philadelphia in early 1755 the Mohawks sachems met with Governor Morris and his council and Hendrick

repeatedly assured the Governor in Council that the Connecticut Purchase was made clandestinely by Mr. Lydius at Albany with a few drunken Oneida Indians without the knowledge and consent of the Six Nations in Council and the signers of the Indian deed had not the least right or claim to the lands they sold. And that on his return he would acquaint the Body of the Confederacy with it and have the purchase made null and void by a public decree of the whole body and ascertain and publish the just claim and property of these lands to the proprietaries of Pennsylvania. Mr. Claus returned with K. Henry by Esopus and Albany where Cap[t] StM[s] fell in love with Ms. Mary Brant who was then pretty likely not having had the smallpox.[29]

Claus and the Mohawks arrived at Albany on February 8, 1755. Stationed at Albany's fort at that time and holding a commission in a New York regiment was twenty-seven-year-old Captain Staats Morris, the governor of Pennsylvania's nephew. Captain Morris was a lively young man who had recently gotten in trouble with one of the Justices of the Peace in Albany, and would be arraigned at the next session of oyer and terminer in June. He was a friend of William Johnson's and had dealings with the Indians who passed through Albany, for Claus himself wrote that "Cap[t] Staats Morris supplied [Scaroyady] with so much money as brought him to Col. [William] Johnson's" just a few weeks before the Mohawk delegation arrived in Albany when Captain Morris saw them

and spoke to Hendrick. Molly Brant was eighteen, and "pretty likely."
Staats Morris is undoubtedly the Cap' StMᵗ Claus meant.[30]

There is a traditional story that at a regimental militia muster an
officer rode around with Molly Brant sitting behind him on his horse.
After this time William Johnson or the officer took her home with him.
In early 1755 Governor-General William Shirley of Massachusetts gave
Captain Staats Morris a commission in the governor's own regiment,
which assembled that summer just outside of Albany. Shirley himself met
New York militia General William Johnson there in early July, but Staats
must have been in Albany earlier for the session of oyer and terminer.
There were several regimental musters that summer. Captain Staats
Morris accompanied Shirley and his force on their unsuccessful
expedition to Oswego and passed through the Mohawk country again
that October, stopping long enough to receive messages from the
Mohawks to be passed on to William Johnson. Shirley sent Captain
Morris on to England with dispatches, and while in Britain Staats married
the dowager duchess of Gordon. Staats and his wife returned to New
York years later and even visited his old friend William Johnson. By then
Molly Brant was William Johnson's common-law wife and the mother of
several of his children. There may have been an additional child of
Molly's, a boy who was to die in the Revolution. He may even have been
the son of Staats Morris.[31]

CHAPTER XIII

Mohawk Leadership and Sir William Johnson

While the Six Nations had been meeting with representatives from the northern colonies in Albany in the summer of 1754 a force of Virginians under George Washington had been meeting with a French force at Fort Necessity in what is now western Pennsylvania. Inexperienced and outnumbered, Washington was forced to surrender and leave the Ohio country in the hands of the French, who built Fort Duquesne at the Forks of the Ohio River.[1]

The government in London, determined not to leave this vital area in French hands, directed Governor Shirley of Massachusetts and Sir William Pepperell of that colony each to raise regiments of 1,000 men and also sent several regiments of British regulars under the command of General Braddock to Virginia the following spring.[2]

Braddock met with the governors of New York, Massachusetts, Virginia, Pennsylvania, and Maryland on April 14, 1755, to plan the overall strategy for the summer campaign. Three thrusts were to be made against the French: one against Fort Duquesne on the Ohio, one against Fort Niagara at the western end of Lake Ontario, and a third expedition from Albany north against the French fortress of Crown Point on Lake Champlain. Braddock would command the first expedition, Governor William Shirley of Massachusetts the second, and William Johnson the third.[3]

The English commander-in-chief had already been directed to appoint William Johnson as sole superintendent of the Indians. At the April conference, which Johnson attended, Braddock issued Johnson a commission as colonel. The governors of New York and Massachusetts made him a major-general of their militia, for he was to command levies raised mostly from the New England colonies in the thrust to Lake Champlain. Shirley, the Massachusetts governor, was to command mostly New York troops. Both expeditions would assemble and set out from Albany, William Johnson's force heading north and Shirley's west through Mohawk and Oneida country to Fort Oswego on Lake Ontario, and from there by boat to Niagara.[4]

It was a situation made for confusion and rivalry as both Shirley and Johnson vied for men, supplies, and Indian auxiliaries. Johnson was supposed to take the bulk of the Six Nations warriors with him, but Shirley would need Iroquois guides through the Six Nations country. Perceiving that Johnson would not be helpful in this matter Shirley turned to John Henry Lydius to aid his recruiting efforts among the Mohawks.[5]

By now Mohawk leadership was solidly behind William Johnson. Abraham Peters Canostens had asked for Johnson's return as Indian Commissioner at the 1754 Albany conference. At a conference with the Six Nations at his home in June, 1755 Johnson told of his new appointment as sole manager of Indian affairs and relayed General Braddock's message to them. In opening the conference, Johnson asked the Iroquois leaders that "you will take care that no snake may creep in amongst us or anything which may obstruct our harmony." He was probably referring to French spies, but one Oneida sachem used this statement to chastise Lydius, who was present at the conference to recruit for Shirley. The Oneida Conochquiesie said to Johnson:

> Brother. You promised us that you would keep this fireplace clean from all filth and that no snake should come into this Council Room. That Man sitting there [pointing to Col. Lydius] is a Devil, and has stole our Lands, he takes Indians slyly by the Blanket one at a time, and when they are drunk, puts some money in their Bosoms, and persuades them to sign deeds for our lands upon the Susquehanna which we will not ratify nor suffer to be settled by any means.

Johnson then forbade Lydius from further recruitment and at the end of the conference went to Albany to oversee the efforts at readying the force for Crown Point.[6]

Lydius, however, sought the help of his fellow Turtle clan brothers. Hance, the son of war captain Seth Thick Lip (probably Seth Karonkyaghonghkwa—see Fig. 4-3) told Lydius at Schenectady in mid-July that the tribe of the tortoise would go with Shirley. At the end of July, Matthew Ferrall (William Johnson's brother-in-law), Arent Stevens (the province interpreter), and John Butler (son of Walter Butler) subsidized a fete and war dance for the warriors who were to go with William Johnson to Crown Point. The fete was held at the house of Thomas Ganughsiddishe, son of Brant Kanagaradunkwa (Fig. 10-1). Thomas was the principal war captain of the Bear clan at Tionondoroge. Lydius and his Turtle clan brother, the war chief Aaron Oseragighte, showed up at the celebration, but Thomas and Little Abraham—Abraham Teyorhansere, the Wolf clan war chief at Tionondoroge—told Lydius not to speak to their men. During the war dance, Aaron forced Ferrall to sit down and then put hot ashes on Ferrall's head to insult him.[7]

This incident, dramatic enough in itself, casts some light on Mohawk leadership. Mohawks, like the other Six Nations, traditionally fought in clans under varying numbers of war captains, each of whom probably had about seven to thirty warriors under their personal leadership. From this account it is evident that Tionondoroge had one man in each clan who functioned as the principal war captain for his clan. Probably Canajoharie had its own principal war captains as well. Like all Mohawk leaders, these men operated through personal influence and common consent.[8]

Aaron, probably the principal Turtle war captain, had previously been referred to as a sachem—if it is the same Aaron (Fig. 7-4). Abraham Teyorhansere or Teyorheasere, called Little Abraham to differentiate him from the older Abraham Peters Canostens, would go on to become one of the two principal sachems at Tionondoroge in the late 1750s. He is probably the Abraham who married Catharine, Kinsiago's daughter on July 11, 1743. Catherine's mother Margaret was the sister of Christina, Brant Kanagaradunkwa's second wife (see Fig. 10-2). Thomas Ganughsiddishe was Brant Kanagaradunkwa's son by his first wife Catharine (see Fig. 10-1), and Aaron Oseragighte was married to Margaret, the sister of Brant Kanagaradunkwa's first wife (see Fig. 7-3). Thus all of these three war leaders at Tionondoroge in 1755 were connected by blood or marriage to Brant Kanagaradunkwa. They or their wives were also connected to the mothers of William Johnson's Mohawk sons Keghneghtaga and Tagawirunte, particularly if Tagawirunte's mother was Esther, Brant Kanagaradunkwa's daughter by his first wife. Doubtless Johnson used these connections to advance his influence among the

Tionondoroge Mohawks, as he used the leadership of the Peters family to influence the Canajoharie Mohawks. That this process worked in the opposite direction is also true, for it was probably by Johnson's influence that Brant Kanagaradunkwa retained his sachemship after his third marriage to Margaret in 1753, though he had to move from Tionondoroge to Canajoharie. Brant's son Nickus Canadiorha also moved to Canajoharie and later became a sachem there. Brant's son Thomas Ganughsiddishe stayed at Tionondoroge, probably because he was already established as the chief Bear clan war captain there. At Thomas's death in 1761 William Johnson referred to him as the chief warrior of the Lower Castle.[9]

Johnson also used his political influence at Tionondoroge in the spring of 1755 to have a Turtle clan Mohawk known as French Peter—Peter Taquayanont—appointed a sachem. Peter had been staying at Tionondoroge since the previous fall and had been spreading pro-French propaganda among the lower Mohawks. The appointment was part of a "deal" worked out between Peter Taquayanont and William Johnson in which Johnson would financially provide for Peter and his family and see him appointed to a sachemship if the Caughnawagan would move himself and his family permanently to the Mohawk valley. Both sides kept their bargain in the years to come, demonstrating the degree of influence Johnson had with the people of Tionondoroge.[10]

Political leadership among the Mohawks of Tionondoroge had changed since the 1740s. In the early and middle years of that decade three distinguished Tionondoroge Wolf clan leaders there had died: Gideon Tonidoge Sharenhowaneh, Cornelius Thaneghwanege, and in August, 1747, Ezras Kanneraghtahare. In 1745 Conrad Weiser was told that the three chiefs at Tionondoroge were Aaron (Oseragighte), Brant (Kanagaradunkwa), and Thomas (probably Thomas Sewatsese or Sewaghsasa). By 1754, when Lydius made another list of Mohawk leaders at the Albany Congress, the Tionondoroge leaders were Tsistarare (Seth Sietstarare, Fig. 3-1, formerly *Dekarihokeh)*, Canadagaye (Johannes Canadagaye, a Bear), Sotsikowano (Johannes Segehowane, Fig. 4-5; a Turtle), and Gaweghnog (Brant Kaweghnoke, Figs. 4-4 and 4-5; a Wolf). With the exception of Seth these men were probably the civil leaders of the three clans at Tionondoroge. Seth Sietstarare remained a key Mohawk leader into his late seventies, for he accompanied Hendrick Theyanoguin and Brant Kanagaradunkwa to

Philadelphia in early 1755. Seth's only surviving son Kiliaen, a "principal warrior" of the Bear clan, died in May, 1755, when Seth and his wife Sara were still alive. Seth Sietstarare survived into 1759, when he was eighty-one.[11]

Johannes Segehowane, Gideon Tonidoge's nephew, had been leader of the Tionondoroge Turtle clan since the late 1720s. He was probably given his formal Mohawk name after the death of Ezras Sogjowanne (or Sonihoware), Canastasi Koaroni's husband (see Fig. 3-2), sometime after June, 1721. Johannes continued to be prominent in affairs as late as 1760 when he led the Tionondoroge Turtles to Montreal. He probably died soon after. His son Jacob is frequently mentioned in the *Johnson Papers* and seems to have had a degree of informal prominence, though not referred to as a sachem or chief. Johannes Segehowane's son Brant Kaweghnoke (Wide-Mouthed Brant, see Fig. 4-5), adopted by Jacamine Tagwanagon, became the leader of the Tionondoroge Wolf clan and died in 1760. It seems probable that Brant Kaweghnoke owed his position to his adoptive mother Jacamine, head woman of Tionondoroge in the 1730s, suggesting that Brant Kaweghnoke was a League sachem.[12]

The other Tionondoroge Mohawk on Lydius's 1754 list, Johannes Canadagaye, was also referred to as Hans de Wilt (Hans the Savage) and could speak Dutch. He acquired his formal name after Kiliaen Canadagaye (baptized in Albany on April 9, 1732) died in February, 1745. Johannes Canadagaye was a noted orator and from 1755 was often referred to as the chief sachem or one of the two chief sachems of Tionondoroge, serving as speaker for the lower Mohawks through the 1760s. Although he worked closely with William Johnson, there is no evidence that Johnson's influence led to his appointment.[13]

Lydius's list of the chiefs at Canajoharie in 1754 differs little from that of 1745: Hendrick, Abraham, and Nickus Peters and William Tarraghioris (Towaraghions). By 1754 these men were in their sixties. Johnson dealt extensively with the Peters' brothers, especially Hendrick and Abraham; the common bond between Johnson and Hendrick and Abraham was their pro-English sentiments. Nickus Peters Karaghiagdatie's sentiments were less certain in the early 1750s because he had been a prisoner for so long in Canada and because his daughter Catharine had married a French Indian. This changed after 1755, when one of his younger sons, either Nickus Anatshiaenghse or Paulus, was killed during the Blood Morning Scout at Lake George. Nickus Peters' daughter

Catharine formed a liaison with George Croghan, Johnson's assistant, in late 1757 (see Figs. 3-1 and 13-1).[14]

Hendrick Theyanoguin was chief sachem of Canajoharie until his death, followed in this position by Abraham Canostens, then by Nickus Karaghiagdatie, each until their deaths. After Nickus' death in 1759 Brant Aroghyiadecka was referred to as the chief sachem of Canajoharie, but generally leadership there was shared between several chiefs, showing that this position was one of personal attainment rather than a formal political office.[15]

After the incident in Thomas Ganughsiddishe's house in July, 1755, Lydius shifted his recruiting efforts to Canajoharie, requesting that Hendrick and his brother Nickus Karaghiagdatie accompany Shirley. Nickus referred the matter to his wife which, since she was the head woman of the Turtle clan—Lydius's clan—was perfectly proper. Daniel Claus persuaded the Peters brothers and most of the other Canajoharies to go with Johnson, however.[16]

After assembling near Albany in July and August, Johnson's forces headed northward along the Hudson to Lydius's house, where the portage to Lake St. Sacrement began. Here Johnson directed that a fort be erected and a road built across the portage to Lake St. Sacrement, which Johnson renamed Lake George. The troops were to pass along the road to Lake George, then embark in bateaux up the lake, make another portage to Lake Champlain, and go on to Crown Point. While the troops were constructing walls around Lydius's original house the first of the Six Nations warriors joined them. On August 23 Abraham Canostens brought in an advance contingent, and two days later Hendrick Theyanoguin came at the head of 200 more. By the time the army was ready to march there were 200 to 300 Indians with the 3,000 troops. Leaving 500 militia at the Lydius fort (soon renamed Fort Edward), Johnson and his men advanced along the newly-made road to the south end of Lake George in early September. Here they cleared an expanse of trees and prepared to build another fort as a base for their boat trip up the lake.[17]

In the meantime a sizeable French force: 200 French regulars, 600 Canadian militiamen, and about 600 Caughnawagas and Abenaki Indians, were marching south from Crown Point to attack the Lydius fort. Led astray by his Caughnawaga guides, the French general, Baron Dieskau, turned his men around and set out to attack Johnson's main force, now

Figure 13-1. Family of Catharine Croghan and Joseph Brant Thayendanegea

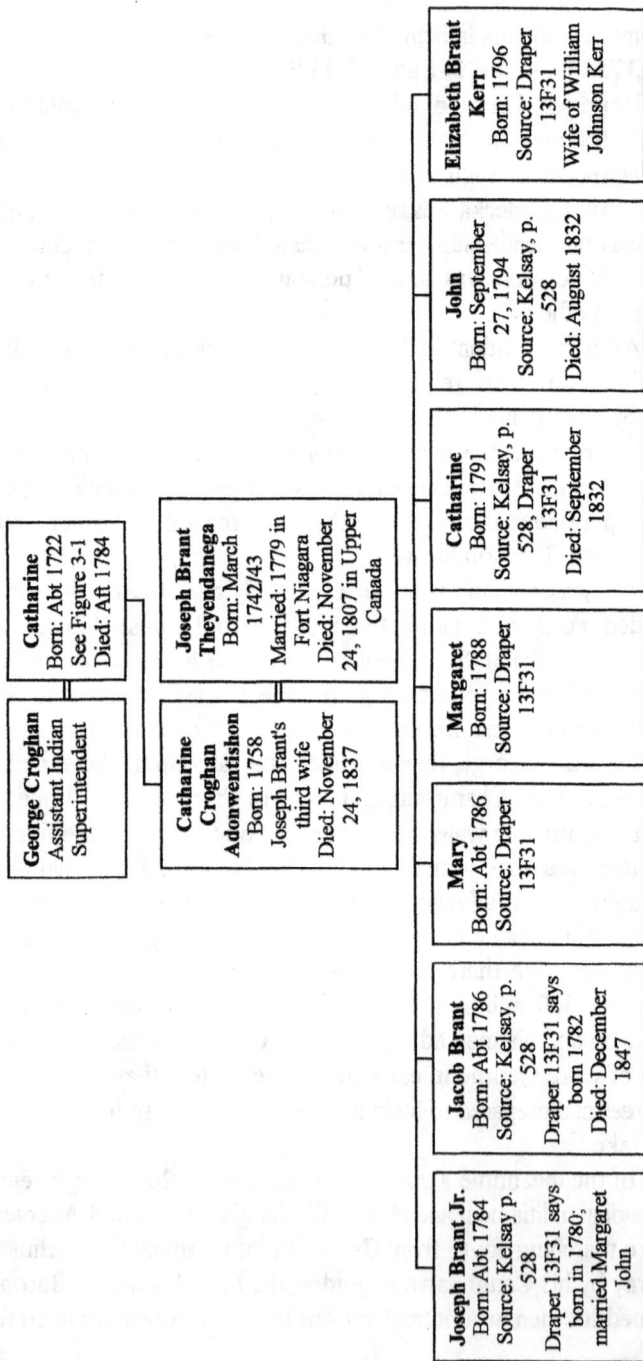

```
┌─────────────────────┐        ┌─────────────────────┐
│  George Croghan     │────────│  Catharine          │
│  Assistant Indian   │        │  Born: Abt 1722     │
│  Superintendent     │        │  See Figure 3-1     │
│                     │        │  Died: Aft 1784     │
└─────────────────────┘        └─────────────────────┘
            │
┌─────────────────────┐        ┌─────────────────────┐
│  Catharine          │========│  Joseph Brant       │
│  Croghan            │        │  Theyendanega       │
│  Adonwentishon      │        │  Born: March        │
│  Born: 1758         │        │  1742/43            │
│  Joseph Brant's     │        │  Married: 1779 in   │
│  third wife         │        │  Fort Niagara       │
│  Died: November     │        │  Died: November     │
│  24, 1837           │        │  24, 1807 in Upper  │
│                     │        │  Canada             │
└─────────────────────┘        └─────────────────────┘
```

Joseph Brant Jr.	Jacob Brant	Mary	Margaret	Catharine	John	Elizabeth Brant Kerr
Born: Abt 1784	Born: Abt 1786	Born: Abt 1786	Born: 1788	Born: 1791	Born: September 27, 1794	Born: 1796
Source: Kelsay p. 528	Source: Kelsay, p. 528	Source: Draper 13F31	Source: Draper 13F31	Source: Kelsay, p. 528, Draper 13F31	Source: Kelsay, p. 528	Source: Draper 13F31
Draper 13F31 says born in 1780; married Margaret John	Draper 13F31 says born 1782 Died: December 1847			Died: September 1832	Died: August 1832	Wife of William Johnson Kerr

at Lake George. On the morning of September 8, after discovering that Johnson was sending a relief force from Lake George to Fort Edward, the French waited in ambush along the road their enemies had just built.[18] Johnson had been sending out scouting parties to warn him of any French movements. On the afternoon of September 7 Thick Lawrence (actually Stout Lawrence from the Dutch *dicke*, probably Lawrence Sanagaris, the Tionondoroge Bear clan leader who signed the July 6, 1754, deed to Pennsylvania; see also Fig. 13-2) and two other scouts reported to Hendrick and Johnson at Lake George that about 600 men were headed from Lake Champlain's South Bay to the Carrying Place (Fort Edward). Johnson called a council of war, and the New England officers proposed sending 500 men to the South Bay to destroy Dieskau's boats and 500 to relieve Fort Edward. When asked, Hendrick is reported to have said of the relief force: "if they are to fight they are too few, if to they are to be killed they are too many." He took three sticks and showed how together they could not be broken, but that separated each could be broken.[19]

With this graphic advice Johnson decided to send all 1000 troops led by Colonel Ephraim Williams Jr. of Massachusetts and 200 Six Nations warriors to the relief of the fort. Williams and Hendrick on horses led the van, the Colonel an old acquaintance of the Mohawk chief from Stockbridge. All three sections of the relief force—van, center, and rear—had their own contingent of Six Nations Indians.[20]

Two or three miles down the road they were ambushed by the French force. The French regulars were drawn up onto the road itself, Canadians and their Indian allies hidden along both sides. Supposedly a whispered conversation between Hendrick and a Caughnawaga hidden in the bushes precipitated the Caughnawaga and Abenaki Indians' fire before Johnson's force was entirely in the trap, but British and Six Nations loses were heavy. Colonel Williams was killed as were many other officers. Hendrick slipped off his horse and made his way through the skirmish line into the woods on the left only to meet the French Indian baggage party composed of women and children. The old chief, too stout to run, was killed and scalped by the women and children. William Tarraghioris, Turtle clan chief of Canajoharie, was also killed, along with one of Nickus Karaghiagdatie's sons. Other Mohawks killed were Waniacoone, Skahijowio, Onienkoto, Thomas, and Scaroyady's son Nica-awna. Cayadanora, a Tuscarora, was also slain. In all, thirty-two

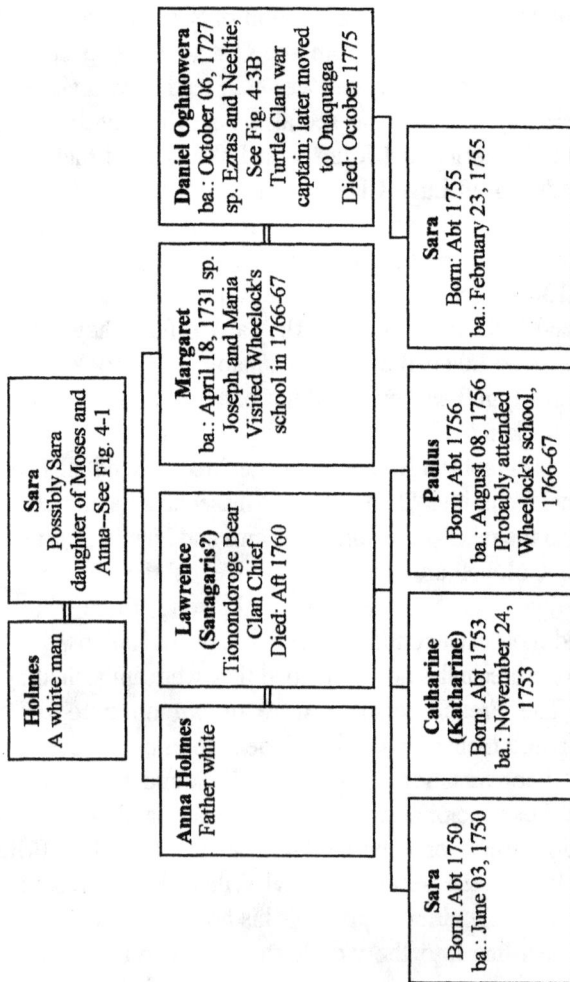

Figure 13-2. Family of Lawrence and Anna Holmes

of Johnson's Indian allies were killed or missing and twelve wounded.[21]

British colonial casualties were even worse, with 120 killed, 801 wounded, and sixty-two missing by the end of the day. These figures include the battle that followed at the lake, for the surviving British militia and Six Nations warriors fled back to the camp at Lake George, pursued by the French. Johnson managed to rally his forces despite receiving a bullet in his thigh, and after several hours of fighting the French retreated, leaving their wounded commander Baron Dieskau on the field. Both sides were too exhausted to continue their campaigns that year.[22]

Although the British heralded the Battle of Lake George as a victory to match the defeat of General Braddock that had taken place on July 9— and rewarded William Johnson with a baronetcy—to the Mohawks it was a disaster. Not only had they lost their greatest speaker and another influential sachem, but in all twelve of their principal men had fallen in the battle. They had also involved themselves in war with their Caughnawaga relatives, a war which would become increasingly bloody in the years to come.[23]

Braddock's defeat on the banks of the Monongahela in July caused great unease among the Mohawks. In November they asked William Johnson to build a fort at Canajoharie and man it with white troops. This fort, and the increased presence of troops at Fort Hunter, led to problems between the garrisons and the Mohawks. In September of the next year Paulus Peters wrote Sir William Johnson about the theft of his keg of rum by the commander of the fort at Canajoharie. Two years later Abraham Teyorhansere reported how soldiers from Fort Hunter had attacked him in his own stable because he found them stealing his horses. Other soldiers from the fort had encountered the wife of one of the sachems and attempted to ravish her. Fortunately she had been out cutting wood and successfully defended herself with the ax she carried. Abraham and the other Mohawks, having been raised in a culture that lacked rape, found the soldiers' behavior incomprehensible.[24]

British attempts to dislodge the French during the years 1756 and 1757 generally met with disaster. During this time Sir William Johnson sent numerous small raiding parties north to Lake Champlain. In 1757 one of these raiding parties led by Moses, probably Moses Nowadarika, met with disaster and "Moses was made a sacrifice of by the enemy," i.e., he was captured by enemy Indians and tortured to death. Moses's wife

Margaret had been attacked by a drunken Indian in 1755 and nearly died of her injuries. Another drunk Indian, Seth, killed the Mohawk Reinier in 1754. This Reinier may have been Christina's brother (see Fig. 10-2).[25]

At Canajoharie Hendrick's son Paulus Peters Saghsanowano was so active in organizing war parties that he neglected his duties as schoolmaster there and had his salary stopped by the Reverend Ogilvie. One scouting party he organized with Brant Kanagaradunkwa and his son Nickus Canadiorha included Aront, Brant's son-in-law. An Aront married Magdalene on July 11, 1742, and this Magdalene was probably Brant's daughter, named for her aunt, Magdalene Kryn (see Figs. 7-3, 10-1, and 13-3).[26]

While war captains were leading their men northward, Johnson's deputy George Croghan was holding a series of conferences in Pennsylvania to try and regain the allegiances of the Delawares and Shawnees. Sir William sent a Mohawk delegation to John Harris' Ferry (Harrisburg, Pennsylvania) in April-May of 1757 to meet with the Delaware leader Teedyuscung. This delegation was led by Jonathan Cayenquerigo, Johannes Canadagaye, Johannes Kryn Anequendahonji or Unaguaandchonge (commonly known as White Hans or Hance Kryn) and four other Bear chiefs and two Wolf chiefs: Abraham Tayorhansere of Tionondoroge and Peter Serehowane of Canajoharie.[27]

Johannes Kryn Anequendahonji was a Tionondoroge sachem baptized in 1722 (see Fig. 7-3) and described as "a whitish Indian living at the Mohawks." He was a brother-in-law of Brant Kanagaradunkwa, which may explain why, many years later, Phillip Schuyler noted Johannes Kryn's "great attachment to the Johnson family." At a meeting with Caughnawaga Mohawks in 1764 Johannes Anequendahonji sang his war song with Sir William Johnson, after which the Caughnawaga Bear clan chief Tom Wildman Keghneghtaga sang his song. Tom Wildman had the same Mohawk name as Sir William's son Brant.[28]

Johannes Anequendahonji's wife was named Neeltie, a member of the Wolf clan. They were married on October 7, 1744, had a son Nickus baptized and buried in February, 1745, and later sons Abraham Sogradisse, Cryn (or Crine, baptized on July 25, 1749), and John (baptized on May 19, 1755). Johannes Anequendahonji tried to remain neutral at the outbreak of the American Revolution and was one of the few Mohawks who eventually took the American side in their struggle for independence (Abraham Tayorhansere was another). In 1780 Johannes

Figure 13-3. Brant Kanagaradunkwa's Children at Canajoharie and Their Families

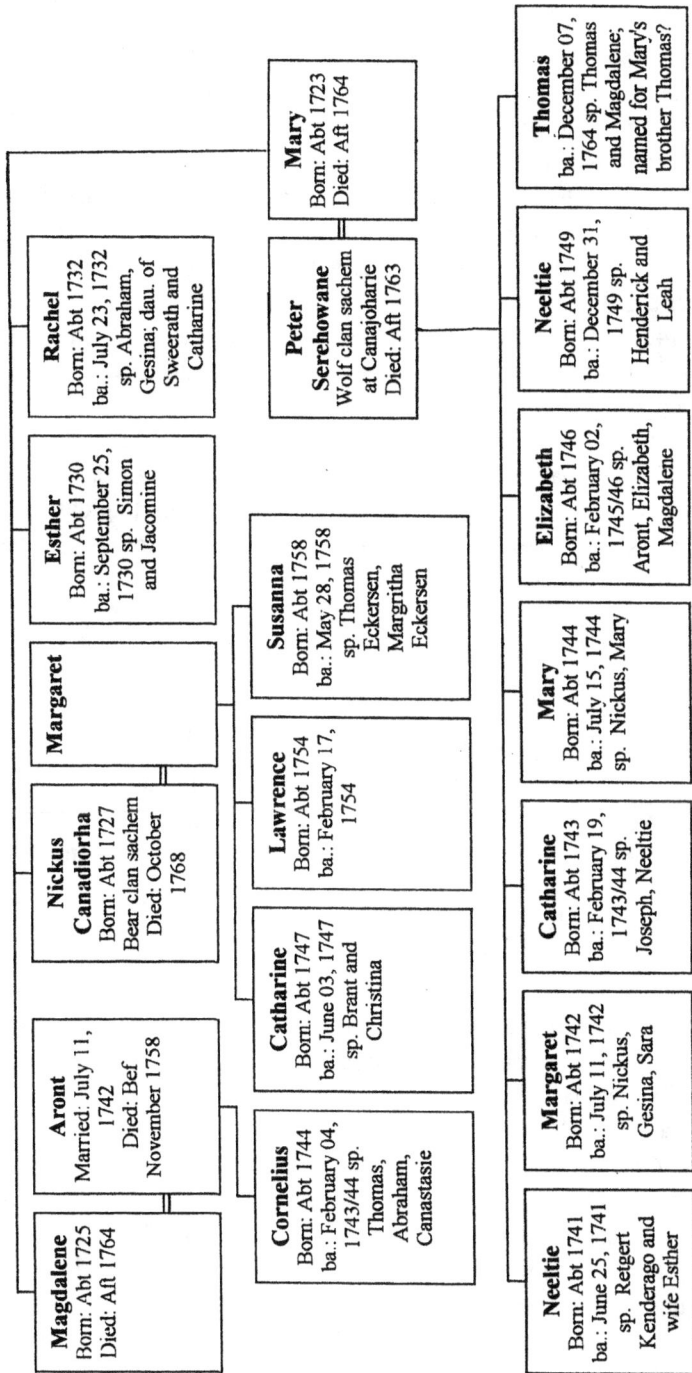

Magdalene
Born: Abt 1725
Died: Aft 1764

Aront
Married: July 11, 1742
Died: Bef November 1758

Nickus Canadiorha
Born: Abt 1727
Bear clan sachem
Died: October 1768

Margaret

Esther
Born: Abt 1730
ba.: September 25, 1730 sp. Simon and Jacomine

Rachel
Born: Abt 1732
ba.: July 23, 1732 sp. Abraham, Gesina; dau. of Sweerath and Catharine

Mary
Born: Abt 1723
Died: Aft 1764

Peter Serehowane
Wolf clan sachem at Canajoharie
Died: Aft 1763

Cornelius
Born: Abt 1744
ba.: February 04, 1743/44 sp. Thomas, Abraham, Canastasie

Catharine
Born: Abt 1747
ba.: June 03, 1747 sp. Brant and Christina

Lawrence
Born: Abt 1754
ba.: February 17, 1754

Susanna
Born: Abt 1758
ba.: May 28, 1758 sp. Thomas Eckersen, Margritha Eckersen

Neeltie
Born: Abt 1741
ba.: June 25, 1741 sp. Retgert Kenderago and wife Esther

Margaret
Born: Abt 1742
ba.: July 11, 1742 sp. Nickus, Gesina, Sara

Catharine
Born: Abt 1743
ba.: February 19, 1743/44 sp. Joseph, Neeltie

Mary
Born: Abt 1744
ba.: July 15, 1744 sp. Nickus, Mary

Elizabeth
Born: Abt 1746
ba.: February 02, 1745/46 sp. Aront, Elizabeth, Magdalene

Neeltie
Born: Abt 1749
ba.: December 31, 1749 sp. Henderick and Leah

Thomas
ba.: December 07, 1764 sp. Thomas and Magdalene; named for Mary's brother Thomas?

Kryn's family was carried to Canada by Loyalists, and after the war he and later his children petitioned the Americans for aid, having suffered a great deal in his efforts to persuade the Mohawks to adopt neutrality.[29]

Peter Serehowane, the Wolf clan Canajoharie sachem who also went to the Harris' Ferry meeting in 1757, appears to have been another son-in-law of Brant Kanagaradunkwa. Margaret, daughter of Peter and Mary was baptized on the same day that Aront married Magdalene, and the latter couple sponsored Peter and Mary's daughter Elizabeth on February 2, 1746. On February 19, 1744, Peter Serehowane's daughter Catharine was baptized, and the next day Thomas Ganughsiddishe's son John was baptized (see Figs. 10-1 and 13-3).[30]

The council fire at Harris' Ferry was shifted to Lancaster in April, 1757, shortly after the arrival of delegates from all of the Six Nations except the Senecas. Still, the Delaware chief Teedyuscung did not come. After weeks of waiting Abraham Tayorhansere suggested that, because the Delawares now only acknowledged the Senecas as their "Uncles," Teedyuscung should be invited by way of the Senecas. Croghan and Conrad Weiser persuaded the Pennsylvania governor to take this sound advice and the conference adjourned. Teedyuscung finally met with the Pennsylvania governor in July, but the result was only a temporary truce with the Susquehanna Delawares.[31]

A far more important conference convened in Easton, Pennsylvania in November, 1758. The principal Mohawk sachem to attend was Nickus Karaghiagdatie. Abraham Peters Canostens had died in January, 1757, and Nickus was the last Peters of his generation, with the exception of a sister (probably Mary) who lived into the 1760s. Nickus' first wife Elizabeth had died in May, 1757, but by late 1758 he had remarried to a woman who had two young sons. Possibly reinvigorated by his new marriage, Nickus blasted Teedyuscung in a speech so vitriolic that it was not put on the official record. Nickus gave a later speech that expressed the Six Nations' lack of support for the Delaware leader seconded by the Seneca chief Tagashata (Kyashuta) and other Iroquois leaders, and the conference ended with the Six Nations and their "Nephews" the Delawares proclaiming their hearty support for the English cause. Immediately afterward Croghan took a delegation of warriors to the aid of British general Forbes, who was able to capture a deserted Fort Duquesne in November, 1758—deserted by the French after they lost the support of the western Delawares. Nickus Karaghiagdatie's effort may have exhausted him, however, for he died in early 1759.[32]

After 1746 the careful records of Mohawk baptisms and marriages kept by the reverends Barclay and Van Driessen were replaced by spotty records in the Schenectady and Albany churches and in 1750 by the register of the new Fort Hunter missionary, Reverend Ogilvie. Ogilvie, although sympathetic to the Mohawks and greatly respected by them, kept poor and incomplete records for the Indians, omitting the names of parents or even the children themselves and never mentioning the sponsors. About 25 percent of his Indian baptisms were not recorded at all. After Ogilvie's departure in 1760 even this inadequate register ended, and none of the records of the successive Fort Hunter missionaries have survived. A few Mohawks continued to go to the Schenectady church or the church at Caughnawaga (Fonda, N.Y.), the Reverend Ehle visited the Canajoharies three or four times a year, and the Schoharie church records continued to include Schoharie and Onaquaga Indians up to the Revolution. Because of this lack of church records, the principal source for information on the Mohawks during this period is the *Johnson Papers*, supplemented by the entries in Jelles Fonda's account books, and these entries are quite limited.[33]

Sir William Johnson's accounts in the late 1750s and early 1760s make it clear that a small group of Mohawk leaders were particularly trusted speakers, agents, and messengers. Brant Kanagaradunkwa, now at Canajoharie, continued as Sir William's close friend into the mid-1760s, and it was at Brant's house during a conference in January, 1759 that Sir William and Molly Brant almost certainly conceived their oldest child, Peter, born the following September. Brant's son Nickus Canadiorha and Hendrick Theyanoguin's son Paulus Peters Saghsanowano were loyal Johnson allies. In return they could count on his financial aid and help in such affairs as the keg of rum stolen from Paulus and the horse stolen from Brant, and in more serious matters such as death threats made against Brant and his wife by drunken Oneidas.[34]

Paulus's cousin, Nickus Karaghiagdatie's oldest son Johannes (or Hance) Dekarihokenh, was also a loyal Johnson ally. Though his position as head League sachem of the tribe undoubtedly carried great weight, it did not prevent Hance from going on a raid in 1757 to find a prisoner or scalp to "put in the room or stead" of his late mother, nor from leading the Canajoharie Turtle warriors who accompanied Sir William at the British capture of Montreal in 1760. At Sir William's specific request

Hance Dekarihokenh led a party of warriors to accompany the Bradstreet expedition to the Ohio country in 1764. Hance also saw that belts and messages from the upper Iroquois tribes were brought to Johnson.[35]

At one meeting at Canajoharie in March, 1763, the "chief sachems" were Brant Aroghyiadecka, Jonathan Cayenquerigo, Paulus Peters Saghsanowano Anahario, Brant Kanagaradunkwa, Peter Serehowane, and Nickus Canadiorha. Of these, only Peter Serehowane was a Wolf, and his wife was a close Bear clan connection of Johnson's (see Fig. 13-3). Hance Dekarihokenh's name was missing from the roll of this meeting, but he led the Canajoharie contingent at the Fort Stanwix Treaty in 1768, with Brant Aroghyiadecka and Paulus Peters (Brant Kana-garadunkwa had probably died in the interim). Johnson's political ties were to the Turtle and Bear clans through Brant Kanagaradunkwa and his Bear clan wives, and through the Peters family (only one of whom, Nickus, was a Wolf), despite the fact that Molly Brant, Johnson's mistress from January, 1759, was a Wolf.[36]

Women played a key role in Mohawk society, and Johnson paid considerable attention to them. In one meeting at Canajoharie in May, 1758 he answered a request from the chief women there that he not go to a meeting at Oneida:

> Dyattego [sister?] your tender and affectionate speech, made some days ago, I have considered, and thereupon have dispatched messengers to Oneida, in order to inquire how things stand there after what happened at the German Flatts, and whether my presence at the meeting would be still necessary. These messengers are returned, and I find by them that the sachems of Oneida likewise disapprove my proceeding any farther, for sundry reasons they give in their reply. Wherefore I shall comply with your request to return, and heartily thank you for the great tenderness and love expressed for me in your speech.

Three days earlier Johnson had condoled the women of Canajoharie for the loss of a member of the Bear clan. One infers that most of the women condoled were Bears, notably Brant Kanagaradunkwa's daughters Mary and Magdalene.[37]

The chief woman of the Wolf clan at Canajoharie in 1761 was named Esther. There are two likely candidates. The first would be the wife of

Abraham Tiurhadaghriyo. Abraham and Esther co-sponsored a child with Peter Serehowane in March, 1741 and had a son Peter baptized on July 14, 1748, sponsored by the Canajoharie Mohawk Nickus Canaquase and his wife Sara. One of the Wolf Canajoharie Mohawks who went to Montreal in 1760 was Lot Tyorhadaghrio, possibly a son of Abraham and Esther. Lot is an unusual name for a Mohawk, the only adult Lot in the church records being Lot Thoroghyonge who co-sponsored Peter Tehonwaghwangeraghkwa and Margaret daughter with Esther Kanoghserightha on January 28, 1742. This Esther, Esther Kanoghserightha, may have been Abraham Tiurhadaghriyo's wife.[38]

A second candidate for the Wolf clan matron was the wife of Rutgert Kenderago. Together Rutgert and Esther sponsored Peter Serehowane and Mary's daughter Neeltie on June 25, 1741. Rut was apparently a Wolf, and his son David Rut Caraghquinty (or Karaghkundy) was likewise grouped with the Canajoharie Wolves in 1760. If Rut and his son David (a war captain in the Revolution) were indeed both Wolves, the marriage of Rutgert Kenderago and Esther is another early instance of individuals marrying within the Wolf clan.[39]

Although Sir William occasionally used Johannes Dekarihokenh as a messenger, he used two Tionondoroge Mohawks as messengers on a regular basis: Aaron Oseragighte and Captain Daniel Oghnowera. These two men, both Turtle clan chiefs, frequently received payment for "sundry services" and often went to Niagara, Detroit, and Fort Pitt for Sir William after these posts came into English hands. One or both of them could speak and write in English, probably the reason they were so often called upon to deliver messages.[40]

After the Easton conference in October, 1758 and the subsequent capture of Fort Duquesne (renamed Fort Pitt), the way was prepared for Indian support of the English forces that took Fort Niagara in 1759 and Montreal in 1760. With peace, however, the perennial problem of old land grants and fraudulent deeds once again plagued the Mohawks.

CHAPTER XIV

Closing Decades at Schoharie

Like the other Mohawks, the Mohawks living along Schoharie Creek felt increased pressures from white settlement as the eighteenth century progressed. The northernmost villages were surrendered early to Palatine settlers. Parcels were sold to individual settlers, such as that to William York, Jacob Lawyer, and Nicholas York in 1723. Between 1730 and 1735 the leaders of the three Mohawk clans at Schoharie—Agarhetonthea (Wolf), Chawanguina (Bear), and Seth (Turtle)—petitioned the governor to void the sale of 6,000 acres of land, mostly along Schoharie Creek, made by a group of River Indians (Mahicans) who had no claim to the land.[1]

By May, 1753 Karighondontee's son Seth Tehodoghwenziageghthe was, like other Mohawk leaders, complaining of the inability of Governor Clinton to act on their complaints against illegal land deals. On June 6, 1754, the Karighondontees, along with Joseph (for the Wolf clan) and Anthony (for the Bear clan, probably the husband of Seth's daughter Mary—see Fig. 14-1), sold a parcel of land to George Zomer and others. In September the Karighondontees petitioned the governor about land claimed by Johannes Lawyer, which the Karighondontees said they gave to Nicolas Mattice.[2]

The Karighondontee extended family was not the only group of Mohawks living at Schoharie. In 1753, while traveling through Schoharie to Onaquaga, Gideon Hawley stayed at the home of Jonah T'hanhanagwanageas (see Chapter 11). He also hired an Indian named Pallas, called Bellis or Pellis Warreson (Paulus, Mary's son) in the Schoharie church records (see Fig. 14-2). Born on Long Island, Pellis had married Anna Karighondontee on October 25, 1741. This man, while under the influence of alcohol, was suspected by Hawley of trying to murder him on the Susquehanna River on the way to Onaquaga.[3]

Table 14-1. Succession of Schoharie Men

Attending the Albany Conference, July, 1754[a]	Accompanying Sir William Johnson to Montreal, 1760[d]	Signing the 1771 Petition[e]
1.Laurus Nahehidaye[b]		
2.Seth *Tekahoghwenziageghthe*[b,c]		
3.John Zininngino[c]		
4.Jacob Anaghgoonighs		
5.Kanigeghare		
6.David Aweahaghse		
7.Hansury Aghsunhaqucks[b]		
8.Jacob Keantslaghroot ?	3.Jacob Otsdoghrodo	Jacob
9.Lawrence Unnghrageaghte	4.Lawrence Onoghrageghte	
10.Joseph Kaneya	6.Joseph Kaneiya	
11.Johannes Deeanajiyasero		
12.Joseph Th'rewaghty	5.Joseph Th'rewaghty	Joseph
13.Joseph Karunghiazigoa		
14.Nicholas Arighwanientha[c]		
15.David Orighuryughsto ?	2.David Otkoghraro	David
	1.Seth Tetsiniyaghko[b]	Seth
	7.Hance Ury Sawanagarady	Hans Ury
	8.Nicolas Seskiye	
	9.William *Tehodoghwenziokoghto*	William

Numbers in columns 1 and 2 show the ordering of each delegation, the most senior and important men first. Seth Tetsiniyaghko, a Turtle Mohawk not on the 1754 Schoharie list, led the 1760 delegation, followed by David, who was last in 1754. Those at the top of the 1754 list had passed on by 1760, while those lower down had moved up, replaced at the bottom by younger men.

[a]*Pa. Col. Rec.* 6:128.

[b]Signed 1754 Petition to the governor of New York using the surname Careke Dunte (Seth Tetsingiyaghko as Seth Careke Dunte Jr.): N.Y. State Arch., Albany, Col. Mss., Land Papers, Vol. 9, 23.

[c]Signed for the three Mohawk clans on the 1731-35 Petition to the governor of New York: N.Y. State Arch., Albany, Col. Mss., Land Papers 1731-35, Vol. 2, 106A-106B.

[d]*JP* 13:177. [e]*JP* 8:20-22.

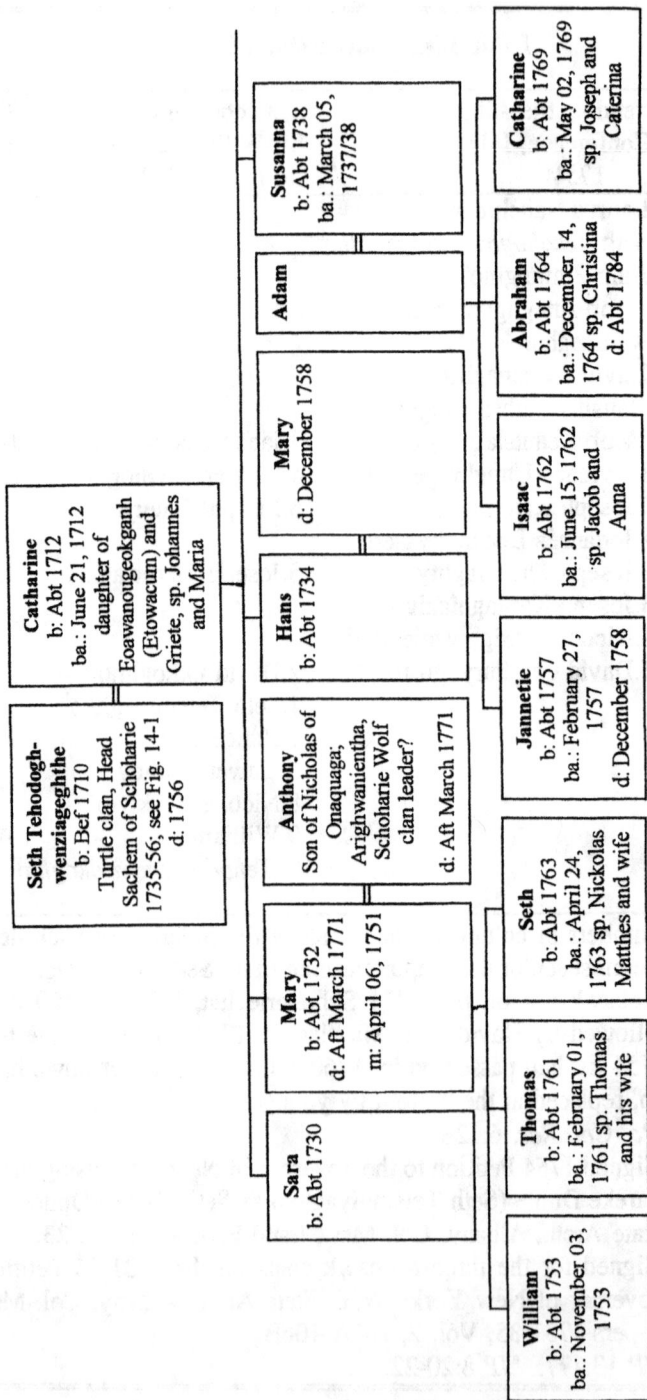

Figure 14-1. Descendants of Seth Tehodoghwenziageghthe and Catharine

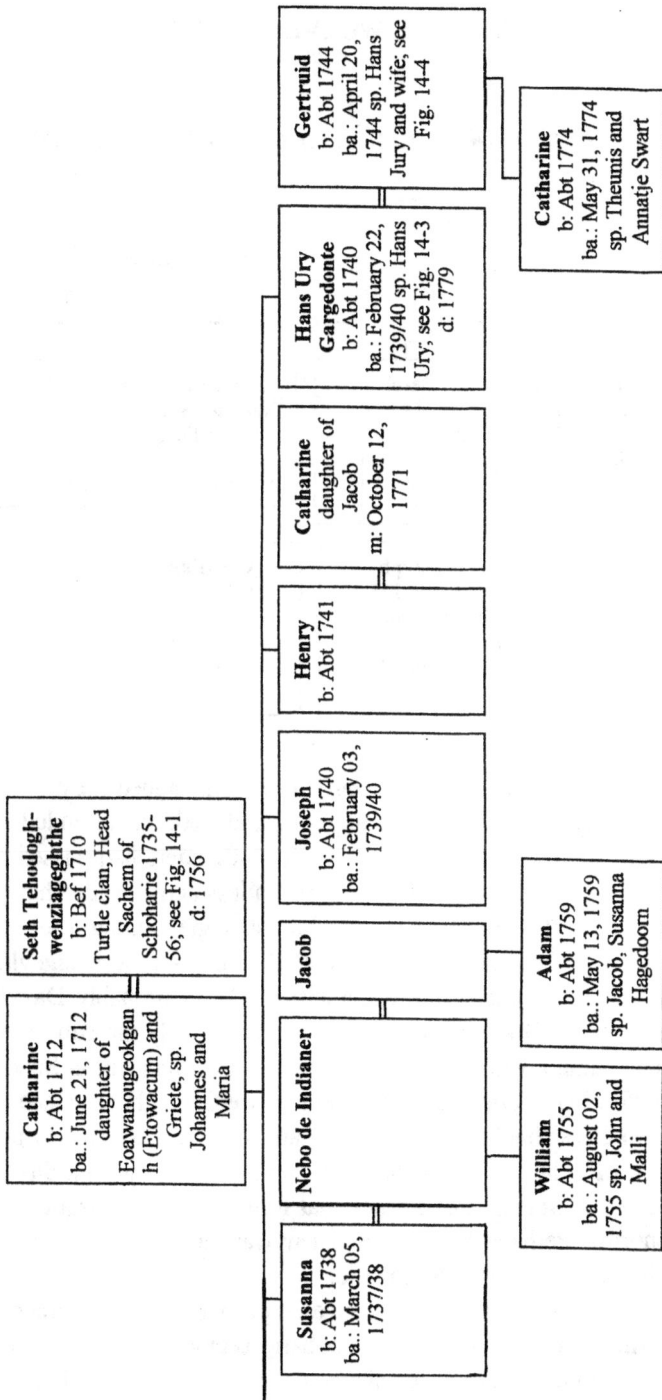

Figure 14-1. Descendants of Seth and Catharine (Continued)

Catharine
b: Abt 1712
ba.: June 21, 1712
daughter of
Eoawanougeokgan
h (Etowacum) and
Griete, sp.
Johannes and
Maria

Seth Tehodogh-wenziageghthe
b: Bef 1710
Turtle clan, Head
Sachem of
Schoharie 1735-
56; see Fig. 14-1
d: 1756

Susanna
b: Abt 1738
ba.: March 05,
1737/38

Nebo de Indianer

Jacob

Joseph
b: Abt 1740
ba.: February 03,
1739/40

Henry
b: Abt 1741

Catharine
daughter of
Jacob
m: October 12,
1771

Hans Ury Gargedonte
b: Abt 1740
ba.: February 22,
1739/40 sp. Hans
Ury; see Fig. 14-3
d: 1779

Gertruid
b: Abt 1744
ba.: April 20,
1744 sp. Hans
Jury and wife; see
Fig. 14-4

William
b: Abt 1755
ba.: August 02,
1755 sp. John and
Malli

Adam
b: Abt 1759
ba.: May 13, 1759
sp. Jacob, Susanna
Hagedoorn

Catharine
b: Abt 1774
ba.: May 31, 1774
sp. Theunis and
Annatje Swart

Figure 14-2. Children of Anna Kargadonte

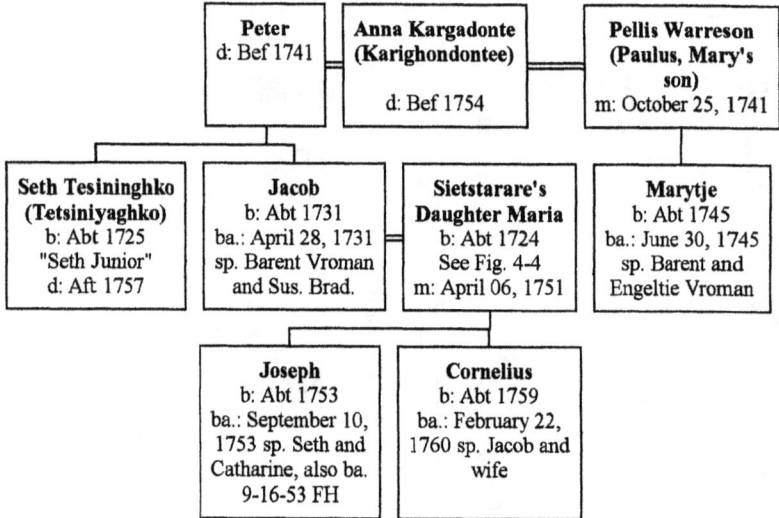

Peter d: Bef 1741	Anna Kargadonte (Karighondontee) d: Bef 1754	Pellis Warreson (Paulus, Mary's son) m: October 25, 1741

Seth Tesininghko (Tetsiniyaghko) b: Abt 1725 "Seth Junior" d: Aft 1757	Jacob b: Abt 1731 ba.: April 28, 1731 sp. Barent Vroman and Sus. Brad.	Sietstarare's Daughter Maria b: Abt 1724 See Fig. 4-4 m: April 06, 1751	Marytje b: Abt 1745 ba.: June 30, 1745 sp. Barent and Engeltie Vroman

Joseph b: Abt 1753 ba.: September 10, 1753 sp. Seth and Catharine, also ba. 9-16-53 FH	Cornelius b: Abt 1759 ba.: February 22, 1760 sp. Jacob and wife

The three of the Schoharie clan leaders who signed the petition in the 1730s—Agarhetonthea, Chawanguina, and Seth—all attended the 1754 Albany conference, but this generation of leaders had passed away by 1760 (see Table 14-1) or had assumed a less active leadership role. By May, 1756 there was a leadership struggle among the Schoharie Mohawks between those under Seth Tehodoghwenziageghthe and another group under the leadership of David probably David Orighuryughsto or Otkoghraro. David was most likely the son of Aquianer born at Antigo who married Sara daughter of John (Jan) at Schoharie on July 25, 1747. Sara was Seth Tehodoghwenziageghthe's niece (Fig. 14-3). On December 26, 1758, Sir William Johnson gave twenty pounds to David of Schoharie to begin settlement at Avigo on the Susquehanna (Avigo was the name of a creek that flowed into the Susquehanna from the north). Perhaps this new settlement was Sir William's attempt to ease the leadership crisis at Schoharie. [4]

Seth Tehodoghwenziageghthe died probably in the summer of 1756, but the political division at Schoharie seemed to have prevented his formal condolence (and replacement) until the following January, when

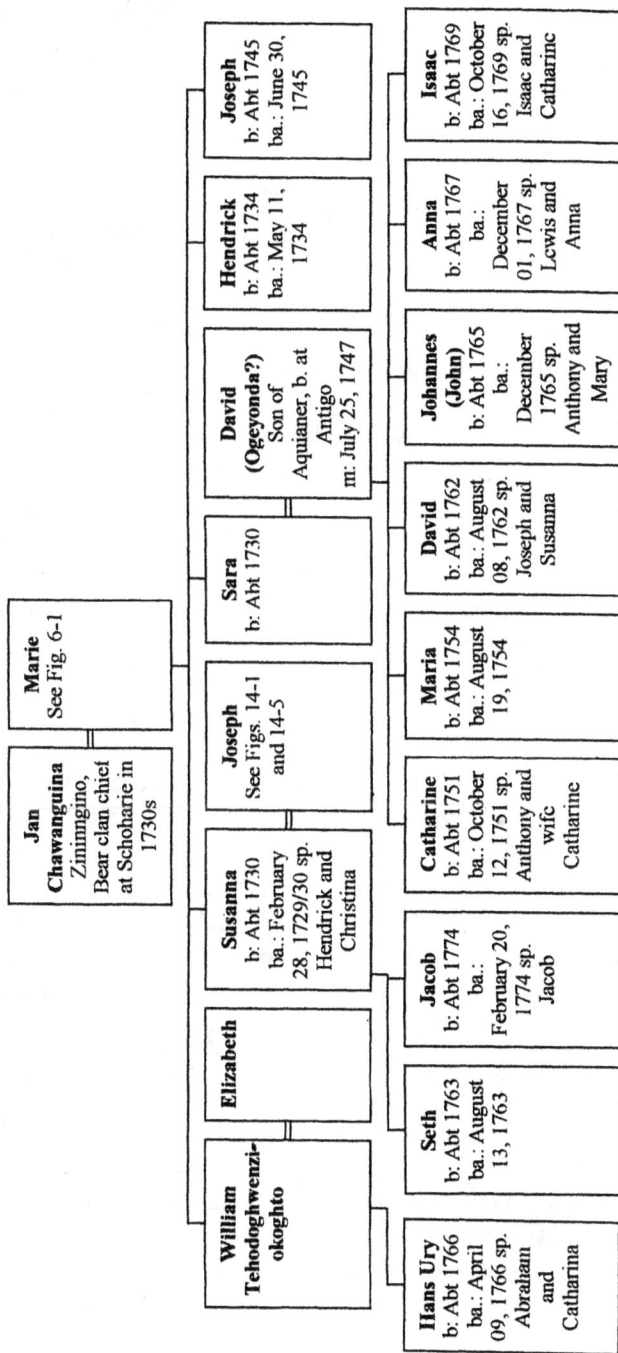

Figure 14-3. Descendants of Jan Chawanguina and Marie

David, now "Chief of the Schoharie Indians," came to Fort Johnson for the condolence ceremony. Dissent probably continued, however, for two groups went out to "replace" Seth Tehodoghwenziageghthe that spring: David in May and Seth (probably Seth Jr. in the 1754 petition, Seth Tetsiniyaghko of the Turtle clan—see Fig. 14-2) in early June. Seth Tehodoghwenziageghthe's brother, Hans Ury Aghsunhaqacks (Fig. 14-5), also led a raid at this time. Seth's oldest son Hans went with Seth Jr.'s group. One of Hans' children died in April, 1756 and his surviving children and wife died in December, 1758.[5]

One of the issues in this leadership struggle was the disposition of the remaining Indian land. The other Mohawks claimed that the Karighondontees had a right only to the land given to Karighondontee's wife for her immediate use, and thus had no right to sell other remaining land. The problem of how much land remained in Indian possession was exacerbated by the late 1750s, when other Indians had joined the original occupants of the Schoharie Valley. To Mohawks and Mahicans were added Tuscaroras, Delawares, and Oneidas. Another settlement, at Brekabeen a mile north of the Wilder Hook, was started not long before the Revolution.[6]

On January 29, 1764, seven Schoharies "waited on Sir William" and notified him that they had appointed Joseph Attrewaghti (Th'rewaghty), a young man, to be their Headman. This Joseph was either Seth Tehodoghwenziageghthe's son, baptized on February 3, 1740 (see Fig. 14-1), or Hans Ury and Susanna's son, baptized on February 28, 1736 (Fig. 14-5); his wife was named Susanna, probably Jan and Marie's daughter (Fig. 14-3). Evidently the Karighondontees had regained the leadership at Schoharie, for in the years before the Revolution the chiefs at Schoharie were this Joseph, Seth (probably Seth Jr.), Hans Ury (Aghsunhaqacks), Seth Tehodoghwenziageghthe's son Henry (see Fig. 14-1), and lastly, "Aggy Awner" David Ogeyonda (see Fig. 14-3). In 1766 Lawrence (Fig. 6-1), referred to by Sir William Johnson as chief sachem at Schoharie and supposedly seventy-eight years old, his wife, and his nephew Nicholas son of Catharine ("chief woman at Schoharie") presented Sir William Johnson with a mine. Lawrence died in August, 1768. Catharine's daughter Elizabeth was married to Lawrence, the son of Isaac Dekayenensere of Onaquaga, one of the many ties the Schoharie Mohawks had with the Onaquagans (see Figs. 14-4 and 11-3).[7]

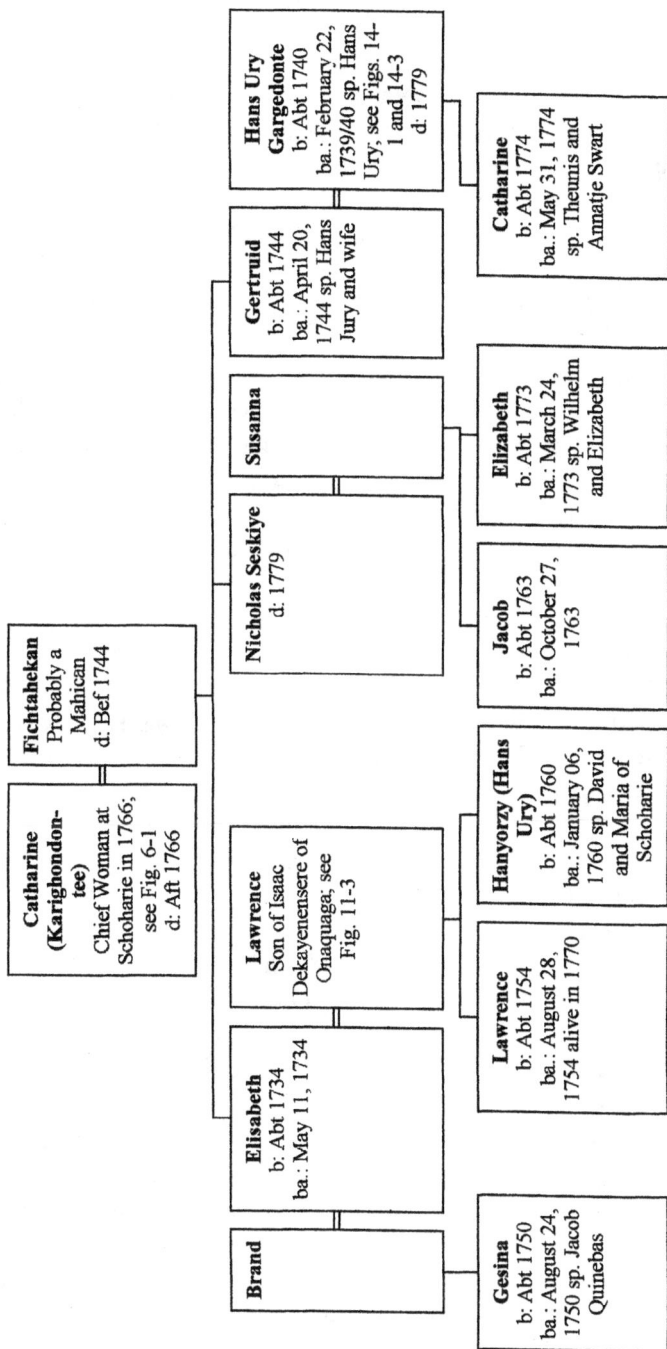

Figure 14-4. Descendants of Catharine and Fichtahekan

Judge Mathias Brown, who was born in 1745 and moved to Schoharie in 1760, left several observations on the Karighondontees. He wrote that William son of Jan killed another Indian named John Coy shortly before the Revolution. This may have been William Tehodoghwenziokoghto, probably a maternal nephew of the first Seth who was given the latter's name after 1756. Judge Brown also wrote that the prominent women amongst the Schoharie Indians just before the Revolution were Hisiquet (Elizabeth), Wawly (Mary), and Catoline (Catharine).[8]

On March 15, 1771, a group of twenty-nine Schoharies, evidently mostly Karighondontees, again made a petition (this time to Sir William Johnson) against the sale of lands by another group of Indians without their knowledge and consent. The petition is headed by Joseph Th'rewaghty and followed by either his wife or sister Susanna.[9]

In August, 1775, an epidemic broke out among the Indians who were attending a meeting with the American Indian Commissioners at the German Flats. Among those who died as a result were a large number of Schoharies, including a Cherokee woman named Warree, aged 105, "the mother of the Schoharies." Although the disease was called "yellow fever" no whites died of it, which may mean it was actually hepatitis A, to which most Europeans were immune but which does involve the liver and causes a yellowish tinge to the skin and the sclera of the eyes.[10]

After this devastation only a few Indians appeared in the Schoharie church records. By 1777 only an Oneida couple and Lewis the Frenchman and his wife Marie brought their children to be baptized at Schoharie; Lewis and Marie's son Marthynes (Martin) on September 12, 1777, and their daughter Elizabeth on May 10, 1778. Whether Lewis was actually an Indian is unclear, but it was probably an earlier Lewis (signer of the 1711 Vrooman deed) whom Judge Brown describes as having captured and scalped a Canadian Indian woman and brought her home to be his wife.[11]

In late 1776 or early 1777, "David Ogeyonda, a subtle Schoharie warrior [David Otkoghraro, the Schoharie war captain?], who had a hut on the lands of Adam Vrooman, and who had been for some time active for the Tories, doing the duties of a runner, spy, etc.," tried unsuccessfully to kill the chairman of the local Committee of Safety, Johannes Ball. The next year David, who was described as a small man, was killed trying to escape a party of Patriot militia and cavalry who had captured him.

Figure 14-5. Families of Hans Ury and Margaret Gargadonte

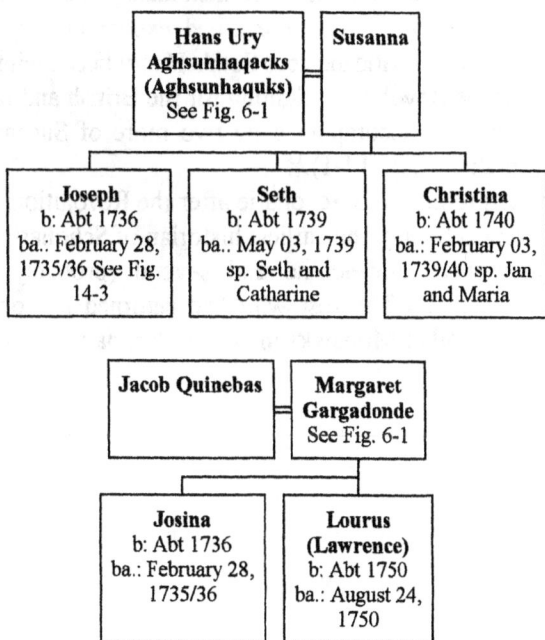

```
                    ┌──────────────────┬──────────────┐
                    │   Hans Ury       │  Susanna     │
                    │ Aghsunhaqacks    │═             │
                    │ (Aghsunhaquks)   │              │
                    │   See Fig. 6-1   │              │
                    └──────────────────┴──────────────┘
        ┌─────────────────┬─────────────────┬─────────────────┐
        │    Joseph       │     Seth        │   Christina     │
        │  b: Abt 1736    │  b: Abt 1739    │  b: Abt 1740    │
        │ ba.: February 28,│ ba.: May 03, 1739│ ba.: February 03,│
        │ 1735/36 See Fig.│  sp. Seth and   │ 1739/40 sp. Jan │
        │     14-3        │   Catharine     │   and Maria     │
        └─────────────────┴─────────────────┴─────────────────┘


                    ┌──────────────────┬──────────────┐
                    │  Jacob Quinebas  │  Margaret    │
                    │                  │═ Gargadonde  │
                    │                  │  See Fig. 6-1│
                    └──────────────────┴──────────────┘
            ┌─────────────────┬─────────────────┐
            │     Josina      │    Lourus       │
            │  b: Abt 1736    │  (Lawrence)     │
            │ ba.: February 28,│  b: Abt 1750    │
            │   1735/36       │ ba.: August 24, │
            │                 │    1750         │
            └─────────────────┴─────────────────┘
```

When David was brought down, wounded, in his flight, the cavalry took turns shooting at the still-conscious Indian until one of them had put a bullet through his head. This David had several sons, one of them called Yon (Jan). David and Sara had a son John baptized in December, 1765, but probably called Jan after Sara's father, Jan Chawanguina.[12]

Seth Tehodoghwenziageghthe's son Henry, "a tall, dark Schoharie chief," with his brother Hans Ury, their maternal nephew (Susanna's son) Adam (Fig. 14-1) and their cousin, Catharine's son Nicholas (Fig. 14-4), captured two men near Harpersfield, New York, in the early spring of 1779. One night at Tioga Point these two men managed to tomahawk all of their sleeping captors. All were killed except Henry, who fled wounded. After this traumatic incident Seth's Henry became infamous in the later years of the Revolution, fighting for the British and raiding the Schoharie settlements, accompanied by two more of Susanna's sons, William and Abraham (Fig. 14-1).[13]

A few Indians returned to Schoharie after the Revolution, including Abraham, but Jeptha Simms, the earliest historian of Schoharie, makes it plain that they were unwelcome and several (probably including Abraham) were killed. The rest who had returned left once again, possibly to join the other Mohawks in Upper Canada.[14]

CHAPTER XV

Closing Decades at Tionondoroge and Canajoharie

Numbers of Mohawks did not survive the difficult years of the late 1750s and early 1760s. As early as 1750 Reverend Ogilvie noted that "the number of Mohawks is very much decreased within these few years," owing to so many having gone to Canada. He reported that there were 204 Mohawks at Tionondoroge and 214 at Canajoharie. In the winter of 1756-57 a severe fever struck the Mohawks, carrying off many of the principal men and women and a great many children. In February of 1759 many of the Tionondoroge Mohawks died of a malignant fever, possibly typhoid. In the winter of 1760-61 another fever struck the Mohawks, killing a number of otherwise healthy adults, including Thomas Ganughsiddishe (see Fig. 10-1). Sir William Johnson's accounts for these years contain a number of dismal entries such as this one on December 13, 1758: "To Seths Hance 3 dollars to redeem 4 strouds he pledged for necessarys to bury his wife and 2 children." Other payments were to widows for coffins.[1]

Their decreased numbers made the Mohawks feel particularly vulnerable to the renewed pressures from speculators to take over the rich agricultural lands of the Mohawk and Canajoharie Flats and their traditional hunting grounds north of the Mohawk River. Each of these three areas came under renewed attacks by unscrupulous whites who tried to gain ownership after 1761 because the governor of New York was instructed by the king not to grant any new licenses to purchase Indian lands. As Sir William Johnson correctly foresaw, this royal directive made the older licenses and deeds, even those of questionable legality, more valuable than ever.[2]

The Kayaderosseras Patent Controversy
The Mohawks' hunting grounds north of Albany (in the present-day Adirondacks) had long been vulnerable to takeover by whites holding

contested deeds to the area—deeds which each succeeding generation of Mohawk leaders claimed were invalid. The controversy over this land, called in the 1750s and 1760s the Kayaderosseras Patent controversy, began with a deed signed in August, 1702. Hendrick Tejonihokarara (with a wolf sign) and Joseph Dehanochrakhas (with a bear sign) signed a deed to David Schuyler (mayor of Albany in 1707) and Robert Livingston Jr. (son of the Secretary for Indian Affairs) for a parcel of land near Saratoga. In this deed the Mohawks were incorrectly named as Hendrick Dehanochrakhas and Joseph Tiojonninhoger. Later Mohawks did not catch this mistake—they thought that "Dehanochrakhas" meant "Tuscarora."[3]

The deed which formed the main bone of contention in the Kayaderosseras controversy was signed on October 4, 1704, to Sampson Broughton and others, interpreted by Hilletie Van Olinda. Joseph, Hendrick, and Cornelius were named in the deed, but the signatories were actually Joseph, Hendrick, Amos, and Gideon. Cornelius was probably Cornelius Tirogaren, a Turtle clan sachem. Hendrick Tejonihokarare and Gideon Tonidoge were Wolves and Joseph Dehanochrakhas was a Bear. All were sachems. Amos was Amos Harogiechta, Canastasi Sr.'s husband, born about 1657 and baptized on December 25, 1697. He may have been the war captain Adoeanoketta, one of the leaders of the summer 1691 raid which assembled at Lac St. Sacrement (see Chapter 3), but he did not appear as a sachem in the councils at Albany.[4]

Many years later the Mohawk representatives said that the Kayanderosseras deed had been signed by only two of the three clans and was thus invalid; thus Amos must have been a member of either the Wolf or Bear clan. This itself is peculiar, for if Amos had signed in the place of Cornelius Tirogaren in the 1704 deed, he should have been signing for the Turtle clan, Hendrick for the Wolf, and Joseph for the Bear (Gideon signed to "confirm" the other three marks as valid, a practice common in late seventeenth-century deeds).[5]

Certainly to be valid the deed would have to be signed by representatives of all three clans. As Sir William Johnson wrote to the Lords of Trade on October 30, 1764:

Each Nation [of the Iroquois] is perfectly well acquainted, with their exact original bounds, the same is again divided into due proportions for each Tribe [clan] and afterwards subdivided into shares to each family, with all which they are most particular; neither do they ever infringe upon one another or invade their neighbors hunting grounds.[6]

The ownership pattern described by Sir William is found as early as the 1670s, when chiefs of the Turtle clan in the first and second castles of Canewage and Canagora signed several deeds. A member of another clan would sometimes sign as a guarantor of the other clan's signings (their marks). The land in these early deeds obviously was part of the *hunting grounds* alotted to the Turtle clan. Other deeds from this time period carry the marks of men from all three clans, indicating that the land in question belonged to all three clans.[7]

According to later Mohawks, the signers of the Kayanderosseras deed were told that the land sold therein was only enough for three or four farms and the payment (sixty pounds in goods) was burned before the Mohawks received it. In any case the land described in the deed was nowhere near the amount granted on the ensuing patent: on November 2, 1708, Lord Cornbury granted a patent of *800,000 acres*.[8]

Nothing was done on this patent for decades, but in the 1754 Albany conference the Mohawks learned of its existence for the first time and demanded that the Crown cancel the grant. This would require action by the New York assembly, who refused to do so, probably because so much money was by then tied up in the patent: by 1763 a one-thirteenth share in this patent was selling for 1,400 pounds.[9]

Sir William held a series of meetings with the Mohawks on this matter, such as the one with the Tionondoroge leaders in September, 1764, attended by Abraham Teyorhansere, Captain Daniel Oghnowera, Hendrick (either Ragosagiaghta—Little Hendrick—like Captain Daniel a member of the Turtle clan, or Hendrick Sadoquiat), Aaron (either Aaron Oseragighte or his oldest son Aaron Kanonnaron, also called Little Aaron or Aaron Hill—see Fig. 7-4), Isaac Anoghsootke (see Fig. 7-1), and Johannes Canadagaye. Finally, after over a decade of effort by Sir William Johnson and Cadwalladar Colden to resolve the matter, the Mohawks ceded the eastern part of the land but retained the western part for hunting. In this settlement they received a payment of 5,000 dollars.[10]

The City of Albany's Attempt to get a Deed to the Mohawk Flats
The city of Albany, after a hiatus of nearly thirty years, tried once again in 1760 to get the Tionondoroge Mohawks to acknowledge the city's rights to the Mohawk Flats. Abraham Teyorhansere brought the matter to Sir William Johnson's attention at a meeting at Fort Johnson on March 20, 1760:

> We are now come to you tears in our eyes, on account of the
> Reports we daily hear among our Bretheren the White people,
> which are, that we are a poor people, having no Land we can call
> our own, for even the Land we plant and live on we are told is
> the Property of the people of Albany, which we are entirely
> ignorant of, and can hardly think it true . . .

Abraham asked Sir William if the depriving of the Mohawks and their children of their little remaining land should be their reward for their faithfulness to the king.[11]

The matter apparently lapsed for more than a decade, but in 1773 the Tiononderoge Mohawks Abraham Teyorhansere, Aaron Kanonaron, Johannes Kryn Aneqwendahonji (Fig. 7-3), Isaac Anoghsootke (Fig. 7-1), Hans (Johannes) Canadagaya, Lawrence (Fig. 13-2), Seth, David Hill Karonyonte, Peter Taquayanont, Abraham Kreyn Sogradisse (Johannes Kryn's son), and Cornelius (probably Peter Taquayanont's son) met with an Albany committee under Sir William's supervision at Johnson Hall.[12]

The Albany committee brought copies of two deeds to Abraham Cuyler signed by Cornelius Thaneghwanege (Fig. 7-4) and by Aaron, Segehowane (Johannes Segehowane), and Collian (Kiliaen), and the 1730 deed to Peter Brown (see Appendix F). They also mentioned another parcel of lands sold to Jan Wemple. These purchasers, the committee said, had taken deeds from the city of Albany and paid the city fathers for this land. Now, however, at least one of the heirs of these purchasers had refused to pay rent to the city of Albany. The committee glibly revised the history of the Mohawk Flats controversy in their presentation speech to the Tionondoroge chiefs, ignored the 1733 grant that entrusted the land to the king, and ended by asking the Mohawks to accept a deed from the city of Albany to the land, with its reversion to the city if the Mohawks themselves ever vacated it.[13]

In his reply Abraham deftly countered the committee's arguments:

"Notwithstanding, Brothers, the Regard you profess, you appear to us to covet the little spot we live upon, which costs you nothing." He continued: "As for your Deeds, or Papers, we really do not [underst]and them.—we refer those matters to our Brother Sir Wm. Johnson our Superintendant, and whom we trust will take Care of our [affairs]."[14]

Faced with having to deal with Sir William, the committee, expressing its regret that the Mohawks were failing to take them up on their "generous offer," abruptly and unceremoniously departed. The city of Albany would have to wait until after the Revolution to gain the Mohawk Flats.[15]

The Livingston Deed to the Canajoharie Flats

The most troublesome and intractable of the land controversies that plagued the Mohawks in the post-French and Indian War years involved the Canajoharie Mohawks' planting grounds and an unscrupulous farmer named George Klock.

The deed that started this long dispute was signed in 1730 by Karagh-kondie, Orighjadichha, Hanaharisso, and Kanaquatho, sachems of the three clans of Canajoharie, to Philip Livingston and others for a large tract of land south and west of "Canajoharie" (see Appendix F). This deed, which contained boundaries vague even by the standards of Indian deeds, included the Canajoharie Mohawks' prime planting grounds. In 1763 Brant Aroghyiadecka ("Orighijadichha") said he did not remember having signed the deed and that if he had he must have been drunk. The marks on the deed are indeed peculiar, for unlike the carefully drawn clan signs typical of most valid deeds the marks of the four Mohawks on the Livingston deed are ambiguous. Karaghkondie's "wolf" has a bear-like body, and what looks to be a second head coming out of the first. The rear of Aroghyiadecka's mark is smeared to illegibility and the body of the "bear" has a line running lengthwise from the head to the mid-torso, ending with a dot. Only turtle signs characteristically were drawn with such lines through the body of the animal, denoting the patterns on the upper shell of a box or snapping turtle. Hanaharisso's turtle has a smeared cross projecting beyond the head of the animal. Kanaquatho's figure is bearlike, with lines on a rounded, turtle-like body. These things considered, one indeed suspects that the men were not sober when they made these marks.[16]

Some years previous to the 1760s Edward Collins (recipient of

Mohawk land gratis with his mother in a 1714 deed) had made a secret nighttime survey of the Canajoharie land and "cut four farms out of it." At the Albany Conference in 1754 the Livingston family had publicly agreed to give up their claim to the land, and afterward the white farmers on the land paid rent to the Canajoharie Mohawks. In the winter of 1761, however, a Livingston heir sold a share of this land to George Klock, a farmer on the north side of the Mohawk River. While Sir William Johnson was at Detroit that year Klock told all the white farmers on the land that they had to leave and must stop paying rent to the Indians. Klock set out to "comfirm" the claim of the original deed by getting as many Canajoharie Mohawks drunk as he could and having them sign deeds giving up their rights. In January, 1762, Jonathan Cayenquerigo (Fig. 4-2) related to Sir William Johnson the activities of Klock and his two partners (one of whom was Jelles Fonda) and how Klock had also accused the Mohawks of aiding warlike Indians in the west, just to stir up trouble between them and the English generals.[17]

Sir William was helpless to stop Klock's nefarious activities. Klock's neighbors, including his own brother, were kept up night after night by the noise of drunken roistering Indians coming from Klock's house. In March, 1763, the governor of New York ordered a formal meeting held to settle the matter of two of Klock's "confirming" deeds and a written declaration that Klock and Fonda had managed to secure from some of the Mohawks.[18]

Jonathan Cayenquerigo spoke at this meeting, declaring that

> liquor hath been always our Ruin, for whenever any of our people go over to the house of Geo. Klock, and we send for them from thence, he fills them more, and by that means detains them . . . as none of our People would otherwise have so acted, neither is it probable that any of our People would sell their Lands twice, For, if the Land in Question had been formerly sold we should not ask a second price for it [in Klock's new deeds].[19]

Jonathan punctuated his speech by throwing down empty liquor bottles instead of the customary wampum. He later added:

> When one Bottle was emptied, another was always filled, and 'twould require a very large Vessell to contain all which hath been

given us—The same Geo. Klock hath (we find) given out that he
hath given us 565 pounds if so, it must have been seen on us. It
is very strange what should have become thereof. You may see
we are all Naked, or must have spent it in the Taverns, which is
not the case and may be enquired into[20]

In June, 1763, the New York courts declared that they could not
consider the matter, leaving the Mohawks no further legal recourse.
Johnson reported that the Mohawks "are now divided into parties . . . &
their whole time is spent quarrelling." By November, however, the
Livingston heirs signed a quitclaim to the leaders of Canajoharie's three
clans: Johannes Dekarihokenh, Jonathan Cayenquerigo, and Rakeridigha
(the Wolf clan leader). Eventually all the white claimants except for
Klock signed the release.[21]

Klock continued his troublemaking ways. In the winter of 1764
Joseph Brant (the brother of Sir William's common-law wife Molly) and
Hance Dekarihokenh intercepted four Mohawks who were being enticed
to Jelles Fonda's house to go to Albany and sign a deed. Joseph and
Hance persuaded three of these men to return to Canajoharie but the last,
Jacob Onoghtoragh, who "wasn't of their clan" (i.e., he was a Bear) left
for Albany. Joseph Brant and Hance addressed the New York governor,
William Tryon, on the matter of Klock on July 28, 1772.[22]

About 1773 Klock induced a young Mohawk to go to England to be
exhibited for a fee. By the spring of 1774 this Mohawk had returned, but
Klock owed him money for his appearances in England and Joseph Brant
led a group of Mohawks to Klock's house in May to get it. That Joseph
and the other Mohawks were also looking for one or more of Klock's
deeds to the Canajoharie Flats is evidenced by the presence in the group
of Paulus Peters and Sir William's Mohawk son Brant Keghneghtaga,
both of whom could read English and hence identify any papers found at
Klock's farm. (Others with Joseph were: Johannes Rut, Jacob
Onoghtoragh who had been enticed to Albany ten years before and his
son Henry, John Peter a Frenchman, Peter "who is living at Brand's
house," Chequa Adam a son of Carestalgee, Elias a son of Eve, Cobes
Rahunsie, and Peter his son.)[23]

The Mohawks made Klock agree to sign the long-sought release
when it could be witnessed by a Justice of the Peace, but when Joseph
Brant came on June 28 with a Justice, Klock had fled to Albany, where

he wrote out a complaint against the Indians. Twice that summer Klock tried unsuccessfully to get Joseph indicted.[24]

The matter was unresolved at Sir William Johnson's death on July 11, 1774 (the very day Hance Dekarihokenh spoke of Klock's actions at a Six Nations conference at Johnson Hall), and was not settled until after the Revolution, when the Canajoharie Mohawks gave a power of attorney to Jelles Fonda to have him get what compensation he could from the new state of New York in payment for their lost land.[25]

Sir William Johnson's motives to help the Mohawks retain their lands contained a large degree of self-interest, for he benefited financially from Indian land grants and politically from his influence with the "keepers of the eastern door" of the Iroquois League. He sacrificed the interests of many southern and western tribes at the treaty of Fort Stanwix (Rome, New York) in 1768 when he drew a new line to mark the limits of white settlement.[26]

In 1763 the British government had declared that white settlement should not extend beyond the Alleghenies. Settlement pressures, particularly in the southern colonies, necessitated a refinement of this line. In 1765 Sir William, as Indian superintendent, had drawn a tentative line with the Iroquois, who claimed ownership of the southern lands by right of conquest in the previous century. In 1768 he met with the Six Nations and other Indians at Fort Stanwix to determine the final demarcation of this line, and he ran it along the Ohio River all the way to the Tennessee River, permitting white settlement in all the lands south and east of these rivers: the present-day states of Kentucky and West Virginia. In fact, most of these lands were claimed by the Cherokee, and some were used as hunting grounds by the Shawnee.[27]

At Fort Stanwix, too, Johnson's long-running dispute with a prominant New England minister and educator came to a head over Iroquois land, in this case Oneida lands and the long-disputed Wyoming Valley.[28]

The Reverend Eleazar Wheelock had established a school at Lebanon, Connecticut, to educate Indian youths to become teachers and Congregationalist missionaries to those Indians living on the frontier. In August, 1761, after appeals to Sir William Johnson, the Reverend received his first Mohawk students: a young man named Sander, another named Nickus, and a third—Joseph Brant. Of these three, only Joseph stayed the course. Nickus and Sander returned to the Mohawk Valley that fall (Sander died soon after). Joseph remained until July 5, 1763; his sister Molly called him home after learning that the Indian boys were required to do farm chores as part of their educational program. Other Mohawk lads had come in the meantime: Moses and Johannes brought by Joseph in November, 1761; Abraham Major, Abraham Minor, and Peter; and in November, 1764 Sir William's Mohawk son William Tagawirunte and two more Mohawks—William Minor and Elias. The baronet described his son to the Reverend Wheelock as "a sensible Smart Boy, but a little wild at present." In March of the following year Wheelock wrote Sir William that "William will likely make a fine Boy. He behaves very well."[29]

In April, 1765, nine of Wheelock's Indian students were approved by the Connecticut Board of Correspondents as either teachers or teaching assistants. Most were sent out to the Six Nations country by the summer, including the two Abrahams and Peter who were to teach among the Mohawks. Moses was sent to Onaquaga but found the Onaquagans had temporarily moved to Lake Otsego and so opened his school there. More information on these young Mohawks is hard to come by, other than statements that the two Abrahams and Peter succumbed to drunkenness and reverted to their native style of life. That Moses was intended for Onaquaga suggests that he may have been an Onaquagan himself, perhaps Adam Addynghkahnorum's grandson Moses, baptized in 1749 (see Fig. 11-2).[30]

Johannes, who like Moses was brought to Reverend Wheelock's school by Joseph Brant in November, 1761, was also approved as an assistant schoolmaster in 1765, but he appears not to have been given a school. He did, however, later serve as an interpeter to Wheelock's missionaries. In 1769 a visitor to Onaquaga met a young Mohawk named John Davies, who claimed to have received his education at the Reverend Wheelock's school. I expect that this was Johannes.[31]

While educating the Indian superintendent's son, Reverend Wheelock put into motion a grand scheme to finance his school by raising funds in Great Britain. He sent his first Indian pupil, the Mohegan minister Samsom Occum, and another minister to England in December, 1765, to raise monies for his Indian school. The missionary board in Boston objected to Occum's going as a representative of the school, and to counteract its influence Wheelock obtained a written commendation from Sir William Johnson.[32]

It would seem that during this time William Tagawirunte developed into a troublesome pupil. In September, 1765, he was drawn into a fight with the Mohegan pupil Joseph Johnson by the name-calling of John Wheelock, the Reverend's younger son, and the match became a general melee between the Iroquois and the Algonquins. In November, 1765, the Reverend's older son Ralph became the Indian schoolmaster. Ralph was blustering, arrogant, and tactless to his pupils, but he seems to have been particularly obnoxious to William, and vice versa. A famous anectdote, related by Joseph Brant, has William refusing to saddle Ralph's horse because he (William) is a gentleman's son. "Do you know what a gentleman is?" asked Ralph. "I do," answered William, "A gentleman is a person who keeps race-horses and drinks Madeira wine, and that is what neither you nor your father do—therefore, saddle your horse yourself!"[33]

Wheelock, possibly because Ralph was an epileptic, refused to believe ill of his son and so doubtless took Ralph's side in the matter. Once the fund-raising in Britain became a success the Reverend tried to dispense with the baronet's troublesome son. Wheelock sent Ralph to Johnson Hall in the summer of 1766 to tell Sir William about William Tagawirunte. As he wrote Johnson:

> William (Major as we call him for distinction sake) is a very good Genius, and capable of making a very likely man; but his Pride and the Violence of his Temper have sometimes rendered him troublesome; and obliged me to use severity with him, of which my son can inform you. Perhaps a Line or Message from You might be of Special service to him.

Evidently the baronet called William home for two or three weeks in September but then sent him back to school. Interestingly, about the same time William Tagawirunte was sent back to school Sir William also sent Wheelock two more Mohawks, a woman named Margaret and a youth named Paulus, with the following note:

> I have but Just time to tell you that the Bearer is Margaret—the Wife of Daniel a Mohock Indian who haveing used her Very ill & Cohabited with a near Relation, she is under a necessity or[of] retiring from his Resentment for a time, & is desirous of making

your house her Assylum, the rather as she has a Young Relation under your Care at present.[34]

From a letter Margaret wrote (in English) to the Reverend Wheelock earlier that summer we know that her maternal niece Katharine was one of the students at the school. Margaret's husband was Captain Daniel Oghnowera. When Margaret arrived at Wheelock's she was put to work in the Reverend's home and Paulus was enrolled as a student. Paulus was thus a youth or boy. There is only one Paulus of the appropriate age in the church records, baptized on August 8, 1756, the son of Lawrence and his half-white wife, Anna Holmes (see Fig. 13-2). Lawrence and Anna had an older child Katharine (Catharine), baptized on November 24, 1753. Paulus was probably Katharine's younger brother, come to see his sister with his aunt ("mother") Margaret; thus Margaret would have been Anna Holmes's sister.[35]

In December of 1766 two other Mohawks named John Green and Seth entered Wheelock's school. Seth was a wholly inappropriate addition to the community of scholars; he had killed and scalped an enemy Indian on a raid and didn't settle down to the strict regime of studies. Possibly it didn't help that he shared a study with William Tagawirunte.[36]

Margaret was homesick (and possibly tired of being the Reverend's scullery maid) and on January 9, 1767, she left with her niece Katharine, Paulus, and another Mohawk girl, Mary. The next month the Reverend was visited by a Mohawk sachem, the father of John Green, and John's mother, sister, and brothers. The sachem, probably Johannes Kryn (Fig. 7-3), told Wheelock that Sir William was getting Episcopal priests as missionaries for all the Indians. Obviously upset with this news, Wheelock used the sachem's leaving on February 16 (with his son John) as an opportunity to get rid of Seth and William Tagawirunte, saying that the latter was "to[o] forward and litegeous to consist with the health and well-being of this school." It was also important to note that Wheelock thought Sir William Johnson's usefulness to him was not nearly so great as it had been, now that thousands of pounds had been gathered in Britain for his school.[37]

Wheelock still needed land in the Six Nations country for the site of the new, larger school he was planning, however. He had been appealing to Sir William Johnson for such a site in the Wyoming Valley since 1761.

Johnson told a correspondent that the Six Nations found the idea obnoxious. Undaunted, Wheelock sent two agents to the Fort Stanwix treaty congress in September-October of 1768 to try and secure land from the Oneidas, who were influenced by the Wheelock-trained missionary, Samuel Kirkland.[38]

Wheelock's chief agent at the congress was the near-demented Reverend Jacob Johnson. Reverend Johnson proved so "eccentric" that all opportunities to influence the Indians were lost and Wheelock incurred the lasting enmity of Sir William Johnson, in part because of the "private instructions" to Reverend Johnson from Wheelock that Sir William had somehow gotten hold of. By the end of the next year all Iroquois pupils had been withdrawn from Wheelock's school, although the Reverend Kirkland was still active at Oneida.[39]

White settlement was officially forbidden beyond the Fort Stanwix treaty line, but scarcely had the ink dried on the treaty (officially signed in 1770) when settlers began to cross it. Johnson and other Crown officials were helpless to stop the encroachments of white settlers pushing west. Conflicts between whites and Indians led to Lord Dunmore's War in Virginia in 1774, in which colonial fighters defeated a force of Indians at the Battle of Point Pleasant. Johnson's death on July 11, 1774, came in the middle of a conference held to discuss incursions on Indian lands beyond the 1768 line.[40]

During the Revolution the Mohawks, with the exception of a few families, became allies of the British in Canada. After the war they ceded all of their remaining Mohawk Valley lands to the Americans and settled in Upper Canada (present-day Ontario), the Tionondoroge Mohawks under their leader Captain John Deserontyn—Thomas Ganughsiddishe's son (see Fig. 10-1)—at the Bay of Quinte. The Canajoharie Mohawks and others of the Six Nations followed Joseph Brant to the Grand River Reserve. The Senecas remained in western New York and northern Pennsylvania. Most of the Tuscaroras formed a settlement outside of Buffalo, New York. Only the Oneidas (and a few Tuscaroras) of the old Iroquois league had favored the American cause in the Revolution. They remained on their old lands in New York through the eighteenth century. In the next century most of the Oneidas moved to the region of Green Bay, Wisconsin, not far from where the Stockbridge Indians finally made their home.[41]

APPENDIX A

First Church in Albany,

Indian Baptisms and Marriages, 1689-1756[a]

Date[b]	Baptismal Name	Parents, Indian Name or Information	Sponsors
12-27-89	**Paulus**	**Ock-Kweese**, he is blind, age 40	
7-11-90	**David**	**Swongara** (Little Board) age c. 40	
	Rebecca	**Kowajatense**, wife of David, age c. 30	
	Isac	**Tekaniadaroge** (Division of the wax?: *lack-scheydinge*) about 22	
	Henderick	**Tejonihokarawa** (Open the door) c. 30	
	Lidia	**Karanondo** (Lifter or sharper: *opligster*) about 50, widow	
	Seth	**Kaadsjihandasa** (Runner from the fire: *vier-uyt loper*) 12 years, son of a deceased daughter of Lidia, now her adopted son	
	Rachel	**Sionheja** (Lively), ca. 25, wife of **Joseph Skanjodowanne** (Eagle's beak) baptized by the Jesuits	
	Manasse	Joseph Skanjodowanne & Rachel Sionheja (c. 4 yrs.)	
	Kanastasis	baptismal name in Canada; widow	
	Jacob	son of Kanastasis, c. 8 years	
	Sara	daughter of Kanastasis, c. 3 yrs	
	Adam	**Sagonorasse** (Fastener: *vast-binder*) parents dead, adopted son of his relatives **Laurens & Maria**, now communicants, 12 yrs.	
8-6-90	**Lea**	**Kwaowarate** (Transition or passage: *overgang*), c. 60, widow	
	Josine	**Wanika** (Loaned) c. 40, widow, sister of Lea	
	Jakomine	dau. of Josine, about 9 years	
	Josua	son of Josine, about 7 years	

207

Date[b]	Baptismal Name	Parents, Indian Name or Information	Sponsors
8-6-90	Eunice	**Karehodongwas** (Plucker of trees: *Bloomplukster*), 16 yrs. daughter of Lea, wife of Isak Tekaniadaroge, mother of Simon	
	Simon	son Eunice and Isak, abt. 9 mos.	
	Alida	**Karehojenda** (Fallen tree) daughter of Lea, wife of a heathen, c. 30 years	
12-1690	Lysbet	(Deer) daughter of Henderick and Catarine pros., & after prev. inst. & conf. baptized at Albany	
6-1-91	Maria	Joseph & Rachel	Laurens & Rebecca
7-5-91	Henry	Laurens & Maria	Gov. Henry Sloughter
10-25-91	Anna	**Skonwakwani**, c. 25 years	
2-7-92	Rebecca	**Jokeyha** (She who shells: *Uytdopster*), 20 yrs.	
	Eunice	**Honiskoö** (Paralyzed in the back), 14 yrs.	
	Sara	3 or 4 mos. old (child of a prosletyte)	
	Cornelis	**Aanasjadago** (Plucker of feathers), 22 yrs.	
	Jan	**Onodaka** (Gamekeeper?: *Koddens*), 16 years	
	Daniel	**Sognihoä** (Sprig), 15 years	
	Abraham	**Hojadio** (Own body), 10 years	
	Jan	**Etsje ni ser** (Sleeper on branches), 12 yrs.	
	Elias	1 year (child of a proselyte)	
3-28-92	Eva	**Jawaandasse** (Who has not any too much to eat), age 35	
	Catarina	**Tokwanaharonne** (Who stands in the midst of the people), 18 years, daughter of Eva Jawaandasse	
	Noach	**Tetsjohoniodaon** (Erected poles), 9 yrs., son of Eva	
	Anna	**Tiosseroage** (Who clings to a dress), daughter of Eva	
	Moeset	**Tsudtakkwe** (Repulsed) 30 years	
	Magdalene	**Koanadakkarrie** (Who has left—or run away from—her castle), 11 years, daughter of Moeset	

Date[b]	Baptismal Name	Parents, Indian Name or Information	Sponsors
3-28-92	Debora	Tsionesse (Lowered again), 8, daughter of Moeset	
	Christine	Skanjadaradi (Across the river), 4 years, daughter of Moeset	
	Grietje	Shohwason (One who always covers herself), 20 years	
	Martyn	Sinonda (A small mountain), 13 years	
	Dorkas	Tionaktiago (One who breaks her sleeping place), 13 years	
	Rut	Hoa (Owl), 12 years	
	Hendrick	Waäms or Waänis (Long bow), 1 year old	
	Cornelia	ch. of Canastasji, 6 weeks old	
8-15-92	Marta	Teianjeharre (Two heights), c. 48 years	
	Alette	Quaktendiatha (One who is being driven), 10 years, daughter of Marta	
	Catarine	Sadiogawa (She has as much, or An equal share), widow, about 33 years old	
1-1-93	Sara	Dekajagentha (Who leaves by two doors), c. 40 years	
	Abraham	Wagwagton (Pushed over), 17, son of Sara	
	Isak	Sirware (Puts the cloth in the water) c. 4 years, son of Sara	
	Jacob	Isack & Eunice, married pros.	
10-29-93	Gideon	Tonidoge (Split moon), 23 years	
	Antoni	Akerrijehe (One who continually turns something around), 15 years	
	Thomas	child of Rebecca ba. 9 -[Feb] 7-92	
	Anna	Joseph & Jacomine	
12-31-93	Agniet	Kajaidahe, c. 40 years, wife of Tjerk	
	Susanna	2 mos. old, daughter of Agniet [and Tjerk]	
	Margriet	Kviethentha, 17 years	
4-11-94	Eva	Sowasthoa (Little one), 49 years	
	Seli	Tejononnaron, 9 yrs, adopted dau. of Eva	
	Anna	Sajogerenha (Little chaser: *opdryvertie*), c. 26 years	

Date[b]	Baptismal Name	Parents, Indian Name or Information	Sponsors
4-11-94	Gerrit	Anna's little child	
	Moses	ch. of Gideon (the mother is not yet baptized)	
	Helena	Joseph & Rachel	
	Hester	Joseph & Rachel	
	Dorothe	Grietie (ba. 3-28-92) (a small child)	
7-8-94	Helena	of a proselyte	
12-26-94	Pieter	**Kanarongwe** (Drawer out of arrows), c. 20 years	
	Sander	**Anoniachtha** (Dancer), c. 20 years	
	Brant	**Thowariage** (One whose fence has been broken), c. 21 years	
	Dorcas	**Sakkoherriho** (One who re-enters the bushes) c. 23 years	
	Christine	**Tsike** (Seer), c. 18 years	
	Amirant	**Kanianaundon** (One who lifts cones: *Kegal steenen*), c. 20 years	
3-17-95	Maria	Kanastasi	
6-23-95	Susanna	**Nikajada** (Thin waist), c. 30 years	
	Jonas	3 years old, son of Susanna	
	Diwer	5 mos. old, child of Susanna	
	Dirk	**Rode** (Stupid), c. 80 years old	
1-1-96	Zacharias	Joseph & Kanastasi (both prev. ba. in Canada)	
	Lucas	**Sondagerakwe** (Who digs up the soil) c. 21 years old, son of Eva (50)	
	Barent	**Tarogiagetho** (Who scrapes the air), 19 yrs.	
	Isak	**Sognaondje** (Who defeats the skeleton), 17 yrs.	
	Jacob	**Kajingwirago** (Large arrow), 22 years	
	Hester	**Toaddoni** (One who cradles), 35 years	
	Debora	**Kahusje** (Long wooden shaft), 13 years, daughter of Hester	
	Frans	6 years old, son of Hester	
	Gerrit	also a little ch. of Hester	
	Agniet	**Katerakse** (Root-eater), 50 years	

Date[b]	Baptismal Name	Parents, Indian Name or Information	Sponsors
1-1-96	Abraham	Sadigniadode (They are alike), 17 years, son of Agniet	
	Marie	Brant & Margriet (a small child)	
	Celie	Wakajesha (In vain), 30 years	
	Seth	a little child of Celie	
4-13-96	Moeset	c. 20 years, kept her original name	
	Neeltie	Kawachkerat (One who is whitish), c. 24 years.	
	Catrina	c. 2, Neeltie's child	
	Sara	Sukkorio (One who has beautiful hair), 15 years, sister of Neeltie	
4-13-96	Jan	Juthori (Cold), c. 22 years	
	Elias	Joseph & Jacomoni	David, Gideon, Josine
6-28-96	Thomas	Gideon & Catrina, 5 years	
	Antonette	Gideon & Catrina, 2 years	
	Johannes	Owajadatferrio (He has been found), c. 26	
	Judik	child of Anne	
	Blandine	Koatkitsquanni c. 37 years	
	Agnis	15 years, daughter of Blandine	
	Clara	12 years, daughter of Blandine	
	Jephta	10 years, son of Blandine	
	Isai	6 years son of Blandine	
9-20-96	Jonatan	Takaradi, c. 20 years	
	Bata	Tejoderondat, c. 36 years	
	Hagar	Dekarogwendats, c. 17 years	
	Sara	Rut & Hester	
	Natan	Gideon & Dorcas	
12-27-96	Johannes	Moeset & a Christian	Hilletje Olinda
	Debora	Jacob (ba. 1-1-96), mother receives inst.	
	Willem	Toadakje (One who is being led)	
1-3-97	Pieter	Pieter & Canastasji (Peter was killed a few months ago)	Rebecca
4-4-97	Daniel	7 yrs., son of Neeltie (ba. 4-13-96)	
	Adam	6 wks., son of Neeltie (ba. 4-13-96)	
	Christine	Johannes (ba. 6-28-96) & Rebecca	

Date[b]	Baptismal Name	Parents, Indian Name or Information	Sponsors
4-4-97	**Brant**	2 mons., son of **Marie Senehanawith** (Who boils maize) baptized in Canada	
	Jacob	Christine (ba. 12-26-94) & husband yet unbaptized	
	Jan	Jan (ba. 4-13-96) & Maria (ba. in Canada) 4 weeks old	
5-13-97	**Reinier**	Tjerk & Agniet	
12-25-97	**Amos**	**Harogiechta** (One who descended dead from heaven), 40 years	
	Asa	**Onasiadikha** (Pasture burner), c. 35 years	
4-25-98	**Jacob**	Brant & Margriet	Canastasji
	Neeltie	Nadikansha & Catrine abt. 10 wks. old	Dorcas
	Marcus	Josina (adptd. mother) abt. 4 mos. old	Martha
7-16-98	**Elisabeth**	Rebecca (adpt. mother)	Marie
9-10-99	**Margriet**	Asag & Maria	Arent, Eva
1-5-1700	**Abraam**	Jacob & Jacomyn	Elisabet Wendels
5-12-00	**Adam**	Arent & Agniet	Rebecca
9-1-00	**Laurens**	Gideon & Dorcas	Pieter Schuyler, Rachel Schuyler, Canastasi
10-6-00	**Isabelle**	**Wothoggen** (*doopster*) 40 years	
	Eva	**Thainchta** 8 years	Martya
	Johannes	**Rotsiho** 12 years, Gideon's adopted son, child of his brother	
	Sara	**Kakenbarontje**, 9 years, adopted daughter of Gideon, child of his brother, named for the mother of Domine LydiusIsabella Lydius	
	Seth	**Anadag**, 5 years, adopted son of Gideon, child of his brother	
	child	Pierre (ba. Canada) & Blandine Quacketsquanni	
	Rebecca	Rebecca & Asa	
3-29-03	**Gideon**	Johannes & Louysa	Gideon, Asa, Dorcas

Date[b]	Baptismal Name	Parents, Indian Name or Information	Sponsors
5-30-03	David	Gideon & Dorcas	Stephanus Groosbeek, Isabelle Lydius
7-4-03	Christine	Karendekchtha, 24	Gideon, Rebecca
	Johannes	Wajadajeeni, 1	Wessel Ten Broek, Hilletje Van Olinda
	Catharine	Asa & Maria Tejoqueetsjveni	Johannes Lydius & Margaret Koasootha
10-3-03	Susanna	Willem & Anna	Jan Jansse Bleecker, Susanna Bleecker
12-26-03	Joseph	Maria	Joseph, Hagar
7-2-04	Anna	Seth (ba. 7-11-90) & Sara (ba. 4-13-96)	Gideon & Dorcas
10-14-05	Pieter	Cornelis & Catharina	Asaph, Rebecca
1-20-06	Jacobus	Pierre (ba. in Canada) & Catharine	Laur. Van der Volge, Marie Van der Volge
	Philip	Joseph Oddaroudagoy & Maria	Philip Schuyler, Sara
4-14-06	Isaac	Jacob Tehotsogtade & Jacomyntje Kowanagwe	Enoch & Rachel
	Jacob	Johannes & Louysa	Jacob Kaniaegkoo, Canastasi
	Dina	Petrus & Catharina	Jonathan Stevens, Christina
	Cornelis	Ruth & Margarita	Johannes Tejassa & Rebecca Jokeyha
	Timotheus	Oujichtanoroh & Anna Hazeankehha	Amos, Canastasi Kanawaakohha
	Margaret	Seri	Esras
7-14-06	Elisabeth	Ezra	Henrik, Catharina
12-29-06	Elisabeth	Kanijngrage & Grietje	Asaph, Maria
1-19-07	Daniel	Johannes & Rebecca	Jacob, Jacomina
4-13-07	Lidia	Seth & Sara	Stephannes Groesbeek, Rebecca
11-2-07	Elisabeth	Brant & Margarita	Johannes Harmanse (Visscher) & Maria

Date[b]	Baptismal Name	Parents, Indian Name or Information	Sponsors
11-9-07	Josua	Ezras & Canastasi	Hendrik, Catharina
	Pieter	Jacob Kayingwirago & Jacomyn	Harman van Slyk & Rebecca Kowtayolduse
2-8-08	Catherina	Arien Egnietha & Maria Kjada	Ezras Sonihowarre, Canastasi Koaroni
3-3-08	Aaron	Cornelis Thannewaneek & Catharine Karhages	Ezras & Martha
4-4-08	Dirk	Gideon & Dorcas	Wessel Ten Broek, Geertruy Schuyler
5-26-08	Catharina	Abraham Dsikereha & Catharine Dewadewa-naghwa	Gerrit Symonse & Tryntje his wife
12-25-08	Isaac	Jacob Anonssontje & Jacomyn Kwanogweech	Robbert Wendel & Rachel Kajodarontje
7-3-09	Adam	Johannes Tejassa & Rebecca Dwssdjchouwe	Ezras, Neeltie Tewaghkerat
4-28-10	Anna	Simon & Chrystyn	Rebecca Jr.
	Marie	Seth & Sara	Jacomine
4-30-10	Elisabeth	Onias	Rebecca Sr. & Kanagthathye Jr.
	Seth	Maria	Gideon, Dorcas, Sara
	Hester	Anna & a heathen	Johs. & Rebecca Jr.
	Elias	Eunice & a heathen	Kanagthathje Sr. & Catharina
5-5-10	Catharyn	Johs. Tejejachso & Rebecca Dewaysidis	Martha Tejongja-ghare & Catharyn Kahichtaginos
3-11-11	Christina Maria (aborigine)		Abraham Schuyler,
4-17-20	Jacob	Catharyna	Rebecka
	Robin	Joseph	Maria
4-18-20	Elizabeth	Jacomyn	Chatarine
5-29-20	Ezras	Corneliz & Maria	Ezras & Neeltie
7-15-20	Zelia	Chaterina	Ezras & Maria
	Daniel	Jannetie	Ezras & Rebekka

Date[b]	Baptismal Name	Parents, Indian Name or Information	Sponsors
8-20-20	Cornelia	Anna	Hendrik & Chatarine
	David	Paulus & Hester	Gideon & Maria
	Aaron	Maria	Cornelis & Catharina
	Esraz	Adam & Elizabeth	Ezras & Neeltie
2-12-21	Thomas	Brant & Catharina	Jakob & Maria
4-7-21	Joseph	Elias & Martyn	Cornelis & Jacomyn
	Susanna	Joseph & Maria	Ezras & Josyna
	Seth	Pierre & Catharina	Sara
	Anna	Johannes & Margariet	Hendrik & Sara
	Moses	Syoteke & Maria	Cornelius & Maria
	Isack	Ajandraaejon & Sara	Chatharina
6-4-21	Catharine	Maria	Pieter & Christyna
	Jacob	Abraham & Chrestyna	Gideon & Chanistasi
	Moses	Anthine & Sara	Paulus & Hester
	Thomas	Nickes & Catharine	Thomas & Canastasi
	Maria	Adam & Chanandekdre	Christyna
7-9-21	Jenik	Simon & Josyna	Ezras & Canastasi
	Josua	David & Annochquisseris	Anthoni
	Thomas	Charadighan & Hilletie	Cornelis & Chatharina
1-28-22	Johannes	Kreyn & Anna	John Collins & Margarita Bleeker Collins
3-25-22	Pieter	Pieter & Elizabeth	Ezras & Josyna
6-24-22	Simon	Sander & Margarita	Simon & Josina
	Christina	Sander & Margarita	Brandt & Christina
	Elizabeth	Johannes & Dyvertie	Gideon
	Margarita	Brant & Jacomyn	Pieter & Alida
9-30-22	Margarita	David & Maria	Ezras & Margarita
	Catharina	Joseph & Agniet	Anthony & Dorcasy
	Hester	Canassaoneha & Jannetis	Pieter & Josyna
1-1-23	Seth	Hendrick & Margarita	
	Seth	Adam & Elizabeth	Seth & Sara
2-10-23	Johannes	Seth & Sara	Gideon & Lydia
5-11-23	Joseph	Christyaen & Maria	Jan & Maria
6-31[sic]-23	Sara	Paulus & Hester	Gideon & Canestasy

Date[b]	Baptismal Name	Parents, Indian Name or Information	Sponsors
6-31[sic]-23	Ezras	Nicholaes & Catharina	Pieter & Margariet
7-28-23	Robbyn	Arens & Sara	Jan Rosie & Sara Kidny
10-13-23	Jacob	Joseph & Maria	John Wendel, Louysa
	Hendrik	Maria Thandrachgua	Ezras & Margariet
	Josua	Pierre & Catharine	Jacomyn
	Joseph	Cornelis & Jacomyn	Thomas & Canastasi
	Eva	Cornelis & Maria	Dorcas
12-26-23	Maria	Jan Kajendaroucho & Maria Kajenjkethachtado	Chrystyaen & Maria
	Sara	Webequey & Maria	Hendrik & Maria
	---	David & Onochquiseris	Gideon & Maria
3-29-24	Aernaet	Sara Evyjachoon	Peter van Driessen
7-5-24	Sara	Sander & Margariet	Canastasi
	Isaac	Elias & Martin	Anthony, Jacomina,
	Jacob	Elias & Martin	& Dorcas
	Laurens	Ezras & Margariet	Ezras & Margariet
	Seth	Pieter & Elyzabeth	Joseph & Louysa
9-20-24	Rebecka	Anthony & Sara	Gideon & Rebecka
10-9-24	Maria	Seth & Margarita	Ezras & Josine
	Hendrik	Adam & Griettie	John & Anna Wendel
11-19-24	Gideon	David & Lydia	Gideon & Dorcas
12-27-24	Thomas	Adam & Elisabeth	Gideon & Dorcas
3-21-25	Joseph	Moses & Alida	Hendrick Cuyler, Jacomyn, a pros.
	Jacob	Simon & Josina	Petr. Van Driesen, Christina, a pros.
6-26-25	Zacharias	Ezras & Elysabeth	Ezras, Josyna
	Pieter	Aquarith & Christina	Quarant & Jacomyn
	Neeltie	Hendrik & Anna	Ezras & Margariet
8-1-25	Joseph	Hendrik & Margarita	Joseph & Zelia
9-5-25	Robert	Arens & Sara	John & Eliza Rosie, Zara Kidny
11-26-25	Anthony	Joseph & Agniet	Anthony & Sara
	Aaron	Tjerk & Katharina	Ezras & Neeltie

Date[b]	Baptismal Name	Parents, Indian Name or Information	Sponsors
11-26-25	Pieter	Johannes & Margariet	Pieter & Maria
	Chatharina	Johannes & Margariet	Chatharina
	Jacob	Johannes & Maria	Jacomina
	Catharina	Margariet	Ezras & Margariet
	Sara		
4-17-26	Maria	Daniel & Susanna	Hendrik & Rebecca
	Joseph	Abraham & Maria	Hendrik & Elyzabeth
5-15-26	Johannes	Seth & Margariet	Ezras, Anna Wendell
7-10-26	Lyzabeth	Paulus & Hester	Ezras & Maria
	Neeltie	Pieter & Chatarina	Hendrik & Zara
	Pieter	Philip & Zaria	Ezras & Canistazy
	Jacob	Ezras & Chatarina	Hendrik & Eva
	Maria	a heathen woman bapt.	
11-6-26	Catharina	Joseph & Maria	Maria
2-22-27	Maria	Cousart & Jannetie	Hendrik & Rebecca
	Maria	Symen & Josyne	Thomas & Canasthazy
4-2-27	Brant	(adopted by Jacomyn) Johannes & Mary	Hendrik & Josine
	Aaron	Sander & Margariet	Jan & Mary
4-9-27	Susanna	Cornelis & Josyna	Jacob & Josyna
5-6-27	David	Jan & Maria	Hendrik, of Isack Kip[c] and Rebecca, pros.
6-9-27	Joseph	Sara	Ezra & Canasthazy
	Moses	Pieter & Elyzabeth	Anthony & Sara
	Jan	Hilletie	Simon & Josyna
7-23-27	Christina	Joseph & Maria	Brant & Chatharina
8-13-27	Zeth	David & Lydia	Seth & Sara
10-6-27	Daniel	Ezras & Elysabeth	Ezras & Neeltie
	Jan	Moses & Alida	Jan & Maria
12-28-27	Anne	Hosonjonda & Madalena	Hendrik & Eva
	Petrus	Daniel & Elyzabeth	Jacomyn
	Ezras	Jooticke & Maria	Thomas & Canastazy
	Laurens	Kenunksies & Anna	Hendr. & Margariet

Date[b]	Baptismal Name	Parents, Indian Name or Information	Sponsors
12-28-27	Maria	Thomas & Alida	Ezra & Maria
7-13-29	Jacob	Symon & Josyna	Thomas & Canastazy
12-13-29	Eliaz	Moses & Alida	Maria
	Nickus & Sara ma. Christians baptized		
	Abraham		
	Cornelis		
	Catharina		
2-13-30	Anna	Hendrik & Anna	Symen & Catharine
2-28-30	Susanna	Jan & Maria	Hendrik & Christina
	Cornelis	Daniel & Elyzabeth	Hendr. & Maria
3-11-30	Adam	Petrus & Elyzabeth	Catharina
	Johannes	Lucas & Sara	Eva
8-30-30	Maria	Hendrik & Maria	Joseph & Maria
9-25-30	Hester	Brand & Catharina	Symen & Jacomyne
	Susanna	Cahousouwane & Catharina	Hendrik & Maria
12-25-30	Canastasy		
	Rebecca		
	Abraham		
	Rachel		
	Sara	Rebecca	Abraham & Josina
	Catharine	Josina	Abraham & Catharina
	Lena	Madelena	Seth & Maria
	Joseph	Abraham & Grietie	Adam & Grietie
	David	David & Margarita	Symen & Esther
	Nikes	Nikes & Elizabeth	Seth & Lydia
	Joseph	Rachel	Joseph & Maria
	Joseph	Rebecca	Gideon & Madalena
	Lidea	Laurens & Rachel	Seth & Sara
4-18-31	Grietie	Sara	Joseph & Maria
	Catharina	Anna	Abraham & Josina
	Cornelis	Margariet	Simon & Maria
	Adam		
	Sara		
	Isaac		
	Abraham		

Date[b]	Baptismal Name	Parents, Indian Name or Information	Sponsors
6-10-31	Grietie	Carroragiera & Susanna	Adam & Margriet
	Rebecca	Elyzabeth	Hendrik &
	Jan	Elyzabeth	Rebecca (for both)
	Jacob	Rebecca	Gideon & Margariet
8-22-31	Paulus	Joseph & Catharina	Simon & Sara
9-26-31	Sara	after prev. confession	Hendrik & Christina
4-9-32	Kiliaen	Canadagaje	
	Catharine	Jan & Anna	Aaron & Christina
5-7-32	Petrus		
	Moses		
	Hester		
	Antony		
	Margarita		
	Maria		
	Catharina		
	Nicolaes		
	Jannetie		
	Brand		
	Catharina		
	Anna		
	Jacomyn		
	Christina		
	Margarita		
	Elyzabeth		
	Maria		
	Margarieta		
	Gideon		
	Lourens	Jonathan & Maria	Hendrik & Josyna
	Thomas	Nicolaes & Jannetie	Nikes & Sara
7-23-32	Adam		
	Paulus		
	Catharina		
	Dyvertie		
	Margarieta		
	Sara		
	Elyzabeth		

Date[b]	Baptismal Name	Parents, Indian Name or Information	Sponsors
7-23-32	Thomas		
	Kiliaen		
	Petrus		
	Jacob		
	Johannes		
	Joseph		
	Rachel	Sweerath & Catharina	Abraham & Josyna
1-7-33	Margarita	Ananias & Sara	Hendrick & Margarita
3-31-33	Joseph	Daniel & Elysabeth	Joseph & Josyna
7-15-33	Aron	Ruth & Elyzabeth	Abraham & Margarieta
	Maria	Jan & Susanna	Brand & Josina
12-21[sic]	Anna	Johannes & Maria	Seth & Anna
[prob.10]-33	Maria	Cornelis & Anna	Thomas & Canastazie
12-19-33	Susanna	Ezras & Maria	Abraham & Christina
6-23-34	Elsie[d]	Isack & Mary	Adr. Bratt, Corn. Busscher
7-12-34	Abraham		
4-4-35	Lidia	Jacob & Diever	Seth & Sara
	Sara	Abraham & Dina	Hendrick & Rebecka
7-2-35	Petrus		
	Brant		
9-14-35	Hendrick		
	Christina		
	child	Hendrick & Christina	Lucas & Maria
7-[sic]26 -36	Catharina	Jacob	Jac. Hilten, Eliz. Goeway
4-10-37	Elyzabeth	Moses & Margariet	Simon & Maria
6-19-37	Catharina	Cornelis & Anna	Aaron & Canastazy
	Gideon	Brant & Rebecca	Joseph & Maria
8-19-37	Ezras	Pieter & Zelia	
1-15-38	Elizabeth	Isaac & Maria	Joseph & Catharine
5-11-38	Johannes	Hendrik & Christina	Johannes E. Wendel Elizabeth Wendel

Date[b]	Baptismal Name	Parents, Indian Name or Information	Sponsors
5-7-41	Zara	Isaac & Maria	Joseph & Catharina
	Josua	Hendrick & Anna	Simon & Maria
4-29-44	Alida	Joseph & Catharine	Hendrik & Jacomyn
	Ephraim	Seth & Margaret	Catharine, Ephraim Wendell
7-10-48	Seth	Johannes & Maria	Nicolaes Lydius, Margaret
7-14-48	Petrus	Abraham & Hester	Niccas & Sarah
12-25-48	Catharina	Jacob Sogwinjewane & Mary Magdalena	Nich. I. & Margarieta Is. Lydius
7-23-49	Anna	Seth & Christina	Seth & Anna
12-31-49	Neeltje	Petrus & Maria	Henderick & Leah
	Christina	Seth & Maria	Ciljaen & Margarita
7-12-50	Maria	Abram & Leah	Moses & Margaret
2-20-51	Gideon	Nicas & Neeltie	Nicas & Christina
7-14-51	Neeltje	Jacob & Magdalana	Cornelis & Neeltjn
8-28-54	Lawrence	Lawrence & Elizabeth	(also in St. Peter's)
10-6-54	Maria	Johannes & Maria	Hendrik & Maria
10-31-56	Nicolaes	Andrew Montour & Sara	Martinus & Sara Maria Lydius

Indian Marriages in the Albany Church Records[a]

Date[b]	Spouse's Name	Spouse's Name
7-7-21	Abraham	Christina
7-22-21	Seth	Margaret
2-10-22	Hendrick	Margaret
1-12-47	Johannes son of Seth	Maria dau. of Aaron
	Joseph son of Hendrick	Christina dau. of Seth

[a]The First Church in Albany records were printed, with certain exceptions, in the *Holland Society Yearbooks*. See Chapter 1, Note 19, for details. Microfilms of the church records (First [Reformed] Church

of Albany, Clinton Square) are also available at the NY State Library, Albany (AFM 229). These microfilms include the Elder Trotter transcriptions of the baptism and marriage records but do not include the original baptism records from 1700-25.

[b]The numeric dates shown here are for the 1600s and 1700s and follow the month-day-year system. Thus 12-27-89 would be December 27, 1689, and 6-12-12 would be June 12, 1712.

[c]This may be a mistake, since the individuals appear to be Hendrick Tejonihokarawa and his wife Rebecca. Isaac Kip was an Albany trader. I believe that Dominie Van Driessen may have left incomplete a second entry, that of one of Isaac Kip's slaves, just after the baptism of an Indian child. Alternatively, this could be a slave baptism, not necessarily of Africans, since Indians were also slaves during this time.

[d]This could be a slave baptism.

First Reformed Dutch Church, Schenectady,

Indian Baptisms and Marriages, 1698-1774[a]

Date[b]	Baptismal/ Sp. Name	Parents, Indian Name, or Spouse Name	Sponsors
10-19-98	Christine	Jan Onoda & Susanna	Gideon & Rebecca
12-28-98	Iosine	Sander & Christine	
	Marta	Johannes & Rebecca	
1-9-00	Joseph	Onigoheriago & Lohwisa	Joseph
5-5-00	Lowisa	Onigogriage & Lowisa	Maset
	Mary	Casseron & Canastatsie	Mary Groot
	Hendrick	Annigagtahouwe & Anna	Cathryn
9-1-00	Christina	Esseron Kanderagtaharre [Neeltie crossed out]	[Anna crossed out]
	David	Adam Senooqquara & Unisse	Anna
	Abraham	Brant Saquainwaraghton & Margrita	Sara
10-5-00	Arie	Maria	Hendrik
	Zara	Maria (same)	Josephus
	Maria	Zara	Hindrik
	Catrina	Zara (same)	Josephus
	James	Maria	Zara
	Rachel	Maria (same)	Canastade
	Kornelus	Arie & Catrina	Rachel
	Hendrik	Arie & Catrina	Marta
12-21-00	Hendrik	Tosistaron	Hindrik
	Aaron	Tagowasce	Joseph
	Rachel		Martha
	Margrieta	Horide	Jakkemeintje
	Catrina	Naetzioni	Catrina
	Jackementje	Ryaende	Jackemeintje

223

Date[b]	Baptismal/ Sp. Name	Parents, Indian Name, or Spouse Name	Sponsors
12-21-00	Maria Christina	Christina Jackameintje	Maria Christina
12-25-00	Elizabet Christina Jackamentje Margrieta	o[sic] Elisabet & Laurens Elisabet & Laurens Elisabet & Laurens	Rachel Canastasee Jakkemeintje Margrita
1/2-1701	Rebecca	Heindaggon & Aandien	Jackmeintje
3-2-01	Neeltje	Rebecka & Johans	Neeltje & Esras
4-19-01	Alida	Annourigta	Alida
	Sara	Kanedkte	Sara
	Margrita	Kanigko	Sara
	Sara	Karigwaderos	Sara
	Christina	Dearennisse	Sara
	Maria	Kariwaenion	Maria
	Katarina	Attaenriagse	Katarina
	Daniel	Katarina	Katarina
	Grieta	Raweton	Loise
	Eunice	Karistasia	Eunice
	Anna	Thanigwanege	Anna
	Hindrik	Anna	Hindrik
	Epraim	Anna (same)	Katrina
	Lea		Lea
	Gesina	Siniregkwisla	Gesina
	Maria Magdalena		
		Kakangserraha	Maria Magdalena
	Isaak	Maria Magdalena	Isaak Swits
	Johannes	Teiaiagse	Johannes
	Anna	Teiaiagse	Loisa
	Grita	Deiudhondawae	Margrita
	Hindrick	Dieudhondawae	Hindrick
	Adam	Deiudhodawae	Adam Vroman
	Essron	Maria	Essron

in kerke Og'niondage (or *Ogniendage*)

| 5-23-01 | Zara | Nigaronda | Kanastasie |

Date[b]	Baptismal/ Sp. Name	Parents, Indian Name, or Spouse Name	Sponsors
5-23-01	Elizabet	Zara	Kanastasie
	Johannes	O [sic]	Kornelius
	Albertus	Nohogsage	Esras
	Abraham	Sakhowanne	Brant
	Harmanus	Kadogo	Esras
	Simon	Kanathonka	Simon
	Josua	Kargigko	Jacob
	Djver	Tiere	Zara
	Arent	Sinienkwine	Asaph
	Gesina	Kaierinigtage	Christina
	Grieta	Joseph	Margreta
	Zacharias	Haiugwagta	Marta

1701 Admitted as members:
> Hendrick & his wife **Catrina**
> Brant & his wife **Margreta**
> Esras & his wife **Kanastasse**
> Amos & his wife **Kanastadse**
> Ezras & his wife **Neeltie**
> Jacob & his wife **Jakkameintje**
> Ruth [Rut] & his wife **Maria**
> Lucas & his wife **Maria**
> Sanders & his wife **Christina**
> Johannes & his wife **Rebekka**
> Johannes & his wife **Louisa**
> Isaak & his wife **Eunice**
> Petrus & his wife **Anna**
> Arieseras & his wife **Katerina**

Date[b]	Baptismal/ Sp. Name	Parents, Indian Name, or Spouse Name	Sponsors
7-13-01	Abraham	Degaragkwoniako	Kornelis
	Jakob	Anatshonti	Adoni
	Petrus	Royaner	Johannes
	Margreta	Ayeendas	Margreta
9-28-01	Maria	Agadsagadda	Margrita
	Arent	Onaaste	Leukas
	Maria	Isaak	Maria

Date[b]	Baptismal/ Sp. Name	Parents, Indian Name, or Spouse Name	Sponsors
11-25-01	**Margreta**	Essras & Kanastase	Laurens Van der Volgen & Volkye Simonse Veeder
	Anna	Sanders & Christien	Iakkameintje
	Thomas	Maria	Amos
	Susanke	Debora	Catrina
	Henoch	**Aglonthaenra**	Hindrik
	Petrus	**Ionniarowanne**	Johannes
12-26-01	**Ruth**		
2-8-02	**Koor Sinnehanawagt** married to **Rachel**		
	Isaak Dekaneedsiaesere married to **Anna Sioddooska**		
5-10-02	**Reinier**	Lauren & Elizabet	Laurens van der Volgen & Grieta Heemstaat
	Jan	Petrus & Anna	Rachel & Margrita
	Neeltie	Aaeniesrase [Ariesras] & Catarina	Lowisa & Ariaente Vissers
	Ariaentje	Arien & Mariane	Anna
	Aletta	Christina	Marta
	Grietje	Arent & Angenieta	Jakameintje
5-30-02	**Giliamus**	Joseph & Jakkamein	Lauren Vander Volgen & Maria
7-10-02	**Pierre** married to **Maria**		
7-19-02	**Johannes**	[Joseph] Thehanoragkwa & Anna	Neeltje
10-3-02	**Sebeveus**	Johannes & Maria	Jakob Kanikooah & Catrina
	Sander	Isaac & Anna	Diver Wendel
10-5-02	**Jesaias**	Anna	Eva Swart
	Maria	**Diaiaenuenondsron** [obs.]	Catrina
10/12-1702	**Willem**	Maria	Jacob Kanikoah & Kanesisy neoni
4-17-03	**Margrieta**	Esras & Neeltie	Sara
	Jacob	Matrees	Jacob Kanikooh
5-8-03	**Kornelia**	Brant & Margrieta	Catarina

Date[b]	Baptismal/ Sp. Name	Parents, Indian Name, or Spouse Name	Sponsors
5-30-03	Elizibet	Aieer [Arie?] & Catarina	Jan Pariss & [his wife] Maria
7-4-03	Barent	Jacob & Jackamientje	Barent Wemp Volkye Symonsen

at Oniagrage:

8-15-03	Rebecka	Johannes & Rebecka	
	Eva	Lukas & Christiena	
	Hendrikus	Jan & Sara	Jan & Christien
10-3-03	Maria	Johannes & Rebecca	Johannes & Maria
10-1703	Sara	Thioheraronge & Nisa	Joseph & Saerai
1/2-1704	Divertje	Sianigora & Anna	Johans Sanders Glen & Divertje Wendel
3-5-04	Lysabet	Katarina	Lysabet Philipsen
	Barend	Isaak & Janisse	Alida
4-15-04	Hendrik	Louris & Mariaiose	Catarina
	Maddelena	Jacob Kanikooah & Trivetthe	Maria
7-8-04	Zacharias	Raksarion & Sara	Jackameintje
7-9-04	Rachel	Enos & Grietje	Christien
10-4-04	Jan Aerahookto married to Sara Konhanegtani		
	Cornelis (or Kees) Takonnigwannege married to Magdalena Keragkwinon		
	Jackob Kanikook married to Sara Nionoendaes		
12-23-04	Sara	Laurens Delagger & Elisabeth	Jan & Kanastasie
4-7-05	Moses	Joseph & Jackomeintje	Catrina
	Esras	Esras & Kanastaesy	Gosina
	Anna	Tehanogiagkhwa & Angenita	Jackameintje
7-1-05	Maria	Arien & Maria anna	Tam Smit & Maria Kobes

(Here ends Freeman baptisms)

11-9-07	Josua	Esras & Canastasi	Henrik & Catharina
	Pieter	Jacob & Jacomyn	Harmen Van Slyk & Rebecca

Date[b]	Baptismal/ Sp. Name	Parents, Indian Name, or Spouse Name	Sponsors
2-8-08	Catharina	Arij Egnidea & Maria Kajada	Esras Sonihomane Canastasi Koukoni
	Anna	Johannes Tahagwende & Josina Kastuie	Henrik & Anna Tejonhohawage
	Margaret	Petrus Katsjehadi & Anna Kaharadask	Margriet Kariootho
5-26-08	Catharina	Abraham Dsikereha & Catharina Dewadewanagkwa	Gerrit Symonse & Tryntje Rottings
10-30-10	Christina	Jacob Depothonthode Jacomyn Chagteljouny	Neeltje Thejouru- thawihong & Esras Kannerachthahere
10-19-11	Ariaantjen	Esras & Neeltjen	Ariaantjen Wendels
	Anna	Seth & Sara	Gidion & Dorkas
	Maria	Cornelius & Maria	Amos & Kanastazi
	Thomas	Catryn	Amos & Kanastazi
	Maria	Cornelis & Catrina	Rachel
	Neeltjen	Anthony & Sara	Sara
10-21-11	Thomas	Maria	Martha
	Susanna	Maria	Susanna
	Maria		Rachel
	Abraham	Angeniet	Sara
2-13-12	Martha	Zander & Christina	Sara
	Jacob	Symen & Christina	Margriet
	Cornelis	Janisse	Johannes & Maria
	Elsjen	Maria	Rebecka
	Maria	Thomas	Sara
6-20-12	Daniel married to Elizabeth		

Petrus Van Driessen en Albany gedoopt [baptized]:

6-21-12	Martha	Johannes & Lossyse	Cornelis & Martha
	Alida	Onihoanhoundi & Anna	Cornelis & Catryna
	Margaret	Onihoanhoundi & Anna	Esras & Neeltie
	Cornelis	Onihoenhoundi & Anna	Griete Vroman &
	kryn		Adam Vroman

Date[b]	Baptismal/ Sp. Name	Parents, Indian Name, or Spouse Name	Sponsors
6-21-12	Catryna	Onihoanhoundi & Anna	Tryntie Vroman & Barent Vroman
	Cornelis	Canatasay & Souttyh	Aergald & Annehe
	Philippius	Abram & Maria	Philip Schuyler & Marya
	Maria	Ersras & Maria	Esras & Anna
	Susanna	Oteyn & Cateryn	Amos & Canastasy
	Laurens	Onichtanerongh & Jacomyn	Canasthasy & Amos
	Anna	Tihuherarounjh & Sara	Elias & Lelia
	Hendrik	Tihuheraroungh & Sara	Hendrik & Anna
	Sara	Theonthehy & Maria	Antony & Tarrohay
	Thomas	Willem & Alida	Simon & Anna
	Catryn	Eoawanougrougany & Griette	Johannes
	Jonathan	Thomas & Chrystyna	Jacob & Susanna
	Dievertie	Zyohanasawon & Maria	Johannes & Jacomyn
10-[1-8]-12	Rachel	Simon & Anna	Arent Zroman & Slyntie Zroman
10-9-12	Jacomyn	Scanadhesse	Esras & Jacomyn
6-29-46	Harmen	Henrik & Christina	Harmen Vedder & Annatje Vedder
8-31-46	Arent	Nikes & Sara	Arent Stastens & Maria
	Maria	Daniel & Neeltie	Meders Wempl & Jacomyn
5-20-47	Peter	David & his wife	Daniel & his wife
6-1-47	Seth	Michael Montour & Hester	Paulus & Hester
6-3-47	Catharine	Nicas Brant & Margritje	Brant & Christina
6-21-47	Louris	Moses & Margaret	Lucas & Margariet
11-4-47	Jacomyntje	Lucas & Margaret	Hendrik & Anna
3-19-48	David	Isaak & Elizabet	Sara Fisher, Johannes

Date[b]	Baptismal/ Sp. Name	Parents, Indian Name, or Spouse Name	Sponsors
2-12-49	**Abraham** married to **Lea**		
5-18-49	**Margaret**	Hans	Moses & Margaret
5-21-49	**Isak**	Thomas & Catharine	Isack, Elisabet, David
6-1-49	**Louris** married to **Jacomyntje**		
6-9-49	**David** married to **Maddelene Creyn**		
7-25-49	**Creyn**	Johannes Creyn & Neeltie	Magdalene
3-11-50	**Lea**	Lucas & Margaret	Albert van Slyk & Jesina
9-29-51	**Nicolaas**	Nicolaas & Rebecca	Arent Stevens & Elisabet Coulons
12-11-57	**Hester**	Hendrik & Mary	Jacob & Hester
6-30-59	**Jacob**	Johannes & Marie	Johannes & Margaret
	Elisabeth	Ruth & Annus	
2-18-60	**Isaac**	Joseph & Jacomyn	
5-22-62	**Isaac**	Pieter & Eva	Christina
6-15-62	**Isaac**	Adam & Susanna	Jacob & Anna
1-21-63	**Jacob**	Jacob & Anna	Joseph & Chrystien
12-29-63	**Joseph**	Thomas & Catharine	Joseph & Mary
6-5-64	**Isaac**	Isaac & Lydia	Aaron & Catarine
6-28-64	**Pieter**	Pieter & Eva	Magdalene
12-7-64	**Thomas**	Pieter & Mary	Thomas & Magdalene
12-14-64	**Abraham**	Adam & Susanna	Christina
1-27-65	**Hendrick** married to **Sarah**		
	Alsook Aaron married to **Susanna**		
11-9-65	**Aaron** married to **Anna**		
9-15-66	**Moses**	Pieter & Eva	Mary
12-1-67	**Anna**	David & Sara	Lewis & Anna
12-3-67	**Killaen**	Brant & Mary	Christien
5-28-68	**Adam**	Adam & Lydea	Margaret
5-2-69	**Catharine**	Adam & Susanna	Joseph & Caterina
10-16-69	**Isaac**	David & Sara	Isaac & Catarien
5-23-70	**Pieter**	Brant & Mary	Adam

Date[b]	Baptismal/ Sp. Name	Parents, Indian Name, or Spouse Name	Sponsors
7-22-70	**Elizabeth**	Adam & Lydea	Elizabeth
10-13-70	**Elias**	Seth & Christina	Mary
11-17-70	**Johannes**	Johannes & Chrysteen	David & Lydia
	Anna	Joseph & Mary	Mary
11-28-70	**Catreen**	Abraham Kreyn & Jacomyn	Elisabeth
2-21-73	**Pieter**	Pieter & Susanna	Pieter & Jannitje
12-14-74	**Magdalene**	Willem & Anna	Joseph Montour & Catrina

[a]Records of the First Reformed Church at Schenectady, New York, 1683-1881, are located at the New York State Library, Albany. The original handwritten records (3 volumes) were filmed by the Genealogical Society of Utah in 1941 (#0017910) and in 1968 (Call Number: US/CAN Film Area 0534207) and are available through the Latter-Day Saints' libraries.

[b]The numeric dates shown here are for the 1600s and 1700s and follow the month-day-year system. Thus 10-19-98 would be October 19, 1698 and 9-1-00 would be September 1, 1700.

Fort Hunter Indian Records, 1712-1759[a]

Date[b]	Baptismal/ Sp. Name	Parents, Indian Name, Age or Spouse Name	Sponsors

Records from the Reverend Andrews:

11-23-12	**Aaron**	Peter & Cornelia—infant	
	Cornelius	Sachtachrogi & Anne—inft.	
1-11-13	**Catharius**	Simon & Josiena—inft.	
	Elizabeth	Onagsakearet & Maria—2 years old	
	Luke	Phillin & Anne—4 years old	
	Ezra	about 22 years old	
1-25-13	**Solomon**	Honeseras Tinhhoraroungewe & Sara—2 years old	
	Anne	Uttagarondagourigh & Anne— 4 years old	
	Sarah	Uttagarondagourigh & wife— infant	
	Zachariah	Joseph Sagot & Hannah—4 years	
	Hannah	Joseph Sagot & Hannah—2 yrs. old	
2-22-13	**Aron**	Ezra and his wife—instant [infant?]	
3-8-13	**Mary**	Ezra & Maria	

Here begins the Barclay Register

4-13-35	**Jacob**	Ezras Teganderassa & Elisabeth	Esras Senior, Mary
	John	Peter Ogoghsano- gethta & Christina	Moses Adiogarondi, Hannah Guanthoha
	Henry	Thomas Sewatsese & Ester	Aron Osaragihta, Mary Teonuleri
	Mary	Cannassware & Margaret	Andrew Agerondongwas, Deborah Teonoonaron

Date[b]	Baptismal/ Sp. Name	Parents, Indian Name, or Spouse Name	Sponsors
4-13-35	**Aaron**	Adam Tegedoonrek & Christina	Thomas Butler, Margaret Gwaghtarani
	Sarah	Joseph Sadagayeenda & Chatarine	Joseph Clement, Anna Clement, Mary Clement
	David	Cornelis Thaneghwa- nege & Anna	Simon Waghnekar- agkwa & wife Gesina
	Aron son of Adam Tegedoonrek deceased		
6-19-35	**Lucas Jughahiese** married to **Margaret Teongosese**		
	Abraham Sghetagearat married to **Jacamine Kaghtenoone**		
7-6-35	son	**Petrus**	
	Joseph	Michael Montour & wife	Joseph Clement, Anna Clement
	Adam Tegedoonrek died about this time		
	Isaack married to **Elizabeth**		
	Petrus married to __		
10-5-35	**Seth**	Paul and Mary	Seth
	Seth married to **Mary**		
	Moses Nowadarike married to __		
	David married to **Sarah**		
12-28-35	**Aron**	Aron Oserageghte & Margaret	Aria, Esras Senior, Anna Aron's sister
	Abraham	Isack Anoghsoohte & Elisabeth	John Segahowane, Brant Kanagaradunkwa, Cath- arina Tagganakwari
1-15-36	**Elizabeth** (by Mr. Ale)	Henry & Anna	Thomas Sewatsese, Mary Conostajee
	Abel married to **Mary** (by Revd. Mr. Ale)		
2-1736	**Henry** married to **Margaret**, Area's granddaughter		
	Isack Simonsson married to **Mary** Gideon's daughter (by Dr. Van Dressen)		
3-3-36	**Gideon**	Joseph & Mary	B. Stoniston, Lois
6-2-36	**Simon**	David Tewaghjewasha & Catharine	Simon, Jacamine Tagwanagon

Date[b]	Baptismal/ Sp. Name	Parents, Indian Name, or Spouse Name	Sponsors
6-2-36	**Paul**	Daniel Aasharego & Elisabeth	Paul Tehoghwhen-geronte, wife Ester
7-18-36	**Rut**	John & Mary	Simon & Margaret Kinsigoo's wife

Henry married to **Mary**
Lucas Jughahahese, **Margaret** his wife, and **Catharine** Stoniston's daughter admitted to communion

| 1-9-37 | **Neeltie** | Abel & Mary | Esras Sr., wife Neeltie |
| 2-4-37 | **Sarah** | Stoniston & Mary | Hendrick, Anna Clement |

Killiane son of Seth Sr. married to **Catharine** Stoniston's daughter

2-12-37	**Jacob**	**Owhensiawane** aged c. 30 ba. at Connajughare Castle	Esras Senior, Abraham of Connajore
3-12-37	**Peter**	Lucas Jughahiese & Margaret	
4-7-37	**Henry**	Seth & Margaret	These by the Revd.
	Isack	Christian	Mr. Ale

Since the Return of Mr. Barclay:

| 5-10-38 | **Joseph** | Jacob Owhensiawane | Cornels. Thanighwanege Moses Uttijagaroondi Mary |

| 7-2-38 | **Seth** and **Mary** his wife and **Lawrence**'s wife admitted to communion |

| 9-3-38 | **Abraham** | Thomas Sewaghsasa & his wife | Lucas Jughahisese, John Sajahawane, Mary Kaheghtaginhase |

| 9-6-38 | **Brant** married to **Lydia** |
| 9-10-38 | **Peter** | Thomas & Catharine | David, Rut, Susannah |

Thomas married to **Catharine**

10-11-38	**Brant** married to **Christina**
1-14-39	**Catharine**	Aron Oseragighte & Margaret	Isack Anoghsookte, wife Elizbeth, Canasteje
1-28-39	**Cornelius** married to **Neeltie**

Date[b]	Baptismal/ Sp. Name	Parents, Indian Name, or Spouse Name	Sponsors
2-4-39	Peter	Sander Kensiagoo & Margaret	Brant Kanagaradunkwa, Moses Nowadariha, Christina Brant's wife
2-18-39	Jacamine	Kayingwerigoo & wife	Joseph Sayoenwese, Mary Kaheghtginhoss
	Johannes Shadidaghko married to **Matin**		
2-25-39	**David Dewayhgiwaghse** married to **Chatharine Oyogoon**		
4-29-39	Catharine	Hendrick & Anna	Margaret Kinsiago, Margaret Jughhahwe
	Sarah	Esras &Elizabeth Teganderasse	Esras Kanenaghtaghare, Seth Karonkyaghragh-kwa & wife Margaret
5-20-39	**Sarah** daughter of Seth buried.		
6-5-39	daughter of Jacob Owhessawane buried. N.B. Two more children of same died this Spring when I was absent.		
6-6-39	**Peter** son of Sander Kinsiago buried.		
6-8-39	**Gesina Tekarrirahon**, aged about 90 years, buried.		
7-8-39	**Abraham** Oneida married to **Christina** Oneida and both baptized		Abraham Canostens & & wife Gesina
	Chatharina	Abraham & Christina	Susannah
9-30-39	Margaret	Christian &Margaret	Gedeon Dewighnidoge, Catharina, Mary Teyonaklyeri
	Seth	David & Sarah	Seth Karonhyaghongh-kwa, Moses Nowadarita, Matarina
10-5-39	son of Daniel Asharego buried.		
10-11-39	**Seth** son of David buried.		
10-14-39	Jacamine	Brant Kaweghnoke & Lydia	Seth Sietstaraonde Karihoge, Mary his dau., Jacamine Brant mother
1-13-40	John	Reynier & wife	Brant Kanadaragunkwa, Moses Utiyagaroondi,
	Rachel	Reynier & wife	Jacamine Kaghteriooni,

Date[b]	Baptismal/ Sp. Name	Parents, Indian Name, or Spouse Name	Sponsors
			Christina Brant's wife
2-10-40	Joseph	Brant Karonkyatikha & Alida	Ezras Senior, Gideon, Mary his daughter
2-24-40	Christina	Cornelius Thanighwan- nege & Anna	Hendrick & wife Christina
	Cornelius	Oderagaurrie (captive, aged 20)	Hendrick, Cornelius Thanighwanege
3-11-40	David the Indian died about this time.		
5-10-40	Moses	Petrus Sagoghsena- gighte & Christina	Moses Addiyagaroonde, Sara
	Martha	Jacob Owhensiawane & wife	Gideon Dewignidoge, Sarah Kahickgoah
5-16-40	Martha daughter of Jacob Owhenawane buried.		
5-25-40	Catharine	Lucas Jughhahiese & Margaret	Johanis Segehowane, Abraham Soherianough, Canastaje
5-26-40	Aron Soghoronnadagawe married to Catherine Kaniharhas		
5-29-40	Catharine daughter of Lucas Jughhahiese buried.		
6-29-40	Kiliane	Seth & Margaret	Kiliane, Joseph Catharine
7-6-40	Jonathan	Paul Tegaghnewadi- ghon & Sara	Abraham Kaneghstase, David Kahowa & wife Susanna
	David	Peter Teyoronkyathe & Mary	Isack Sinhagtontho, David Soregwaghskon, Margaret Garonkyaghkon
8-14-40	Cornelius	John Shaddidaghton & wife Martina	
8-18-40	Lot	Joseph Thahoweanoghte & Margaret	Abraham Kanostens, Brant Jogawe, wife Rebecca
9-2-40	Jacamine	Moses Nowaderika & Margaret	Gedion Sr., Jacomine, Sr., Christina Brant's wife

Date[b]	Baptismal/ Sp. Name	Parents, Indian Name, or Spouse Name	Sponsors
9-28-40	John	David & Catharine	Kiliaen, Joseph, Catharine
	Jacob	Jacob Jorane & Eve	Lasarus Ajenowiesaks, Elizabeth wife of Daniel Asharego
	Mary	Michael Montour & wife	Ezras Teganderasse, Anna Clement, Mary
10-9-40	Anthony	Seth & Mary	Seth Dekarihoge, Cornelius, wife Neeltie
	Zacharias	Cornelia	Sander Kinsiago & Margaret Jughahise
10-26-40	Mary	Cornelius & Neeltie	Seth, Canastaje
12-25-40	Lydia	Kiliane & Catharine	Seth Sietstararne, Sara his wife
3-1-41	Abraham	Abraham Asharego & Margaret	Abraham Tiurhadagh-riyo, wife Ester, Peter Serehowane
	Margaret	Anthony Oniyingodon & Margaret	John Garihotea, Susanna Kanighsentha, Jannitie Kannoenoah
3-15-41	Cornelius	Joseph Decasonyorea & Margaret	Araon Oseragighte, Cornelius Thanigh-wanege, Catharina
5-24-41	Thomas	Joseph Seyoenwese & Mary	Lucas Jughahiese, & wife Margaret
5-31-41	David	Hendrick & Christina	Kiliane & wife Catharine
	Jacob	Johannes & Mary	Mary Sajoenwese
6-21-41	Paul	Henricus & Margaret Margaret died in childbed.	Paulus
6-25-41	Henderick	Nicus & Sara Kanaghkwase	Henderick Kaghsogh-yaetha, wife Christina
	Jacob	Peter Kanagagrongo & Mary	Gidion Sehonjowane, wife Catharine
	Neeltie	Petrus Serehowane & Mary	Rutgert Kenderago, wife Ester

Date[b]	Baptismal/ Sp. Name	Parents, Indian Name, or Spouse Name	Sponsors
7-18-41	Mary	Daniel Asharego & Elisabeth	Aron Oseragighte, Canestagie
	Lucas	Jacob Tagaghroryaethe & Kagoghyadon	Lucas Jughahiese, wife Margaret, Cornelius Tewanighwanege
	Jacob	Peter Tehonawaghkwan- geraghkwa & Margaret	Jacob, Jacamine Kaghteneni
7-20-41	Asa married to Cornelia		
7-28-41	Seth married Sara		
9-3-41	Moses	Lucas Jughahiese & Margaret	Lawrence, Susanna
9-20-41	Hendrick	Jacob Owensiawane	Kahickgo, Elizabeth Asharego's wife
10-4-41	---	Jan & Anna	Aron Oseragighte, Alida
10-18-41	William married to Mary Magdalene Paul married to Christina		
1-3-42	Jacob	Isaac & Elizabeth	John Sejehowane & wife
1-28-42	Christina	Peter Tehonwaghwan- geraghkwa & Margaret	Lot Thoroghyonge, Ester Kanoghserightha, Maria
4-23-42	John	Aron & Margaret	Isaac Anoghsookte, Alida
4-24-42	Adam	Brant & Lydia	Seth Sietetarare, Esras Sr., daughter Margaret
5-8-42	Paul son of Paul buried.		
5-9-42	son	Paul & Ester	Abraham Canostens, Gesina
6-13-42	Ester	Jacob & ---	Hendrick Peterie, Gesina
	Brant	Brant & Christina	Seth, his wife Margaret
7-11-42	Margaret	Peter & Mary	Nicus, Gesina, Sarah
	Susanna	Ester	Cornelius Thanighwa- nege, Catharina, Alida

Isaac married to Magdalene
Aront married to Magdalene
Daniel married to Sarah

Date[b]	Baptismal/ Sp. Name	Parents, Indian Name, or Spouse Name	Sponsors
1-16-43	Mary	Moses Nowadorika	Mary
2-19-43	A daughter of Noah was buried.		
4-24-43	David	David & Angeniehe	Esras Sr., Moses Adiayaroondi,Margaret
5-29-43	Eve	Petrus Patrey	Seth, Neeltie
6-5-43	Ann daughter of Hendrick & Ann buried.		
7-11-43	Abraham married to Catharina Kinsiagoe's daughter		
7-12-43	Jacob	Isaac	Joseph, Catharine
1-8-44	Cornelius	Michael Montour	John Sejehowane, Brant, Margaret
1-15-44	Henry	Asaph & Cornelia	Michael Montour, Rynier, Kisiago's wife
1-22-44	Seth	Kiliaen & Catharine	Seth Sr., daughter Lydia
2-4-44	Cornelius	Aront & Magdalene	Thomas, Abraham, Canostaje
	Paul	David & Sarah	Seth Caronkjcent, Sarah
	Catharine	Lazarus & Mary	Rineer, Agnes
2-5-44	---	Joseph	
2-19-44	Chatarine	Peter Serehowane	Joseph, Neeltie
2-20-44	John	Thomas, Brant's son	Seth, Nicus, Alida
5-27-44	David	Nicus	Paulus, Seth, Neeltie
	John	Paulus & Christina	Hendrick Petersse, Brant, Mary Peterse
	Peter	Cornelius & Neeltie	Cornelius Thanighwa- nege, Abraham Peterse, Mary S
	Thomas	Christina	William, Christian, Gesina
	Sarah	Jacob Owhensiawane	Joseph, Rebecca, Sarah
6-10-44	Sarah	Margaret	Daniel, Sarah
6-17-44	Cornelius	Joseph Sonhahtowane	Cornelius, Anna
[prob. all	David	John Seghnegearat	Abraham, Catharine
Oneidas]	Anna	Cornelius Kaghneghtagan	James, Magdalene
7-15-44	Mary	Petrus & Mary	Nicholaus, Mary
	Magdalene	Rut & Ester	Abraham, Gesina

Date[b]	Baptismal/ Sp. Name	Parents, Indian Name, or Spouse Name	Sponsors
7-22-44	**Margaret**	Hendrick & Leah	Aron Oseragighta, Mary
9-9-44	daughter	Lucas Jughahiese	Moses Nowadarika & wife
10-7-44	**John Quaqua** married to **Neeltie**		
10-14-44	son	Isaac Onoghsoohte	
10-23-44	**Brant**	Brant Junior	Seth Karihoge, Seth Junior, Mary
1-13-45	**Peter**	Aron & Margaret	Brant, Margaret
	Eva	Rebecca	John Sejehowane
2-10-45	**Isaac**	Hendrick & Anna	Simon, Gesina
2-17-45	**Nicus**	John Guagua	Seth, Joseph, Alida
2-24-45	**Killiaen** was buried.		
2-28-45	**Nicus** son of John Guagua died.		
5-26-45	2 children out of Old Simon's family buried.		
5-30-45	**Simon** son of the Blind Woman buried.		
6-20-45	**Seth**	Jacob Ohwhensiawane	Seth, Anthony's son & his wife
	---	Abraham & Catharine	
6-23-45	**Elizabeth**	Brant Karonkyahkha	Abraham Canostens, Elizabeth
	Nicus	**Onweriyongsere** aged about 25 years	Thomas Thayonusyo
	Anna	**Kaniyoghsawere** (aged 14)	Joseph Onondagera
	Christian	adopted son of Brant	Christian, Jannetie
6-30-45	**Sarah**	John___	Daniel Asharego, Sarah Paulus's
9-15-45	---	Moses Nowadarika	
	---	Petrus Sagoghsenagighte	
	Elizabeth	daughter of ___ Wolf ___	
10-10-45	**Jacobus**	Joseph & Margaret (at Albany)	Adam, Jury, Mary
10-16-45	**Jacob**	**Sayighranoka** Tuscarora aged c. 40	Hendrick Thayanoge, Abraham Kanostens, Mary

Date[b]	Baptismal/ Sp. Name	Parents, Indian Name, or Spouse Name	Sponsors
1-12-46	**Seth**	Jacob Tagwaynont	Seth (Mary—scratched out), Magdalene
	David	Aron	David Laroy, Isaack, Elizabeth
1-19-46	daughter	Joseph at Connajughare	Daniel
2-2-46	**Joseph**	John Kanadagaye & Mary	Moses, Thomas, Canasteje
	Elizabeth	Petrus & Mary	Aront, Elizabeth, Magdalene

Here begins Rev. Ogilvie's Register of Indian Children and Marriages

4-22-50	**Ezras**	John & Anna	
6-3[5?]-50	**Sarah**	Lawrance & Anna	
6-7-50	**Daniel** married to **Margaret** daughter of _		
	Petrus married to **Anna** daughter of Kanatagai		
6-17-50	**Esras**		
2-2-51	**Anna**	John & Anna	
	Peter	infant captive from the Flat-Heads [Catawbas]	
2-17-51	**Isaac**	infant, names of parents forgot	
3-3-51	**Cornelius**	Hendrick & Magdalene—child	
3-17-51	**Lawrance** married to **Anna Holmes** daughter of a white man		
10-6-51	**Sausannah**	Thomas & Cathrine	
	Sarah	Moses & Margaret	
	Hannah	Seth & a Flat-Head Squaw	
1-19-52	**Johannes**	John & Wari [Mary]	Seth & Mary
2-16-52	**Mary**	Indian child of Oneida, baptized at Canijohare	
2-23-52	**Wari**	parents not present	
	Hester	parents not present	
2-27-52	**Christian**		
	[Christina]	Arent & a squaw of Canijoharie	
2-28-52	**Elizabeth**	Petrus & Anna	
3-2-52	**Joseph** son of Margaret widow married to		
	Catharine daughter of Anna widow		
	Arie son of Hendr. married to		
	Lydia adopted daughter of Daniel		

Date[b]	Baptismal/ Sp. Name	Parents, Indian Name, or Spouse Name	Sponsors

3-2-52   **Watijaas** son of a French Indian married to
         Wari daughter of Seth a sachem
3-15-52 **Christian**
         [Christina] Cornelius & Susannah
6-8-52   **Joseph**   Esras & Anna
8-9-52   **Zacharias**   parents forgot
3-4-53   **Hendrick**   a French Indian & Cathrine—
                         aged 14 years
         Jacob   Margt. widow of Lykas &
                         Brant of Canijohare
         Jacob married to **Margaret** both from Kiahega
3-18-53 **Ananias** a French Indian married to
                         Magdalene datr. of Seth a Sachem
                         from this castle [Tionondoroge]
7-6-53   **Anthony**   Kelian
9-9-53   **Brandt** a Sachem of this Castle married to
                         Margaret a widow from Canijohare Castle
9-16-53 **Joseph**   Jacob & Mary Jestarhare's daughter
9-20-53 **Jacob**   Arie & Lydia
10-22-53 **Thos.**   Thos. & Cathr.
11-24-53 **Cathr.**   Lawrence & Anna Holmes
         Margaret   Joseph & Jacomine
         Elizabeth   Nicholas & Anna
2-17-54 **Kellian**   Joshua & Margaret
         Lawrence   Nickus & Margaret
         Mary   Seth's Hans & Mary
         Jacomine   Watijaas & Mary
2-24-54 **Mary**   Cornelius & Susanna
         Hendrick   an aged Indian a Captive from the
                         Southern Nations
         Isaac married to **Catharine** widow of Joseph
6-30-54 **Nicholas**   Hendrick & Rachel of
                         Canajohare, baptized at Albany
         David   Petrus & Anna daughter of Kanatagoi
7-27-54 **Jacob** married to **Catharine** [both of Tionondoroge]

Date[b]	Baptismal/ Sp. Name	Parents, Indian Name, or Spouse Name	Sponsors
7-29-54	**Joseph** married to **Elizabeth**		
8-28-54	**Lawrence**	Lawrence & Elizabeth	
10-7-54	**Mary**	Hans Jury & Mary	
10-14-54	**Ann**	Johannis & Hester	
	Daniel	Jan & Hester	
12-2-54	**Neeltie**	Michael & Hester	
1-7-55	**Jacob**	Nickus & Magdalene	
2-23-55	**Sarah**	Daniel & Margaret	
5-19-55	**Johannes**	Johannes Crine & Neeltie	
6-1-55	**Abraham**	Johannes & Wari	
6-22-55	**Cathrine**	Cornelius & Maria of Schoharie	
	David	Sias & Sarah of Onoghquaga	
6-29-55	**Jacob Sejohowana** (son of a principal Sachem) married to **Anna** of Fort Hunter		
12-5-55	**Daniel**	Peter & Sarah	
	Christeen	Thomas & Catharine	
12-25-55	**Lawrance**	Abraham & Leah	
2-8-56	**Margaret**	Joseph & Elizabeth	
	Catharine	Moses & Margaret	
2-15-56	**Neeltie**	Monacatitha [Scaroyady] & Eve	
	Aaron	Monacatitha [Scaroyady] & Eve	
	Aaron	Johannes & Mary	
2-25-56	daughter	Daniel (principal man of Oneida) & Anna (of Oneida)	
	Isaac	Isaac & Cathrine	
	Daniel	Peter & Sarah	
3-28-56	**Rowanas**	Arie & Lydia	
8-3-56	**Moses**	Hendrick & Rachel (in Albany)	
8-8-56	**Paulus**	Lawrence & Anna Holms	
8-10-56	**Mary**	David & Margaret	
2-10-57	**Elizabeth**	an adult, with her two children:	
	David	Elizabeth (in Albany)	
	Elizabeth	Elizabeth (in Albany)	
	Anthony	about 13 years old	
2-13-57	**Eve**	John & Jacomine	

Date[b]	Baptismal/ Sp. Name	Parents, Indian Name, or Spouse Name	Sponsors
2-13-57	**Mary**	Jacob & Hester	
8-5-57	**Mary**	Hendrick & Magdalene	
	Jacob	John & Anna	
	David	Joseph & Josyna	
1-15-58	**Cornelius**	Jacob Sejehowana & Anna	
1-22-58	**Cornelius**	Seth & Christiana	
	Peter of Canijohare married to **Sarah** of this castle		
2-8-58	**Mary**	Thomas & Cathrine	
2-9-58	**Abraham**	Isaac & Cathrine	
2-14-58	**Cathrine**	Johannes & Mary	
3-5-58	**Cathrine**	Johannes & Anna	
4-14-58	**Hester**	Louis & Sarah (in Albany)	
2-11-59	**Jacomine**	Arie & Lydia	
2-12-59	**Abraham Isaac's** married to **Jacomine Brandt's**		
3-4-59	**Abraham** married to **Mary**		

[a]The Reverend Andrews' list was published in *The New York Genealogical and Biographical Record* 105 (1974): 117. Reverend Barclay's Register is at the New York Historical Society, New York City. (see Chapter 9, Note 30). The Reverend Ogilvie's Register was published in the *Bulletin of the Ft. Ticonderoga Museum* 10 (1961): 382-85.

[b]The numeric dates shown here follow the month-day-year system. Thus 1-11-13 would be January 11, 1713, and 4-13-35 would be April 13, 1735.

Schoharie Indian Baptisms and Marriages, 1731-1778[a]

Date[b]	Baptismal/ Sp. Name	Parents, Sp. Name, or Information	Sponsors or Birthplace
4-28-31[c]	Jacob	Peter & Anna	Bar. Vroman & Sus. Brad
5-11-34[d]	Hendrick	Jan and Maria	Mar. Ryckaart, Elyz. Rickaart
	Elyzabeth	Fichtahekan & Catharina	Nic. Jorck, Margr. Zee
2-28-36[e]	Joseph	Hans Jurriaan & Susanna	H. Mathias, El. Mathias
	Josyna	Jacob & Grietie	Johs. Ingoold & M. Ingoold
3-13-37	child	Adam & Eva	-----
3-5-38	Zusanna	Seth & Catharina	Conradt Rickedt with Elisab.
	Seth	Johan Georg	Seth & Catharina
2-3-40	Joseph	Seth & Catharina	Robbyn Frieman & Malli Vrieman
	Christina	John Georgie & Susanna	John & Maria
2-22-40	Hans Jurria	Hans Jurrie	
	Set [Seth]	John. Eckker	
	Maria	dau. of an Indian	Lauris
	Maria	Jantie	
8-1-41	Peter & wife	Maria (baptized)	Dirck Hagedoorn
10-25-41	Pelles Warresen of Schoharie		b. Long Island
	married to	Anna Kargadonte the Indian, of Schoharie	b. Mohawks land
4-20-44	Eva	Jayas	Pellis Warrison & Anna his wife
	Geertruid	father dead & Catharin	Hans Jury & wife
6-30-45	Marytie	Bellis Warreson & Anna	Barent Vroman Engeltie his wife

Date[b]	Baptismal/ Sp. Name	Parents, Sp. Name, or Information	Sponsors or Birthplace
6-30-45	Joseph	John & Maria	Pieter Snyder Elise Kathryn his wife
7-18-46	John		
12-26-46	Hendrik	Piter & Maria	Niclaas & wife Jannitye
6-26-47	Jacob		Lourens
	Jeremias		Lourens
	Willem		Lourens
	Jannitje		Lourens
	Jantie Ju[nior]		Lourens
	Catrin (a child)		Lourens
	Neeltie (a child)		Lourens
7-25-47	David of Schoharie son of Aquianer		b. Antigo
	married to	Sara daughter of John	b. Schoharie
1-1-49	Piter	Piter & Dorothea	Jacob Diderich & wife
3-19-49	Moses	John and wife	Salomon Meyer
at Wysersdorp:			
7-16-49	Susanna	(a child)	Adam
	Catharina	(a child)	Dirk Hagedoorn
	Anna	(a child)	Jonar.
	Henderick	(a child)	Hendrick
	Catharina	(a child)	d: Hagedoorn
	Sara	(a child)	d: Haged.
	Rachel	(a child)	Thomas Eckkerson
	David	(a child)	David
	Niclaas	(a child)	Jonar
	Maria	(a child)	Maria Vroman
	Pect: Thimothey (a child)		Bartholomaus Vroman
	Geertruid	(a child)	Jesaias Swart
	Johan	(a child)	Jonathan
8-24-50	Lourus	Jacob Quinebes & Margarith Gargadonde	Lourens Lawyer & wife Catharine
	Gesina	Brand & Elisabeth	Jacob Quinebes

APPENDIX D   249

Date[b]	Baptismal/ Sp. Name	Parents, Sp. Name, or Information	Sponsors or Birthplace
1-15-51	**Jacob**	son of Eva married to	
		Cornelia daughter of Wouder the Indian	
4-6-51	**Anthony** of Schoharie son of Niclaas b. Oqkwaka		
	married to	**Maria** of Schoharie dau. of Seth b. Schoharie	
	Jacob son of Anna married to		b. Schoharie
		Maria dau. of Seth	b. Mohawks land
7-13-51	**Maria**	Jonathan & Elisabeth	Henderick Hagedoorn & wife Susanna
	Sara	Jonar & Sara	Jacob & wife Maria, John Eckkerson & wife
	Cornelia	Moses & Cornelia	Jonar Larrown Catharina Hagedoon
	Moses married to **Cornelia**		
7-20-51	**Henderick** son of Jantjie married to		
		Elisabeth dau. of Adam b. Ogkwago	
8-30-51	**Jantie**	Abraham & Margarith	Pellis
10-12-51	**Catharina**	David & Sara	Anthony & wife Catharine
12-2-51	**Jan**	Jacob s. Hans Jurri & wife Eva	Niclaas Mathesse & his wife
8-22-52	**Lourens** married to		
		Margarith dau. of Isaac Kayanoosah	
9-14-52	**Janneke**		Henderick & wife
10-25-52	**Christina**	David & Anna	
9-10-53	**Joseph**	Jacob & Maria	Seth & wife Catharine
11-3-53	**Willem**	Anthony & Maria	Lourens Layer & wife Elisabeth
3-23-54	**Abraham** the Makickkander E		
8-11-54	**Neeltie**	Moses & Margarith	Neeltie & Theunis
	Thomas son of Alida married to		
		Elisabeth daughter of Isaac	

Date[b]	Baptismal/ Sp. Name	Parents, Sp. Name, or Information	Sponsors or Birthplace
8-19-54	Maria	David & Sara	Johan Larrown & Maria Hagedoorn
8-21-54	Adam		John Ecker & Marytie Veeder
	Zeth	Zeth de Diskororis & wife Sara	daughter of Seth
	Anna	Adam & Lea	Maria Seybel
8-24-54	Adam		
	Margaritha	David & Alida	Lourens Isaac's son-in-law & Margaritha
2-17-55	Jacob	Piter & Christina	
8-2-55	Dirck	Jeremias & Anna	Dirck Hagedoorn
	Maria	Piter & Jantjie	Theunis the Indian & Catharina Hagedoorn
	Willem	Nebo the Indian & Susanna	John the Indian & Malli
8-14-55	Willem	Jonar the Indian & Elisabeth	Theunis & wife Neeltie
	Susanna	Talas Sytockha & Elisabeth	Catharin, Sets wife
	Catharin	Talas Sytockha & Elisabeth	Catharin, Sets wife
10-23-55	Lourens	Peregirnes & Sara	Joseph & Sara, Seth's daughter
12-30-55	David	Maria	
5-9-56	Maria	(b. Apr. 11) Lorentz & Margaret	Jurgen Werner & wife, Isaac the Indian
8-15-56	Susanna	Lorentz Jun. & Sara	Lorentz & wife
9-5-56	Susanna	Tinus (deceased) & Nelje	Johs. Lawyer, Susanna
9/10-1756	Susanna	Joseph & Maria	Joseph & Marie
11-21-56	Cornelius	Jacob & Christina	
2-27-57	Jannetje	Jan & Marie	
3-27-57	Seth	Anthony & Catharina	Christian Bauch & wife

Date[b]	Baptismal/ Sp. Name	Parents, Sp. Name, or Information	Sponsors or Birthplace
3/4-1757	Janneje		Gertraut Mathees
5-1-57	Susanna	David & Susanna	Jacob Schafer & Eva Schafer
8-1-57	Jonert	(an adult)	Jacob Fr. Lawyer and wife
	Jacobus	Jonert	Martinus Schafer & wife
	Sara	Jonert	Eva, dau. of Isaac & a son of Richtmeir
	Nelje	(an adult)	Richtmeier & his wife
8-7-57	Christina	Adam & Sophia	Christina & her husband
8-28-57	Lorentz	Laurentz & Rachel	
12-11-57	Catharina	Abraham	Matthes Bauman and Catharina Kayser
3-3-58	Christina	Arend & Rosina	Nicholas & Margaret from Canajoharie
3-3-58	Thomas married to Anna		
5-28-58	Johannes of Onaquaga married to		b. at Onaquaga
	Catharine of Onaquaga		b. at Onaquaga
	Susanna	Nicholaas & Margrith	Thomas Eckersen & Margritha Eckersen
	Grittie	Abraham & Catharina	John Van deyk & Cornelia Van deyk
	Adam	Hendrik & Elisabeth	Adam & wife Eva
	Elisabeth	David & Alida	Hendrik & Elisabeth
	Elisabeth	Abraham & Catharina	David & Alida
	Nicolaas	Jacob & Cornelia	Josiahs Swart & Gertruyd Swart
6-25-58	Barend	Jonathan & Maria	Barend Keyser & Maria Barbar Keyser
7-20-58	Quites	Crains & Catharina	Moses & Maria
8-6-58	Lorentz	Peter & Anna	Isaac & Susanna

Date[b]	Baptismal/ Sp. Name	Parents, Sp. Name, or Information	Sponsors or Birthplace
9-17-58	**Maria**	Pieter & Jannetie	Samuel Vrooman & Derkie V. Alstein
11-2-58 (birthdate)	**Catharina**	Peter & Maria	Matthas Baumann & wife
12-10-58	**Joseph** married to **Sara**		both b. at Canajoharie
1-23-59	**Henerich**	Thomas & Anna	Henerich & Gertruyd Heeger
3-18-59	**Josina**	Jacob & Margritta	Pieter & Wary Achquagers
4-24-59	**Johan Jost Johannes**		
5-5-59	**Jacob** married **Eva** daughter of Isaac the Agquager		
5-13-59	**Adam**	Jacob & Susanna	Jacob the Indian, Sussnna Hagedoorn
8-26-59	**Jacob**	Adam & Lea of Oghquaga	Jacob, Adam's son, Catrina Loow
9-11-59	**Daniel**	Daniel & Rachel of Oghquaage	Pitter & Cristina
9-23-59	**Moses**	Joseph & Sara	
9-30-59	**Jan**	(an old Indian)	Peter & wife Christina Jan Vrooman
	Jan married **Catharina**, daughter of Johan Jurgen & Eva of Aquaka		
11-1-59	**Maria**	Henerik & Eva	Jan & Maria
11-16-59	**Pitter**	Pitter & Dorthee Oqhquagers	Pitter & Margritt Mann
11-25-59	**Wilhelm**	Quites & Catharin	
1-6-60	**Hanyorzy**	Lourentz & Elisabeth	David & Maria Indians of Schoharie
2-8-60	**Margareth**	Hannes Bier & Jannetie	Peter Mann Margreth Mann
2-22-60	**Cornelis**	Jacob & Maria	Jacob & wife
4-3-60	**Christina**		

Date[b]	Baptismal/ Sp. Name	Parents, Sp. Name, or Information	Sponsors or Birthplace
5-12-60	Peter		Matthes Baumann & his wife
8-21-60	Isac	(an adult)	
	Isac married to Sophia		
	Jacob married to Margaret		
	David		
12-6-60	Isaac	Jacob and Margareth	Isaac
12-27-60	Hans Jurgen	Hans Jurg & Catharina	Jacob & Jannetje
2-1-61	Thomas	Anthony & Maria	Thomas & wife
2-15-61	Seth		
	Jonathan	Sara	
	Cornelia		
2-18-61	Rosina	Akus & Sara	Christopher Rettig & wife
2-23-61	Peter	Jacob & Christina	David & wife Sara
6-14-61	Elisabeth	Crenius & Catharina	Jurgen Henrich Stubrach & his wife
7-1761	Jan	Jonas	
8-1761	Henrich	Sawatis & Wark	
8-27-61	Wilhelm baptized and married to Anna		
9-6-61	Jan baptized and married to Elisabeth		
9-9-61	Alers	an old Aquejanis (fellow tribesman)	Joseph & Susanna
5-6-62	Jacob	Jacob of Aquage	Jacob & wife Eva
	Eva	Cornelia	Jacob & Margareth
5-25-62	Johannes	Johannes & Dorothea	Johannes Zahe & wife
7-18-62	Quari (adult)		
	Elisabeth (little girl)		
8-8-62	David	David & Sara	Joseph & Susanna
8-1762	Jacob	Wilhelm	
12-9-62	Johannes	son of Jacob baptized and	
	married to	Maria	
	Catharine	Peter & Maria	

Date[b]	Baptismal/ Sp. Name	Parents, Sp. Name, or Information	Sponsors or Birthplace
3-27-63	Jan	Levinus, a Frenchman and Maria	Lorentz Lawyer & wife
4-24-63	Seth	Anthoni	Nickel Matthes & wife
5-8-63	Anthoni	Anthoni & wife	Barent Kayser & wife
7-12-63	Joses	Louis Scherean & Anna	Tobias & Christina
8-13-63	Seth	Joseph & Susanna	
9-11-63	Sara	Akus father	
	Nicolas	Jacob father	
	Nelje	Henrich father	
10-1763	Ari	Cornelius & Grit	David & wife
10-27-63	Jacob	Niclas & Susanna	
6-4-64	Jan	Henrich & Lakus	
8-5-64	Margrit	an aged Indian	
	Jacob	an Indian boy	
8-29-64	Susanna	an Indian little girl	
2-13-65	Catharina	Peter & Christina	
3-7-65	Isaac	Wilhelm & Hanna	
4-17-65	Sara	Louis & Maria	Jan & wife Maria
12-1765	Johannes	David & Sara	Anthoni & Wari
12-25-65	Jan	Grenis & Gretje	Louis
4-8-66	Anthony	Peter & Maria	Anthoni & wife Catharina
4-9-66	Hans Jurg	Willelm & Elisabeth	Abraham & Catharina
4-20-66	Martinus	Abraham & Catharine	
	Abraham	Anthon & Cunigund	
6-1766	Wilhelm	Louis & Maria	Wilhelm Bauch & wife
5-10-67	Lollis	(Indian boy from Aquake)	
8-8-67	Merje	Johannes	
		(after this the writing is not Domine Sommers')	
10-19-67	Cornelis	Isaac & wife	Cornelis Vroman & daughter

Date[b]	Baptismal/ Sp. Name	Parents, Sp. Name, or Information	Sponsors or Birthplace
10-9-68	Christina	Peter & Maria	Lorentz Lawyer & wife
7-29-69	Jantje	Jan of Ogkwake & Susanna	Theunas Swart & Jantje Swart
10-28-69	Marthynes	Lavines & Maria	Martynes Siele & wife
11-12-69	Jantje	Willem & Anna	Joh. Lourence Layer Jantje Vroman
5-6-70	Moses	David & Wari	John Vroman & wife Maria
1-21-71	Willem	Pitter Smert & Wari	Willem de I. & wife
3-9-71	Elisabeth	Alexies & Sara	Sose & Elisabet
10-12-71	Henrick	son of Seth married to Catharina daughter of Jacob	b. at Schoharie
1-5-72	Anna	Hans Jurrie & Theroki	Jacob
2-11-72	Louis	Louis & Maria	Henrich & w. Catharine
6-20-72	Eva	George & Anna	
8-2-72	Jacob	Anthony & Geertruid	Johannes & Maria
	Anna	Thomas & Geertruid	Theunis & Maria Vroman
8-8-72	Johannes	Gideon & Catharin	Hannes & Maria Bellinger
	Willem	Moses & Margarith	Willem & Maria
8-13-72	Sara	Jacob de Makikkanger Christina	Marthynes & wife Elisabeth
9-21-72	Elisabeth	Georg Meyer de Indian his wife Margareth	Piter Smart & wife & Maria
11-21-72	Piter	Joseph & Catharin	Piter & wife Maria
3-24-73	Elisabeth	Nicolas & Susanna	Wilhelm & Elisabeth
4-1773	Jacob	(Indian child)	Louis the Frenchman
8-1-73	Peter		Adam of Ogk[waga]
	Elizabeth	his daughter	Piter Ganoenti
	Jacob		

Date[b]	Baptismal/ Sp. Name	Parents, Sp. Name, or Information	Sponsors or Birthplace
9-24-73	Johannes	Lourus & Margarita	Johannes Bekker & wife Maria
10-9-73	Piter b. 9-21	Wilem & Sophia	Piter Schneider Jr. & wife Maria Catharine
12-29-73	Jantje	Piter & Elizabeth	Jesias Swart & wife Geertrud
2-20-74	Jacob	Joseph & Susanna	Jacob
5-31-74	Catharin	Hans Jurrie Gargedonte & wife Geertruid	Theunis Swart & wife Annatje
7-31-74	Peter	Peter & Catharine	
2-5-75	Elizabeth	Jacob, Adam's son & Margareth, Isaac's dau.	Lauris Isaac & Elisabeth Isaac
3-28-75	Maria	Louis & Maria	Jan, son of David & wife
	Jan	(an adult Indian)	Chatharina
7-23-75	Neeltje	Niclaas & Elisabeth	Peter, Neeltie grandmother
8-4-75	Gritgen	George & Anna	Lowise & Maria
	Kneles	Kneles & Susanna	Jan & Susanna
8-6-75	Sara	Moses & Cornelia	Lodewyk Schneider & wife Sara
9-25-75	Catharin	Hendrik & Anna	
2-2-76	John	a converted Indian	David & wife Sara
2-12-76	Wari	Cornelis & Wari	Adam & Susanna
5-17-76	Henrich	John & Malli	Henrich & wife
5-24-76	Sara	Joseph & Eva	
6-15-76	Alida	Willem & Sophia	Joseph Beving & wife Alida
6-22-77	Jacob	Jacob de Onyder & wife Catharin	Jacob & Jantje
9-12-77	Marthynes	Lowis & Maria	Marthynes Ziele & wife Maria
5-10-78	Elizabet	Lowis & Maria	Lorens Lawyer & wife Eliz.

ªThese entries are taken from "Records of the High and Low Dutch Reformed Congregation at Schoharie (now the Reformed Church)," New York Genealogical and Biographical Society, New York, 1917, vol. 1 (pt. 1) and "Records of St. Paul's Evangelical Lutheran Church, Schoharie, New York," New York Genealogical and Biographical Society, New York, 1914.

ᵇThe numeric dates shown here are follow the month-day-year system. Thus 3-13-37 would be March 13, 1737.

ᶜEntries with a nonitalicized date are from the High and Low Dutch Reformed Congegration (now the Reformed Church) at Schoharie.

ᵈEntries with an italicized date come from St. Paul's Evangelical Lutheran Church, Schoharie.

ᵉEntry appears in both the records of St. Paul's Lutheran Church and the Reformed Church at Schoharie.

Miscellaneous Indian Birth and Marriage Records,

1758-1792

Date[a]	Baptismal Name	Parents, Indian Name, or Information	Sponsors

from the Reformed Protestant Dutch Church of Caughnawauga, New York[b]:

Date	Baptismal Name	Parents, Indian Name, or Information	Sponsors
[1758][c]	**Aaron**	Aaron & Susanna	Mary
[1758][c]	**Mary**	Johannes & Mary	Sarah
9-12-62	**Johannes**	Johannes & Anna	Cornelius & Neeltie
5-17-63	**Mosis**	Mosis & Annies	Christien
	Lea	Paulus the Frenchman & Christina	Annes
5-13-64	**Johannes**	parents unrecorded	Margaret
	Johannes	parents' illegible	Catarien

from the German Flats Reformed Church (Fort Herkimer Church), New York[d]:

Date	Baptismal Name	Parents, Indian Name, or Information	Sponsors
8-28-62	**Christian** (b. Mar. 3)	Major John Chamble & Sara Monduir of Fort Stanwix	Lt. Albert Brown Mrs. Brown
2-7-86	**Dorthea** (b. Dec. 1, 1785)	Jacob Dachstaeder the Indian & Lea	John Denie & Dorthea
5-27-87	**Sara** (b. May 6)	John Tenny, Indian & Dorthea	Joh. Georg Dachstader & Sara, both Indians
	Georg (b. Feb. 25)	Jacob Dachstaeder & Lea	Joh. Georg Smarth & Catharina, both Indians
8-12-88	**John** (b. June 24)	Georg Martin (Indian) & Catharin (white)	Johannes Hess, Indian
1-26-90	**Abraham** (9 mos.-1 yr.)	John Deny & Dorthea both Indians	Abraham & Catharin

Date[a]	Baptismal/ Sp. Name	Parents, Spouse Name, or Information	Sponsors
1-26-90	**Dorthea** (9 mos.-1 yr.)	Jacob Dachstaed & Lea	John & Dorthea
3-1-92	**John** (b. Oct. 2, 1791)	John De Ny & Dorthea	David, Indian, & Maria De Ny

from Trinity Lutheran Church, Stone Arabia, New York[e]:

11-26-70	**William** Asarad sohn[?] married to Adam's daughter of Onaquaga		
4-10-72	**Jacob Arosckerisch** Indian married to **Maria Aroschkerisch** Indian		
[7][c] -1772 (b. Jan. 19, 1772)	**John**	William an Indian & Catharina	Sir William Janson, *absent.*, Joh. Valentin Casparus & wife

from the Register-Book of Old Christ Church, Philadelphia, by the Rev. Peters at Fort Stanwix, New York, September and October, 1768[f] (during the Fort Stanwix Congress):

Baptismal/ Sp. Name	Parents, Spouse Name, or Information
William, 12 mos.	Rut, a Tuscarora Indian
Mary 1.5 yrs.	Nichas, an Oneida
Teasanickta	adult Tuscarora
William 8 yrs.	Teasanickta
Elizabeth 4 yrs.	Teasanickta
John 27 yrs.	Teasanickta
Attohichon 14 yrs.	a Delaware Indian girl
Catharine 12 yrs.	sister of Attohichon
Sarah 3 yrs.	an Indian
Peter 9 mos.	an Indian boy
John Harris 18 yrs.	Tuscarora Indian
David 30 yrs.	adult Tuscarora
son 3 mos.	Henry & Sarah, Mohawks
Thomas b. Oct. 1, 1768	Adam an Oneida

Baptismal/ Sp. Name	Parents, Spouse Name, or Information
Dorothy b. Sept. 17, 1768	Henry & Margaret of Oneoquago
John 5 mos. (twins)	Sagiatunka, a Shawaness
Elizabeth 5 mos.	Sagiatunkau
daughter b. Oct. 26, 1768	Henry & Mary
Carastaatzi b. Oct. 28, 1768	Joseph a Mohawk & Carastaatzi, a Conewago Indian
Anna 25 yrs.	Tuscarora woman
Mary 18 mos.	Augustus & Anna (above)
daughter b. Oct. 1768	Seth & Christiana, Indians of Oneoquago
Mary	wife of William, an Oneoquago Indian
son b. June 1, 1768	said William & Mary

[a]The numeric dates shown here follow the month-day-year system. Thus 2-7-86 would be February 7, 1786.

[b]Royden W. Vosburgh, ed., "Records of the Reformed Protestant Dutch Church of Caughnawauga," New York Genealogical and Biographical Society, 1917, vol. 1.

[c]Inferred date.

[d]Royden W. Vosburgh, ed., "Records of the Reformed Protestant Dutch of German Flatts in Fort Herkimer, town of German Flats, Herkimer County, N.Y.," New York Genealogical and Biographical Society, 1917.

[e]Royden W. Vosburgh, ed., "Records of Trinity Lutheran Church of Stone Arabia in the Town of Palatine in Montgomery County, N.Y.," New York Genealogical and Biographical Society, 1914.

[f]Carousso, D. H., contr., "Fort Stanwix (Rome, New York) Indian Baptisms, 1768," *New York Genealogical & Biographical Record* 103 (1972):154.

Mohawk Signers of Deeds, 1700-1749

Signer	Sign[a]	Year	Deed[b]	For Lands
Aaron	X	1730	J	near Ft. Hunter
Abraham	bear	1732	L	near Canajoharie
Adam	turtle	1732	L	near Canajoharie
Adiriejagtha (Adirsaghtha)	wolf	1717	F	at Schoharie
Adjagoroende	squiggle	1717	F	at Schoharie
Adrejochta	turtle	1729	H	E of Schenectady
Amos Socerheit (Socerhat)	Unkn.	1700	A	Mohawk woodlands
Amos the Indian	Unkn.	1711	D	W of Schoharie Crk
Anharissa	turtle	1723	G	on Schoharie Creek
Annanias	bear	1732	L	near Canajoharie
Anthony	wolf	1732	L	near Canajoharie
Anthony	bear	1714	E	W side Mohawk R.
Argiadihha	turtle	1732	L	near Canajoharie
Aria	Unkn.	1733	M	the Mohawk Flats
Aria Canoghow (Canaghowende)	bear?	1717	F	at Schoharie
Asaf Onasiadickha (Onasiadrickha)	Unkn.	1700	A	Mohawk woodlands
Asarus. See Esrus				
Arongegtha (Anongightha)	squiggle	1717	F	at Schoharie.
Aulida	tortoise	1714	E	W side Mohawk R.
Aurie	X	1714	E	W side Mohawk R.
Brant	wolf	1714	E	W side Mohawk R.
Brant Sagayengarechta (Sagayengaragta)	Unkn.	1700	A	Mohawk woodlands
Cagnawadyggria (Cagnawadigtha)	bear	1717	F	at Schoharie
Canadagaie	Unkn.	1732	K	near Ft. Edward
Canaghquase	wolf	1717	F	at Schoharie
Canasquisacha (Canasguisacka)	wolf (with big feet)	1717	F	at Schoharie
Canneragtaharie [see also Esron and Esras]	Unkn.	1732	K	near Ft. Edward
Canquothoo [see also Kanaquatho]	Unkn.	1711	D	W of Schoharie Crk
Caregohe	Unkn.	1732	K	near Ft. Edward

Signer	Sign[a]	Year	Deed[b]	For Lands
Carogjarageon	Unkn.	1732	K	near Ft. Edward
Christian Diaryhogan	turtle	1749	Q	western lands
Cornelis	tortoise	1714	E	W side Mohawk R.
Cornelis	turtle	1717	F	at Schoharie
Cornelis	Unkn.	1711	D	W of Schoharie Crk
Cornelis Tereigaren (Tesiagaran)	Unkn.	1700	A	Mohawk woodlands
Cornelis Tirogaren	turtle	1701	B	beaver hntng. grds.
Cornelius	Unkn.	1733	M	Mohawk Flats
Crine	tortoise	1714	E	W side Mohawk R.
Dagnatagonghe (Dagnatagunoke)	cross	1723	G	on Schoharie Creek
Danagerane	head	1723	G	on Schoharie Creek
Davet (David)	wolf	1730	J	near Ft. Hunter
DeGarydonde (Degarytunteey)	bear	1723	G	on Schoharie Creek
Dehanadasse (Ganadasse)	cross	1717	F	at Schoharie
Donachqua	wolf	1723	G	on Schoharie Creek
Egnitee	Unkn.	1732	K	near Ft. Edward
Eliza [prob. Elias]	wolf	1732	L	near Canajoharie
Erras	Unkn.	1733	M	Mohawk Flats
Eseras Sogjowanne	turtle	1717	F	at Schoharie
Esras	X	1714	E	W side Mohawk R.
Esras	"elk"	1714	E	W side Mohawk R.
Esras (Eseras)	large wolf)	1717	F	at Schoharie
Esras (Asarus)-1	Unkn.	1733	M	Mohawk Flats
Esras (Asarus)-2	Unkn.	1733	M	Mohawk Flats
Esras (Asarus)	bear?	1735	O	Ft. Hunter woods
Esras the Indian	Unkn.	1711	D	W of Schoharie Crk
Ezras	"snake"	1714	E	W side Mohawk R.
Esras	cross	1717	F	at Schoharie
Esras Tikjerere	bear	1740	P	near Ft. Hunter
Esron (Isran) Kanneratahera	Unkn.	1700	A	Mohawk woodland
Ganadasse [see Dehanadasse]				
Gesina (Eusena)	X	1714	E	W side Mohawk R.
Gideon (Gydeon)	"deer"	1714	E	W side Mohawk R.
Gideon	wolf	1717	F	at Schoharie
Gideon (Gideyon)	wolf	1730	J	near Ft. Hunter
Gideon	turtle	1732	L	near Canajoharie

Signer	Sign[a]	Year	Deed[b]	For Lands
Gideon (Gidion)	Unkn.	1733	M	Mohawk Flats
Gideon (Gidion)	wolf	1735	O	Ft. Hunter woods
Gidion Dewighnidoge	wolf	1740	P	near Ft. Hunter
Hanneyarhi..	bear	1735	N	near Canajoharie
Hanaharisso	turtle	1730	I	Canajoharie Flats
Hendrick	wolf	1701	B	beaver hntg. grds.
Hendrick	wolf	1714	E	W side Mohawk R.
Henderyck	H	1730	J	near Ft. Hunter
Hendrick	bear	1732	L	near Canajoharie
Hendrick Deganadhiondagqua	Unkn.	1700	A	Mohawk woodlands
Hendrick Ingan [Indian]	wolf	1729	H	E of Schenectady
Hendrick the Indian	Unkn.	1711	D	W of Schoharie Crk
Hendrick Tieonienhokaranas	Unkn.	1701	A	Mohawk woodlands
Hendrick Tiojonninhoge	wolf	1702	C	N of Mohawk R.
Hendrik Teoniahigarawe	wolf	1701	B	beaver hntg. grds.
Jacob	"deer" or "elk"	1714	E	W of Mohawk R.
Jacob Johagigtariego	Unkn.	1700	A	Mohawk woodlands
Jacob the Indian	Unkn.	1711	D	W of Schoharie Crk
Jacomin	Unkn.	1733	M	Mohawk Flats
Jan	wolf	1732	L	near Canajoharie
Johannes	turtle	1714	E	W of Mohawk R.
Johannes	turtle	1730	J	near Ft. Hunter
Johannes	turtle	1732	L	near Canajoharie
Johannes the Indian	Unkn.	1711	D	W of Schoharie Crk
Johannis	turtle	1735	O	Ft. Hunter woods
Johannis Ingan [Indian]	turtle	1729	H	E of Schenectady
Johanus-1	Unkn.	1733	M	Mohawk Flats
Johanus-2	Unkn.	1733	M	Mohawk Flats
John Sejehowane	turtle	1740	P	near Ft. Hunter
Joseph	?	1735	O	Ft. Hunter woods
Joseph Anograckhas [see also Tanochrachoss]	Unkn.	1700	A	Mohawk woodlands
Joseph Dehanockrakhas [see also Tanochrachoss]	bear head	1702	C	N of Mohawk R.
Kaderade (Taderade or Taderase) [see also Kangdade]	squiggle	1717	F	at Schoharie
Kahenterunkqua	Unkn.	1711	D	W of Schoharie Crk

Signer	Sign[a]	Year	Deed[b]	For Lands
Kanaquatho	bear	1730	I	Canajoharie Flats
Kanastasi	wolf?	1730	J	near Ft. Hunter
Kangade (Karigade)	wolf	1735	N	near Canajoharie
Karaghkondie (Karahkondie)	bear?	1730	I	Canajoharie Flats
Kawnawahdeakeoe	Unkn.	1711	D	W of Schoharie Crk
Koor Jinhanawaght	Unkn.	1700	A	Mohawk woodlands
Lawrence [see Sourance]				
Leweas the Indian	Unkn.	1711	D	W of Schoharie Crk
Louris	circle & bar	1730	J	near Ft. Hunter
Lucas	bear	1714	E	W of Mohawk R.
Luycas	bear	1717	F	at Schoharie
Mary	oval	1730	J	near Ft. Hunter
Moses	wolf	1732	L	near Canajoharie
Nicolaes	turtle	1732	L	near Canajoharie
Nintie	bear head	1730	J	near Ft. Hunter
Oneedyea	Unkn.	1711	D	W of Schoharie Crk
Onightanorum (Ouigtenorum)	Unkn.	1717	F	Schoharie
Onichemorum	bear	1732	L	near Canajoharie
Onucheranorum	bear	1701	B	beaver hntg. grds.
Onnadahsea	Unkn.	1711	D	W of Schoharie Crk
Onnowarage (Onowaroge)	turtle or bear	1717	F	at Schoharie
Orighjadickha	bear	1730	I	Canajoharie Flats
Pennonequieeson [see also Sinonquireso]	Unkn.	1711	D	W of Schoharie Crk
Peter	Unkn.	1733	M	Mohawk Flats
Peter Ontachsax	wolf?	1749	Q	western lands
Ragsotjata	Unkn.	1732	K	near Ft. Edward
Rebecca (Rebeckka)	wolf	1730	J	near Ft. Hunter
Rowagniodarie (Rowagjoidarie)	squiggle	1717	F	at Schoharie
Sagonadietha	Unkn.	1711	D	W of Schoharie Crk
Sander	"hedge hog"	1714	E	W of Mohawk R.
Sander	Unkn.	1733	M	Mohawk Flats
Satergusqua	?	1723	G	on Schoharie Creek
Sara	cross	1730	J	near Ft. Hunter
Schaveghneguese	turtle	1714	E	W of Mohawk R.
Seth	tortoise	1714	E	W. of Mohawk R.

Signer	Sign[a]	Year	Deed[b]	For Lands
Seth	bear	1732	L	near Canajoharie
Seth	turtle	1717	F	at Schoharie
Sett	Unkn.	1733	M	Mohawk Flats
Sett	Illeg.	1735	O	Ft. Hunter woods
Sinonquireso	bear	1701	B	beaver hntg. grds.
Sogohondightha	wolf or bear	1717	F	at Schoharie
Sonhe Wannah	Unkn.	1711	D	W of Schoharie Crk
Soonhagtowane	Unkn.	1701	A	Mohawk woodlands
(Sionhagtowane)				
Sourance	wolf	1732	L	near Canajoharie
Symon	"fox"	1714	E	W of Mohawk R.
Symon	wolf	1732	L	near Canajoharie
Taderade (or Taderase) see Kaderade.				
Tanochrachoss	bear head	1701	B	beaver hntg. grds.
[see also Joseph Dehanochrakhas]				
Tangijon [see William Tanjijon]				
Targions (Targiors)	turtle?	1717	F	at Schoharie
Targioris	bear	1732	L	near Canajoharie
Tejase	Unkn.	1732	K	near Ft. Edward
Tejonjagarawe	Unkn.	1732	K	near Ft. Edward
Thanighnawege	wolf	1717	F	at Schoharie
Testarrajie	Unkn.	1732	K	near Ft. Edward
Tewagnidoge	Unkn.	1732	K	near Ft. Edward
Tharojons (Thanajons)	wolf or bear	1717	F	at Schoharie
Thomas	Unkn.	1735	O	Ft. Hunter woods
Togwayenant	squiggle	1714	E	W of Mohawk R.
Tosoquatho	bear	1701	B	beaver hntg. grds.
Totquanese (Tot-quaiorese)	turtle	1717	F	at Schoharie
Tsinago	turtle	1701	B	beaver hntg. grds.
Tuquaw-in-hunt	Unkn.	1711	D	W of Schoharie Crk
Tucktahraessoo	Unkn.	1711	D	W of Schoharie Crk
Turthyowris	Unkn.	1711	D	W of Schoharie Crk
Wadonce	squiggle	1717	F	at Schoharie
Whisaw	Unkn.	1733	M	Mohawk Flats
Willem	turtle	1732	L	near Canajoharie
William Tangijon	turtle	1735	N	near Canajoharie
Yohhawhezah	"deer"	1714	E	W of Mohawk R.

[a]Signs with quotation marks are those given in Stone's *Life of Brant* 1:498–99. The author was not aware that the Mohawks were depicting turtles, wolves, and bears, and thus came up with such guesses as "deers," "elks" and "hedgehogs." These animals were either wolves or bears, while the "fox" must have been a wolf. He also made a distinction between tortoises and turtles, which was not necessary.

[b]Deeds listed by letters are described below:

A: Deed of the Mohawk woodland, December 26, 1700 (copies in English and Dutch), enclosed with: *Calendar of State Papers*, 1701, Item no. 38:33–37 (IIDH Reel #6 16 January 1701).

B: Deed of beaver hunting lands to the king, July 19, 1701: *DRCHNY* 4:910.

C: Indian land grant to Robert Livingston and David Schuyler, August 26, 1702 Albany County Clerk's Office, Albany, Deed Bood 4, p. 241 (IIDH Reel #6 26 August 1702 [II]).

D: Deed of August 22, 1711 to Adam Vroman of Schenectady for 260 acres of land in Schoharie: J. R. Simms, *History of Schoharie County and the Border Wars of New York* (1845), 55.

E: Deed to Margaret and Edward Collins, November 16, 1714: "Appendix: Family Name of Brant," in *Life of Brant* by W. L. Stone (1861 ed.) 1:498–99.

F: June 5, 1717 deed to Myndert Schuyler and others for lands at Schoharie: County Clerk's Office, Albany, Deed Book 5, p. 370-71 (IIDH Reel # 8 15 June 1717 [III]).

G: Indian deed . . . to William York, Jacob Frederic Lawyer, and Nicholas York, February 6, 1723: New York State Archives, Albany, Land Papers, Vol. 9, p. 23.

H: Deed to lands east of Schenectady to Hendrick Hagedoon, 1729: County Clerk's Office, Albany, Deed Book 7, p. 449 (IIDH Reel #28 10 Sept 1766 [III]).

I: Deed from four Mohawk sachems of Canajoharie: New York State Historical Association, Cooperstown, Special Collections, Files from the Indian Museum (IIDH Reel #10 16 February 1730).

J: Deed of land near Fort Hunter from Mohawks to Peter Brown, July 7, 1730:
      County Clerk's Office, Albany, Deed Book 7, p. 361-62 (IIDH Reel #27 3
      May 1765).

L: Mohawk Indian Land Grant to Petrus Van Driessen and Johannes Ehl, May
      9, 1732: St. Johnsville, N.Y., *Enterprise and News*, June 18, 1932.

M: 1733 Deed Conveying the Mohawk Flats to the King: *DRCHNY* 6:15-16.

N: Deed of land from sachems of Canajoharie to Jacob Glen: Newberry
      Library, Chicago, Illinois, Ayer Manuscripts N.A. 420 (IIDH Reel #10, 9
      June 1735).

O: Deed from Mohawks to Walter Butler, Dec. 24, 1735: New York State
      Archives, Albany, Colonial Mss., Land Papers, 1735-38, Vol. 12, p. 36.

P: Deed of land to Reverend Henry Barclay, November 24, 1740: New York
      Historical Society, New York, Horsmanden Papers, Selections Relating to
      the Six Nations, p. 80 (IIDH Reel #38, 9 May 1786).

Q: Indian deed to Thomas Penn for lands between Delaware and Susquehanna
      rivers: *Pa. Archives* (Ser. 1) 2:33-37 (IIDH Reel #14 22 August 1749).

Notes

Works frequently cited have been identified by the following abbreviations:

ERNY: Hugh Hastings, compiler, *Ecclesiastical Records of the State of New York* (Albany, State of New York, 1901).

DHNY: E. B. O'Callaghan, ed., *Documentary History of the State of New York* (folio) (Albany, State of New York, 1849–51).

Draper F   Lyman Copeland Draper, compiler, Joseph Brant Papers, F Series (Madison Wisconsin, Historical Society of Wisconsin, n.d.).

DRCHNY: E. B. O'Callaghan and B. Fernow, eds., *Documents Relative to the Colonial History of New York* (Albany, State of New York, 1853–87), 13 volumes.

IIDH: Francis Jennings, et al., eds., *Iroquois Indians: A Documentary History of the Diplomacy of the Six Nations and Their League* (Woodbridge, CT, Research Publications, 1984-85), microfilm reels 1–38.

JP: James Sullivan, Alexander C. Flick, and Milton Hamilton, eds., *The Sir William Johnson Papers* (Albany, State University of New York Press, 1929–65) 14 volumes.

LIR: Lawrence H. Leder, ed., *The Livingston Indian Records, 1666–1723* (Gettysburg, Pa., Pennsylvania Historical Association, 1956).

Pa. Arch.: Samuel Hazard, ed., *Pennsylvania Archives, 1st Series* (Joseph Severn & Co., Philadelphia, 1851–56).

Pa. Col. Rec.: *Minutes of the Provincial Council of Pennsylvania from the Organization to the Termination of Proprietary Government* (Thomas Fenn & Co., Harrisburg, PA, 1851).

CHAPTER 1

1. B. James Bartlett and J. Franklin Jameson, eds., *Journal of Jasper Danckaerts 1679–1680* (New York: Charles Scribner's Sons, 1913), 202.

2. Ibid.

3. Johannes Megapolensis, Jr., "A Short Account of the Mohawk Indians, their Country, Language, Stature, Dress, Religion and Government," in J. Franklin Jameson, ed., *Narratives of New Netherland, 1609–1664* (New York: Charles Scribner's Sons, 1909), 178.

4. B. James Bartlett and J. F. Jameson, *Journal of Jasper Danckaerts*, 201; Austin A. Yates, *Schenectady County, New York, Its History to the Close of the Nineteenth Century* (New York History Company, 1902), 6, 16, 26; A. J. F. van Laer, ed., *Van Rensselaer Bowier Manuscripts* (Albany: University of the State of New York, 1908), 255–57, 809; A. J. F. van Laer, ed., *Minutes of the Court of Rensselaerswyck 1648–1652* (Albany, The University of the State of New York, 1922), 128–29; Jonathan Pearson, *Contributions for the Genealogies of the First Settlers of the Ancient County of Albany from 1630 to 1800* (Baltimore: Genealogical Publishing Co., 1978), 134.

5. Harriet Bowers Mumford Paige, "The Diaries of H. B. M. Paige," (8 handwritten volumes in the Schenectady County Historical Society, c. 1860), 4:176–78. Paige is quoting a tradition from Giles F. Yates. The Yates family is descended from both Otstock, through Jacques van Slyck, and Keuntze, through Captain Andreas Bradt; see A. A. Yates, *Schenectady County* 17; see also Boyd Ehle, "The Mohawk Valley Ehles," Saint Johnsville, New York, *Enterprise and News*, June 4, 1930, chap. 1, Palatine line. The Ehles are descended from Cornelius van Slyck's brother. A. A. Yates in *Schenectady County*, 16, incorrectly names Keuntze's "husband" as a nonexistent Andries Andrieson Bradt. He was probably Arent Andriesson Bradt, brother of Albert Andriesson Bradt who came to New Netherland in 1634. Arent Bradt married Catalina DeVos in 1648 and died in 1662 (ibid., 231; see also A. J. F. van Laer, *Van Rensselaer Bowier Manuscripts* 810).

6. Marcel Trudel, *Histoire de la Nouvelle-France 2, Le Comptoir 1604–1627* (Montréal: les Editions Fides, 1963), 368–69; Barbara Graymont, *The Iroquois* (New York: Chelsea House, 1988), 47–48, 57.

7. Adrien Bergeron, *Le Grand Arrangement des Acadiens au Québec: Notes de Petite-histoire Genealogies, Trance-Acadie-Québec de 1625 á 1925* (Montreal: Editions Elysee, 1981), 4:222–226; René Jetté, *Dictionnaire Généalogique des familles du Québec, des Origines á 1730* (Montreal: University of Montreal Press, 1983), 566; Trudel, *Histoire de la Nouvelle-France 2*, Appendix E (Tableau des Hiverne-

ments), 498; Benjamin Sulte, *Histoire des Canadiens-Français 1608–1860* (Montréal: Wilson & cie, 1882), 1:14—Sulte also says Hertel came to New France "perhaps" as early as 1613, but this seems a bit too early; Hubert Charbonneau and Jacques Légaré, eds. *Répertoire des Actes de Baptême Mariage Sépulture et des Recensements du Québec Ancien, XVII siècle* (Montreal: University of Montreal Press, 1980), 4 (B601):1637-12-20 baptism of Nicole Essibranchich (there are no page numbers in the volumes prior to 1700).

8. Trudel, *Histoire de La Nouvelle-France 2, 390–91* and *3: La seigneurie des Cent-Associés, 1627–1663* (Montréal, Fides, 1979), pt. 1:138; Reuben Gold Thwaites, ed., *The Jesuit Relations and Allied Documents, Travels and Explorations of the Jesuit Missionaries in New France, 1610–1791* (Cleveland: Burrows Brothers, 1896–1901), 4:261, 9:305; H. Charbonneau and J. Légaré, *Répertoire des Actes* 4 (B601)—Jacques Hertel sponsored at least eight and as many as twenty AmerIndians between 1636-04-23 and 1650-11-10 at Trois-Rivières.

9. Trudel, *Histoire de la Nouvelle-France 2*, 369; Samuel Eliot Morison, *Samuel de Champlain: Father of New France* (Boston: Little, Brown and Co., 1972), 179–80.

10. Morison, ibid., 180; W. D. LeSueur, translator, *The Works of Samuel de Champlain, Volume 5, 1620–29* (Toronto: The Champlain Society, 1933), 214–23.

11. Bergeron, *Des Acadiens au Québec* 4:223–24; Jetté, *Dictionnaire Généalogique* 566; *DRCHNY* 3:132–33, 4:122; Cadwallader Colden, *The History of the Five Indian Nations of Canada* (New York: New Amsterdam Book Co., 1902), 1:130.

12. B. J. Bartlett and J. F. Jameson, *Journal of Jasper Danckaerts* 205–10.

13. Jonathan Pearson, ed., *Early Records of the City and County of Albany and Colony of Rensselaerswyck 1656–1675* (Albany: J. Munsell, 1869), 1:354, 436; Jonathan Pearson and A. J. F. van Laer, eds., *Early Records of the City and County of Albany and Colony of Rensselaerswick* (New York: University of the State of New York, 1918–19), 3:85–86, 172; 4:119–21; Joel H. Monroe, *Schenectady Ancient and Modern* (Geneva, NY: W. F. Humphrey, 1914), 25, 40; H. B. M. Paige, "Diary,"4:176–78; A. A. Yates, *Schenectady County* 26–27; *LIR* 29, 31, 40, 45, 111, 113, 127, 129–30, 131, 133, 139, 140.

14. A. A. Yates, ibid., 224; Yates states explicity that Leah was

Hilletie's sister. Jonathan Pearson, in *Contributions for the Genealogies of the First Settlers of the Ancient County of Albany* 134, says that Leah was "perhaps" Hilletie's sister.

15. A. A. Yates, ibid., 223–24; J. M. Monroe, *Schenectady Ancient and Modern* 39; J. Pearson, *Early Records of Albany* 436; *LIR* 29, 34.

16. *ERNY* 2:768–71, 813–17, 857–62, 880–86, 898–900, 902–04, 910, 936, 945, 947, 957; *DHNY* 3:533–38.

17. Floyd Lounsbury, "Iroquoian Languages," *in* Bruce G. Trigger, ed., *Handbook of North American Indians: Volume XV, Northeast* (Washington, DC: Smithsonian Institution, 1978), 334–37; for an in-depth study of a modern Mohawk dialect see Nancy Bonvillain, "A Grammar of Akwesasne Mohawk," *National Museum of Man, Ethnology Division Paper* 8 (Ottawa: 1973); Gunther Michelson, "A Thousand Words of Mohawk," *National Museum of Man, Ethnology Division Paper 5* (Ottawa: 1973) gives a brief overview and a useful word list. Henry R. Schoolcraft, *Notes on the Iroquois; or, Contributions to the Statistics, Aboriginal History, Antiquities, and General Ethnology of Western New-York* (New York: Bartlett & Welford, 1846), 264–281, contains Iroquois translations of several hundred English words; the quote is from J. Megapolensis, "A short account of the Mohawk Indians," 172.

18   Quote from *DRCHNY* 3:777.

19. *ERNY* 2:1003, 1007; The Holland Society, "Records of the Reformed Dutch Church in Albany," *Holland Society Yearbook for 1904* (New York: The Knickerbocker Press, 1904), 17:1–83. The first volume of the First Church in Albany (its present name) records is actually a copy, made by Dellius in 1699, of an earlier record begun in 1683. In the copy Dellius inserted other important church documents, including membership lists and lists of communicants. This record goes to mid-1700 and takes up the first part of the book. About midway through this book are recorded original baptisms beginning in 1725 and going to 1763, and marriages from 1750–60. This volume is in the possession of the First Church in Albany. The records 1683 to mid-1700 are printed in the *Holland Society Yearbook for 1904*, while the 1725–63 records are printed in the *Holland Society Yearbook for 1906* and *Yearbook for 1907*. A second book was used from 1700 through 1724 to record baptisms and marriages. It is labeled 1700–1749 [*sic*] and is in the vault of the New York State Library at Albany ("Church Records, SC 17568,

Box 1, vol. 2"). It is printed in the *Holland Society Yearbook for 1905* but **the Indian baptisms have not been printed**. A third volume, also in the State Library vault, contains First Church records from 1760 to 1830 (Robert S. Alexander, historian of the First Church, personal communications, August 9 and 23, 1989). The New York State Library, Albany, also has microfilms (AFM229) of volumes 1 and 3 and of the Elder Trotter transcription of volume 2.

20. Holland Society, *Yearbook for 1904*, 7, 49.

21. Ibid.; Jonathan Pearson and A. J. F. Van Laer, eds., "Early Records of the City and County of Albany II: Deeds 3 & 4, 1678–1704," *New York State Library History Bulletin 9* (Albany: State University of New York Press, 1916), 276. The name Ock-kwese may mean partridge (C. Colden, *History of the Five Nations* 1:61, 130); Evert Wendell, Indian Account Book 1695–1726, Misc. Microfilms, Micro Reel #71, New York Historical Society, New York, 44, 61; see also footnote 3 in Chapter 3.

CHAPTER 2

1. On the date of the founding of the League, see Elisabeth Tooker, "The League of the Iroquois: Its History, Politics, and Ritual," in Bruce G. Trigger, ed., *Handbook of North American Indians: Volume XV, Northeast* 418–22; on Iroquois prehistory, see Dean Snow, "Iroquois Prehistory" in Michael K. Foster, et al., eds., *Extending the Rafters: Interdisciplinary Approaches to Iroquoian Studies* (Albany: State University of New York Press, 1984), 254–57 and James A. Tuck, "Northern Iroquoian Prehistory," in Bruce G. Trigger, ed., *Handbook of North American Indians, Volume XV: Northeast* 322–333. A recent volume by Dean R. Snow, *The Iroquois* (Oxford, UK, and Cambridge, Mass.: Blackwell, 1994) contains a synopsis of archeologic, ethnohistoric, linguistic, and cultural information on the prehistoric Iroquois.

2. Graymont, Barbara, *The Iroquois* (New York: Chelsea House, 1988), 13–15, 18–26, 28–33; Elizabeth Tooker, "The League of the Iroquois," 422. There are many books and articles on the founding of the League, including: Horatio Hale, "A Law Giver of the Stone Age," *Proc. American Assoc. Advancement of Science* 30 (1881):324–41 (see also Chapter 2 in Hale's *The Iroquois Book of Rites* [Philadelphia: D. G. Brinton, 1883], reprinted by the University of Toronto Press, 1963); Arthur C. Parker, *The Constitution of the Five Nations; or, The Iroquois*

Book of the Great Law (New York State Museum Bulletin 184, 1916, reprinted in *Parker on the Iroquois* edited by William N. Fenton, Syracuse University Press, 1968), 7–158; J. N. B. Hewett, "Legend of the Founding of the Iroquois League," *American Anthropologist* 5 (1892):131–48; C. H. Henning, "The Origin of the Confederacy of the Five Nations," *Proceedings of the American Association for the Advancement of Science* 47 (1898):477–80.

3. Lewis Henry Morgan, "Laws of Descent of the Iroquois," *Proceedings of the American Association for the Advancement of Science* 11, no. 2 (1858):132–48; J. N. B. Hewitt and William N. Fenton, "Some Mnemonic Pictographs Relating to the Iroquois Condolence Council," *Journal of the Washington Academy of Sciences* 35:301–15; Daniel K. Richter, *The Ordeal of the Longhouse: The Peoples of the Iroquois League in the Era of European Colonization* (Chapel Hill: University of North Carolina Press, 1992), 1; William N. Fenton, "Problems Arising from the Historic Northeastern Position of the Iroquois," *Smithsonian Miscellaneous Collections* 100 (1940):201; D. R. Snow, *The Iroquois* 86; David Guldenzopf, "Frontier Demography and Settlement Patterns of the Mohawk Iroquois," *Man in the Northeast* 27 (1984):80.

4. Elisabeth Tooker, "The League of the Iroquois," 424–25; J. M. B. Hewitt and William N. Fenton, "The Requickening Address of the Iroquois Condolence Council," *Journal of the Washington Academy of Sciences* 34 (3):65–85.

5. J. N. B. Hewitt, "A Constitutional League of Peace in the Stone Age of America: The League of the Iroquois and its Constitution," *Smithsonian Institution Annual Report 1918* (Washington, DC: 1919), 527–45 (quote from 530).

6. J. N. B. Hewett, ibid., 530–31; Lewis Henry Morgan, *Laws of Descent* 133–35; A. A. Goldenweiser, "On Iroquois Work, 1912," *Summary Reports of the Geological Survey of Canada, 1912* (1913), 468–69. The women's right of ownership included the longhouse, the village, and the cleared fields around the village. The men had jurisdiction over the woodlands. The concept that the women owned the agricultural land was often rejected by whites. For example, Judge John M. Brown in 1823 said that the Mohawk women "always *pretended* [my italcs] to have the exclusive title to the soil" (*Brief Sketch of the First Settlement of the County of Schoharie by the Germans* [Schoharie, NY:

L. Cuthbert, 1823], 19). Deeds were signed almost exclusively by male Mohawks, because they were for uncleared woodland. Women affixed their signs to a few, for example, the November 16, 1714, deed to Margaret and Edward Collins found in William L. Stone's *Life of Brant*, (2d ed., Albany: Munsell, 1865), 1:498–99, which was signed by Aulida [Alida], Rebecca, and Eusena. This land must have included already cleared agricultural areas—the flatlands prized by both whites and Indians.

7. Daniel K. Richter, *Ordeal of the Longhouse* 18–24; William N. Fenton and Elisabeth Tooker, "Mohawk," in Bruce G. Trigger, ed., *Handbook of North American Indians, Volume XV: Northeast* 467. For a narrative reconstruction of the life of these early Mohawk villagers, see Joseph Bruchac, "A Mohawk Village in 1491: Otstungo," *National Geographic* (October 1991):68–83.

8. Daniel K. Richter, *Ordeal of the Longhouse* 20; Johannes Megapolensis, "A Short History of the Mohawks," 178–79; William Fenton, "Problems Arising from . . .," 203–09; D. R. Snow, *The Iroquois* 39, 62, 228 n.8.

9. William Fenton, ibid., 205–06; D. Guldenzopf, "Frontier Demography," 79–94; Barbara Graymont, *The Iroquois in the American Revolution* (Syracuse, NY: Syracuse University Press, 1972), 147, 219; Hugh Hastings, ed., *The Public Papers of George Clinton, War of the Revolution Series* (Albany: State of New York, 1900), 4:222; Maryly Penrose, *Indian Affairs Papers* (Franklin Park, NJ: Liberty Bell Associates, 1981), 125, 129–30.

10. Examples of deeds signed with clan symbols are found in Jonathan Pearson and A. J. F. Van Laer, eds., *New York State Library History Bulletin* 9:152–53, 195–97, 276, 340, and in IIDH reels 6, 8, 10, 27, 28, and 38—see *Guide to the Microfilm Collection* for specific listings. One early council where names of chiefs and their clan symbols are preserved is found in *DRCHNY* 4:910; the list from the 1754 Albany conference is in *Pa. Col. Rec.* 6:127–28; Sir William Johnson's list appears with clan affiliations in *JP* 13:173–75.

11. *DRCHNY* 4:43; Paul A. Wallace, *Conrad Weiser 1696–1760, Friend of Colonist and Mohawk* (Philadelphia: University of Pennsylvania Press, 1945), 200; C. Colden, *History of the Five Nations* 1:xvii.

12. Archer Butler Hulbert and William Nathaniel Schwartz, eds., "David Zeisberger's History of the Northern American Indians," *Ohio*

Archaeological and Historical Quarterly 19 (1910):1–189 (quote from 101).

13. Quote from *DHNY* 2:271. Gideon Tonidoge's League name of *Sharenhowaneh* (Wolf clan) and Seth Sietstarare's *Dekarihokenh* (Turtle) appear only in Henry Barclay's Register Book: "A register of Baptisms, Marriages, Communicants & Funerals begun by Henry Barclay at Fort Hunter, January 26th 1734/5" (New York, New York Historical Society), 17, 34–35. Hendrick Peters Theyanoguin's formal name of Saquainquaragton is mentioned only from nineteenth century tradition quoted in H. R. Scoolcraft's *Notes on the Iroquois* (Albany: Munsell, 1847), frontispiece. For an in-depth study of Mohawk leadership in the eighteenth century see Mary A. Druke, "A Study of Leadership in mid-eighteenth Mohawk and Oneida Society," Ph.D. dissertation, The University of Chicago, Department of Anthropology, 1981.

14. League sachems in the records of the First Church in Albany include Isaac Dekarihokenh, Seth Dekarihokenh (Turtles), Gideon Sharenhowaneh (Wolf), and Petrus Royaner. Seth and Gideon also appear in Henry Barclay's Register Book, as does David Leroy (possibly standing for le royaner)—See Appendices A and C. The association of chiefs with Christian religious ceremonies goes back to the missionary efforts of the Jesuits, when Iroquois leaders sought to associate themselves with the priests and their spiritual power (see Daniel K. Richter, "Iroquois versus Iroquois: Jesuit Missions and Christianity in Village Politics, 1642–1686," *Ethnohistory* 32(1):5.

15. L. H. Morgan, "Laws of Descent," 136; Goldweisser, "On Iroquois Work, 1912," 471.

16. P. A. Wallace, *Conrad Weiser* 203–04; Records of the Society for the Propagation of the Gospel Letterbooks (ser. A), 11:323–26, 12:318–40 (quoted in Daniel K. Richter, *Ordeal of the Longhouse* 233).

17. Examples of adoptions by a couple (Adam, adopted son of Laurens and Maria, baptized July 11, 1690) are found in Holland Society, *Yearbook for 1904* 51, and by women (Lydia, adoptive mother of Seth, baptized July 11, 1690, Seli Tejononnaron, adopted daughter of Eva, baptized April 11, 1694, Elizabeth, adopted daughter of Rebecca, baptized July 16, 1698) in ibid., 51, 64, 78; a probable adoption of five children by a couple (Grita, Hindrick, Adam, Johannes, and Anna, by Teiaiagse and Deiudhondawae on April 19, 1701) is found in Jonathan Pearson, ed., "Extracts from the Doop-Boek, or Baptismal Register of

the Reformed Protestant Dutch Church of Schenectady, N.Y.," *New England Historical and Genealogical Register* 18 (October, 1864):357; three children referred to as adopted children of Gideon: Johannes Rotsiho, Sara Kakenbarontje, and Seth Adanho (children of Gideon's brother) were baptized in Albany on October 6, 1700 (see Chapter 4 for a discussion of this last adoption).

18. Barbara Graymont, *The Iroquois* 58–59; Elisabeth Tooker, "The League of the Iroquois," 430.

19. "Narrative of a Journey into the Mohawk and Oneida Country, 1634–1635," in J. Franklin Jameson, ed., *Narratives of New Netherland, 1609–1664* (New York: Charles Scribner's Sons, 1909), 137–57.

20. Daniel K. Richter, *Ordeal of the Longhouse* 55–57, 61–65; Barbara Graymont, *The Iroquois* 63–67; Bruce G. Trigger, *The Children of Anahaentsic* (Montreal: McGill-Queen's University Press, 1976), 2:725–92.

21. Daniel K. Richter, ibid., 58–59; D. Guldenzopf, "Frontier Demography," 80; Reuben Thwaites, *Jesuit Relations* 49:233, 51:187.

22. William Fenton, "Problems Arising from . . .," 207–08; Reuben Thwaites, ibid., 51:81–85.

23. W. N. Fenton and E. Tooker, "Mohawk," 469–70; William Fenton, ibid., 208; *DRCHNY* 3:250.

24. Daniel K. Richter, *Ordeal of the Longhouse* 137–38.

25. Daniel K. Richter, ibid., 142, 144; see also Thomas Donohue, *The Iroquois and the Jesuits: The Story of the Labors of Catholic Missionaries among These Indians* (Buffalo: Catholic Pub. Co., 1895), 187–88.

26. Richard Aquila, *The Iroquois Restoration: Iroquois Deplomacy on the Colonial Frontier 1701–1754* (Detroit: Wayne State University Press, 1983), 44–45.

27. *DHNY* 2:95; *DRCHNY* 3:713n; Daniel K. Richter, *Ordeal of the Longhouse* 136; Neal Salisbury, "Toward the Covenant Chain: Iroquois and Southern New England Algonquians, 1637–1684," in Daniel K. Richter and James H. Merrell, eds., *Beyond the Covenant Chain: The Iroquois and Their Neighbors in Indian North America 1600–1800* (Syracuse: Syracuse University Press, 1987), 71.

28. Jerome R. Reich, *Leisler's Rebellion: A Study of Democracy in New York 1664–1720* (Chicago: Univ. Chicago Press, 1953), 1, 55–58,

64–66, 81–83; C. Colden, *History of the Five Nations* 1:108–11; *DHNY* 2:73

29. *DHNY* ibid.

30. Ibid.

31. *DRCHNY* 3:696.

32. C. Colden, *History of the Five Nations* 1:139–42; *DHNY* 1:186, 191, 193–94, 2:91; *LIR* 158–60.

33. *DHNY* 2:91–95; Sinonquireso (Sinnonquirese) and Tosoquatho signed the July 19, 1701, grant of Iroquois beaver hunting grounds to the king of England (*DRCHNY* 4:910) with bear signs (Tosoquatho is mislabeled a Seneca). They (and Oquedagoa) were also among the Mohawk sachems present at a council on August 27, 1700 (*DRCHNY*, 4:728) and the council with New York governor Lord Cornbury on July 18, 1702 (*DRCHNY* 4:985)—see table 5-1. In April, 1700, Sinnonquirese is termed a principal sachem of the Mohawks, not a Christian (*DRCHNY* 4:654, 657). Rode was baptized on July 23, 1695, at aged eighty (Holland Society, *Yearbook for 1904* 68). He signed (with what appears to be a standing tortoise) two deeds on March 4, 1682, as a sachem of the first castle, another on July 26, 1683, as a sachem of Cagnewage to Jan Quackenbos, and others on August 1, 1684, to Gov. Dungan, on May 8, 1686 to Teunis Slingerlant and Johannes Appel, on September 25, 1689 to Reynier and Jan Quackenbos, and on August 15, 1698, to Cornelius Van Dyck et al. (J. Pearson and A. J. F. Van Laer, *New York State Museum Bulletin* 9:151–53, 195–97, 229–30, 276–77, 363–64; Saggoddiochquisax also signed the July 26, 1683, and August 15, 1698, deeds and a November 4, 1689, deed. He may have been Sagoestesi, the Mohawk chief mentioned in the 1671 Albany Court Minutes (A. J. F. Van Laer, ed., *Minutes of the Court of Albany, Rensselaerswyck and Schenectady 1668–1673* [Albany: State University of New York Press, 1926], 1:257). Thodorasse, or Todorasse, signed (with a snake-like figure) the March 4, 1682 deed confirming a deed of 26 July/5 August 1667. His grandfather Caniachko was probably the Canachquo or Canaghko who signed two deeds in July, 1672 with what appear to be tortoises (*DRCHNY* 13:465 and IIDH Reel #2, 18 July 1672).

34. *DRCHNY* 3:751–53; Holland Society, ibid., 51.

CHAPTER 3

1. All quotations in this chapter about the July 11, 1690, Mohawk converts are taken from the Holland Society, *Yearbook for 1904* 51.

2. William N. Fenton, "The Roll Call of the Iroquois Chiefs: A Study of a Mnemonic Cane from the Six Nations Reserve," *Smithsonian Miscellaneous Collections* 111 (1950): 59.

3. Holland Society, *Yearbook for 1904* 7–10, 11–20 contains a list of communicants and church members found in volume 1 of the First Church in Albany records. After some individuals' names is a note, usually "dead," in a different handwriting than the list itself (which was done by Dominie Dellius). Inspection of a microfilm copy of these records and some of the 1701–1710 baptisms by Dominie Johannes Lydius shows that the later notes are in Lydius' handwriting. Since Dominie Lydius died in March, 1710 (*ERNY* 3:1810), the notations of death of communicants and members must have been made before this time. Isaac and Eunice's son Barend (Brant) was baptized on March 5, 1704, at Schenectady, so Isaac must have died after this date.

4. *DRCHNY* 4:728, 730–31, 743, 758, 897, 910, 985; Richmond P. Bond, *Queen Anne's American Kings* (Oxford: Clarenden Press, 1952), 39–40, 64; Holland Society, *Yearbook for 1904* 19, 52.

5. *DRCHNY* 4:539–41; Holland Society, ibid., 8 (David, Rebecca and Lydia were admitted to Communion together on October 22, 1691).

6. Holland Society, ibid., 8, 55, 76, 78; Church Records, SC 17568, Box 1k vol. 2 (pages are unnumbered); W. L. Stone, *Life of Brant* 1:499; Calvert Papers, Ms. 194 #1093, Maryland Historical Society, Baltimore (IIDH Reel #10 12 December 1734).

7. Daniel K. Richter, *Ordeal of the Longhouse* 107–08, Chapter 6.

8. Holland Society, *Yearbook for 1904* 8, 51, 64; J. Pearson, "Extracts from the Doop-Boek," 18:235, 19:72.

9. Holland Society, ibid., 51, 53; Records of the First Reformed Church of Schenectady, New York, vol. 1, pt. 2:156 (see Appendix B, note "a").

10. Holland Society, ibid., 8, 12, 20, 51, 57; Church Records, SC 17568, Box 1, vol. 2; J. Pearson, "Extracts from the Doop-Boek," 18:234, 358, 19:69, 70, 72; First Reformed Church, Schenectady, vol. 1, pt. 1:126, 141, 166; June 15, 1717 deed to Myndert Schuyler and others, Albany County Clerk's Office, Deed Book 5, 370–71 (IIDH reel #8, 15 June 1717 [III]).

11. Holland Society, ibid., 52.

12. W. L. Stone, *Life of Brant* 1:498–99; Boyd Ehle, "The Mohawk Valley Ehles," Saint Johnsville, New York, *Enterprise and News*, June 18, 1930; William Fenton, "Problems Arising from . . .," 208; *DRCHNY* 3:250.

13. A. B. Hulbert and W. N. Schwartz, eds., "David's Zeisberger's History," 82–83.

14. *DRCHNY* 3:732, 752–53; *DHNY* 2:144–45; Holland Society, *Yearbook for 1904* 52–53; *ERNY* 2:1010–11.

15. *ERNY* 2:1016–17; *DRCHNY* 3:771–72; *DHNY* 2:205, 213–15.

16. *DRCHNY* 3:777–80.

17. *DRCHNY* 3:800–05.

18. *DRCHNY* 3:814–18. Quotes from (1st) 817 and (2nd) 816.

19. *ERNY* 2:1065–66; Lois M. Feister, "Indian Dutch Relations in the Upper Hudson Valley: A Study of Baptism Records in the Dutch Reformed Church, Albany, New York," *Man in the Northeast* 24 (1982):90.

20. Caristase (Cristagie) served as a messenger for Arent Viele from Onondaga to Albany in the spring of 1690 (*DHNY* 2:144). The name Caristagia (Caristase) appears seventy-four years later at the Upper Castle of Canajoharie and, ironically, in 1768 was the baptismal name given to the son of a Caughnawaga Mohawk woman (*JP* 11:984; "Fort Stanwix [Rome, New York] Indian Baptisms, 1768," *New York Genealogical and Biographical Record* 103 [1972]:154; Appendix E); *DRCHNY* 3:815, 4:346.

21. Holland Society, *Yearbook for 1904* 8, 53–57, 62, 72, 74; J. Pearson, "Extracts from the Doop-Boek," 18:232; First Reformed Church, Schenectady, vol. 1, pt. 1:109, 117, 126, pt. 2:133, 134, 145; Church Records, SC 17568, Box 1, vol. 2; *Pa. Col. Rec.* 6:128; *JP* 13:173; Henry Barclay, Register Book, 65.

22. Albany County Clerk's Office, Deed Book 7:361–62 (IIDH Reel #27, 3 May 1765).

23. *DRCHNY* 4:897, 910; IIDH Reel #6, 16 Jan. 1701; W. L. Stone, *Life of Brant* 1:498–99; Jeptha Simms, *Frontiersmen of New York* (Albany: 1882-3), 1:130–31; Albany County Clerk's Office Deed Book 5:370–71 (IIDH Reel #8, 15 June 1717); First Reformed Church, Schenectady, vol. 1, pt. 2:175; Church Records SC 17568 Box 1, vol. 2.

24. J. Pearson, "Extracts from the Doop-Boek," 18:232; Simms, ibid.

25. Holland Society, *Yearbook for 1904* 17, 58, 78; Church Records, SC 17568, Box 1, vol. 2; J. Pearson, ibid., 234, 235, 358, 19:72; First Reformed Church, Schenectady, vol. 1, pt. 2:139, 144.

26. On the tradition of Hendrick Peters' adoption see: Milton W. Hamilton, "Theyanoguin," *Encyclopedia of Canadian Biography* 3 (Toronto, University of Troonto Press, 1979):622–24; on the tradition of Hendrick having a Mahican father and a Mohawk mother see "Language of the Mohegans," *Mass. Historical Society Collections* (1st ser.), 9:97 and *DRCHNY* 6:297; on Hendrick Peters' age: Reverend Gideon Hawley, who knew both Hendrick and his brother Abraham at Stockbridge, Mass., stated that "neither of them were seventy at their deaths" (*Mass. Hist. Society Collections* [3rd ser.], 1:151). Also, Joseph Burt, an eyewitness to Hendrick just before his death at Lake George in 1755, told Timothy Dwight that Hendrick was between 60 and 65 years of age at his death (Timothy Dwight, *Travels in New York and New England* [New Haven, 1821], 262); On Hendrick's clan see Boyd Ehle, "The Mohawk Valley Ehles," Saint Johnsville *Enterprise and News*, June 18, 1930, and *Pa. Col. Rec.* 6:127; other references to Hendrick's life and position (to name only a few) are found in: *JP* 1:278, 9:30, 231, 238, 357, 10:337, 13:15–19; H. R. Schoolcraft, *Notes on the Iroquois* (Albany: Munsell, 1847), frontispiece and 415–16; H. R. Schoolcraft, *History of the Indian Tribes of the United States* (Philadelphia: Lippencott, 1857), 6:220.

27. Holland Society, *Yearbook for 1904* 60.

28. *DRCHNY* 4:17.

29. W. Fenton, "Problems arising from. . .," 209; W. Fenton and E. Tooker, "Mohawk," 474–75; names of Mohawk towns appeared to change frequently in the seventeenth century, but during the eighteenth century the names Tionondoroge (spelled in various ways) and Canajoharie remained in general use. Holland Society, *Yearbook for 1904* 62; Henry Barclay, Register Book, 35.

30. Holland Society, ibid., 71.

31. Anthony signed the Margaret and Edward Collins (Nov. 16, 1714) deed with a bear (W. L. Stone, *Life of Brant* 1:498–99). Another Anthony, living at Canajoharie between 1732 and 1760, was a member of the Wolf clan—Boyd Ehle, "The Mohawk Valley Ehles," Saint Johnsville *Enterprise and News*, June 18, 1930; *JP*, 13:175.) The earlier Anthony appears with Dorcas sponsoring Jacob and Isaac, twin sons of

Elias and Martin[a] in 1724, suggesting a brother-sister relationship, at least in the Mohawk sense: Church Records, SC 17568, Box 1, vol. 2; for his descendants see Fig. 4-5.

CHAPTER 4

1. Holland Society, *Yearbook for 1904* 10, 66, 69.

2. Brant, in a letter to the Archbishop of Canterbury in 1710, signs with the Bear totem and is pictured with a bear in portraits (R. P. Bond, *Queen Anne's American Kings* 40 and plates facing pages 8 and 48). Lucas signs the June 15, 1717, deed to Myndert Schuyler for lands at Schoharie with a bear (Albany County Clerk's Office, Deed Book 5:370–71 and IIDH Reel #8 15 June 1717 [III]). For Dorcas as a Bear, see text and footnote 3, this chapter. J. Pearson, "Extracts from the Doop-Boek," 18:234; *Ontario Historical Society Papers and Records* 12 (1914):102; Holland Society, *Yearbook for 1904* 10; Church Records, SC 17568, Box 1, vol. 2.

3. Holland Society, *Yearbook for 1904* 64, 72; Church Records, SC 17568, Box 1, vol. 2; *JP* 3:153, 157, 9:626, 722, 10:17, 125, 128, 308, 410, 12:900, 13:174; P. A. Wallace, *Conrad Weiser* 348, 432; Henry Barclay, Register Book, 5.

4. Holland Society, ibid., 71, 73.

5. Ibid., 71 (the original records also contain the statement in Dutch that Neeltie Kawachkerat and Sara Sukkorio were sisters), 74; J. Pearson, "Extracts from the Doop-Boek," 18:234 (Neeltie is crossed out in the original entry); First Reformed Church, Schenectady, Vol. 1, pt. 1:126, pt. 2:145.

6. Holland Society, ibid., 9, 10; *DRCHN,* 4:59–62, 77, 93, 125, 281.

7. Holland Society, ibid., 68; New York State Archives, Albany, Colonial Manuscripts, 40:72, 75 (IIDH Reel #5, 19 and 28 September 1695); *DRCHNY* 4:363.

8. Great Britain, Public Record Office CO5/1063 (IIDH Reel #14, 2 Aug 1750 [II]); *ERNY* 2:1169; *DRCHNY* 4:177, 345–47, 363; IIDH reel #5, 6 June 1698; Georgiana C. Nammack, *Fraud, Politics, and the Dispossession of the Indians* (Norman: University of Oklahoma Press, 1969), 11.

9. *DRCHNY,* 4:346; Holland Society, *Yearbook for 1904* 69–78.

10. Daniel K. Richter, *Ordeal of the Longhouse* 187–88, 191–92, 356; *DRCHNY* 4:340–41, 347–51.

11. *DRCHNY* 4:345–47, 362–66; *ERNY* 2:1224.

12. *Propositions Made by the Five Nations of Indians . . . the 20th of July, Anno Dom. 1698* (New York: 1698), 3–4; *DRCHNY* 4:364, 510, 565–66; Daniel K. Richter, *Ordeal of the Longhouse*, 192.

13. *DRCHNY* 4:539-41;

14. Ibid.; *ERNY* 2:1318-20.

15. *DRCHNY* 4:488–90, 533–36; *ERNY* 2:1305–14, 1316–17, 1320–25, 1329–31, 1335, 1394–1422.

16. R. Aquila, *The Iroquois Restoration* 45, 47; *DRCHNY* 4:648, 730–31; Holland Society, *Yearbook for 1904* 10, 63, 75 (Agnes is not noted as having gone to Canada).

17. R. Aquilia, ibid., 46, 48–54, 55-66; *DRCHNY* 4:654, 657, 896–911.

18. G. C. Nammack, *Fraud* 16; Daniel K. Richter, *Ordeal of the Longhouse*, 212.

19. *ERNY* 2:1308–09, 1316–17, 1336–37, 1365.

20. Ibid., 1340–45, 1350–51, 1359–60, 1386–88.

21. Ibid., 1371–74.

22. Ibid., 1388–90.

23. Ibid., 1371–74 (quotes from 1373); *DRCHNY* 4:727–46.

24. *Calendar of State Papers*, 1701, Item no. 38:33–37 (in IIDH Reel #6, 16 Jan 1701 [II], quote from 33–34); *DRCHNY* 4:835.

25. Deeds (in English and Dutch) enclosed with *Calendar of State Papers*, 1701, Item no. 38 ibid.

26. Jonathan Pearson, *Three Centuries: The History of the First Reformed Church of Schenectady 1680–1980, Volume I* (written by Pearson in 1880, reprinted 1980), 77; John Garratt, "The Four Kings, An Historical Essay," in *The Four Kings* (Ottawa: Public Archives of Canada, 1985), 4; Daniel K. Richter, *Ordeal of the Longhouse* 365 n.15.

27. J. Pearson, ibid., 74; *DRCHNY* 4:815 and *DHNY* 3:540–41; J. Pearson, "Extracts from the Doop-Boek," 18:357–58; First Reformed Church, Schenectady, vol. 1, pt. 2:145.

28. *DRCHNY* 4:906.

29. First Reformed Church, Schenectady, vol. 1, pt. 1:109, 111, 113–17, 118, 121–24, 126, 129, pt. 2:132, 133–36, 139–41, 144–46, 156, 160, 166, 169–78; Pearson gives a different set of figures (J. Pearson, *Three Centuries* 1:80): 20 Indian couples married, 101 Indians baptized, and 14 professed church members. The main descrepancy is

whether the couples on p. 126 were being admitted as members or married (see LDS Microfilm #0534207, Table of Contents, 2).

30. Church Records, SC 17568, Box 1, vol. 2; *DRCHNY* 4:988.

31. Church Records, ibid.

32. John Segehowane and his wife Mary had a son Jacob baptized (sponsor, Jacamine) in Albany on Nov. 26, 1725, and were almost certainly the John and Mary parents of Brant who was baptized on April 2, 1727, and adopted by Jacamine (Holland Society, *Yearbook for 1906* 20, 26). This Brant—Brant Kaweghnoke—married Lydia, Seth Sietstarare's daughter, on September 6, 1738 (Henry Barclay, Register Book, 9). Since Lydia was baptized on April 13, 1707 (Church Records, SC 17568, Box 1, vol. 2), Brant must have been born about 1710 or so and Johannes Segehowane born about 1690—he is still active in 1760 (*JP* 13:173). Johannes Rotsiho (b. 1688) is the only Johannes (or Jan, for that matter), born about this time. Ezras Kanneraghtahare's daughter Margaret was baptized on April 17, 1703 (First Reformed Church, Schenectady, vol. 1, pt. 2:145). Of the two Seths chronologically right to be her husband, Seth son of Celie Wakajesa seems related only to a couple, Henry and Margaret, who married in 1722 and had a son Seth baptized on January 1, 1723 (Church Records, SC 17568, Box 1, vol. 2). He may have died young. The other is Seth Adanho. Span of children baptized (1711–1724), sponsors, and the close family tie make it likely that Anthony's wife was Sara Kakenbarontje (b. 1691). The 1748 baptisms are in Holland Society, *Yearbook for 1906* 122, 124.

33. *JP* 1:645; *DRCHNY* 6:659; Milton Hamilton, *Sir William Johnson, Colonial American* (New York: National University Publications and Kennekat Press, 1979), 63, 343; "The Colden Papers, Vol. II—1730–1742," *New York Historical Society Collections* 51 (1918):52–54 (quotes from 52); Holland Society, ibid., 45.

34. *JP* 1:786, 9:489; Julian Boyd, ed., *The Susquehannah Company Papers Volume I: 1750–55* (Ithaca, NY: Cornell University Press, 1962), lxxxiv–lxxxviii.

35. *ERNY* 3:1639–45; *DRCHNY* 5:227 (quote); *DHNY* 3:541.

36. John W. Lydekker, *The Faithful Mohawks* (Cambridge: University Press, 1938), 14–23, J. Garratt, "The Four Kings," 4–5; Daniel K. Richter, *Ordeal of the Longhouse* 222.

37. Church Records, SC 17568, Box 1, vol. 2; *DHNY* 3:540–41.

CHAPTER 5

1. *DRCHNY* 4:994; *LIR*, 185–86.
2. *DRCHNY* 5:65; *LIR* 9, 201; C. Colden, "The Letters and Papers of Cadwallader Colden, Vol. IX," *New York Historical Society Collections* 68 (1935):363–64; Daniel Richter, *Ordeal of the Longhouse* 216.
3. David Hawke, *The Colonial Experience* (New York: Bobbs-Merrill, 1966), 332; R. Bond, *Four Kings* 22–24;
4. *LIR* 202–06; R. Bond, ibid., 27–29.
5. D. Hawke, *Colonial Experience* 332; J. Garratt, "The Four Kings," 6; R. Bond, ibid., 34.
6. R. Bond, ibid., 31–33, 35, 113.
7. *DRCHNY* 4:907–08; Daniel K. Richter, *Ordeal of the Longhouse* 197.
8. J. Lydekker, *Faithful Mohawks* 21–24; Rev. Thomas Barclay called the Mohawks "so ignorant and Scandalous that they can scarce be reputed Christians" (*DHNY* 3:541). This does not auger well for a good relationship.
9. J. Munsell, ed., "The City Records from 1705–1710," *Annals of Albany* 5:186.
10. *DRCHNY* 4:279, 281, 346, 728, 730–31, 743, 758, 897, 985; IIDH Reel #14, 2 August 1750 (II).
11. *DRCHNY* 4:728, 897, 985. Awanay and Joseph were probably baptized in Canada.
12. R. Bond, *Four Kings* 116. Hendrick later learned to speak some English (ibid., 64).
13. *DRCHNY* 4:730–31, 994; R. Bond, ibid., 28–29; Draper 15F19.
14. Holland Society, *Yearbook for 1904* 10, 66, 70, 77; Church Records, SC 17568, Box 1, vol. 2; First Reformed Church, Schenectady, vol. 1, pt. 1:106, pt. 2:145; J. Pearson, "Extracts from the Doop-Boek," 18:234.
15. J. Pearson, ibid., 18:233, 234, 357; Church Records, SC 17568, Box 1, vol. 2; First Reformed Church, Schenectady, vol. 1, pt. 1:106, pt. 2:139; Patrick Frazier, *The Mohigans of Stockbridge* (Lincoln: University of Nebraska Press, 1992), 9.
16. *DRCHNY* 3:802; *LIR* 172; First Reformed Church, Schenectady, vol. 1, pt. 2:139.
17. R. Bond, *Four Kings* 1–2; Lydekker, *The Faithful Mohawks*

27-28; J. Garratt, "The Four Kings," 8.

18. J. Lydekker, ibid., 28-31; R. Bond, ibid., 7-9, 59-60; J. Garratt, 9-10.

19. R. Bond, ibid., 3-15; J. Garratt, ibid., 8-9.

20. Church Records, SC 17568, Box 1, vol. 2; Holland Society, *Yearbook for 1906* 24, 27, 40, 42, 67; Henry Barclay, Register Book, 6, 26, 33; *Pa. Col. Rec.* 6:127; Martin Kellogg, "An account What I have Done for the Mohawk in the Year 1750 and 1751," [actually extends to 1752], Connecticut Archives, Indians (1st Ser.), 2:72a; Boyd Ehle, "The Mohawk Valley Ehles," Saint Johnsville, New York, *Enterprise and News*, June 18, 1930; *JP* 3:156, 157, 9:782; Treaty between the Indians formerly resident at the Mohawk Castle, Fort Hunter, New York . . . 1789, Public Archives Canada, MG 19 F 21 (1 page).

21. Beatrice Mattice, *They Walked these Hills Before Me: An Early History of the Town of Conesville* (Cornwallville, NY: 1980), chptr. 2: 2; P. Frazier, *Mohigans of Stockbridge* 9, 36.

22. R. Bond, *Four Kings* 40; J. Lydekker, *Faithful Mohawks* 32; W. L. Stone, *Life of Brant* 1:2; I. T. Kelsay, *Joseph Brant 1743-1807 Man of Two Worlds* (Syracuse: Syracuse University Press, 1984), 51-53.

23. *The London Magazine* 45 (July, 1776):339; Barbara Graymont, "Theyendanegea," *Dictionary of Canadian Biography* 5 (Toronto: University of Toronto Press, 1983):803; Draper 1F33, 13F21.

24. Carl F. Klinck and James J. Talman, eds., *The Journal of Major John Norton 1816* (Toronto: University of Toronto Press, 1970), 105, 109, 270; Holland Society, *Yearbook for 1904* 10, 63; Daniel K. Richter, "Iroquois versus Iroquois," 71.

25. *JP* 3:395, 12:457.

26. I. T. Kelsay, *Joseph Brant* 177, 208; Sir Frederick Haldimand, Unpublished papers, British Museum Additional Manuscripts, vol. 21774:56; Draper 13F135-2; see also Chapter 12.

27. Charles A. Strange, contributor, "Excerpts from the Records of the Society for the Propagation of the Gospel in Foreign Parts," *New York Genealogical and Biographical Record* 105 (1974):117; *Pa. Col. Rec.* 6:128.

CHAPTER 6

1. W. A. Knittle, *Early Eighteenth Century Palatine Emigration*

(Philadelphia, Dorrance & Co., 1937), 2–5, 12-22, 47, 52–65 (this scholarly treatment is still an excellent source for the history of the Palatine immigrations).

2. Ibid., 66–68, 124–31, 144–46; P. A. Wallace, *Conrad Weiser* 6–8.

3. *LIR* 214–15.

4. Ibid., 215–16 (quote is from the latter page).

5. Ibid.

6. G. Nammack, *Fraud*, 18; Peter Wraxall, *An Abridgment of Indian Affairs* (Cambridge, MA: Harvard Historical Studies 21, 1915), 75; New York Council Minutes 10: 529–30 (IIDH Reel #7, 20 June 1710).

7. Albany County Clerk's Office, Deed Book 5:227 (IIDH Reel #8, 28 May 1714).

8. *DHNY* 3:338.

9. P. Wraxall, *Abridgement* 79; G. Nammack, *Fraud* 19; W. A. Knittle, *Palatine Emigration* 152.

10. P. Wraxall, ibid.; W. A. Knittle, ibid., 156–57, 160, 165, 169–70.

11. Jeptha R. Simms, *History of Schoharie County and Border Wars of the Revolution* (Albany: Munsell & Tanner, 1845), 54–56; P. A. Wallace, *Conrad Weiser* 28; New York Council Minutes 11:235–36 (IIDH Reel #8, 10 April 1714).

12. P. A. Wallace, ibid., 11–13, 15–16; Sanford Cobb, *The Story of the Palatines* (New York: G. P. Putnam's Sons, 1897), 211–13; W. A. Knittle, *Palatine Emigration* 173–77, 188.

13. P. A. Wallace, ibid., 16–17 (quote 17).

14. *DRCHNY* 4:978–79; J. R. Simms, *History of Schoharie* 55; W. L. Stone, *Life of Brant* 1:498.

15. J. Lydekker, *Faithful Mohawks* 37, 40; Jeptha R. Simms, *Frontiersmen of New York* (Albany: 1882-3), 1:75.

16. J. M. Brown, *Brief Sketch of the First Settlement of the County of Schoharie by the Germans* 5, 19; J. R. Simms, ibid., 74, 76.

17. J. R. Simms, *History of Schoharie* 55; New York State Archives, Albany, Colonial Manuscripts, Land Papers, vol. 9:23; Church Records, SC 17568, Box 1, vol. 2; New York State Archives, Albany, Land Papers 1731-35, vol. 2:106A–106B; *JP* 9:589.

18. J. R. Simms, *Frontiersmen* 1:75; Beatrice Mattice, *They Walked these Hills before Me* chptr. 2:2; R. W. Vosburgh, ed., "Records of the High and Low Dutch Reformed Congregation at Schoharie (now the

Reformed Church)," (New York Genealogical and Biographical Society, New York, 1917), vol. 1, pt. 1:1, 10, 31, 34 265; R. W. Vosburgh, ed., "Records of St. Paul's Evangelical Lutheran Church, Schoharie, New York," (New York Genealogical and Biographical Society, New York, 1914), vi, viii, ix, xi, 19; New York State Archives, Land Papers 1731–35, ibid.; *Pa. Col. Rec.* 6:128; Petition from the Mohawks of Schoharie against Johannes Lawyer for claiming land given to them to Nicholas Matice, New York State Archives, Albany, Colonial Manuscripts 81:135 (IIDH Reel #16 Sept. 1754); J. M. Brown, *Brief Sketch of the First Settlement of the County of Schoharie by the Germans* 8, 35; *JP,* 12:96.

19. P. A. Wallace, *Conrad Weiser* 17–18, 25, 578–79; W. A. Knittle, *Palatine Emmigration* 192–93. Weiser wrote in 1750 of the Karighondontees: "they being my old acquaintence, as I had lived from the year 1714 till the year 1729 within two miles of their town" (*Pa. Col. Rec..* 5:471). He did not mention his 1713 stay with the Mohawks in relation to the Karighondontees.

20. W. A. Knittle, ibid., 191.

21. Sanford Cobb, *Story of the Palatines* 281. W. A. Knittle (ibid., 200–01) says that it was Nicholas Bayard's grandson, also named Nicholas, who executed this maneuver. New York Council Minutes 11:235–36 (IIDH Reel #8 10 and 22 April 1714); J. R. Simms, *History of Schoharie* 62–63; Albany County Clerk's Office Deed Book 5:370–71 (IIDH Reel #8 15 June 1717 [III]).

22. W. A. Knittle, ibid., 204–09; P. A. Wallace, *Conrad Weiser* 30–31.

23. Albany County Clerk's Office Deed Book 5:370–71 (IIDH Reel #8 15 June 1717 [III]); *DRCHNY* 4:910.

24. Leah Stevens interpreted the 1711 and 1714 deeds to Adam Vrooman (J. R. Simms, *History of Schoharie* 56), the February 6, 1722/3 deed to William York, Jacob Frederick Lawyer and Nicholas York (N.Y. State Archives, Albany, Colonial Manuscripts, Land Papers vol. 9: 23), and the 1722 deed to John Conrad Weiser Junior and others for land on both sides of the Mohawk River (N.Y. State Archives, ibid., vol. 8:168). Paulus Peters, son of Hendrick Peters Tiyanoga, signed several documents with his name, such as the July 5, 1754, grant of land near Canada Creek from the Indians of Canajoharie: Albany County Clerk's Office Deed Book 7:52 (IIDH Reel #23 2 April 1760); he also wrote

several letters to Sir William Johnson and Arent Stevens (*JP* 2:293, 714–15, 4: 165–66, 9:534, 546–48) and was schoomaster to Mohawk children at Canajoharie: "The Reverend John Ogilvie, D.D.," *Ontario Historical Society Papers and Records,* 22:314, 316, 319; on Mohawk literacy in their own language see Richard Smith, *A Tour of Four Great Rivers* (edited by Francis W. Halsey, New York: Scribner's, 1906), 86.

CHAPTER 7

1. J. Lydekker, *Faithful Mohawks* 32–33 (quotes from 33n).

2. Ibid., 33–34. The earliest surviving records for St. Peter's are found in "A Register of Christnings Kept By The Revd. John Ogilvie begun June ye 9th 1749," *New York Genealogical and Biographical Record* 67 (1936):204–216, 369–86.

3. J. Pearson, "Extracts from the Doop-Boek," 19:71; First Reformed Church, Schenectady, vol. 1, pt. 2:173, 177.

4. Church Records, SC 17568, Box 1, vol. 2; J. Pearson, ibid., 18:235, 358; First Reformed Church, Schenectady, vol. 1, pt. 1:126.

5. *JP* 13:174; Draper 13F86, 88–89; Henry Barclay, Register Book, 4, 35.

6. Holland Society, *Yearbook for 1904* 69, 73, 82; First Reformed Church, Schenectady, vol. 1, pt. 2:145; Church Records, SC 17568, Box 1, vol. 2.

7. *DRCHNY* 4:38; *JP* 9:626; Henry Barclay, Register Book, 6, 17; Holland Society, *Yearbook for 1906* 20, 26; *DRCHNY* 6:15–16.

8. J. Munsell, "Table of Dutch Baptismal Names with the corresponding English Names," *Annals of Albany* 3:114–115; First Refirmed Church, Schenectady, v1, pt. 2:139; W. L. Stone, *Life of Brant* 1:498-99; L. Feister, "Indian Dutch Relations," 107; *JP* 8:955, 965; Barbara Graymont, *The Iroquois and the American Revolution* 225–28; David Faux, "Johannes Crine: A Traitor among the Mohawks," *The Loyalist Gazette* 19(1):5–6.

9. Henri Béchard, "Togouiry," *Dictionary of Canadian Biography* 1 (1969):650.

10. Elisabeth Tooker, "The League of the Iroquois," 424; C. A. Westlager, *The Delaware Indians* (New Brunswick, NJ: Rutgers University Press, 1972), 71–72.

11. *JP* 13:174; D. Faux, "Johannes Crine," 5; Evelyn H. C. Johnson, "Chief John Johnson" *Ontario Historical Society Papers and Records* 12

(1914):102, 104; Seth Newhouse, "Cosmogony of Dekanawida's Government of the Iroquois Confederacy: The Original Historical Narratives of the Iroquois Confederacy," Public Archives of Canada, MG 19 F26, 246.

12. Petition from the Mohawks of Schoharie against Johannes Lawyer for Claiming land given to them to Nicholas Mattice, New York State Archives, Albany, Colonial Manuscripts, 81:135 (IIDH Reel #16 Sept. 1754); *Pa. Col. Rec.* 6:122–23, 127 contains one example of Abraham, Nickus and Hendrick using the surname Peters; for Paulus Peters, see footnote 24, Chapter 6.

13. First Reformed Church, Schenectady, vol. 1, pt. 2:178.

14. J. Lydekker, *Faithful Mohawks* 34–35; *Annals of Albany* 6:58–60 and *DHNY* 3:542–43; P. A. Wallace, *Conrad Weiser* 17.

15. *Annals of Albany*, ibid., 59.

16. C. Colden, *History of the Five Indian Nations* 2:221–22 (quote from 222); "Expenses of an Indian Treaty," *Annals of Albany* 4:276; J. R. Simms, *History of Schoharie* 27, 55; IIDH Reel #8 15 June 1717 (III); *LIR*, 218; "The Mohawk Valley Elhes," Saint Johnsville, New York, *Enterprise and News*, June 4, 1930.

17. *Annals of Albany* 6:59–60.

18. J. Lydekker, *Faithful Mohawks*, 35.

19. Ibid., 34–38; Records of the Society for the Propagation of the Gospel, Letterbooks (series A), 8:257, 304–05, 9:227–28, 10:190, 219, 11:355–56, 12:411, 13:326–29, 337, 487.

20. J. Lydekker, ibid., 39–40 (quote from 40).

21. Ibid., 40, 49; *DRCHNY* 5:372–76; Church Records, SC 17568, Box 1, vol. 2; R. Bond, *The Four Kings* 94; D. Landy, "Tuscarora among the Iroquois" in Bruce G. Trigger, ed., *Handbook of North American Indians, Volume XV: Northeast* 518–24.

22. *DRCHNY* 5:372; Holland Society, *Yearbook for 1904* 66; J. Pearson, "Extracts from the Doop-Boek," 18:232, 358; First Reformed Church, Schenectady, vol. 1, pt. 2:177; W. L. Stone, *Life of Brant* 1:498–99.

23. *LIR* 205; W. L. Stone, ibid.; J. Lydekker, *Faithful Mohawks* 55; J. Pearson, ibid., 18:235; Evert Wendell, Indian Account Book, 1695–1726, Misc. Microfilms #71, New York Historical Society, 106; First Reformed Church, Schenectady, vol. 1, pt. 2:133.

24. First Reformed Church, Schenectady, vol. 1, pt. 2:160, 176; J.

Pearson, ibid.; J. Lydekker, ibid.; Holland Society, *Yearbook for 1906* 51, 67; Henry Barclay, Register Book, 3, 20, 56.
   25. *DRCHNY* 5:372–76.
   26. Daniel K. Richter, *Ordeal of the Longhouse* 231; *DRCHNY* 5:569.
   27. *JP* 3:162, 163, 166, 10:105, 11:659, 12:261, 13:173, 177; J. R. Simms, *History of Schoharie* 165, Henry Barclay, Register Book, 67; Gideon Hawley, unpublished diary and papers in the collection of the Congregational Society of Boston (microfilm copy owned by Broome County Historical Society), 49.
   28. SPG Letterbooks (series A), 9:227–28; J. Lydekker, *Faithful Mohawks* 47–48, 50 (quote).
   29. Daniel K. Richter, *Ordeal of the Longhouse* 232–33; J. Lydekker, ibid., 51.

CHAPTER 8
   1. C. Colden, "Letters on Smith's History of New York," *New York Historical Society Collections* 1 (1868):200.
   2. "Witham Marshe's Journal," *Mass. Historical Society Collections,* 1st ser.), 7: 189–91.
   3. William Darlington, ed., *Christopher Gish's Journals and Biographies of His Contemporaries* (Pittsburgh: J.R. Weldin, 1893), 154.
   4. William A. Hunter, "Elizabeth? Couc," *Dictionary of Canadian Biography* 3(1971):147–48.
   5. H. Charbonneau and J. Légaré, *Répertoire des Actes,* 4 (B601): 1651-8-27, and 1652-11-1, 4 (M601):1657-4-16; Benjamin Sulte, "The Montour Family," in William H. Engle, ed., *Notes and Queries Historical, Biographical, and Genealogical Relating Chiefly to Interior Pennsylvania* (4th ser.), 2:327–29.
   6. B. Sulte, ibid., 327 (quote); H. Carbonneau and J. Légaré, ibid., 4 (B601):1657-4-16.
   7. B. Sulte, ibid.; H. Charbonneau and J. Légaré, ibid. 4 (B601):- 1657-7-14, 1659-11-27, and 1664-6-1.
   8. M. Trudel, *Histoire de la Novelle-France 3,* pt. 2:459, 584–85.
   9. B. Sulte, "The Montour Family," 328; Thomas-M. Charland, *Histoire de Sainte François-du-Lac* (Ottawa: Dominican College, 1942), 21, 23.

10. H. Charbonneau and J. Légaré, *Répertoire des Actes* 5 (B471):1677-12-31, 6 (C601):1664-5-22; T.-M. Charland, ibid., 29.

11. T.-M. Charland, ibid., 30–31.

12. Ibid., 30; B. Sulte, "The Montour Family," 328.

13. Archives nationales de Quebec (Montreal), ACTES: Pierre Couc 1711-6-14: Contrat de mariage entre Joseph Grinhil . . . et Marie-Louise Paillé; Emma L. Colman, *New England Captives Carried to Canada* (Portland, ME, The Southworth Press, 1925), 1:128-29, 417; H. Charbonneau and J. Légaré, *Répertoire des Actes* 8:565, 9:367.

14. *DRCHNY* 9:138–39 (quote from 139).

15. H. Charbonneau and J. Légaré, *Répertoire des Actes* 5 (B471 and M471):1682-8-30, 5 (B471):1684-9-21 and 1686-7-25, 4 (B631):-1688-6-26 and 1690-1-1, 12 (B601):253, 287.

16. H. Charbonneau and J. Légaré, ibid., 4 (B601):1684-5-1, 4 (B631):1687-11, (M631):1688-1-1; Cyprien Tanguay, *Dictionaire Généalogique des Familles Canadiennes* (Montreal, Eusebe Senécal et Fils, 1887), 3:160; T.-M. Charland, *Histoire de Saint François* 17; William A. Haviland and Marjory W. Power, *The Original Vermonters* (Hanover, NH: University Press of New England, 1981), 227; T. Pownall, *A Topographic Description of the Dominions of The United States of America* (Pittsburgh: University of Pittsburgh Press, 1949), 155–56; the editor of this volume presumes that Montour's Creek is present-day East Creek, but an old map reproduced on the wall of the museum in Whitehall, New York, shows it to be in the location of Metawee Creek ("Skenesborough, heretofore Montours Creek"); R. Jetté, *Dictionnaire Généalogique* 278.

17. H. Charbonneau and J. Légaré, *Répertoire des Actes* 5 (M471): 1684-4-30 and 6 (NOT):1684-4-26; R. Jetté, ibid., 490.

18. Memorandum of M. de la Mothe concerning the establishment of Detroit, written November 19, 1704 in "Cadillac Papers," *Michigan Pioneer Collections* 33 (1903):237–38.

19. Ibid.; for an evaluation of Cadillac and the trustworthiness of his writings, see Y. Zoltvany, "Laumet," *Dictionary of Canadian Biography* 2 (1969):352, 356.

20. *Mich. Pioneer Coll.* 33:238.

21. Ibid., 270; "The Mackinac Register," *Wisconsin Hist. Collections* 19 (1910):1; R. Jetté, *Dictionnaire Généalogique* 278, 795; *Mich. Pioneer Coll.* 33:270; Y. Zoltvany, "Laumet," 352–53 (quote from 353).

22. R. Jetté, ibid., 278, 490. Jetté equates the separate references to Marie Anne Germaneau (or Montour) to three people: Louis Couc's daughter, Isabelle's natural daughter, and Isabelle and Joachim's daughter. They are obviously one individual, Isabelle's natural daughter. Marie Anne gave her age as thirty in 1727 when she became the servant of M. Lamy and as thirty-five in 1730 when her son Jean Baptiste was baptized. This son was not the child of her husband Jean Montari (or Montary) Jolicoeur. A Jolicoeur was one of the soldiers who deserted with Isabelle in 1706 (see note 33). Marie Anne died April 22, 1730, having married Montari three months previously on January 30. On August 26, 1730, Montari was remarried to Marie, daughter of Joseph Lafleur and his wife Elizabeth—Joseph was Louis Couc's son baptized in November, 1687; his wife Elizabeth a Huron from Detroit: H. Charbonneau and J. Légaré, *Répertoire des Actes* 13 (B391):117, 177, 233, 18:4, 267, 269, 357. For Michael Germaneau see ibid., 13:151, 237, 288. Michael gave his parents' Christian names as Pierre and Marie (actually, his maternal grandparents Christian names). For Marguerite Germaneau, wife of Jean Renault Langlois, see ibid., 13:243.

23. *Mich. Pioneer Coll.* 33:238, 268.

24. Ibid., 238 (quote). The "Techenet" to whom Isabelle was married may have been one of the two elder sons of Alexandre Téchenay (who came to New France with the Carignan Regiment in 1665): Jean, born in 1669 or Pierre, born in 1671 (R. Jetté, *Dictionnaire Généalogique* 1065).

25. *Mich. Pioneer Coll.* 33:432–36. Outchipouac, one of the Ottawa war chiefs who was supposed to have been betrayed by Isabelle and her collaborators Quarante Sous (a Huron) and Bourgmont, was the Indian who later guided Marguerite Turpin to the English. Perhaps Cadillac was again slanting the story told to d'Aigremont.

26. B. Sulte, "The Montour Family," 327 (quote); *Mich. Pioneer Coll.* 33:260–61, 493; Marcel Fournier, *De La Nouvelle Angleterre et la Nouvelle-France* (Soc. Généalogique Canad.-Français, 1992), 167; H. Charbonneau and J. Légaré, *Répertoire des Actes* 4 (S631):1690-4.

27. *Mich. Pioneer Coll.* 34 (1904):234–36, 306; Henry D. Brown et al., eds., *Cadillac and the Founding of Detroit* (Detroit Historical Society and Wayne State University Press, 1976), 67.

28. *DRCHNY*, 9:138–39, 601, 839, 4:940; Y. Zoltvany, "New France and the West," *Canadian Historical Review* 46 (1968):301–22.

29. H. Charbonneau and J. Légaré, *Répertoire des Actes* 4 (S601): 1697-2-26, 12 (S601):297, 28:242, 247, 492; *DRCHNY* 9:138–39.

30. Y. Zoltvany, "Laumet," 353–55; *Mich. Pioneer Coll.* 33:425.

31. Y. Zoltvany, ibid., 354–55; *Mich. Pioneer Coll.* 33:441; P. Wraxall, *Abridgement* 50.

32. Y. Zoltvany, ibid., 354 (1st quote); *Mich. Pioneer Coll.* ibid. (2nd quote).

33. *Mich. Pioneer Coll.* 34:233–36. The statement by Jacques Lucas in this "Judgment rendered by the Council of war against Bertellemy Pichon," (November 7, 1707) is somewhat ambiguous and not well translated, since it implies that the three chief deserters had been brought in when in fact they had not. The deserter Pichon's statement is also not entirely clear (possibly by design). But when he says "he [Pichon] could not get him [Jolicoeur] to return, so he left him . . ." implies that Pichon came back to Detroit alone, unaided by soldiers from the fort, and because of the new intelligence he brought concerning Bourgmont a force was being sent out that day to capture the remaining deserters. Despite his apparently voluntary return, Pichon was executed.

34. *Mich. Pioneer Coll.* 34:307; *Pa. Col. Rec.* 3:295. All of Isabelle's full sisters are accounted for, but it is remotely possible that Latort is referring to an older Indian half-sister.

35. *DRCHNY* 5:65.

36. *DRCHNY* 9:830, 902.

37. C. Colden, "Papers, Vol. IX," *New York Historical Society Collections* 68 (1935):370–72; P. Wraxall, *Abridgement* 65–67.

38. C. Colden, ibid.; *Pa. Arch.* (1st ser.), 1:241.

39. *DRCHNY* 5:278–79; New York State Archives, Council Minutes, 11:100–03 (IIDH Reel #7 June 14, 1712); New York State Archives, Colonial Manuscripts, 57:169, 170 (IIDH Reel #7 June 16, 1712); W. Darlington, *Christopher Gish's Journals* 154; Daniel K. Richter, *Ordeal of the Longhouse* 240.

40. William C. Reichel, *Memorials of the Moravian Church* (Philadelphia, 1870), 97n; *JP* 10:148, 2:768; W. A. Hunter, "Elizabeth? Couc," 147; Richard E. Day, *Calendar of the Sir William Johnson Manuscripts in the New York State Library* (Albany: New York State Library, 1909), 205, 206, 208; *DRCHNY* 7:172.

41. W. C. Reichel, ibid., 95; P. A. Wallace, *Conrad Weiser* 353.

42. *Pa. Col. Rec.* 3:295; W. C. Reichel, *Memorials* 96–96; P. A. Wallace, *Conrad Weiser* 80, 139 (quote), 195.

43. W. C. Reichel, ibid.

44. "Witham Marshe's Journal," 189–91; W. A. Hunter, "Elizabeth? Couc," 147.

45. P. A. Wallace, *Conrad Weiser* contains numerous references to Andrew Montour with accompanying citations as does Albert T. Volwiler's *George Croghan and the Westward Movement* (Cleveland: Arthur H. Clark Co., 1926) and Nicholas B. Wainwright's *George Groghan, Wilderness Diplomat* (Chapel Hill: Univ. North Carolina Press, 1959—see p. 284 for Andrew's death); Holland Society, *Yearbook for 1907* 52; *JP* 2:522; 3:734, 925, 9:632, 634, 700, 804; 10:148; P. A. Wallace, *Indians in Pennsylvania* (Harrisburg: Pennsylvania Historical and Museum Commission, 1961), 175–76; Earl P. Olmsted, *Blackcoats among the Delaware: David Zeisberger on the Ohio Frontier* (Kent, Ohio: Kent State University Press, 1991), 129.

46. P. A. Wallace, *Conrad Weiser* 345, 368; *Pa. Col. Rec.* 5:689–700; Pennsylvania Prov. Records M:231-37 (IIDH Reel #15 4 October 1753); *Bull. Ft. Ticonderoga Mus.* 10 (5):385; *JP* 10:481, 12:357; Walter Pilkington, ed., *A Journal of the Reverend Samuel Kirkland* (Clinton, NY: Hamilton College, 1980), 34; Milo Quaife, ed., *The John Askin Papers* (Detroit Library Commission Burton Historical Collection, 1928), 1:194; R. D. Vosburgh, ed., "Records of the Reformed Protestant Dutch Church of German Flats, in Herkimer, town of German Flats, Herkimer County, N.Y." (New York, New York Genealogical and Biographical Society, 1917).

47. *Mich. Pioneer Coll.* 34:260–61, 264–65; R. Jetté, *Dictionnaire Généalogique* 758; M. Fournier, *De La Nouvelle Angleterre et La Nouvelle-France* 167.

48. *Mich. Pioneer Coll.* 33:583; P. A. Wallace, *Indians in Pennsylvania* 172–73; *Pa. Arch.* (1st ser.), 3:741.

49. *Pa. Arch.* (1st ser.), 3:558 (quote); P. A. Wallace, ibid., 173; Eugene F. Bliss, ed., *Diary of David Zeisberger among the Indians of Ohio* 1 (Cincinatti: Hist. and Philosophical Soc. of Ohio, 1885):148–49; W. C. Reichel, *Memorials* 330–31; Oscar J. Harvey, *History of Wilkes-Barre* 1 (Wilkes-Barre: 1909):207.

50. O. J. Harvey, ibid.; F. Bliss, ibid., 149.

51. "Witham Marshe's Journal," 189–91; W. H. Engle, *Notes and*

Queries . . . Relating Chiefly to Interior Pennsylvania (Harrisburg Pub. Co., 1897), Annual Volume 1896, 102; O. J. Harvey, ibid., 1026–27; E. A. Cruikshank, *The Story of Butler's Rangers and the Settlement of Niagara* (Welland, Ontario: Lundys Lane Historical Society, 1893), 66, 82; F. Bliss, *David Zeisberger* 1:148–49; *A Narrative of the Captivity and Sufferings of Benjamin Gilbert and His Family; Who Were Surprised by the Indians and Taken from Their Farms on the Frontiers of Pennsylvania. In the Spring, 1780* (Philadelphia and London, 1790), recounts the capture of the Gilbert family by Roland Montour and his brother John. It was noteable that due to the raiders' care everyone, from Benjamin Gilbert in his sixties to the youngest grandchild, an infant, arrived safely at Niagara. Roland's death is reported in Sir Frederick Haldimand papers (British Museum Additional Manuscripts volumes 21760 and 21842.

52. "Calendar of Council Minutes 1668–1783," *New York State Library Bulletin* 58 (1902):302; C. Tanguay, *Dictionnaire Généalogique des Familles Canadiennes* 3:160; "Minutes of the Council of Indian Affairs," Public Archives Canada, RG10, vol. 1819:137a–138.

53. *Pa. Arch.* (2nd ser.), 7:156.

54. Henry Barclay, Register Book, 4, 28, 51; *Bull. Ft. Ticonderoga Mus.* 10(5):383; First Reformed Church, Schenectady, vol. 2 (1728–1785), pt. 1:41

55. Henry Barclay, ibid.; Jelles Fonda, Indian Book for Jelles Fonda at Cachnewago (Fort Johnson, NY, Montgomery County Historical Society MSS 1-647), index.

56. P. A. Wallace, *Indians in Pennsylvania* 172; O. J. Harvey, *History of Wilkes-Barre* 984–85.

57. O. J. Harvey, ibid.

58. Henry Barclay, Register Book, 52; First Reformed Church, Schenectady, vol. 2, pt. 2:248.

59. *Dictionnaire National des Canadiens Français 1608–1760* 2 (Institut Généalogique Drouin, Montreal, 1965), 934; H. Charbonneau and J. Légaré, *Répertoire des Actes* 23:415; R. Jetté, *Dictionnaire Généalogique des Familles* 795; Archives nationales du Quebec (Montreal), ACTES: Montour 23-07-1765 (TR), 26-07-1729, 12-4-1747, 18-09-1756, 02-11-1758, 24-04-1759, 12-03-1753, 20-03-1753, 06-03-1759.

CHAPTER 9

1. George Sheldon, *History of Deerfield, Massachusetts* (Deerfield: E. A. Hall & Co., 1895), 1:389–92 (quote from 392).

2. *LIR* 231–33; George Sheldon, ibid., 404; R. Bond, *Four Kings* 64.

3. George Sheldon, ibid., 400.

4. Ibid., 409, 435.

5. George Sheldon, ibid., 226–27, 403–07; Timothy Hopkins, *The Kelloggs in the Old World and the New* (San Francisco, Sunset Press, 1903) vol. 1; Emma Lewis Coleman, *New England Captives Carried to Canada* 2:97–101; Marcel Fournier, *de la Nouvelle Angleterre à la Nouvelle-France* 152; *Journals of the House of Representatives of Massachusetts 1727–1729 Volume 8* (Massachusetts Historical Society, 1927), 110–11, 238, 364.

6. George Sheldon, ibid., 422–23, 426–27, 435; James Baxter, *The Pioneers of New France in New England* (Albany: Munsell, 1894), 237, 241–42; Church Records, SC 17568, Box 1, vol. 2; Henry Barclay, Register Book, 7, 17.

7. Church Records, SC 17568, Box 1, vol. 2; Holland Society, *Yearbook for 1904*, 74; First Reformed Church, Schenectady, vol. 1, pt. 2:143.

8. Holland Society, ibid., 52; George Sheldon, *History of Deerfield*, 415; Church Records, SC 17568, Box 1, vol. 2.

9. Church Records, ibid.

10. Ibid.; J. Pearson, "Extracts from the Doop-Boek," 18:234.

11. Church Records, ibid.; Holland Society, *Yearbook for 1906* 21, 40, 42; Maryland Historical Society, Baltimore, Calvert Papers, Ms. 194 #1093 (IIDH Reel #10, 12 December 1734).

12. Holland Society, ibid., 29, 37, 49; Henry Barclay, Register Book, 6, 35; J. Lydekker, *Faithful Mohawks* 55.

13. "The Mohawk Valley Ehles," Saint Johnsville, New York, *Enterprise and News*, June 4, 1930; W. J. Hinke, "Letter to the Editor," *Enterprise and News*, June 21, 1932.

14. Ibid., June 4, 1930; J. R. Simms, *Frontiersmen of New York*, 1:61–62.

15. *Enterprise and News*, ibid.; Holland Society, *Yearbook for 1906* 36, 40, 41, 45, 46. Isabel T. Kelsay, in "Karaghtadie" *Dictionary of Canadian Biography* (1974), 3:322, confuses Nickus Canaquase with

Nickus Karaghiagdatie. Both are from Canajoharie, but Nickus Peters Karaghiagdatie was a Wolf clan sachem and Nickus Canaquase probably the Turtle Nickus in the 1732 Van Driessen/Ehle deed and the "Big Nickus" who signed a deed in 1751 with a turtle—*JP*, 13:18.

16. Saint Johnsville, New York, *Enterprise and News*, June 4, June 11, and June 18, 1930.

17. Ibid., June 18, 1930.

18. *JP* 13:113, 9:357, 391; *Pa. Col. Rec.* 6:127; Mohawk Land Grant to William Brown and William Burnet January 8, 1753, Albany County Clerk's Office Deed Book 6:452 (IIDH Reel #15 28 June 1753); C. Colden, *History of the Five Nations* 2:221–22.

19. Saint Johnsville, New York, *Enterprise and News*, June 4, 1930; *DRCHNY* 4:907, 6:784; *DHNY* 4:660; W. M. Fenton, "Problems Arising from . . .," 209; J. R. Simms, *Frontiersmen of New York* 1:60–62; David Faux, "Iroquoian Occupation of the Mohawk Valley during and after the Revolution," *Man in the Northeast* 34 (1987): 31.

20. Deed from four Mohawk sachems of Canajoharie, New York State Historical Assoc., Cooperstown, Spec. Collections, Files from the Indian Museum (IIDH Reel #10 16 February 1730); Deed of land from sachems of Canajoharie to Jacob Glen, Newberry Library, Chicago, Illinois, Ayer Manuscripts N.A. 420 (IIDH Reel #10, 9 June 1735); *JP*, 13:15–19, 175; J. R. Simms, *History of Schoharie* 55; New York State Archives, Albany, Land Papers, 9:23.

21. G. Nammack *Fraud*, 22–23; *JP* 8:957, 960; Albany County Clerk's Office, Deed Book 7, 361–62 (IIDH Reel #27, 3 May 1765).

22. *DRCHNY* 5:960–62, 6:6; Nammack, ibid., 23–24; Great Britain, Public Record Office, Colonial Office Papers 5/1093 (IIDH Reel #10, 12 September 1733); *JP* 8:957–58. Aria Canoghowende signed, with probably a bear, the June 15, 1717 Schoharie deed (IIDH Reel #8, 15 June 1717 [III]) and the 1734 petition (see footnote 26) also with a bear.

23. *DRCHNY* 6: 15–16; Holland Society, *Yearbook for 1906*, 26; Henry Barclay, Register Book, 9, 17, 40; *JP* 1:405, 3:997; Account Book, probably Jelles Fonda's, 1755–1775 Caughnawaga, N.Y. (microfilm copy at Cornell University library, Ithaca, New York), 46, 51, 54, 67, 73, 87.

24. *DRCHNY* 6:16; Ezras Tekjerere signed the deed to Rev. Henry Barclay for the Bear and Johannes Segehowanne for the Turtle clan on November 24, 1740 (New York Historical Society, New York,

Horsmanden Papers, Selections Relating to the Six Nations, 80) (IIDH Reel #38, 9 May 1786).

25. Other references to Johannes Segehowane include: *JP*, 3:163, 9:498, 567, 588, 645, 728, 795, 13:173. Hendrick is labeled "ye chief sachem," in the petition to the King of December 12, 1734 (see following footnote).

26. A copy of this petition is found at the Maryland Historical Society, Baltimore, Calvert Papers, Ms. 194, #1093 (IIDH Reel #10, 12 December 1734); G. Nammack, *Fraud* 24–25 covers the Albany efforts to regain possession of the land. For Brant Kanagaradunkwa, see Chapter 10.

27. New York Colonial Manuscripts, Land Papers, 1735–38, 12:86 (IIDH Reel #10 24 December 1735); J. Lydekker, *Faithful Mohawks* 53; James T. Flexner, *Lord of the Mohawks* (Rev. Ed., Boston: Little Brown & Company, 1979), 11.

28. Samuel Hopkins, *Historical Memoirs Relating to the Housitanic Indians* (1911 reprint of 1753 original), 27.

29. J. Lydekker, *Faithful Mohawks* 53–54; S. Hopkins, ibid.

30. The original of Henry Barclay's Register Book, Fort Hunter 1734/5 is in the collections of the New York Historical Society, New York City. A photostat copy (taken by the New York State Library, December 9, 1935) is in the Montgomery County Archives, Fonda, New York. I have used a xerox copy of the Montgomery County's photostat of Barclay's original.

31. J. Lydekker, *Faithful Mohawks* 54–55; H. Barclay, Register Book, 7

32. J. T. Flexner, *Lord of the Mohawks* 13–15; M. Hamilton, *Sir William Johnson, Colonial American* 8–11.

CHAPTER 10

1. M. Hamilton, *Sir William Johnson, Colonial American*, 8–22, 45.

2. Ibid., 33–34, 339; Henry Barclay, Register Book, 22, 25, 38, 39, 60; *JP* 1:8, 102–3, 113n, 180, 249, 2:636.

3. Henry Barclay, Register Book, 10; Holland Society, *Yearbook for 1904* 74.

4. W. L. Stone in his *Life of Brant* 1:4–5, 10 combines Brant Kanagaradunkwa with his son, Nickus Canadiorha, with Nickus Peters Karaghiagdatie, and with Brant Aroghyiadecka. Isabel T. Kelsay, in

Joseph Brant 50–51 and 666 n.5, straightens out this mess, except that Brant Aroghyiadecka is sometimes referred to as Brant Senior, but after 1753 the Old Brant of Canajoharie is usually Brant Kanagaradunkwa. See also P. A. Wallace, *Conrad Weiser* 227, 338.

5.   Church Records, SC 17568, Box 1, vol. 2; *JP* 3:355, 10:224; Henry Barclay, Register Book, 10; Holland Society, *Yearbook for 1906* 27, 39, 46; First Reformed Church, Schenectady, vol. 1, pt. 2:139; White Hans, the youngest son of Kryn Onihoandhoundi and Anna, is referred to by Sir William Johnson as Nickus's uncle: *JP* 13:240.

6.   Henry Barclay, ibid., 5.

7.   P. A. Wallace, *Conrad Weiser*, 326; First Reformed Church, Schenectady, vol. 1, pt. 2:141; Henry Barclay, ibid., 18; an Adjagoroende signed the June 15, 1717 Schoharie deed with what looks to be the profile of a swimming turtle.

8.   Holland Society, *Yearbook for 1904* 66; *Yearbook for 1906*, 17; Church Records SC 17568, Box 1, vol. 2. Sara and David were married on the same day as Moses Nowadarika married, and Moses sponsored their first child, Seth—see Henry Barclay, Register Book, 4, 17.

9.   Holland Society, *Yearbook for 1906* 26; First Reformed Churhc, Schenectady, vol. 1, pt. 2:145; see also Henry Barclay, Register Book, 17.

10.   Henry Barclay, ibid., 11, 26; see also footnote 38.

11.   See Chapter 2 for a discussion of Iroquois kin relationships.

12.   Henry Barclay, Register Book, 42. Uncertainty over Brant Keghneghtaga's birthdate occurs because his age is given as 35 in 1783 ("Census of Niagara, 1783," *Ontario Register* 1 (1968):210). This census was actually a ration list used to determine food allotments, and recorded ages of family heads were sometimes made younger to allow those individuals more rations. Many interviews in Draper 13F refer to Brant Johnson and Margaret Campbell (with varying degrees of accuracy). For Brant's real age see Mrs. Priscilla Dilke's (Brant's granddaughter) statements in Draper 13F115. On the meaning of Brant's name see Draper 14F27 and 13F43. The accounts of Margaret (or Peggy) Campbell's capture can be found in Draper 13F47, 115–17; I. T. Kelsay, *Joseph Brant* 110. On the possible connection with Arthur Campbell and his capture in Augusta County, Virginia in 1757 see his petition of May 4, 1765, in John P. Kennedy, ed., *Journals of the House of Burgesses of Virginia 1761–1765* 10:187 (the 1758 date in the

petition is incorrect), *An Account of the Remarkable Occurrances in the Life and Travels of Colonel James Smith* (Philadelphia: Grigg and Elliot, 1834), 22, 56; Draper 10DD25, 42, and 1QQ82–83; J. A. Waddell, *Annals from Augusta County, Virginia, 1726–1871* (2nd. ed., Staunton, Va.: C. Russell Caldwell, 1902), 144, 157. Moses Nowadarika's daughters are recorded in: Holland Society, *Yearbook for 1906* 67; Henry Barclay, ibid., 26, 46; and *Bull. Ft. Ticonderoga Mus.* 10 (5):382.

13. Henry Barclay, ibid., 56, 65. The Christian who sponsors both of these boys was also a member of the family into which Conrad Weiser was adopted (Chapter 11 and Fig. 11-4), which strengthens the probability that their birth mother was a close relative of Christina's (the Seth who sponsored Brant Keghneghtaga was also a member of this family, being Gideon Tonidoge's nephew and adopted son—see Chapter 4).

14. *JP* 1:900, 9:17.

15. P. Wraxall, *Abridgement* 191; Holland Society, *Yearbook for 1906* 57; H. R. Schoolcraft, *Notes on the Iroquois* 415–16.

16. On religious revitalization movements see Anthony Wallace, "Revitalization Movements: Some Theoretical Considerations for their Comparative Study," *American Anthropologist* 58 (1958):264–81. John Demos in *The Unredeemed Captive* (New York: Knopf, 1994), 128, has also suggested that a revitalization movement took place among the Caughnawaga Mohawks under the religious leadership of Kateri Tekawitha. Both proposed seventeenth-century Mohawk revitalization movements fall into the "vitalization" subcategory—an importation of alien ideas. This is interesting in light of Wallace's delineation of North America as a "revival area" where old customs, rather than alien ideas, predominated. The portrait by John Faber is reproduced in R. Bond, *The Four Kings*.

17. Hendrick Peters Theyanoguin's 1740 portrait is reproduced in Milton Hamilton's *William Johnson, Colonial American*, plate 10. Other portraits of Theyanoguin are found in H. R. Schoolcraft, *Notes on the Iroquois*, frontispiece (with his formal Mohawk name) and in J. T. Flexner's *Lord of the Mohawks* (by T. Jeffries), following p. 146.

18. Holland Society, *Yearbook for 1906* 38; I. T. Kelsay, *Joseph Brant* 50; *JP* 2:293; 4:5, 55, 9:24, 11:984, and 13:175; Stockbridge Book of Records, 1739–59 (Town Hall, Stockbridge, Massachusetts—microfilm copy at the Newberry Library, Chicago); *Mass. Historical Society Collections* (1st Ser.), 9:97.

19. Carl Bridenbaugh, ed., *Gentleman's Progress: The Itinerarium of Dr. Alexander Hamilton, 1744* (Charlotte: North Carolina State Press, 1948), 112–13; F. G. Walett, ed., *The Diary of Ebenezer Parkman 1703–1782, Volume 1* (Worcester, MA: Am. Antiquarian Society, 1974), 100 (quote).

20. F. G. Walett, ibid.; J. T. Flexner, *Lord of the Mohawks* 45–48; P. A. Wallace, *Conrad Weiser* 226–28.

21. J. T. Flexner, ibid.; P. A. Wallace, ibid.; J. Lydekker, *Faithful Mohawks* 56–57; Public Archives of Canada, RG 10, vol. 1821:20–22 (IIDH Reel #12 1 February 1745).

22. Public Archives of Canada, RG 10, vol. 1821:29, 40–46 (IIDH 1 March and 17 April 1745).

23. *DRCHNY* 6:295; Daniel Horsmanden, "Papers Relating to the Provincial History of New York," New York Historical Society, no. 26, 115; P. A. Wallace, *Conrad Weiser* 227–28.

24. Henry Barclay, Register Book, 5; Draper 13F40; Account Book, Probably Jelles Fonda's 1755-1775, Caughnawaga, N.Y. I particularly wish to thank David Faux of Hagersville, Ontario (a descendant of Aaron Oseragighte's through his son David Karonyonte and daughter Mary) for his letters and source materials that were especially helpful in reconstructing aspects of Aaron's family tree and clan relationships. My interpretation of the available evidence is in some cases different from Dr. Faux's.

25. Church Records SC 17568, Box 1, vol. 2; First Reformed Church, Schenectady, vol. 1, pt. 2:139; that Margaret, Kryn Onihoanhoundi's daughter eventually became Aaron Oseragighte's wife is attested to by a statement by Aaron and Margaret's son Aaron Kanonraron (Kanonaron) in the Claus Papers, (Public Archives of Canada, MG 19, ser. F1, vol. 2:165). Aaron Kanonraron refers to the four Iroquois peacemakers at Fort Niagara in February, 1780: his uncle, Dayohensere (Little Abraham), Agwirondongwas (Good Peter), and Oghskennondonogh (Skenadon). This uncle thus was the fourth known peacemaker, Johannes or Hance Crine (or Kryn) Aneqwenahonji. (David Faux, pers. comm., September 7, 1994). Hance Kryn was the son of Kryn Onihoanhoundi and Anna, baptized in 1722 (Church Records, ibid.). For Aria, see Chapter 8, footnote 22; J. Pearson, "Extracts from the Doop-Boek," 18:235; and Evert Wendell, Indian Account Book 1695–1726, New York Historical Society Misc. Microfilms, Micro Reel #71, 106.

26. Henry Barclay, Register Book, 4, 37, 60; Draper 13F86–89.

27. Church Records SC 17568, Box 1, vol. 2; *JP* 13:174; Henry Barclay, ibid., 5. For John Segehowane, see footnotes 24 and 25 in Chapter 9. Brant Kanagaradunkwa signed the 1734 petition to the king (see Chapter 9, footnote 26) with, seemingly, a turtle.

28. P. A. Wallace, *Conrad Weiser* 227–28; "The Examination of John Lydius", 1745, Daniel Horsmanden Papers, Selections Relating to the Six Nations, 3 pages.

29. Daniel Horsmanden Papers, ibid. and "Deposition of Peter Macgrigorie" 9 May 1745; *DRCHNY* 6:291; M. Hamilton, *Sir William Johnson, Colonial American* 63, 80.

30. P. A. Wallace, *Conrad Weiser* 230; J. T. Flexner, *Lord of the Mohawks* 48; *DRCHNY* 6:290–95.

31. *DRCHNY* 6:294; Daniel Horsmanden, Papers, no. 26, 115; *JP*, 1:56; C. Colden, *History of the Five Indian Nations* 2:214, 221.

32. C. Colden, ibid., 214.

33. Henry Barclay, Register Book, 51–68; J. Lydekker, *Faithful Mohawks* 58–59.

34. M. Hamilton, *Sir William Johnson, Colonial American* 43–44, 54, 56-57; C. Colden, *History of the Five Indian Nations* 2:218–221; P. Wraxall, *Abridgement* 248 n.1.

35. *JP* 9:18, *DRCHNY* 6:512; M. Hamilton, "Theyanoguin," *Dictionary of Canadian Biography* 3 (1974):623; I. T. Kelsay, "Karaghtadie," *Dictionary of Canadian Biography* 3:322; C. J. Russ, "Louis La Corne," *Dictionary of Canadian Biography* 3:331.

36. *JP* 1:146–47, 9:8, 19, 20, 22, 23; M. Hamilton, *Sir William Johnson, Colonial American* 58–59.

37. A. B. Hulbert and W. N. Schwartz, eds., "David Zeisberger's History of the Northern American Indians," 101; Henry Barclay, Register Book, 7; *JP* 3:355, 10:224.

38. *DRCHNY* 6:512.

39. It was long believed that Catharine Weisenberg had died in 1745, when Johnson was offered a room in Albany (*JP* 1:42). Milton Hamilton established that she died in 1759 (*Sir William Johnson Colonial American* 34), but by 1748 Catharine and her children were no longer living with Johnson (J. T. Flexner, *Lord of the Mohawks* 49; *JP*, 1:179, 249). On Mary McGrah, see W. L. Stone, *Life and Times of Sir William Johnson, Bart.* (Albany: J. Munsell, 1865), 2:498; Henry Barclay,

Register Book, 1, 19, 54, 55; and *JP* 1:167, 206, 214, 9:65, 12:1071; *DRCHNY* 6:590.

40. Microfilm edition of the Papers of Eleazar Wheelock (Hanover, NH: Dartmouth College Library, 1971) #765429.1; *JP* 1:270, 10:181; *Pa. Col. Rec.* 6:128; W. L. Stone, *Life and Times of Sir William Johnson* 2:493; I. T. Kelsay, "Tagawirunte," *Dictionary of Canadian Biography* 4 (1979):731; Church Records SC #17568, Box 1, vol. 2; Holland Society, *Yearbook for 1906* 39.

41. *JP* 1:168, 169; *DRCHNY* 6:589-90.

CHAPTER 11

1. *DRCHNY* 6:294; P. Frazier, *Mohegans of Stockbridge* 5; for 1688 raid, see Chapter 8; Holland Society, *Yearbook for 1904* 51.

2. Holland Society, ibid., 57.

3. Holland Society, ibid., 73; J. Demos, *Unredeemed Captive* 287 n.40; *Mass. Historical Society Collections*, (1st ser.), 9 (1804):97. If my theory that Canastasi was Hendrick's and Abraham's mother is correct, then either the statement by contemporary observers that Abraham was Hendirck's older brother or the Dellius note that Canastasi was a widow in 1690 would have to be wrong. Other possibilities are that Abraham was Canastasi's son (baptized in Canada) but not Peter's or that Canastasi was not married to Peter in any formal sense (his formal wife would then have been Nickus Karaghiagdatie's mother). These uncertainties illustrate the problems of interpreting the church records in light of the somewhat less formal Mohawk marriages. A possibility that a few men (Peter? Ezras Kanneraghtahare? Gideon Tonidoge?) had more than one wife concurrently also exists.

4. *Pa. Arch.* (1st ser.), 2:174; Holland Society, ibid.; *Pa. Col. Rec.* 5:470; Connecticut Archives Indians (1st ser.) 2:72a. The Peter baptized on January 3, 1697, probably died before 1707, when Rebecca Kowtayolduse (Kowajatense) sponsored another Peter, son of Jacob Kayingwirago and Jacomine. The Mohawks seemed to have "requickened" Christian baptismal names in the sense that a child would be named for a recently deceased person who'd had that name. This practice did not follow clan lines, however, but often the sponsor seems associated with the baptismal name.

5. Patrick Frazier's *The Mohicans of Stockbridge*, offers the best

modern description of founding of the Stockbridge mission and the Mahicans who settled in Stockbridge. An early (and reprinted) version on the founding is in Samuel Hopkins, *Memoirs of the Housitanic Indians*; for the early baptisms see P. Frazier, ibid., 36 and Stockbridge Record Book 1739–1759.

6. P. Frazier, ibid., 39–51, 98–99; John Warner Barber, *Historical Collection of Every Town in Massachusetts* (Worcester, MA: Warren Lazel, 1844), 94–95, 99; *JP* 1:234 (quote).

7. P. Frazier, ibid., 82, 99; *JP*, 9:62; *DRCHNY* 6:589–90; Conn. Archives Indians (1st ser.) 2:72a; in discussing the Mohawks at Stockbridge Electa Jones (*Stockbridge, Past and Present*, Springfield, MA: Samuel Bowles & Co., 1854), 74, says that Molly Brant was Hendrick's sister (she wasn't). I take this to mean that Hendrick's sister was Molly or Mary, probably the Mary Canastasi who sponsored Elizabeth, daughter of Henry and Anna at Canajoharie on January 15, 1735 (H. Barclay, Register Book, 5).

8. P. Frazier, ibid., 88–91, 101.

9. *Mass. Historical Society Collections* (1st ser.), 10:142–45.

10. Ibid., 145.

11. *Pa. Col. Rec.* 5:645.

12. *JP* 9:52–54 (quote from 52); "The Reverend John Ogilvie, D.D.," *Ontario Historical Society Papers and Records* 22:310, 312.

13. *Mass. Historical Society Collections* (1st ser.), 10:145 (quote), 146–48; *Ontario Hist. Soc.*, ibid., 311.

14. Conn. Archives Indians (1st ser.), 2:24b, 74c, 74d; P. Frazier, *Stockbridge* 99. Isaac and Adam's Indian names are mentioned in *JP* 11:38–41 and in James D. McCallum, ed., *The Letters of Eleazar Wheelock's Indians* (Hanover, NH: Dartmouth College, 1932), 79, 80–81.

15. Holland Society, *Yearbook for 1906* 41; *Ontario Hist. Soc Papers and Records.* 22:311; W. Pilkington, *A Journal of the Reverend Samuel Kirkland* 86 nn.38 and 39; *JP* 12:270. There is a modern tradition that Abraham Peters Canostens had two wives, the second a Dutch woman (Ethel Brant Montour, *Famous Indians: Brant, Crowfoot, Oronhyatekha* [Toronto: Clarke, Irwin, 1960], 14). Possibly the ethnic appelation was due to Gesina's distinctly Dutch name—there is no reference to her being anything but Indian in contemporary documents.

16. Conn. Archives Indians (1st ser.), 2:74b; R. W. Vosburgh, ed.,

"Records of the High and Low Dutch Reformed Congregation at Schoharie," vol. 1, pt.1:38, 49; *Mass. Historical Society Collections* (1st ser.), 4:53.

17. Conn. Archives, ibid., 74c, 74d.

18. P. Frazier, *Stockbridge* 99, 101–02; *Mass. Historical Society Collections* (1st ser.), 10:153.

19. *Mass. Historical Society Collections* (1st ser.), 4:51–58; Diary and Papers of the Reverend Gideon Hawley, 1752–1807, 84–85.

20. F. H. Halsey, "The Pioneers of the Mohawk," in Richard Smith's, *A Tour of Four Great Rivers: Hudson, Mohawk, Susquehanna and Delaware* liv; J. T. Flexner, *Lord of the Mohawks* 23; R. Smith, ibid., 67-68; G. Hawley, Diary and Papers, 269; Foster Disinger, "Gideon Hawley at Onohoquage," *Bulletin of the Broome County Historical Society* 1 (1953):9; Marjory Barnum Hinman, *Onaquaga: Hub of the Border Wars of the American Revolution in New York State* (Valley Offset, 1975), 2; *JP* 9:909, 11:43, 48–50, 12:864.

21. R. W. Vosburgh, "Records of St. Pauls Evangelical Church, Schoharie," xi, 41; R. W. Vosburgh, "Records of the High and Low Dutch Congregation at Schoharie," vol. 1, pt. 1:46, 55.

22. R. W. Vosburgh, "Records of the High and Low Dutch Congregation at Schoharie," vol. 1, pt. 1:31, 291, 297; G. Hawley, Diary and Papers, 29, 30, 157, 168; *JP* 4:101, 10:44, 48, 657, 11:58, 85, 13:175, 507, 508; *The Sullivan Clinton Campaign in 1779* (Albany: University of the State of New York, 1929), 107–08; Account Book, Probably Jelles Fonda's, 1755–1775, Caughnawaga, N.Y., 24, 73; *Pa. Arch.* (1st ser.), 4:450; O. J. Harvey, *History of Wilkes-Barre* 828–30; Draper 9F90–91, 9F207, 17F94a, 143a; R. W. Vosburgh, "Records of Trinity Lutheran Church of Stone Arabia, in the town of Palatine, Montgomery County, N.Y." (New York Genealogical and Biographical Society, 1914), vol. 1, pt. 2:282. The entry is: *"Adams Tocher von Ochquaga mit William, Asarad sohn Wilden."* Vosburgh notes that the word "sohn" is illegible and in doubt—I believe that it was actually Reverend England's attempt to render Asarad*ong*was, the name found in Fonda's accounts; R. W. Vosburgh, "Records of the High and Low Dutch Congregation at Schoharie," vol. 1, pt. 1:91, 105.

23. *JP* 12:271; Conn. Archives Indians (1st ser.), 2:74c; R. W. Vosburgh, "Records of the High and Low Dutch Congregation at Schoharie," vol. 1, pt. 1:39, 47, 53, 54, 55, 297; R. W. Vosburgh,

"Records of St. Pauls Evangelical Lutheran Church, Schoharie," 31, 41, 43, 50, 125; I. T. Kelsay, *Joseph Brant* 99–100, 129–31, 133–34; "The Mohawk Valley Ehles," Saint Johnsville, New York, *Enterprise and News*, June 11, 1930.

24. *JP* 1:130, 9:716 (quote); *Mass. Historical Society Collections* (1st ser.), 4:56.

25. G. Hawley, Diary and Papers, 17, 39, 189; *Bull. Broome County Hist. Soc.* 1:10.

26. G. Hawley, ibid., 114–16, 681–82; *Bull. Broome County Hist. Soc.*, ibid.

27. G. Hawley, ibid., 80-81, 97. Hawley also recorded the baptisms of several Tuscaroras.

28. *Pa. Col. Rec.* 6:68; Church Records SC 17568, Box 1, vol. 2; Holland Society, *Yearbook for 1906* 45; R. W. Vosburgh, "Records of St. Pauls Evangelical Lutheran Church, Schoharie," 297; P. A. Wallace, *Conrad Weiser* 380, 435.

29. *Diary of Ebenezer Parkman 1703–1782* 100; *Pa. Col. Rec.* 4:538, 5:685, 7:64–65, 68–69; P. A. Wallace, ibid., 248, 368, 374, 380, 389, 395, 433.

30. *Pa. Col. Rec.* 4:538, 6:141, 159, 160, 162, 7:70; P. A. Wallace, *Conrad Weiser* 365, 432; *JP* 2:438; Holland Society, *Yearbook for 1904* 64 (Moses is referred to as a child in 1694); *Bull. Ft. Ticonderoga Mus.* 10 (5):384; *JP* 13:173.

31. Jelles Fonda Indian Book, 5, 9, 48; Account Book, Probably Jelles Fonda's, 1755–1775, Caughnawaga, N.Y., 14, 15, 47, 65.

32. Church Records SC 17568, Box , vol. 21; SPG Letterbooks (series A), 8:304–05; H. Barclay, Register Book, 17.

33. *JP* 2:621, 3:155, 4:50, 52–53, 56, 59, 9:626, 655, 10:364, 571, 900, 12:288; Richard Day, *Calendar of the Sir William Johnson Manuscripts* 212.

CHAPTER 12

1. M. Hamilton, *William Johnson, Colonial American*, 63–65.

2. *JP* 1:340 (quote); M. Hamilton, ibid., 80.

3. New York State Library, Albany, Manuscripts 1-670 (IIDH Reel #14 23 May 1750); *Pa. Col. Rec.* 5:644, 6:128, 291; *JP* 12:269–70.

4. *JP* 13:15–19; Albany County Clerks Office Deed Book 6:452

(IIDH Reel #15 28 June 1753), 7:425–26 (IIDH Reel #28 9 October 1765).

5. *DRCHNY* 6:783–85; see also "Cadwallader Colden Papers, Vol. IX," *New York Historical Society Collections* 68 (1935):129–34.

6. Petition of Hendrick, Abraham Peterson and others to George Clinton, George Clinton Papers, vol. 14, Clements Library, University of Michigan (IIDH #15 8 February 1753); *JP* 1:368.

7. *DRCHNY* 6:781–88 (quote from 783).

8. Ibid., 783–85.

9. Ibid., 785–88 (quote from 788).

10. M. Hamilton, *William Johnson, Colonial American* 100–01.

11. Ibid., 102, 110, 348 n.15.

12. Ibid., 104–05, 348–49 n.29; *DRCHNY* 6:869-70 (quotes).

13. O. J. Harvey, *History of Wilkes-Barre* 1:268–69; *Pa. Col. Rec.* 6:116, 119; Julian P. Boyd, ed., *Susquehannah Co. Papers* 1:125 (quote here and on 269 of Harvey).

14. *Pa. Col. Rec.* 6:119–23; P. A. Wallace, *Conrad Weiser* 358–59.

15. *Pa. Col. Rec.* 6:124–27.

16. Copies of the deed can be found in *Susquehannah Co. Papers* 1:101–115; *Pa. Arch.* (1st ser.), 2:147–58, and O. J. Harvey, *History of Wilkes-Barre* 1:271–76.

17. *Susquehannah Co. Papers* 1:lxxiv-lxxxi and accompanying numbers in volume.

18. *Susquehannah Co. Papers* 1:123-27; *Pa. Arch.* (1st ser.), 2:174–76.

19. For a pro-Connecticut version, see O. J. Harvey, *History of Wilkes-Barre* 1:269–70; for a pro-Pennsylvania version, see W. R. Shepherd, *History of Proprietary Government in Pennsylvania* (Columbia Univ. Studies in History, Economics, and Public Law 6), 146–160; see also *Susquehannah Co. Papers* 1:lxxxiv, 207; *DRCHNY* 6:984 (quote; for a discussion of this incident, see M. Hamilton, *William Johnson, Colonial American* 130, 352 nn.25, and 26).

20. "Memoir of Daniel Claus, His Descent and How he came to America with a Concise Account of his Adventure and Services," Claus Papers, Public Archives Canada, MG 19, Ser. F1, vol. 23:1–8 (IIDH Reel #36 after 1782); P. A. Wallace, *Conrad Weiser* 304–07, 326.

21. P. A. Wallace, ibid., 326, 338–39; *Susquehannah Co. Papers* 1:83.

22. *Pa. Arch.* (1st ser.), 2:174-76; see also *Susquehannah Co. Papers* 1:130-33.

23. Ibid.

24. *Susquehannah Co. Papers* 1:137, 140-41, 151, 155-59, 189, 211-215; *JP* 1:433, 441; *Pa. Col. Rec.* 6:291. The list of Mohawks attending the Philadelphia meeting has several errors due to miscopying. The first two sachems are named correctly, but Seth should have had no accompanying Mohawk name and Otchenuchyata is probably Joseph's name. Sagotenyuchta was Jacob's name (*Pa. Col. Rec.* 6:128); Cachucko was Young Brant Keghneghtaga's name. "Abram" remains a mystery. The final three Mohawk names on the list are for the three whites: Claus, William Johnson, and Lydius. Joseph Brant is not named as having gone to the conference, but his mother got a gift from the Pennsylvanians, and Claus's Memoir (PAC MG 19, ser. F1, vol. 23:20) names Molly Brant with the party that came from Philadelphia.

25. I. T. Kelsay, *Joseph Brant* 39-43; H. Barclay, Register Book, 4, 35, 38.

26. W. L. Stone (*Life of Brant* 1:3) reports that Joseph's father's name was Tehonwaghwengaraghkwin, a member of the Wolf clan. Another Tehonwagherengaraghkwen, Thomas Davis, was a Wolf clan war captain and a cousin of Joseph Brant's (*Dictionary of Canadian Biography* 6:758). Margaret was a Wolf because her son Joseph was (*JP* 13:175). I. T. Kelsay (*Joseph Brant* 41) suggests that sponsors of Peter and Margaret's children are obscure, but Esther Kanoghserightha who sponsors their daughter Christina may be Esther "the first woman of the Wolf tribe" from Canajoharie noted by Sir William Johnson in 1761. This Esther is the *only* woman in the *Johnson Papers* to receive a clan designation (*JP* 10:227). See also H. R. Schoolcraft, *Notes on the Iroquois* 440.

27. I. T. Kelsay, *Joseph Brant* 43-44; *JP* 9:61; First Reformed Church, Schenectady, vol. 2, pt. 1:42, 49; Leah and Jacomine were names in the Wolf clan family baptized at Albany on August 6, 1690 (see Chapter 3). Leah's (ba. March 17, 1750) sponsors were Albert Van Slyck and Jesina. Another Jesina (Josine) was likewise in this 1690 group, which I have suggested had clan and possibly *ohwachira* ties to Hilletie Van Slyck Van Olinda. Thus Margaret, Joseph Brant's mother may also have been related to this early Wolf clan family.

28. I. T. Kelsay, ibid., 45, 52-53; *Bull. Ft. Ticonderoga Mus.* 10

10 (5):383, 385., W. L. Stone, *Life of Brant* 1:3–4.

   29. Claus Papers, Public Archives Canada MG 19, Ser. F1, vol. 23:20.

   30. *Pa. Col. Rec.* 6:292–93 (quote 292); *Pa. Arch.* (1st ser.), 2:233; *Susquehannah Co. Papers* 1:236.

   31. W. L. Stone, *Life and Times of Sir William Johnson* 1:327–28; "Letter of Sir Charles Hardy to William Johnson," *New York History* 60 (1979):94. *JP* 2:450, 498, 516, 3:229n, 6:618–19, 12:713, 754, 767. Claus Papers, Public Archives Canada MG 19, Ser. F1, vol. 25:63–64 contains this excerpt to Claus from W. Taylor and his partner Duffin at Niagara on 24 Nov. 1778:

> Since we delivered the letter to Miss Mary Brant which came enclosed to us from you, she sent for our W. Taylor and told him she is under a great concern at the loss of her two sons being dear to her as being her children and a loss to her that as she cannot write her thoughts herself nor has she anybody to apply to to do it. For her, they were still alive, she thinks one of them might be with her some times . . .

Peter Johnson, Molly's oldest son by Sir William, was granted a commission as ensign in Lord Adam Gordon's Regiment, the 26th Foot, in 1776 and died at Mud Island near Philadelphia in 1778 (I. Kelsay, *Joseph Brant* 272; John Ferguson [Peter's brother-in-law], Petition on loses 3/4/1793 in the Geovernor George Clinton Papers; W. C. Ford, *British Officers Serving in the American Revolution* [Brooklyn: Historical Printing Club, 1897], 5, 102). Lord Adam Gordon was the brother-in-law of the dowager dutchess of Gordon, Staats Morris' wife. The second son Molly refers to in 1778 is otherwise unknown.

CHAPTER 13

   1. Milton Hamilton, *Sir William Johnson, Colonial American*, 113; D. Hawke, *The Colonial Experience*, 384–85; J. T. Flexner, *Washington: The Indispensible Man* (New York, New American Library, 1984), 14–16.

   2. M. Hamilton, ibid., 114–16.

   3. J. T. Flexner, *Mohawk Baronet*, 124–25; M. Hamilton, ibid., 117; D. Hawke, *The Colonial Experience*, 388.

4. M. Hamilton, ibid., 117-18.

5. The most complete, albeit pro-Johnson, discussion of the Johnson-Shirley controversy is given in Milton Hamilton, ibid., 122-23, 129-38, 180-81, 183, 189-91, 193-95, 198-99 and accompanying references. In his Appendix 2 (328-29) Hamilton discusses the assertions of the numerous pro-Shirley historians; as early as 1757 pro-Shirley tracts were being printed containing charges against Johnson (M. Hamilton, ibid., 199).

6. *DRCHNY* 6:870-71, 964-89 (1st quote, 965, 2nd quote, 984; *JP* 9:193-203. Claus's version (*JP* 9:199-20) and shows more manipulation of the situation by Johnson than does the official transcript.

7. *JP* 1:738-39, 786, and 807-08.

8. M. Druke, "Structure and Meanings of Leadership," 15, 163-64, 166.

9. *DRCHNY* 7:174; *JP* 3:355, 694, 704, 714, 9:468, 489, 10:99, 224, 11:984, 13:140; Henry Barclay, Register Book, 49. Abraham Teyorhansere probably had a second wife, Lea, to whom he was married on February 12, 1749 ("First Dutch Reformed Church of Schenectady, New York—Marriage Records," *New York Genealogical and Biographical Record* 73 [1942]:48). Their daughter Maria was baptized on July 12, 1750 (this baptism is not published but can be seen on the microfilm copy [AFM 229] at the New York State Library, Albany), and son Lawrence on December 25, 1755 (*Bull. Ft. Ticondroga Mus.* 10 [5]:384). Abraham was probably the "chief sachem of the Mohawks" whose house burned down with everything in it in early February, 1769 (*JP* 13:30) and lost his wife by March of the same year (*JP* 13:758); I. T. Kelsay, *Joseph Brant* 52-53; P. A. Wallace, *Conrad Weiser* 339. There is no evidence to indicate that he was Abraham Peters' son or Joseph Brant's maternal uncle, as some have claimed (J. Lydekker, *Faithful Mohawks*, 194-96; Ralph T. Pastore, "Teyorhansere," *Dictionary of Canadian Biography* 4 [1979]:730).

10. *JP* 1:489-90, 634, 2:569, 3:162, 163, 167, 10:105, 766, 11:659, 13:173.

11. Gideon Tonidoge Sharenhowaneh last appears in Barclay's Register Book in June, 1741 (p. 35) and Cornelius Thaneghwanege in the spring of 1744 (p. 56, 57); *JP* 9:29 mentions the burial of Ezras "ye great Mohawk sachem"; P. A. Wallace, *Conrad Weiser* 227; *Pa. Arch.* (1st ser.), 2:174; *Susquehannah Co. Papers* 1:117-18, 131; *Pa. Col. Rec.*

6:291; *JP* 2:568, 3:156, 158, 168, 7:579.

12. Albany County Clerk's Office Deed Book 7:449 (IIDH Reel #28, 10 Sept. 1766 [III]); *JP* 1:405, 3:153, 155, 163, 172, 997, 9:567, 588, 596, 632, 728, 795, 13:173.

13. Daniel Horsmanden, "Papers Relating to the Province of New York," no. 26, 115; Holland Society, *Yearbook for 1906* 45; Henry Barclay, Register Book, 62; *JP* 1:638, 2:374, 3:151, 164, 155, 168, 8:935, 9:17, 217, 347, 463, 588, 596, 647, 937, 10:482, 586, 589, 11:660, 817, 12:628, 797, 798, 13:174.

14. *Pa. Arch.* (1st ser.), 2:174; P. A. Wallace, *Conrad Weiser* 226; *Bull. Ft. Ticonderoga Mus.* 10 (5):383; *JP* 13:113; N. B. Wainwright, *George Croghan* 138.

15. *JP* 3:162, 4:50, 9:238, 357, 621, 650, 10:44, 57, 87, 106, 571.

16. M. Hamilton, *Sir William Johnson, Colonial American* 133–35; I. T. Kelsay, "Karaghtadie," 322.

17. M. Hamilton, ibid., 145–49, 152, 157.

18. *DRCHNY* 10:316–21.

19. M. Hamilton, *Sir William Johnson, Colonial American* 157–59; Jelles Fonda's accounts mention Dicke Lawrence with no special label (Account Book, probably Jelles Fonda's 1755–1775, 1, 110, 116), indicating that he was probably a Tionondoroge Mohawk. There were two Tionondoroge Mohawks named Lawrence: Aquilaighse, a Wolf clan chief, and Sanagaris, a Bear (*JP* 13:174, 9:780). Aquilaigse was called Squint or One-Eyed Lawrence or Lawrence Claes (possibly indicating that the early eighteenth century interpreter Lawrence Claes was his father); see also David Faux, "Iroquois Occupation of the Mohawk Valley during and after the Revolution," *Man in the Northeast* 34:29-30. Thus Thick Lawrence was most likely Sanagaris; Claus Papers, Public Archives Canada MG19, ser. F1, vol. 23:31–32; *JP* 2:16–17; W. L. Stone, *Life and Times of Sir William Johnson* 1:512–13.

20. M. Hamilton, ibid., 159.

21. M. Hamilton, ibid., 159–61; M. Hamilton, "Theyanoguin," *Dictionary of Canadian Biography* 3:623; *DRCHNY* 10:317, 321–22, 342; Claus Papers, Public Archives Canada MG19, ser. F1, vol. 23:35–37; *JP* 9:238, 357.

22. M. Hamilton, *Sir William Johnson, Colonial American* 162–66.

23. Braddock had been mortally wounded and his entire force routed not far from Fort Duquesne on July 9, 1757; for mention of the Mohawk

dead see *Ontario Historical Society Papers and Records* 22:316 (Ogilvie also reported that six of the twelve Mohawks slain had been constant communicants of the church); Johnson received news of his baronetcy the following spring: *DRCHNY* 6:1020; *JP* 2:343–48.

24. *JP* 2:293, 9:546–48, 13:105.

25. *JP* 9:820; *Bull. Ft. Ticonderoga Mus.* 10 (5):346, 352.

26. *Ontario Historical Society Papers and Records* 22:319; *JP*, 2:780, 792; Henry Barclay, Register Book, 42; *New York Genealogical and Biographical Record* 73 (1942):50.

27. N. Wainwright, *George Croghan* 122–25; *JP* 9:626, 655, 727–33; *Pa. Col. Rec.* 7:498–510.

28. *JP* 9:795, 11:208; Papers of the Continental Congress and Constitutional Convention, M247, r165, i151 (quote).

29. Henry Barclay, Register Book, 59, 62; First Reformed Church, Schenectady, vol. 2, pt. 1:47; *Bull. Ft. Ticonderoga Mus.* 10 (5):383; David Faux, "Johannes Crine," *Loyalist Gazette* 19(1):5–6; Barbara Graymont, *The Iroquois and the American Revolution* 225–28; Draper 11F89; *JP* 8:965, 13:174; New York State Archives Legislative Assembly Papers 40:41–44 (IIDH Reel #39 January 1788).

30. *JP* 9:729 (Peter's name is misrepresented as "Sogehowana" but Sir William says only Bears and Wolves attended: *JP* 9:626); Henry Barclay, ibid., 42, 54, 68.

31. *Pa. Col. Rec.* 7:498–510, 527; N. Wainwright, *George Croghan* 122, 124, 127–34.

32. A full account of the Easton conference and its preliminaries can be found in P. A. Wallace's *Conrad Weiser* Chapters 59–61. See also N. Wainwright's *George Croghan* 143–51. Croghan's and Weiser's biographers do not agree on which of these two agents had greater influence at the conference, but both describe the crucial role Nickus Karaghiagdatie played. See also *JP* 2:873, 890–91, 3:1–4, 10:44–48; and *Pa. Col. Rec.* 8:190–203. For a somewhat more sympathetic view of Teedyuscung see Anthony Wallace's *King of the Delawares: Teedyuscung 1700–1763* (Philadelphia: University of Pennsylvania Press, 1949). For the deaths of the individuals mentioned see *JP*, 3:162, 9:621, 650, 767. Gideon Hawley mentioned seeing a sister of Hendrick's and Abraham's in 1765 (*Mass. Hist. Soc. Collections* [3rd ser.], 1:151).

33. The number of children in Ogilvie's "Register" (*Bull. Ft. Ticonderoga Mus.* 10 (5):382–85) is short by about twenty-five percent

of the totals he reported to the Society for the Propagation of the Gospel *(Ontario Hist. Society Papers and Records* 22:308–20); for the Caughnawaga, New York, church records see R. W. Vosburgh, ed., "Records of the Reformed Protestant Dutch Church of Caughnawauga" (New York Historical Society, 1917), vol. 1; Account Book, Probably Jelles Fonda's 1755–1775; Indian Book for Jelles Fonda at Cachnewago (Fort Johnson, New York, Montgomery County Hist. Soc. mss 1-647).

34. *JP* 2:579, 610, 4:165–66, 9:546–48, 10:87, 564; M. Hamilton, *Sir William Johnson, Colonial American* 377 n.38.

35. *JP* 9:651, 767, 10:723, 726, 11:514, 581, 12:734, 798, 13:97, 175.

36. *JP* 4:50, 12:628; That Serehowane's Christian name was Peter is shown in Barclay's Register Book, 31, 35, 55.

37. *JP* 12:112–13. The names of Indian women so rarely appear in the *Johnson Papers*, but a widow named Modalena (Magdalene) is found three times between December, 1758, and February, 1759 (*JP* 3:152, 156, 158). In the last of these three entries, on February 13, 1759, a payment to Brant Kanagaradunkwa's son Nickus is followed immediately by one to "Margaret, Modalena, and Mary 3 Mohawk squaws" for two pounds, eight shillings. This almost certainly represents a visit of Molly Brant's mother Margaret and Molly's stepsisters Magdalene and Mary, Nickus's sisters, possibly with the news that Molly was pregnant with Sir William's child.

38. *JP* 10:227, 13:175; vol. 2, Church Records, SC 17568 Box 1; Henry Barclay, Register Book, 31, 38.

39. Henry Barclay, ibid., 35; *JP* 13:175; British Museum Additional Manuscripts 21765:48, 60, 104; Barbara Graymont, *The Iroquois and the American Revolution* 225, 245.

40. *JP* 2:626, 3:151, 153, 157, 159, 160, 161, 165, 5:686, 9:972, 10:560, 606, 870-72, 935, 939, 11:11, 359–61, 13:146, 265; Michael Day, *Calendar of the Sir William Johnson Papers* 177; *Pa. Col. Rec.* 6:127; Benson Lossing, *A Pictorial Field-Book of the Revolution* (New York: Harper and Brothers, 1850), 256. Captain Daniel later moved to Onaquaga.

CHAPTER 14

1. J. M. Brown, *A Brief Sketch of the First Settlement of the County of Schoharie by the Germans,* 19; New York State Archives, Albany,

Col. Mss., Land Papers 1730–1735, v. 2:106A–106B, v. 9:23.

2. Notes of Cadwallader Colden, George Clinton papers, Clements Library, University of Michigan (IIDH Reel #15 10 May 1753); *JP*, 11:945–47; J. R. Simms, *History of Schoharie* 95–96; Petition of the Mohawks as Schoharie, New York State Archives, Albany, Col. Mss. 81:135 (IIDH Reel #16 September 1754).

3. *Mass. Historical Society Collections* (1st ser.), 4:53, 61, 63–64; R. W. Vosburgh, "Records of the High and Low Dutch Reformed Congregation at Schoharie," vol. 1, pt. 1:285.

4. *Pa. Col. Rec.* 6:128; *DRCHNY* 7:110–11; R. W. Vosburgh, ibid., 288; *DHNY* 4:660; *JP* 3:153.

5. *JP* 2:611, 3:153, 9:589, 770, 781, 782; J. R. Simms, *History of Schoharie* 206.

6. J. R. Simms, ibid., 94, 206; *DRCHNY* 7:113; J. M. Brown, *A Brief Sketch of the First Settlement of the County of Schoharie*, 19.

7. *JP* 11:34, 12:96, 646; R. W. Vosburgh, "Records of the High and Low Dutch Congregation at Schoharie," vol. 1, pt. 1:vi, 10, 92, 98; R. W. Vosburgh, "Records of St. Paul's Evangelical Lutheran, Schoharie," vol. 1:56; J. M. Brown, ibid.

8. J. M. Brown, ibid., 11, 19; J. R. Simms, *History of Schoharie* 103.

9. *JP* 8:20–22.

10. J. Simms, *History of Schoharie* 207–08; J. M. Brown, *A Brief Sketch of the Settlement of the County of Schoharie* 17; Arthur E. Spiess and Bruce D. Spiess, "New England Pandemic of 1616–1622: Cause and Archaeological Implication," *Man in the Northeast* 34 (1987):71–83.

11. J. R. Simms, ibid., 55, 104; R. W. Vosburgh, "Records of the High and Low Dutch Reformed Congregation at Schoharie," vol. 1, pt.1: 109.

12. J. R. Simms, ibid., 213 (quote), 214, 241, 244–47; R. W. Vosburgh, "Records of St. Paul's Evangelical Lutheran Church, Schoharie," vol. 1:73.

13. J. R. Simms, ibid., 290–93, 368, 370–72, 378, 380–81, 412, 437, 511; J. M. Brown, *A Brief Sketch of the Settlement of the County of Schoharie* 17–18.

14. J. R. Simms, ibid., 529–31.

CHAPTER 15

1. *Ontario Hist. Soc. Papers and Records* 22:310; J. Hooper, *A History of St. Peter's Church in the City of Albany* (Albany: Fort Orange Press, 1900), 95; *Bull. Ft. Ticonderoga Mus.* 10 (5):381; D. Guldenzopf, "Frontier Demography," 86; *JP* 3:153, 10:224, 13:194, 199, 207.

2. *JP* 3:642-43, 10:340-42.

3. *DRCHNY* 4:978-994; Albany County Clerk's Office Deed Book 4:241 (IIDH Reel #6 26 August 1702 [II]); *JP* 12:531.

4. G. Namack, *Fraud* 54; *JP* 12:531; Holland Society, *Yearbook for 1904* 76; *DRCHNY* 3:802.

5. *DRCHNY* 7:576, 671; G. Namack, ibid.; C. Colden, "Letter Books, Vol. II," *New York Hist. Soc. Collections* 10 (1878):392-93; for signers confirming other signers of deeds see: "Early Records of the City and County of Albany 2: Deeds 3 and 4, 1678-1704," *New York State Library History Bull.* 9:196-97 (IIDH Reel #2 26 July 1683) and *DRCHNY* 13:465.

6. *DRCHNY* 7:672.

7. *New York State Library History Bull.* 9:152-53, 197, 200-01, 339-40 (IIDH Reel #2 3 July 1672, 18 July 1672, and 26 July 1683); *DRCHNY* 13:573.

8. *DRCHNY* 7:576, 671; G. Namack, *Fraud* 54, 56-58; *DHNY* 2:392. The Mohawks' contention (in 1763) that the goods representing the purchase price were destroyed in the burning of Schenectady is false, since the town was attacked and burned in 1690. It is possible, however, that a later, smaller-scale fire destroyed the goods there, and that these two incidents became merged in the popular memory including, in 1754, a latter-day holder of the patent.

9. *DRCHNY* 7:671; G. Namack, ibid., 58-61.

10. *JP* 11:358-62; G. Namack, ibid., 68-69.

11. *DRCHNY* 7:435-36, 577.

12. *JP* 8:955-65; J. Munsell, *History of Albany* (Albany: Munsell, 1865), 1:357-59.

13. *JP* 8:956-60.

14. *JP* 8:961 (1st quote), 962 (2nd quote), 965-68.

15. *JP* 8:963; Treaty between the Indians formerly resident at the Mohawk Castle, Fort Hunter, New York . . . 1789, Public Archives of Canada, MG19, F21 (1 page).

16. New York State Historical Association, Cooperstown, Spec.

Collections, Files from the Indian Museum (IIDH Reel #10 16 February 1630); *JP* 4:54.

17. W. L. Stone, *Life of Brant* 1:498-99; *JP* 3:564, 613 (quote), 619, 10:336-39, 364-67; *Pa. Col. Rec.* 6:93.

18. G. Namack, *Fraud* 49, describes in detail the various legal proceedings that led up to the March meeting; *JP* 4:50-61, 10:621-22.

19. *JP* 4:53.

20. Ibid.

21. *JP* 4:176-77 (quote from 176), 10:717, 927-92; G. Namack, *Fraud* 50.

22. W. L. Stone, *Life and Times* 2:352; *JP* 11:555-56, 13, 175; I. T. Kelsay, *Joseph Brant* 123.

23. I. T. Kelsay, ibid., 136-37, 141; Draper 2F53.

24. I. T. Kelsay, ibid.

25. *DHNY* 2:582, 583; G. Namack, *Fraud* 50-51; Power of Attorney to Jelles Fonda to Recover Lands Granted to Abraham Van Horne and others, July 6, 1789, New York Hist. Soc. Misc. Manuscript Collections, John Lansing, Jr. Papers, Nov. 13, 1781.

26. The largest land grant given to Sir William Johnson by the Mohawks eventually became the "Royal Grant" or Kingsland, which was comprised of 80,000 acres north of the Mohawk River (see M. Hamilton, *Sir William Johnson, Colonial American* 299-301, 376 and references therein); J. T. Flexner, *Mohawk Baronet* 296-97, 315.

27. J. T. Flexner, ibid., 324-26, 229-30; *DHNY* 2:528-32, 544-46, 4:249-50; *JP* 6:406-08, 519-20, 8:76; *DRCHNY* 8:111-37, 316.

28. For a more complete description of Sir William Johnson's struggles with Wheelock and the Reverend Samuel Kirkland see J. C. Guzzardo, "The Superintendent and the Ministers: The Battle for Oneida Allegiances, 1751-1775," *New York History* 57 (July 1976):255-83.

29. I. T. Kelsay, ibid., 71-76, 82-85, 87-89; J. D. McCallum, *Letters of Eleazar Wheelock's Indians* 293-94; *JP* 4:598 (1st quote), 10:279; *DHNY* 4:315 (2nd quote); Microfilm Edition of the Papers of Eleazar Wheelock: Together with the Early Archives of Dartmouth College and Moor's Indian Charity School (Hanover, NH, Dartmouth College Library, 1971), Reel #14—Vault, "List of Indian Pupils." Kelsay assumes that Sander and Nickus are Sander Kaghiyokandas and Nickus . . . who appear just above and below Joseph Teyendanega (Brant) on the 1760 Montreal list (*JP* 13:175).

30. J. D. McCallum, *Letters of Eleazar Wheelock's Indians* 25; E. Wheelock, *A Continuation of the Narrative of the Indian Charity School at Lebanon, in Connecticut from Nov. 27th, 1762 to Sept. 31, 1765* (Boston, 1765 and Rochester Reprints 2), 8; Letters of Eleazar Wheelock #765429.1; R. W. Vosburgh, "Records of the High and Low Dutch Congregation at Schoharie," vol. 1, pt. 1:31; Account Book, Probably Jelles Fonda's, 1755–1775, Caughnawaga, N.Y., 24.

31. Papers of Eleazar Wheelock, Reel #14—Vault, "List of Indian Pupils"; E. Wheelock, ibid.; W. D. Love, *Samson Occom and The Christian Indians of New England* (Boston and Chicago: The Pilgrim Press, 1899), 68; R. Smith, *A Tour of Four Great Rivers* 47.

32. J. D. McCallum, *Letters of Eleazar Wheelock's Indians* 18–19; J. D. McCallum, *Eleazar Wheelock* (Dartmouth College Ms. Series No. 4, 1939), 151–58; *JP* 4:812, 814, 5:222, 11:339, 858, 12:144n.

33. J. D. McCallum, *Letters of Eleazar Wheelock's Indians* 76–77; W. L. Stone, *Life of Brant* 1:23; the estimation of Ralph's behavior toward the Indians is given in J. D. McCallum, *Eleazar Wheelock* 126.

34. J. D. McCallum, *Eleazer Wheelock* ibid.; W. Pilkington, *Journal of Samuel Kirkland* xviii; *DHNY* 4:367–68 (1st quote); Papers of Eleazer Wheelock, Reel #14—Vault, Daybook 1765–67, "List of Indian Pupils"; *JP* 12:183 (2nd quote).

35. Papers of Eleazer Wheelock, #766458.1 and Reel #14—Vault, Daybook 1765–67; *JP* 5:343–44; *Bull. Ft. Ticonderoga Mus.* 10 (5):383, 384.

36. Papers of Eleazar Wheelock, #767163 and Reel 14—Vault, "List of Indian Pupils," and Daybook 1765–67.

37. Ibid. (quote from #767163); W. D. Love, *Samson Occom* 68. Wheelock later encountered difficulties in getting the money for his use, particularly that from Scotland, which he never recovered save for a small annual stipend (J. D. McCallum, *Eleazar Wheelock* 159–60, 164–65).

38. J. D. McCallum, ibid., 113–16; J. D. McCallum, *Letters of Eleazar Wheelock's Indians* 21, 22–23; J. T. Flexner, *Mohawk Baronet* 326–27; *JP* 5:388–89, 6:472.

39. J. D. McCallum, *Letters of Eleazar Wheelock's Indians* 22–24, 26; J. D. McCallum, *Eleazar Wheelock* 123–26; *JP* 6:457, 472; *DHNY* 4:244–50; J. T. Flexner, ibid., 327–28.

40. J. T. Flexner, ibid., 338–39, 346–47; I. T. Kelsay, *Joseph Brant* 135–36; B. Graymont, *Iroquois and the American Revolution* 48–49; W.

Pilkington, *Diary of Samuel Kirkland* 120; *JP* 12:850; *DRCHNY* 8:244.

41. For a history of the Mohawks in the Revolution, see Barbara Graymont's *The Iroquois in the American Revolution* and Isabel Kelsay's *Joseph Brant, Man of Worlds 1743-1807.* The years 1775 to 1778 are extensively covered, for all the northern Indian tribes, in Paul L. Stevens' Ph.D. dissertation, "His Majesty's 'Savage' Allies: British Policy and the Northern Indians during the Revolutionary War: The Carleton Years, 1774-1778" (SUNY Buffalo and University Microfilms, Ann Arbor, Michigan). The role of the Stockbridge Indians in the Revolution and later is chronicled in W. D. Love's *Samson Occom and the Christian Indians of New England.*